Making a Global Immigrant
Neighborhood

D1572338

In the series *Asian American History and Culture,*

edited by SUCHENG CHAN, DAVID PALUMBO-LIU, MICHAEL OMI,
K. SCOTT WONG, AND LINDA TRINH VÕ

Also in this series:

Ruth Mayer, *Serial Fu Manchu: The Chinese Supervillain and the Spread of Yellow Peril Ideology*

Karen Kuo, *East Is West and West Is East: Gender, Culture, and Interwar Encounters between Asia and America*

Kieu-Linh Caroline Valverde, *Transnationalizing Viet Nam: Community, Culture, and Politics in the Diaspora*

Lan P. Duong, *Treacherous Subjects: Gender, Culture, and Trans-Vietnamese Feminism*

Kristi Brian, *Reframing Transracial Adoption: Adopted Koreans, White Parents, and the Politics of Kinship*

Belinda Kong, *Tiananmen Fictions Outside the Square: The Chinese Literary Diaspora and the Politics of Global Culture*

Bindi V. Shah, *Laotian Daughters: Working toward Community, Belonging, and Environmental Justice*

Cherstin M. Lyon, *Prisons and Patriots: Japanese American Wartime Citizenship, Civil Disobedience, and Historical Memory*

Shelley Sang-Hee Lee, *Claiming the Oriental Gateway: Prewar Seattle and Japanese America*

Isabelle Thuy Pelaud, *This Is All I Choose to Tell: History and Hybridity in Vietnamese American Literature*

Christian Collet and Pei-te Lien, eds., *The Transnational Politics of Asian Americans*

A list of additional titles in this series appears at the back of this book

Making a Global Immigrant Neighborhood

Brooklyn's Sunset Park

TARRY HUM

TEMPLE UNIVERSITY PRESS
PHILADELPHIA

TEMPLE UNIVERSITY PRESS
Philadelphia, Pennsylvania 19122
www.temple.edu/tempress

Library of Congress Cataloging-in-Publication Data

Hum, Tarry, 1961-
Making a global immigrant neighborhood : Brooklyn's Sunset Park / Tarry Hum.
    pages cm — (Asian American history and culture)
  Includes bibliographical references and index.
ISBN 978-1-4399-1090-0 (hardback : alk. paper)
ISBN 978-1-4399-1091-7 (paper : alk. paper)
ISBN 978-1-4399-1092-4 (e-book)
  1. Sunset Park (New York, N.Y.)—History.   2. Community development—New York
(State)—New York—History.   3. Ethnic neighborhoods—New York (State)—New York—
History.   4. Immigrants—New York (State)—New York—History.   I. Title.
HN80.N5H845 2014
307.1'4120974723—dc23

                                                                        2014004476

♾ The paper used in this publication meets the requirements of the
American National Standard for Information Sciences—Permanence
of Paper for Printed Library Materials, ANSI Z39.48-1992

Printed in the United States of America

2 4 6 8 9 7 5 3 1

Contents

Acknowledgments

This book would not be possible without the generosity and dedication of Sunset Park's community leaders and visionaries, including Reverend Samuel Wong, Elizabeth Yeampierre, David Galarza, Chang Xie, Daniel Wiley, May Chen, Wing Lam, Wendy Cheung, Leticia Alanis, Reverend Juan Carlos Ruiz, May Lin, Eddie Bautista, Reverend Samuel Cruz, and Occupy Sunset Park. I am inspired by their tireless activism for immigrant and worker rights, community empowerment, and social and environmental justice. I am also indebted to Jeremy Laufer, Community Board 7; Andrew Genn, New York City Economic Development Corporation; Renee Giordano, Sunset Park 5th Avenue Business Improvement District; and Kathryn Wylde, Partnership for New York City. I am thankful to all the neighborhood residents and organizational staff for sharing their experiences and views in interviews and for their dedication to building community among Sunset Park's multiple publics. While we may not always agree, I am deeply appreciative for our shared enthusiasm and belief that Sunset Park has a rich and important story to tell.

The idea for a book originated with my chapter in *Intersections and Divergences: Contemporary Asian Pacific American Communities,* edited by Linda Trinh Vo and Rick Bonus. This book may not have come to fruition if not for Linda's enduring support for a manuscript-length community study. I fondly recall our meetings at the annual Association of Asian American Studies conferences to discuss my progress. Her recommendations as the series editor at Temple University Press were invaluable in improving the final manuscript. I am indebted to Janet Francendese, editor in chief, for her expert guidance and orchestration of a seamless review process. Her exceptional dedication to advancing scholarship on urban and community studies is much appreciated. I am also thankful for Sara Cohen's cheerful and kind assistance in the final stages of manuscript preparation.

I am grateful for the friendship and support of my City University of New York (CUNY) colleagues. At Queens College, I am especially thankful to Alice Sardell, Stephen Steinberg, Leonard Rodberg, Donald Scott, and Elizabeth Hendrey, who helped advance this work with encouraging conversations and data and grant support. A special thanks to CUNY friends, including Lynn McCormick, Peter Kwong, Edwin Melendez, Immanuel Ness, and Hector Cordero-Guzman.

I have benefited from many academic mentors, but one stands out above all others: Melvin Oliver. First as a dissertation adviser at UCLA and later as a Ford Foundation vice president, Melvin supported my early research investigating the concept of global neighborhoods defined by dynamic demographic change, economic globalization, promarket urban policies, and related consequences for everyday life. He demonstrated by example the exacting qualities and standards of scholarship and mentorship. I appreciate this opportunity to acknowledge Melvin's influence in shaping my academic work.

I thank my father, Shee Hong Hum, and my late mother, Sik So Lee, for bringing our family to Sunset Park, where they hoped that a home purchase would put an end to neighbor complaints of their four rambunctious kids. I am fortunate for the love and support of my sisters, Ellen and Lana, and my brother, Carl. Carl's professional appointments in Mayor Michael Bloomberg's administration overlapped with my research interests, and I have benefited from his insights on city economic development and industrial policies. I am especially grateful for the love and support of my husband, Robert Sanborn, a fellow urban planner who began visiting Sunset Park in 1986 when it was still a fairly quiet neighborhood and later marveled at its dramatic growth, especially the numerous ethnic banks and new developments that seemed to appear overnight. I am most indebted to our children, Malcolm and Kaela Sanborn-Hum, whose visits to Gong Gong's house have often ended up at an environmental justice protest or a community event or in heated discussions about our observations of race, space, and inequality as we traveled to and from Sunset Park along the Gowanus Expressway. I dedicate this book to Malcolm and Kaela and to Latino-Asian Sunset Park.

Making a Global Immigrant Neighborhood

Introduction

In a world city renowned for its distinctive neighborhoods, Sunset Park exemplifies the transformative trends that are shaping New York City's future. Situated in southwest Brooklyn, Sunset Park is a densely concentrated working-poor and racially diverse immigrant neighborhood that shares borders with affluent and largely white neighbors to the north and south. Sunset Park's namesake is a heavily used twenty-four acre park that offers panoramic views of the Upper New York Bay and the Lower Manhattan skyline. For more than a century, Sunset Park's two-and-half-mile waterfront was a "centerpiece of industrial and maritime activity" that supplied thousands of blue-collar jobs to immigrant New Yorkers (New York City Economic Development Corporation 2009, 3). Similar to many local neighborhoods, Sunset Park is at a crossroads, as transnational capital, market-driven pressures, and city planning and economic development policies are positioned to remake and gentrify its landscape. The future of Sunset Park depends on Asian and Latino immigrant collaboration in advancing common interests in community building and civic engagement.

On a hot and humid August day in 2009, a small crowd of Chinese and Latino residents gathered on the steps of Sunset Park's United Methodist Church to protest a neighborhood rezoning proposed by the New York City Department of City Planning, which they claimed would displace them from their homes (Figure I.1). Echoing protests that have taken place in other largely nonwhite New York City neighborhoods, community residents held signs in multiple languages and chanted, "Sunset Park is not

Figure I.1 Chinese Staff and Workers' Association and SPAN Rally on the New York City Department of City Planning's proposed Sunset Park rezoning, August 2009. (*Photo taken by Tarry Hum.*)

for sale." Community organizers, church leaders, and residents voiced their fears that poor people are being forced out and affirmed Asian and Latino unity in the fight to protect Sunset Park. A resident of Manhattan's Lower East Side, speaking in Spanish, called for immigrant solidarity and city-wide neighborhood actions against gentrification. On behalf of this grass-roots alliance, staff attorneys of two legal service organizations—the Asian American Legal Defense and Education Fund and the South Brooklyn

Legal Services—elaborated on a lawsuit filed against the city demanding a full environmental impact study of the proposed Sunset Park rezoning (Jessica Lee 2009; Edroso 2009).

Less than a month earlier, Mayor Michael Bloomberg, elected officials, and economic development leaders had gathered on Sunset Park's waterfront just a few blocks away from the site of the protest to unveil a plan to remake Sunset Park as a "sustainable urban industrial district."[1] With spectacular views of New York Harbor and Lower Manhattan as a backdrop, Bloomberg announced a comprehensive plan and committed millions of dollars in public funds to reactivate and redevelop Sunset Park's industrial waterfront. As part of the lauded Vision 2020 waterfront planning initiative, which lays out a comprehensive approach for remediating the city's extensive inventory of dormant and decaying industrial waterfront facilities, Sunset Park remains integral to policy strategies for diversifying the city's economy to include postindustrial production sectors and an active port economy. Alluding to the opposition of immigrant community stakeholders, Bloomberg stated in his waterfront address that the city's proposed rezoning would protect Sunset Park's neighborhood character and provide opportunities for affordable housing development.

These two public events illuminate the challenges and prospects that working-class immigrant neighborhoods face in a quintessential gateway city. Given the frequent criticism of Mayor Bloomberg's real estate–driven and corporatist approach to community economic development, the Sunset Park rally is notable not for its protest of a progrowth agenda and state-subsidized gentrification but rather for the unified political action by working-poor Chinese and Latino immigrants to protect their shared neighborhood. Although such actions may be episodic, the mobilization of working-class immigrant Asians and Latinos is momentous because their collaboration serves to "destabilize the structure and relationships in the official public space and release possibilities for new interactions, functions and meanings" (Hou 2010, 15). While demographic trends portend the emergence of Sunset Park as an epicenter in shaping the urban Asian American experience, its neighborhood spaces and its future as a home to working-class Asian immigrants are intertwined with the experiences and prospects of its Latino majority. Historically Puerto Rican, Sunset Park is now Pan-Latino, with the largest national group being among the neighborhood's newest arrivals: Mexican immigrants.

Sunset Park was once an industrial working waterfront employing thousands of local residents. Its future as a "sustainable urban industrial district" depends on retrofitting the waterfront's massive industrial infrastructure to support small artisanal manufacturers that produce value-added goods for New York City's elite consumer markets. Recent news that the world-famous chocolatier Jacques Torres is relocating his DUMBO factory to Sunset Park's Brooklyn Army Terminal was celebrated on an HGTV website, which noted that the new addition "bodes well for the neighborhood's long-term desirability" (Hochberg 2013). Remaking Sunset Park's industrial waterfront as a hub for designer production exists in a parallel universe with its designation as an overburdened site of environmental pollution and toxic facilities. Moreover, Superstorm Sandy exposed the grim and devastating realities of global climate change and a new normal in severe weather patterns.[2] This parallel universe underscores the fact that urban policy and planning initiatives for sustainability and resilience must foreground racial equity and justice in Sunset Park's revalorized local landscape of postindustrial economic development and post–Hurricane Sandy rebuilding.

Asian New Yorkers have continued their dramatic growth; according to the 2010 U.S. census, they numbered more than one million, making New York City the densest Asian metropolis in the continental United States. While the Asian population in historic immigrant enclaves such as Manhattan's Chinatown has declined, signaling neighborhood gentrification, the growth rate for Sunset Park's Asian population exceeded the citywide average, positioning Sunset Park to eclipse Manhattan's Chinatown as the city's core center for working-class Chinese immigrants (Table I.1). Analysis of demographic trends also showed that Sunset Park anchored the rapid spread of Chinese immigrants to surrounding South Brooklyn neighborhoods such as Bensonhurst and Dyker Heights. Accordingly, Asian American advocates successfully convinced the New York State Legislative Task Force on Redistricting to create a new Asian-majority State Assembly District by uniting Sunset Park and Bensonhurst as a "community of interest" (Asian American Legal Defense and Education Fund 2012; Durkin 2012).

Long referred to as a satellite Chinatown, Sunset Park has been a majority-Latino neighborhood since the late 1970s. However, dramatic Asian growth over the past three decades has resulted in near parity in population shares. By 2010, Latinos represented 44 percent and Asians 38 percent of the neighborhood population, which has led some to refer to Sunset Park as a Chino-Latino neighborhood.[3] Once majority Puerto Rican, Sunset Park has a Latino population that includes Dominicans and, increasingly, Mexicans. The rate of Puerto Rican decline was 7 percent from 1980 to 1990, 28 percent from 1990 to 2000, and a dramatic 39 percent from 2000 to 2010.[4] Even with continued Mexican migration steadily replacing the Puerto Rican population, Sunset Park's total Latino population dipped slightly in 2010. One of

TABLE I.1 ASIAN POPULATION CHANGE IN NEW YORK CITY'S CHINATOWNS, 1990–2010

	1990			2000			2010			Asian Population Change	
	Total Pop.	Asian	% Asian	Total Pop.	Asian	% Asian	Total Pop.	Asian	% Asian	1990–2000	2000–2010
New York City	7,322,564	508,408	7%	8,008,278	787,047	10%	8,175,133	1,038,388	13%	55%	32%
Brooklyn	2,300,664	106,022	5%	2,465,326	184,291	7%	2,504,700	260,129	10%	74%	41%
Sunset Park	84,147	12,971	15%	102,644	26,175	26%	109,973	41,013	37%	102%	57%
% Population	4%	12%	—	4%	14%	—	4%	16%	—	—	—
Manhattan	1,487,536	106,306	7%	1,537,195	143,291	9%	1,585,873	177,624	11%	35%	24%
Chinatown	113,949	52,505	46%	115,637	59,167	51%	108,921	51,900	48%	13%	-12%
% Population	8%	49%	—	8%	41%	—	7%	29%	—	—	—
Queens	1,951,598	229,830	12%	2,229,379	389,303	17%	2,230,722	508,334	23%	69%	31%
Flushing	121,316	40,631	33%	139,747	67,659	48%	133,185	84,308	63%	67%	25%
% Population	6%	18%	—	6%	17%	—	6%	17%	—	—	—

Source: U.S. census data for 1990, 2000, and 2010 retrieved from Queens College Social Explorer.

New York City's densest immigrant neighborhoods, Sunset Park's future is decidedly Chinese and Mexican. While the dominant urban and community studies approach to Chinese neighborhood formations employs enclave or ethnoburb theorizations (Li 2009; Lin 2011; Zhou, Chin, and Kim 2013), Sunset Park tells a different story as an immigrant global neighborhood by emphasizing the local and concrete forms of globalization in its dynamic migrant demography; a neighborhood economy once anchored in industrial manufacturing and now centered largely on immigrant markets, including transnational real estate investments; and increasingly complex race and class contestations about neighborhood identity and development trajectories.

Although multiethnic immigrant neighborhoods are not a new phenomenon, contemporary immigrant neighborhoods are global in unprecedented ways. First, in contrast to the economic expansion and industrialization at the turn of the century that provided scores of entry-level jobs for non-English-speaking immigrants, a postindustrial and service-based economy marked by extraordinarily high levels of income and wealth inequality now exists. Second, the racial and ethnic diversity and class bifurcation of post-1965 immigrants from Asia, Latin America, and the Caribbean is unparalleled. Moreover, the treatment of undocumented immigrants, especially in a post-9/11 environment, reflects more restrictive citizenship criteria and heightened marginalization of some immigrant groups. Third, neoliberal policies promote a probusiness governance approach that celebrates immigrant entrepreneurship while criminalizing informal sectors and practices that are integral to advanced urban economies. Sunset Park is an ideal site for investigating the role of these economic and political conditions in shaping community formation and intergroup relations in racialized neighborhood spaces.

Racializing Space and Spatializing Race

The literature on global cities provides rich insights and analysis of new economic arrangements that reproduce uneven development and complex patterns of social and economic polarization (Sassen 1991; Abu-Lughod 1999; Brenner and Keil 2006). However, this extensive literature has neglected an investigation of racialized immigrants and the transformation of local neighborhood spaces—in other words, the positioning of immigrant neighborhoods within a reconfigured urban "landscape of power" (Zukin 1991). As a dense multiracial immigrant neighborhood, Brooklyn's Sunset Park gives us insight into the processes of Asian and Latino urbanization and the contested racial politics of spatialization in hyperdiverse neighborhoods. A 2008 special issue of *Amerasia,* a premier Asian American studies journal, posed the question of how Asian Americans create places, and in their introductory essay, UCLA sociologist Kyeyoung Park and *Amerasia* editor Russell Leong argued for alternatives to the widely accepted nomenclature of enclave. To signal how Asian neighborhoods represent the "frontiers" of globalization and transnationalization, they proposed ethnic nexus or global ethnic hubs (Park and Leong 2008).

Community and regional studies are critical in grounding macroprocesses in everyday lived experiences and illuminating the ways that "the lived experience of race has a spatial dimension, and the lived experience of space has a racial dimension" (Lipsitz 2007, 12). The interdisciplinary field of Asian American community studies has engaged in uncovering the intersection of racial ideologies (and racialization processes) and spatially based labor and housing markets, public spaces, and neighbor relations. Asian American scholars have revised and enriched ethnic enclave approaches by emphasizing the urban political economy, the construction and mobilization of race and class identities and alliances, and local politics and multiple forms of civic engagement. Notable examples include Los Angeles (Kurashige 2008a, 2008b), San Diego (Vo 2004), Orange County (Vo 2008; Aguilar–San Juan 2009), and Monterey Park (Saito 1998) in California; Dorchester (Aguilar–San Juan 2009) and Chinatown (Lowe and Brugge 2007; Leong 1997) in Boston; and Manhattan's Chinatown (Kwong 1987; Lin 1998) in New York City.

These studies examine how place remains central to Asian American community building and identity formation. The research concretizes transnational practices, including capital and labor flows in shaping new institutions, labor market conditions, and forms of local placemaking. Moreover, these studies underscore how immigrants, including undocumented immigrants, are key place-based stakeholders and strategic actors in local planning and policy debates and initiatives. Asian American community studies examine how social relations are spatialized by documenting how "race, class, and gender relations and conflicts are acted through spatial and social means" (Gotham 2002, 86).

Asians have resided and continue to reside in racially mixed neighborhoods, but these neighborhoods are understudied and need to be at the foreground of the ongoing theorization of Asian American community formations. Discrimination and racialization that position Asian Americans as the Other have resulted in segregated spatial patterns, and while isolated enclaves have received much focus as a primary residential and economic form, Asians have a long history in multiracial neighborhoods that were prominent particularly in major West Coast cities such as Los Angeles and

San Francisco. Lai (2012, 153) argues that few "Anglophone" geographers (from the United States and the United Kingdom) have looked at the spatialization of race as a "multivectored, relational one involving multiple racialized groups." In addition to Lai's research on urban renewal in San Francisco's Fillmore District, Asian American community studies that focus on multiracial neighborhoods include historic Los Angeles (Kurashige 2004, 2008a, 2008b) and contemporary suburbs in the San Gabriel Valley (Cheng 2013). By moving beyond an enclave perspective of Asian American community formations, these researchers reject the spatial assimilationist trajectory that has dominated the study of race, ethnicity, and spatial formations and heed Kurashige's (2004, 57) argument that the transformation to a majority-minority society "must be taken as a challenge to do more than simply add new story lines to a preexisting narrative."

A well-documented historic example of multiracial neighborhoods in which Asians were a significant population share is Boyle Heights in East Los Angeles (Sanchez 2004). In 2002, the Japanese American National Museum organized an exhibition titled *Boyle Heights: The Power of Place* and a series of public talks with University of Southern California history professor George Sanchez that documented daily life and interactions in a diverse neighborhood space for much of the twentieth century.[5] Sanchez's exhibition text explained that Boyle Heights as a focus for study is significant because "the dynamics and hierarchies of racial power and differentiation were played out in neighborhood politics and personal relationships" (Sanchez 2001). Moving beyond a black-white binary of race relations and residential patterns, these community studies document Asians as key community stakeholders and actors in creating and engaging in a critical space for cross-racial interactions and understandings that shape urbanization processes and the urban experience.

These seminal place-based community studies that reveal the complex and dynamic multiracial landscape of Asian neighborhoods are largely centered on West Coast neighborhoods that reflect distinct histories and spatial patterns of Asian immigration to the United States. Important studies, however, have sought to correct the putative chronology and linearity of Chinese migration from west to east due to rising anti-Chinese violence and the subsequent formation of bachelor-society Chinatowns by documenting the presence and engagement of Chinese immigrants in New York City's early port economy and China trade in the 1700s (Tchen 1999). Moreover, the momentous demographic force of sustained post-1965 international migration and transformative spatial change underscores the relative dearth of contemporary Asian community studies in the quintessential immigrant gateway of New York City. International immigration not only saved New York City from urban decline during the 1970s, but the diverse racial and ethnic composition of contemporary migrants distinguishes this period from historic immigration waves (Lobo and Salvo 2013). While most immigrants to Los Angeles are Mexican, there is no one dominant group in New York City (Foner and Waldinger 2013). New York City's numerous hyperdiverse immigrant neighborhoods include Sunset Park.

The study of contemporary Asian community formations in New York City requires an approach that engages the city's multiracial composition and examines the differential spatial racializations of shared neighborhood places. *New York and Los Angeles: The Uncertain Future* (Oxford University Press, 2013) includes a chapter prepared by sociologists Min Zhou, Margaret M. Chin, and Rebecca Y. Kim on the transformation of Chinese American communities in both cities. Although they acknowledged that immigrant settlement and spatial assimilation models may be dated, the authors continued to employ an enclave and ethnoburb construction even though their research observations about Chinese communities, including Sunset Park, suggested that these concepts are inadequate. While they do describe Sunset Park as a "global" neighborhood because it is transnational and multiethnic (Zhou, Chin, and Kim 2013, 380), this observation was not developed, which resulted in a community narrative consistent with the dominant racialization of urban Chinese immigrant communities as isolated and insular enclaves. Historically, this type of study reinforced the sense that Chinese are "unfit for citizenship in an industrialized democracy" (Lui 2003, 174), and as such it is incumbent upon urbanists and sociologists to advance the theorizing of Asian immigrant community formations. Ultimately, Zhou, Chin, and Kim (2013) conceded this need by concluding their chapter with the following sentence: "As immigration continues into the twenty-first century with its long-lasting impacts on American cities, *a reconceptualization of neighborhood change and residential mobility is much needed*" (381, my emphasis).

An enclave narrative homogenizes the racial composition and depoliticizes class tensions and conflicts. Moreover, it does not adequately capture community life or complex social and political contestations that shape daily lived experiences in these neighborhoods. My work seeks to contribute to a community studies that engages in a deeper and richer understanding of Asian spaces as multiracial and contested spaces in order to uncover potential relationships and leadership models that advance a more just future for Sunset Park's multiple publics. In my study, I seek to better understand the challenges as well as the potential for multiracial alliances and coalition building, because Sunset Park and many Asian urban neighborhoods are shaped by these relationships. As Kurashige (2004, 57) observed, "the new quest for integration depends less on the spatial distribution of whites and blacks and more on the relationships among ethnic and racial communities." As a strategic site of transnational migration and economic globalization, Sunset Park provides contemporary insights into the daily lived experiences of a globalizing urban landscape and its implications for racial and ethnic relations, community building, immigrant incorporation, and civic engagement. As a multiracial, multiethnic neighborhood, it is a potent site to investigate the uneven inclusion of Asian and Latino immigrants in postindustrial cities and, more important, to locate areas of common concern and conditions for social mobilization and activism.

Methodology

In my study of Sunset Park, I employed a qualitative case study methodology based on the principles and practices of action research and participant observation. Simply defined, action research is a "bottom-up approach to inquiry which is aimed at producing more equitable policy outcomes" (Silverman, Taylor, and Crawford 2008, 73). Its core principles include reflexive inquiry, local knowledge, collaboration, case orientation, and social action goals (Greenwood, Whyte, and Harkavy 1993). As a paradigm of praxis, action research utilizes social science methodologies to understand lived socioeconomic and political conditions in order to solve real problems (O'Brien 1998). My action research in Sunset Park formally commenced in 1996 when I returned to New York City as a newly minted Ph.D. in urban planning.

Over the years, I have attended and participated in countless community board meetings, public hearings, and forums, including at the New York City Council. I have formally interviewed senior staff at city agencies, such as the New York City Economic Development Corporation, the Department of City Planning, the Department of Small Business Services, the Mayor's Office of Manufacturing and Industrial Businesses, and the Mayor's Office of Immigrant Affairs. I have conducted hundreds of in-depth interviews with Sunset Park stakeholders, including residents; Community Board 7 members and the district manager; elected officials such as Congresswoman Nydia Velázquez, New York state assemblyman Felix Ortiz, and City Council member Sara Gonzalez; and executive directors and senior staff of nonprofit organizations, including the Brooklyn Chinese American Planning Council, the Brooklyn Chinese-American Association, Asian Americans for Equality, Neighbors Helping Neighbors, La Unión, the United Puerto Rican

Organization of Sunset Park (UPROSE), the Chinese Staff and Workers' Association, the Sunset Park 5th Avenue Business Improvement District, the Garment Industry Development Corporation, the Southwest Brooklyn Industrial Development Corporation, the New York Environmental Justice Alliance, the Fifth Avenue Committee, the Center for Family Life, and the Hispanic Young People's Alternatives.[6]

My interviews of key neighborhood stakeholders included religious leaders, such as Reverend Samuel Wong of the Chinese Promise Baptist Church, Reverend Juan Carlos Ruiz and council president Lelia Johnson of St. Jacobi Evangelical Lutheran Church, and Reverend Samuel Cruz of Trinity Lutheran Church; Lutheran Medical Center senior representatives; and numerous neighborhood activists, including organizers with Sunset United, the Sunset Park Alliance of Neighbors, Occupy Sunset Park, Rice and Dreams, and the Raza Youth Collective. I have also interviewed May Chen, former international vice president of UNITE HERE and manager of Local 23-25, which in the 1980s was the largest International Ladies' Garment Workers' Union affiliate representing New York City's Chinese immigrant garment workers; Education Director Lana Cheung; Saul Nieves with SEIU 32BJ; local business owners, including garment subcontractors and realtor agencies; executive senior staff of ethnic banks, including Amerasia Bank, First American International Bank, Cathay Bank, and United Commercial Bank; and Kathryn Wylde, president and CEO of Partnership for New York City.

To supplement my fieldwork and qualitative interviews, I used secondary data from the decennial U.S. Census and the American Community Survey as well as data from the New York State Department of Labor's Quarterly Census of Employment and Wages (formerly ES 202) to conduct an empirical analysis of Sunset Park's changing demography and neighborhood economy. I used multiple municipal data sources to document land use, property ownership, and development projects. These databases include the New York City Department of Finance's Automated City Register Information System, the Department of City Planning's PLUTO (Primary Land Use Tax Lot Output) data, and the Department of Buildings' Buildings Information System. My research on land use and development also employed the New York Department of State Division of Corporations' State Records and UCC database on Corporations and Businesses. Finally, I analyzed the 2000–2011 Home Mortgage Disclosure Act (HMDA) data to document home mortgage lending patterns. I used the online databases of the Federal Deposit Insurance Corporation and the Federal Financial Institutions Examination Council to obtain bank data, loan portfolios, and Community Reinvestment Act ratings and reports.

On a final note, my family moved to Sunset Park in 1974 near the height of New York City's fiscal crisis. My parents were employed in typical immigrant niches. My mother was a sewing machine operator in Manhattan Chinatown's sweatshop garment industry, and my father worked in an industrial laundry in Greenpoint, Brooklyn, and on weekends worked as a cook in a Chinese restaurant. We were the first Chinese family on our block at a time when Sunset Park (above 5th Avenue) was still a largely white ethnic neighborhood. Over the decades, we witnessed the near complete exodus of Italian, Irish, and Norwegian neighbors as 8th Avenue emerged as Brooklyn's Chinatown in the early 1990s. We shopped on 5th Avenue, at the time the commercial center of Sunset Park's Puerto Rican community, and observed the growing presence of Mexican flags decorating local storefronts and homes. My father still resides in the modest two-family row house he purchased four decades ago. My deep personal relationship with Sunset Park provides me with a special lens and an investment in community issues and development. As a Sunset Park stakeholder, I prepared this book with the hope that my research will deepen and enrich our understanding of immigrant urbanization, advance immigrant Latino-Asian civic engagement and common interests, and aid progressive planners in our work for racial justice and equity in urban economic development and city building practices.

Overview of the Book

This book is organized into six chapters and a conclusion. Based on a review of contemporary theorizations of immigrant neighborhoods, Chapter 1 argues that immigrant communities represent new and distinct formations because they are embedded in the mass migration of racialized minorities in a postindustrial economic context. Some researchers propose new neighborhood formations such as ethnoburbs and ethnic communities, but these typologies do not situate Asians in urban multiethnic, multiracial neighborhoods (Maly 2005; Cheng 2013; Lai 2012; Kurashige 2008a, 2008b). While the "new" urban sociology has generated tremendous insight into the consequences of economic restructuring and social polarization in global and world cities, the significance of immigration, race, and ethnicity in reproducing new and old forms of urban inequality need further investigation (Samers 2002). Chapter 1 proposes a new framework of immigrant global neighborhoods that positions immigrant Latino-Asian neighborhoods within a reconfigured urban "landscape of power" (Zukin 1991).

Chapter 2 tells the evolution of Sunset Park as an ethnically diverse white working-class industrial waterfront neighborhood to its federal poverty-area designation in the late 1960s, when Sunset Park's Puerto Rican population was growing, to its recent revival as one of New York City's most diverse and vibrant immigrant neighborhoods. Integral to the "ethnic succession" of Sunset Park are urban development policies and projects, such as the Gowanus Expressway and its lingering effects on neighborhood deterioration and environmental conditions. Sunset Park's history also includes Federal Housing Authority abuses that heightened the neighborhood's racial transition. Institutions such as the Lutheran Medical Center figured prominently in the stabilization of Sunset Park because of their priority access to federal antipoverty funds. As home to a high-security federal prison, the Metropolitan Detention Center, Sunset Park is also the site of globalized political protests, including demonstrations against the U.S. Navy's bombing of the Puerto Rican island of Vieques and the 9/11 immigrant detentions. This political economic history provides a context for subsequent chapters on opportunities and challenges for Latino and Asian civic engagement and current debates about Sunset Park's informal economy, neighborhood development and rezoning, and designation as a sustainable industrial urban district.

Much of the emphasis on immigrant economies in both the scholarly and policy arenas highlight their "exceptionalism" in generating entrepreneurship, ethnic solidarity, and economic opportunities and propose to replicate small business development as a strategy for asset building in other disadvantaged communities. Although Asian and Latino immigrant-owned businesses play a central role in the reversal of neighborhood economic decline, many of these new enterprises have thrived on a foundation of poverty-level wages, casual employment relations, and nonunion shops. Sunset Park's immigrant ethnic niches include a downgraded garment-manufacturing sector and an informal economy that is most visibly marked by street vendors. In contrast to earlier periods of industrialization and city building, new immigrant groups are creating marginal niches in a postindustrial urban economy. Chapter 3 documents the declining garment industry and and recent legislative efforts to regulate street vendors and examines the related consequences for immigrant economic incorporation and access to public space.

Chapter 4 investigates the paradox of Sunset Park's large working-poor population amid the relatively high volumes of capital represented by numerous banks located in the neighborhood. U.S. banking deregulation and the growing influx of Chinese capital, especially since the early 1990s, have resulted in the establishment of numerous ethnic banks in Sunset Park. The substantial research on immigrant financial capital and access has focused on consumer services and predatory lending. However, the increasing presence of ethnic banks defined as U.S.-based banks established by ethnic minorities has largely been overlooked. Sunset Park is considered an underserved community, but it is also the site of a fairly extensive banking infrastructure, including several mainstream banks. Chapter 4 examines the role of ethnic banks in facilitating homeownership and community development in Sunset Park. An analysis of 2000–2011 HMDA data finds that despite the concentrated presence of ethnic banks in immigrant neighborhoods, they make few home purchase loans or substantive community reinvestments. Rather, they figure prominently as part of an immigrant-based urban growth machine that is transforming Sunset Park through commercial real estate development. Economic development policies such as New York state's banking development districts should incorporate a more complex and dynamic view of the economic landscape of immigrant neighborhoods in order to promote fair access to capital and equitable community investment.

The Bloomberg administration has initiated an unprecedented number of rezonings that cumulatively represent a dramatic reconfiguration of land use in New York City. Community boards—the most decentralized body of urban governance—serve as a conduit for public review and oversight of the development process. Chapter 5 examines the race and class politics in framing the community's concerns about overdevelopment and gentrification and community reactions to the Department of City Planning's proposed rezoning of Sunset Park. This chapter finds that community boards often legitimate and advance a neoliberal agenda in part by marginalizing poor people and people of color. In failing to provide a public forum that meaningfully engages stakeholders, including immigrants in neighborhood planning and development, Sunset Park's rezoning debate underscore the importance of a migrant civil society in building multiracial alliances to define neighborhood space and identity and exercise claims for economic justice and equity in urban development.

Chapter 6 examines the prospects for Sunset Park's waterfront in a postindustrial urban economy. As a mixed-use neighborhood with historically weak political representation and organization, Sunset Park has been scarred by highway construction, and its waterfront has served as a dumping ground for a meatpacking plant, waste transfer stations, power plants, a federal prison, and sex shops. Waterfront reclamation and redevelopment are central to remaking New York City's global city status, and several new developments in Sunset Park, including plans for a waterfront park on the contaminated Bush Terminal piers, are part of this development vision. While Sunset Park's maritime and manufacturing roots are currently protected by city initiatives and zoning designations that recognize the existence of an industrial cluster at the core of the local economy, Chapter 6 examines how the prospects for Sunset Park's waterfront redevelopment in a postindustrial urban economy will be decided in part on the success of environmental justice and sustainable development discourses and actions to shift from noxious threats to countering a neoliberal development agenda that advocates waterfront residence, tourism, and creative industries. Superstorm Sandy has forced the issue of climate change and the devastating impacts of severe weather patterns. While Mayor Bloomberg's leadership on environmental sustainability is much lauded, this chapter examines how his approach to rebuilding and promoting a resilient New York is consistent with a market-driven development agenda.

The book concludes with examples of Sunset Park initiatives that advance social and economic justice. Specifically, the concluding chapter investigates the challenges of and the potentiality for transformative neighborhood change in three central areas: immigrant entrepreneurialism, creating space for Latino-Asian immigrant activism, and just sustainability planning.

1
Immigrant Places

Toward a Theory of Global Neighborhoods

The sociospatial geography of New York City has always been distinguished by dynamic and evolving patterns that demarcate complex race, ethnic, and class compositions and relationships. The processes of immigration and city building are intricately linked, and their study formed the foundational basis for urban sociology. The once-dominant ecological model of neighborhood change based on invasion and succession is premised on the Chicago School of Sociology theory of early twentieth-century race relations, and increasingly its explanatory relevance and robustness fails to capture contemporary dynamics (Ward 1971; Dear 2002). Most notably, the theoretical framing of invasion and succession as the central force facilitating neighborhood change neglects to identify key individual and organizational actors—including real estate developers, financiers, government officials, and residents—and other institutional factors in the production of space and spatial patterns (Gotham 2002).

Competing urban theories have coalesced around the study of paradigmatic and racially diverse metropolises such as Los Angeles, Miami, and New York City, cities that represent "the most dramatic and concentrated expressions of the perplexing theoretical and practical urban issues that have arisen at the end of the twentieth century" (Scott and Soja 1998, vii). The theorization of world and global cities provides rich insights and analyses of emergent economic arrangements that reproduce uneven development and complex patterns of social and economic polarization but neglects to fully investigate the neighborhood formations of racialized immigrants and their positioning in a reconfigured urban landscape of power (Zukin 1991; Samers 2002).

Building on the observation that immigrant urbanism is marked by unprecedented racial and ethnic diversity, this chapter reexamines the dominant sociological lens applied to spatial formations represented by such terms as "enclave," "ethnoburb," "barrio," "colonia," and "ghetto," which are most significant in their implicit and evaluative references to racialized spaces and populations. As Neil Smith (2002, 430) contends, "Globalization takes place through specific social and economic complexes rooted in specific places," and this chapter details how economic restructuring, immigration policies, and neoliberal urban governance shape localized placemaking in diverse neighborhoods.

Immigrants are reinventing urban working-class neighborhoods, and these community formations represent new and enduring forms of marginality as well as potential sites for multiracial alliances and new forms of community building. After a brief review of dominant theorizations of immigrant neighborhoods, this chapter proposes an analytical approach that emphasizes immigrant formations as being embedded in the mass migration of racialized minorities in a global and postindustrial context, thereby countering assumptions of an assimilationist urban narrative premised on the "uplifting effects of an ethnic, immigrant economy" (Smith 1996, 80). Neighborhoods are an integral aspect of the immigrant experience (Irazábal 2012; Logan, Alba, and Zhang 2002). Place is important because local, territorially defined, spatial neighborhoods remain central to how people organize their daily lives and serve as focal points for economic opportunity, political and civic engagement, and cultural and social life (Dreier, Mollenkopf, and Swanstrom 2001; Gottdiener and Hutchison 2000).

Theorizations of neighborhood spaces as enclaves, barrios, slums, or ghettos are socially constructed to evoke particular meanings of race and place and often encapsulate a set of state policies that support a racial hierarchy and its attendant racial categories (Anderson 1987). For example, a legacy of urban renewal policies is the use of the term "blighted" to degrade particular neighborhood places (and by association their residents) and rationalize their destruction for redevelopment or highway construction (J. M. Thomas 1994). State-supported slum clearance leveled urban landscapes in preparation for the mass infusion of private capital and public subsidies to reinvent and revitalize neighborhood spaces. To date, the largest rezoning in New York City's history will remake downtown Jamaica, part of concentrated black southeastern Queens, into an airport village. The catalyst for the state-sanctioned hotel and commercial transformation relied on designating the mixed-use industrial area as blighted.[1]

The social constructions of contemporary urban immigrant neighborhood formations alternate between the term "enclave" and "ghetto." The seminal work of Alejandro Portes and his colleagues developed the concept of a context of reception to describe the key mechanisms that shape the incorporation of new immigrants (Portes 1981; Portes and Bach 1985; Portes and Rumbaut 1990; Portes and Zhou 1992). Immigration is a social process facilitated by ethnic-based networks, and these largely informal networks also promote a particular set of conditions for socioeconomic integration in the host country through the formation of immigrant enclaves and occupational niches (Portes and Bach 1985; Portes and Rumbaut 1990; Waldinger 1996). A critical component of the context of reception is the establishment of an ethnic community, especially one with a large coethnic entrepreneurial base. Immigrant enclaves serve as stepping-stone or port-of-entry communities, providing necessary social, economic, and cultural resources to help facilitate the settlement and integration of new immigrants and subsequent generations (Portes and Bach 1985; Portes and Rumbaut 1990; Marcuse 1997).

While the spatial agglomeration of immigrant-owned businesses is an important defining characteristic, the benefits of enclave residence and employment are an outcome of ethnic-based social structures that mediate labor market processes and community institutions (Waldinger 1996; Zhou 2001). Enclave economies provide opportunities for social mobility through informal hiring and training practices, flexible work environments, self-employment possibilities, and protection from interracial competition, discrimination, and government surveillance and regulations (Zhou 1992). As Sassen (2000a, xii) notes, "Immigrant communities offer an advantage, given the intensity of their networks and the channeling of newly arrived and long-term resident immigrants into immigrant-dominated labor markets."

Proponents of immigrant enclaves contend that the reproduction of ethnic communities does not necessarily indicate the persistence of involuntary segregation but instead represents the capacity for ethnic solidarity and social networks to facilitate economic mobility, community life, and cultural continuity (Zhou and Logan 1991; Zhou 1992; Li 2009). Enclave residence is not the sole option for new immigrants but is a superior option, since enclaves provide "a means of enhancing their [residents'] economic, social, political, and/or cultural development" (Marcuse 1997, 225). Even those no longer faced with constrained residential choices because of a language liability (lack of English proficiency) or limited class resources prefer to cluster in suburban ethnic communities (Logan, Alba, and Zhang 2002) or ethnoburbs (Li 2009).

The enclave construction is consistent with the immigrant assimilationist narrative. According to the Manhattan Institute, "Immigrants saved many American cities, but none perhaps so clearly as New York" (Vitullo-Martin 2008). The immigrant population as the rescuer of urban America is often contrasted with the social disorder and debilitating poverty of a largely native-born black and Puerto Rican urban underclass. Immigrant incorporation is evidence of a neoliberal urbanism premised on an imagined trajectory of unfettered mobility for those able and willing to seize market opportunities (Muller 1993; Moss 2006). The mutuality of immigration and New York City's economic vitality was evidenced when Mayor Michael Bloomberg invited five diverse immigrant families to share the stage at the Queens Museum of Art for his 2008 State of the City speech. All five families lived in Flushing, Queens, a paradigmatic immigrant enclave neighborhood.[2] There is no doubt that their attendance was an affirmation of New York City's racial and ethnic diversity, but more important, they exemplified the palpability of the American Dream. In case the visual symbolism was not apparent, Bloomberg extolled, "Their presence is a two-way street. New York gives them unlimited opportunities and these families help make New York the nation's economic engine, its financial hub, its fashion center, its media mecca, and its cultural capital" (Anon. 2008c).

Other researchers view immigrant community formations on a continuum of urban and social restructurings rather than as a process of ecological and economic successions (Kwong 1987; Lin 1998; Sassen 1991). Enclaves represent sites of production and social reproduction that are integral to an evolving landscape of urban inequality. These scholars reject voluntary segregation and note that ethnicity often masks class divisions and conflicts. Immigrant enclaves are concentrated in industry niches where minimal profits for risk-taking immigrant business owners are based on squeezing coethnic labor. The spatial agglomeration of ethnic resources and institutions does not necessarily promote upward mobility but does buffer unemployment and underemployment and the impacts of working poverty (Ong 1984). The social isolation of immigrant enclaves enables ethnic institutions, including nonprofit organizations and ethnic media, to dominate community politics and business development (Kwong 1987; Kwong and Miscevic 2005). In enclave communities, class divisions rather than bounded solidarity are evident in the degree of labor exploitation found in many workplaces (Light and Bonacich 1988; Lin 1998).

Immigrant neighborhoods are alternately viewed as ghettos, and Kay Anderson (1987) in her classic article "The Idea of Chinatown" describes how racial ideology is embedded in the social significance of urban places. Anderson argues that the social construction of the term "Chinatown" reinforced notions of Chineseness as clannish and unassimilable and Chinese immigrants as perpetual foreigners or symbolic "aliens." Contemporary examples include Chinatown's extensive informal economy. Restaurant and garment sweatshops sit along street vendors who hawk counterfeit goods, but police raids have increasingly pushed this trade underground (Hauser 2008; Chan 2008). Chinese women now stop potential customers near subway stations to show them laminated photos of knockoff handbags and other illicit products stored in the basements of nearby buildings. The conflicting accounts of activities in an East Broadway building are another example of the criminalization of perceived Chinese cultural proclivities (Semple and Singer 2012). Federal and state law enforcement officers raided a building that they claimed was the site of illegal gambling and money laundering, but residents insisted that the activities were social and recreational pursuits among immigrant laborers and retirees. These realities represent an economic underside of Chinatown that is used to evoke long-standing perceptions of Chinese criminality, illegality, and marginalization (Light 1974).

The racialization of black underclass ghettos and Latino barrios coheres with the dominant racial hierarchy (Wacquant 2004; Diaz 2005). In his neighborhood typologies of a post-Fordist city, Peter Marcuse (1997) differentiates a classic and outcast ghetto to underscore the heightened marginalization of poor African Americans and their neighborhood spaces. Marcuse describes how classic ghetto residents were historically engaged in economic transactions with society at large even though they were segregated and discriminated against. In contrast, outcast ghettos, or hyperghettos, are severed from any meaningful connection to mainstream society as a result of the related processes of de-civilizing and demonization (Wacquant 2004), which renders outcast ghettos (and their residents) increasingly isolated and irrelevant to the postindustrial city.

Latino barrios are also shaped by enduring state-sponsored housing and labor market discrimination (Massey and Denton 1993; Diaz 2005). Barrios are increasingly transformed in part by growing numbers of ethnically diverse Latino immigrants from Latin America and the Caribbean (Davila 2004; Miyares 2004; Lobo, Flores, and Salvo 2002). New York City Latino neighborhood formations include immigrant hubs such as Jackson Heights, Corona, and Elmhurst in Queens that do not have historic origins as Puerto Rican colonias or barrios. These neighborhood formations represent new globalized localities because of the unprecedented racial and ethnic diversity and the extensive transnational ties and social practices. The prevalence and persistence of discrimination against blacks finds Latinos and Asians most likely to co-reside in these new immigrant global neighborhoods (Logan and Zhang 2010; Fasenfest, Booza, and Metzger 2004; Davis 2000).

Neighborhoods are not merely spatially defined areas but instead consist of social networks, including those that cross national borders. The compression of time and space made possible by technological innovations facilitates ongoing engagement with the home country, and these transnational social practices and relationships mediate contemporary immigrant incorporation experiences (Cordero-Guzman, Smith, and Grosfoguel 2001; Foner 2001; Levitt 2001). Rejecting a simple assimilationist trajectory, transnationalist scholars document and theorize "an alternative form of adaptation" that entails "cross-border economic, political, and cultural activities" (Portes, Guarnizo, and Haller 2002). Transnationalism is creating new and distinct forms of urbanization in part through the heightened circulation of capital, including the remittances of transmigrant laborers, and the economic enterprises of the professional and entrepreneurial elite, which includes transnational corporations and ethnic banks (Castells 1998; Mitchell 2004).

Toward building a theory that encompasses new forms of American urbanism, including immigrant global neighborhoods, this chapter seeks to locate neighborhood formations and change in a broad context that elaborates on the postindustrial urban economy; racialized immigrants, including a large undocumented population; and a neoliberal policy environment. Post-1965 immigrant neighborhoods are global in unprecedented ways that reflect both new and enduring forms of urban inequality. The restructured metropolitan economy and demography has reconfigured race- and class-based spatial patterns in such a way that a new theoretical construct of immigrant urban neighborhoods beyond enclaves, barrios, and ghettos is necessary.

Postindustrial New York

Immigrants at the turn of the twentieth century were largely absorbed into a great industrial machine and found work in city building, manufacturing, and maritime-related industries. Waves of European immigrants worked the docks, built the city infrastructure, and provided the labor power that made New York City the nation's manufacturing capital (Freeman 2000). Beginning in the 1960s, urban economies underwent a fundamental restructuring from manufacturing goods to services (Bell 1973; Bluestone and Harrison 1982). International competition posed by the emergence of postwar industrialized nations led to the steady decline of American manufacturing because of technological innovations and abundant cheap labor. U.S. employers responded by adopting flexible labor schemes that increased joblessness and employment insecurity at home and embarking on a global search for more profitable conditions (e.g., cheap labor, inexpensive land, and unregulated environments). Policies and institutions that supported fair labor standards and wages in the United States succumbed to corporate downsizing and attacks (Harrison and Bluestone 1988).

While manufacturing as an economic anchor was greatly diminished, a bifurcated service economy facilitated a fundamental transformation of work and urban life in the United States. This new economy has been termed "postindustrial" and "post-Fordist," although some scholars, such as the noted urban geographer Allen J. Scott (2006), argue that these terms are insufficient to capture the radical changes. According to Scott, "The peculiar forms of economic order that are in the ascendant today represent a marked shift away from the massified structures of production and the rigid labor markets that typified fordism, and they appear to be ushering in an altogether new style of urbanization that is posing many unprecedented challenges to policy makers around the world" (4).

As the world economy became dominated by transnational corporations and integrated global labor and capital markets, global cities evolved as a spatial form for this new period of economic globalization (Sassen 1991). Global cities coordinate the geographic dispersal of economic activities by concentrating command functions and also serve as postindustrial production sites for advanced producer services (Sassen 1991, 1994). New York City's transition to a postindustrial economy is evident in the data presented in Table 1.1, which tracks the industry shares of private-sector employment from 1975 to 2005. In 1975, one in five New Yorkers remained employed in the manufacturing sector; however, over the next few decades, manufacturing employment fell by 79 percent, from more than 500,000 workers to approximately 114,000 in 2005. By 2010, the number of manufacturing workers, at roughly 76,000, was nearly halved in just five short years. The two sizable sectors of New York City's much diminished manufacturing base are nondurable products in apparel and food, where location and proximity to consumer markets matter. From 1970 to the early 1990s, New York City had lost the greatest absolute number and share of manufacturing jobs among all other U.S. cities (Fitch 1993, 22). The only industry sector with outstanding employment growth during this period was services, in which employment numbers nearly tripled to 1.7 million, representing a majority 59 percent of all private-sector employment in New York City by 2005.

As the largest source of private-sector employment, the service sector is highly bifurcated or bimodal, generating high-wage, high-skill jobs requiring specialization and technology in addition to a massive base of low-wage, low-skill jobs. During the 2000s, New York City's top three employment sectors were professional and business services, health and social assistance, and accommodation and food, representing the highest-skilled and -paid as well as the lowest-skilled and -paid service jobs. While the city's 1975 economy was diverse, with clusters of firms and workers in multiple industry sectors, its postindustrial economy is anchored by a tripartite of retail, services, and finance, insurance, and real estate (FIRE) sectors. Moody (2007, 125) warned that the "growing dependence on Wall Street and real estate weakened the city's economy by creating a sort of monoculture" and "greatly strengthened the hand of capital and its various organizations to a degree that few understood."

Post–World War II suburbanization promoted a high demand for standardized production in tract homes and durable household goods, which helped sustain U.S. manufacturing infrastructure and growth. In contrast, post-1970s economic restructuring marked the dominance of finance and specialized advanced services, with distinct consumption and spatial patterns in real estate development and urban gentrification that are heavily reliant on labor-intensive processes in the production of customized goods and services (Sassen 1990; Zukin 1987). This fundamental restructuring represents an economic regime that creates the conditions and tendency for informalization (Sassen 1994).

A structural feature of advanced urban economies is labor market informalization and unregulated work in an expansive underground or informal economy (Portes, Castells, and Benton 1989; Sassen 1994). The competitive drive to lower labor costs has led to the reemergence of sweatshop conditions in numerous New York City growth industry sectors, including retail, home health care, restaurants, construction, personal services, food and apparel production, and building maintenance and security (Bernhardt, McGarth, and DeFilippis 2007). The informal sector, or the unregulated economy characterized by extensive violations of basic labor laws and the casualization of employment relations, draws from an immigrant workforce and subcontractors, including independent contractors (Ness 2005). The economic arrangements of a postindustrial economy underscore the interconnectedness between advanced producer services and their corporate headquarters, informalization, downgraded manufacturing, and immigrant economies. These seemingly contradictory aspects of world cities represent "how global processes are actually constituted in the urban economy and in urban space" (Sassen 1996, 25).

TABLE 1.1 NEW YORK CITY PRIVATE-SECTOR FIRMS AND EMPLOYMENT, 1975–2005

Industry	1975				1990				2005				Change from 1975 to 2005	
	Firms[a]	Workers[a]	% Firms	% Workers	Firms[a]	Workers[a]	% Firms	% Workers	Firms[a]	Workers[a]	% Firms	% Workers	Firms	Workers
Total Industries	193,655	2,665,233	100%	100%	194,071	2,902,948	100%	100%	215,603	2,896,794	100%	100%	11%	9%
Services	62,031	743,998	32%	28%	71,879	1,124,007	37%	39%	105,185	1,723,062	49%	59%	70%	132%
Retail trade	41,376	376,444	21%	14%	38,373	382,170	20%	13%	28,065	269,576	13%	9%	-32%	-28%
FIRE[b]	28,138	415,271	15%	16%	26,242	512,045	14%	18%	29,209	419,651	14%	14%	4%	1%
Wholesale trade	23,211	247,390	12%	9%	20,850	208,341	11%	7%	16,114	136,114	7%	5%	-31%	-45%
Manufacturing	21,695	533,429	11%	20%	13,606	335,216	7%	12%	7,300	113,707	3%	4%	-66%	-79%
Construction	8,301	76,051	4%	3%	10,753	109,383	6%	4%	11,054	103,696	5%	4%	33%	36%
Transportation, utilities	7,042	262,019	4%	10%	7,404	219,882	4%	8%	4,390	36,710	2%	1%	-38%	-86%
Agriculture, mining	1,861	10,627	1%	0.4%	4,964	11,878	3%	0.4%	57	241	0.03%	0.01%	-97%	-98%

[a] The columns for firms and workers do not add up because a small number of unclassified firms are not included, and in some cases data was suppressed for confidentiality purposes.
[b] FIRE represents finance, insurance, and real estate.
Source: ES 202 Data, New York State Department of Labor.

The restructuring of urban economies has led to a resurgence in income and wealth inequality. Corporate strategies such as the creation of two-tier wage systems, outsourcing, antiunion tactics, and expansion of contingent work lead to a "Great U-Turn" in earnings (Harrison and Bluestone 1988). In the past few years, employment outsourcing has extended beyond manufacturing production, back-office work, and call centers and has moved up the skill ladder. Wall Street firms among others now outsource jobs related to research and development in banking, finance, and computer technology industries, referred to as "knowledge process outsourcing" and "high-value outsourcing" (Timmons 2008; Giridharadas 2007). New York City's new gilded age is marked by the greatest income gap in the United States. This is most extreme in the borough of Manhattan, where the average salary in 2000 for the top quintile was $365,826—fifty-two times the amount earned by the lowest quintile, whose average earnings was $7,047 (Roberts 2005). Widening economic and social divides have become particularly acute under Mayor Michael Bloomberg, as noted by the collection of essays in an April 2013 issue of *The Nation* titled "The Gilded City—Bloomberg's New York."

Racially segmented labor markets are reinforced by economic restructuring, which has heightened joblessness and marginalization of low-skill African Americans while absorbing immigrants in numerous occupational and industry sectors that are reliant on subcontracting and unregulated work (Johnson and Oliver 1989; Ness 2005). By 2000, nearly half (47 percent) of New York City's resident workforce was foreign-born, with an overwhelming majority representing part of the city's indispensable low-wage labor force (Hum 2005; Fiscal Policy Institute 2007). The explosive growth of immigrant-owned small businesses in New York City is largely concentrated in marginal niches distinguished by ethnic markets and low entry barriers (Zhou 1998; Hum 2006). As the city's "industrial topography" has declined, immigrant neighborhoods have evolved into a prominent feature of the new social geography of work (Ness 2005, 22). Immigrant neighborhoods, as sites of production and social reproduction in a postindustrial economy, are integral to urbanization processes that reproduce race and class inequality.

Immigration, Citizenship, and "Enemy Aliens"

President Lyndon B. Johnson's signing of the 1965 Hart-Celler Act at the base of the iconic Statue of Liberty initiated a dramatic remaking of American demography. The 1965 immigration act repealed the racist quotas established by the 1924 Johnson-Reed Act, also known as the National

Origins Quota Act, that limited immigration largely to those coming from northwestern Europe and wholly excluded Asians for four decades (Ngai 2007). Prior to the Johnson-Reed Act, immigration to the United States remained fairly open except for Chinese "coolies" (who were barred by the 1882 Chinese Exclusion Act) and other "undesirables" inflicted with mental or health deprivations (such as smallpox and typhus, among other infectious diseases), prostitutes, and "idiots, lunatics, convicts, and persons likely to become public charges" (Abbott 1924). The Johnson-Reed Act was enacted to stem the mass influx of immigrants from southern and eastern Europe at the turn of the twentieth century by consolidating a "bureaucratic state regime based on border control, numerical quotas, and removal of illegal aliens" (Ngai 2007, 12).

Although not intended as a "revolutionary bill," the Hart-Celler Act had a transformative impact by unleashing a massive human in-migration from Asia, Latin America, and the Caribbean (Anon. 1965). Premised on principles of family reunification and skill preferences, the Hart-Celler Act had an unforeseen consequence: the dominance of racialized nonwhite migrants from a range of developing countries. Relative to other key U.S. gateway cities, the sheer volume and diversity of immigrants makes New York City the most "pluricultural" of all metropolitan areas (Davis 2000). No single immigrant group dominates or constitutes a majority of the city's foreign-born population, in contrast to Los Angeles where the immigrant population is majority Mexican.

In contrast to the "huddled masses" of late nineteenth-century immigration, post-1965 immigration is marked by high levels of class bifurcation, constituting a "brain drain" for many source countries. For example, the Philippines is a primary source of professional personnel notably in medicine, such that Filipinos are the "most highly visible foreign-trained nurses in the United States" (Ong and Azores 1994, 164). Immigration policies since 1965 have heightened economic bifurcation particularly among Asian immigrants, with significant implications for neighborhood dynamics, institutional leadership, and prospects for interracial alliances (Park and Park 2005; Espiritu and Ong 1994; Kim and Lee 2001). The Immigration Act of 1990 increased family preference visas modestly compared to employment-based visas, which jumped from 34,000 to 140,000, representing a threefold increase (Lobo and Salvo 1998, 746). Moreover, the number of employment preference categories expanded from two to five, including a new investors category (Lobo and Salvo 1998, 740). The trend toward a class-based policy favoring immigrants with exceptional skills and/or wealth is evident in the ongoing debate about immigration reform and in proposals for a point system that rewards those with human and financial capital (Migration Policy Institute 2007).

Even before the 9/11 tragedies, a priority of U.S. immigration policy was to tighten national borders and harden the distinction between legal (i.e., deserving) and illegal (i.e., criminal and undeserving) immigrants. The 1996 Illegal Immigration Reform and Immigrant Responsibility Act (IIRIRA) and the Anti-Terrorism and Effective Death Penalty Act (AEDPA) legislated comprehensive and punitive measures that significantly eroded immigrant access and rights. Signed by President Bill Clinton, these acts reinforced the U.S.-Mexican border (in part by constructing a wall), restricted public benefit eligibility for new immigrants, imposed harsh penalties for unlawful presence, mandated the deportation of legal permanent residents with criminal convictions, and significantly expanded the grounds for mandatory deportation (Fragomen 1997; Morawetz 2000).

A consequence of the 9/11 tragedies was the unprecedented expansion of executive powers and state surveillance as part of a domestic war on terrorism that has fundamentally threatened civil liberties in the United States and promotes the criminalization of racialized immigrants, especially undocumented immigrants (Chang 2002; Akram and Johnson 2002). The USA PATRIOT Act of 2001—whose acronyms stand for "Uniting and Strengthening America by Providing Appropriate Tools Required to Intercept and Obstruct Terrorism"—set in motion unprecedented compromises in civil liberties and abuses of documented and undocumented immigrants in the United States through special registrations, absconder initiatives, detentions, and deportations. The institutional framework for administering and enforcing U.S. immigration laws changed to respond to the post-9/11 environment. The U.S. Immigration and Naturalization Service was dissolved, and its functions were restructured under the Department of Homeland Security (DHS) in three agencies: U.S. Customs and Immigration Services, which administers immigration and naturalization services and establishes immigration policies and priorities; U.S. Immigration and Customs Enforcement (ICE), which enforces immigration and customs laws; and U.S. Customs and Border Protection, which has a priority mission of keeping terrorists and their weapons out of the United States while also securing the border, facilitating lawful international trade and travel, and enforcing U.S. laws and regulations, including immigration and drug laws. As a key component of the DHS's layered-defense approach to national security, ICE advances an aggressive program that targets and criminalizes undocumented immigrants and sanctions their inhumane treatment.[3]

The effects of the domestic war on terrorism were acutely felt in Brooklyn's immigrant neighborhoods with large South Asian and Arab American populations (Bayoumi 2006). In November 2002, the George W. Bush administration implemented the National Security Entry-Exit Registration System, also known as the Special Registration Program, that required men and boys over the age of sixteen from twenty-five countries—all predominately Muslim countries in Asia and Africa except for North Korea—to report to immigration offices to be fingerprinted, photographed, and interrogated under oath.[4] Thousands were arrested, detained, or forced into deportation proceedings for minor visa violations that are typically ignored (Asian American Legal Defense and Education Fund 2004). The program essentially "cleared the streets" of community residents (Bayoumi 2006). A *New York Times* account of the program's impact on Brooklyn's Little Pakistan in the Midwood neighborhood reported that eight thousand Pakistani residents were either deported or had left the country voluntarily (Afridi 2005). Despite the interrogation and registration of more than eighty thousand men, none were found to have any links to terrorism (Swarns 2004). The program represented the first time that the federal government allowed local police to enforce immigration law and amass a database that enables states to track and monitor specific immigrant groups.

Racial profiling also targeted Sikhs, who are not Muslim; however, their religious attire includes turbans and beards for men, which made them a highly visible target (Goodstein and Lewin 2001; Lewin and Niebuhr 2001). In response to several violent incidences, the Sikh community in Queens prepared informational pamphlets that were adorned with small red, white, and blue ribbons and noted basic facts about the Sikh community. The pamphlets were distributed near key neighborhood institutions, including the Gurdwara Sikh Temple Society in South Richmond Hill. The Sikh Coalition, which formed to advocate for victims and their families and work on civil rights concerns of the community, produced a research report and held a rally protesting several bias incidences in the New York City public schools (Sikh Coalition 2008). Community leaders noted that many bias incidences are simply not in the public record because of an intensifying fear of government authorities and possible detainment and deportation.

The fear of unwarranted government surveillance was substantiated by a series of investigative articles by the Associated Press that exposed the New York City Police Department's Muslim surveillance operation.[5] As part of the department's counterterrorism activities, the New York City Police Department has been monitoring mosques; neighborhood businesses, especially dollar stores; and law-abiding citizens such as Muslim students in area universities, including the City University of New York (Powell 2012). In defending the operation, Police Commissioner Raymond Kelly was quoted in the *New York Times* as proclaiming that "people have short memories as to what happened here in 2001" (Goldstein 2012).

In the aftermath of the 9/11 tragedies, the DHS contracted with federal, local, and private detention facilities throughout the United States to jail detainees. Eighty-four detainees designated as "high interest" by the Federal Bureau of Investigation (FBI) were brought to Sunset Park's Metropolitan Detention Center (MDC) in the immediate months after the terrorist attacks. The MDC was one of two federal prisons investigated by the Department of Justice's Office of Inspector General in 2002 because "they held the majority of September 11 detainees and were the focus of many complaints about detainee mistreatment."[6] The extensive abuses of immigrant detainees were documented in several reports.[7] According to the Department of Justice investigation, "The September 11 detainees held at the MDC were locked down 23 hours a day, were placed in four-man holds during movement, had restricted phone call and visitation privileges, and had less ability to obtain and communicate with legal counsel."[8] Advocacy groups also claimed that the MDC's windows were painted black so detainees would have no natural sunlight.

Despite these alarming findings, the Justice Department's civil rights division and U.S. attorney Roslyn Mauskopf in Brooklyn declined to press charges against the MDC prison guards. While some of the guards have since left MDC employment and will never be held accountable for their actions, others remain on the payroll, including an abusive guard found guilty of criminal behavior in another incidence (Bernstein 2004a). These atrocities led a *New York Daily News* reporter to describe the MDC as Brooklyn's Abu Ghraib (Cohler-Esses 2005). The parallels are troubling. Sergeant Gary Pittman was convicted in September 2004 for abusing Iraqi prisoners at Abu Ghraib; his civilian job was as a guard at Sunset Park's federal prison (Gendar 2004). Videos were also taken of Sunset Park MDC guards engaged in prisoner abuses, but with the exception of a few frames, the hundreds of tapes that were filmed remain hidden from the public (Moses 2004; Bernstein 2004a, 2004c).

In 2002, the Center for Constitutional Rights filed a class-action civil rights lawsuit on behalf of 9/11 detainees against U.S. attorney general John Ashcroft, FBI director Robert Mueller, former INS commissioner James Ziglar, and employees of the MDC for violations of detainees' rights under the First, Fourth, and Fifth Amendments and international human rights law.[9] However, a 2006 decision in *Turkmen v. Ashcroft* by U.S. district court judge John Gleeson recognized and upheld the expansion of state powers to indefinitely detain noncitizens of particular religions, races, or national origins without a specific reason and ultimately to deport them without notification (Bernstein 2006a).

Sunset Park resident and filmmaker Konrad Aderer produced *Enemy Alien,* which documents the detainment of and the subsequent struggle to release Farouk Abdel-Muhti, a Palestinian activist and assistant producer for the local Pacifica radio station, WBAI.[10] Abdel-Muhti was arrested on April 26, 2002, ostensibly for a deportation order issued in 1995. In addition to the ICE detainment of high-interest individuals, a 2002 Absconder Apprehension Initiative sought to apprehend, interview, and deport approximately 314,000 people described as "absconders" or "fugitive aliens." Absconders are defined as individuals who had been ordered deported by an immigration judge but remained in the United States. This program was yet another tool to target and remove several thousand Arab and Muslim immigrants who were from countries with or suspected of an Al Qaeda presence.

Abdel-Muhti's activism and his publicizing of the names of ICE detainees on WBAI made him a highly visible target for apprehension and deportation (Aderer 2013). Aderer's film documented Abdel-Muhti's two year detention ordeal, which began at ICE's New York City Office of Enforcement and Removal Operations, located at 26 Federal Plaza, where he was interrogated, beaten, and threatened. Aderer documented Abdel-Muhti's relocation to seven different county jails in New York, New Jersey, and Pennsylvania that were part of ICE's extensive prison network. In telling Abdel-Muhti's ordeal, which included physical abuse and solitary confinement, Aderer explores the parallels between the post-9/11 roundups of Arab and South Asian immigrants and the internment of Japanese Americans during World War II. Of Japanese descent, Aderer interweaves his grandparents' experiences, including interviews with his grandmother, who was interned for three and a half years in Utah (where Aderer's mother was born), and images of his grandfather's photographs, taken secretively because cameras were banned in the camps. Aderer's film makes a powerful point in underscoring the ways that immigrants are easily scapegoated during periods of political and economic crisis; as racialized Americans, they are predisposed to an inevitable and dubious designation as "enemy aliens." Abdel-Muhti was eventually released upon a federal judge's ruling that his imprisonment was unconstitutional. His tragic death of a heart attack three months later was believed to have been hastened by the harsh conditions of his detainment, which greatly diminished his physical health.

Approximately half of the estimated eleven million undocumented immigrants in the United States are "illegal" because they overstayed their visas, meaning they entered lawfully but did not leave when their visas expired (Pew Hispanic Center 2006). Nearly all undocumented men in the United States are in the labor force (Passel, Capps, and Fix 2004). As an indispensable workforce for numerous economic sectors, undocumented immigrants also help keep social welfare programs such as Social Security and Medicare solvent through tax deductions, which they will never benefit from (Porter 2005; Anon. 2008b). Increasingly draconian immigration policies and enforcement actions, however, have led to mass workplace and neighborhood raids to round up and detain hundreds of harmless immigrants for seemingly insignificant violations, including photographing sensitive areas.[11] In his personal account of the May 2008 ICE sweep in Postville, Iowa, of hundreds of Guatemalan and Mexican immigrants at the nation's largest kosher slaughterhouse and meatpacking plant, Florida International University professor Camayd-Freixas (2008) describes "the saddest procession I have ever witnessed" of immigrants "shackled at the wrists, waist and ankles" at their court arraignment. The cases of innocent detainees who have been deported or have died while in U.S. custody highlights a growing concern with the dehumanizing treatment of undocumented immigrants in a highly decentralized and secretive detention system. ICE released an account of the 131 immigrants who died in U.S. custody from October 7, 2003 to December 6, 2012. For each detainee, ICE provided name, date and place of birth, gender, cause of death, and detention facility. It is particularly alarming that 13 percent of the detainees died of asphyxia.

Federal policies continue to promote new social exclusions based on migrant status. The Real ID Act of 2005 imposes new federal standards for the issuance of state driver's licenses and creates a multitiered system with different types of licenses for lawful permanent residents (i.e., U.S. citizens, green card holders, and asylees and refugees) and immigrants with temporary visas, including noncitizens who are in the United States legally.[12] In 2012, the Barack Obama administration expanded the controversial Secure Communities program, which entails the sharing of local and state police information, such as fingerprints, with the FBI and the DHS. Under the program, the FBI automatically sends fingerprints to the DHS to check against its immigration databases. According to the DHS, "If these checks reveal that an individual is unlawfully present in the United States or otherwise removable due to a criminal conviction, ICE takes enforcement action."[13] Secure Communities has resulted in historic numbers of noncriminal deportations. DHS statistics indicates that in fiscal year 2009, approximately 129,000 immigrant fugitives were deported. Immigrant fugitives are those whose only crime was committing fraud by returning to the United States after having been "previously removed" or "who flagrantly ignore an immigration court's order to leave the country."[14] President Obama is frequently criticized for the unprecedented level of immigrant deportations during his administration. The relatively high and increasing share of non-criminal deportees is especially troublesome (Lopez and Gonzalez-Barrera 2013; Preston 2012).

In June 2012, President Obama granted a reprieve to young undocumented persons by deferring their deportation and granting them the right to study and work in the United States (Compton 2012). While the president's Deferred Action for Childhood Arrivals (DACA) provides "temporary relief from deportation," there is still no permanent solution to the undocumented status of close to 1.7 million young immigrants who have no pathway to establish a permanent "lawful presence" in the United States. These young adults are granted a two-year reprieve to allow them to continue their productive engagement as students or workers, but basic citizenship rights such as health care coverage are still denied (Pear 2012).

Sunset Park is an epicenter of undocumented Latino and Asian immigration, so citizenship rights and immigration reform are central themes in its political landscape. Youth activist Citlalli Negrete founded the Raza Youth Collective to mobilize and educate Sunset Park residents about ongoing federal level immigration debates. She is an ardent critic of DACA because it fails to provide a substantive or permanent solution for undocumented immigrants. The goal of immigration reform should be citizenship for all, according to Negrete, and subsequently she rejects the leadership of established groups such as the New York Immigration Coalition and National Council of La Raza because they advocate for interim provisions, such as the DREAM (Development, Relief, and Education for Alien Minors) Act. Since early 2013, the Raza Youth Collective has been involved in citywide actions and coalition building (the collective is a member of the Migrant Power Alliance), but Negrete "feels the need to come back to Sunset Park" (Negrete 2013). Through her personal network, she heard that ICE raids have taken place at Sunset Park workplaces and that workers have been deported. She shared that some Raza Youth Collective activities in the planning stages include a speak-out on 5th Avenue and conducting know-your-rights political education.

New York University's Mitchell Moss (2006) argues there is no public policy more important to cities than federal immigration policy. These policies underscore the national ambivalence toward immigrants. Targeting undocumented immigrants as a key strategy in the domestic war on terrorism helps to maintain a hyperexploited and malleable workforce. The current conditions push undocumented immigrants further underground and has long-term adverse impacts on the civil rights of noncitizens and citizens alike (Akram and Johnson 2002). The criminalization of undocumented immigrants is furthered by efforts to deputize local municipal and town police to enforce immigration laws. Undocumented immigrants as an "illegal" subclass status means that "more than ever, they're on their own" (Segal 2003). Some scholars observe an incremental but transformative shift in immigration policies toward more restrictive citizenship criteria premised on financial and human resources rather than a willingness to work hard (Park and Park 2005). This dual context of heightened enforcement and selective migration impacts the composition and contour of immigrant community formations and a sense of membership and belonging in the United States. Urban fault lines based on racial boundaries are further complicated by citizenship rights, because undocumented immigrants have few if any legal basis for claiming political, social, and economic rights.

The Entrepreneurial City: "No Small Plans"

Post-1965 immigrants settled in New York City during a defining period of urban crisis marked by an international oil embargo, economic restructuring, a massive loss of manufacturing jobs, and white flight. These conditions diminished the city's tax base and municipal services as well as the political will to address rising social needs and unrest. By the mid-1970s, New York City symbolized urban dysfunction and chaos. The strategy to prevent the city's financial collapse was premised on the retrenchment of social welfare programs (including tuition-free higher education at the City University of New York), whose recipients were increasingly African American and Puerto Rican. The gains of social democratic institutions such as unions were eroded through massive layoffs and wage freezes. User fees for a variety of services, including public transportation, were raised repeatedly (Freeman 2000). In sum, New York City avoided default via a fundamental shift in power as the municipal government aligned with the private sector to reduce labor costs and social expenditures and increase support for leading economic development sectors, particularly the FIRE sector (Hackworth 2007; Freeman 2000; Fitch 1993; Moody 2007). As Freeman (2000, 258) described, "Financial leaders saw an opportunity to undo the past, to restructure New York along lines more to their liking than those drawn by decades of liberalism and labor action."

Immigrant assimilation is integral to a neoliberal urbanism that emphasizes individualism. Neoliberalism is defined simply as the ideology that human interests are best served by unfettered entrepreneurial freedoms in an institutional environment that upholds private property rights, free markets, and free trade (Harvey 2003). An immigrant narrative of hard work, sacrifice, and self-reliance fits well with New York City's recovery, which is based on state retrenchment and market ascendance (Vitullo-Martin 2008; Moss 2006). Asian and Latino immigration is integral to urban restructuring by replenishing and transforming the urban population base and providing a vital labor source for a restructuring economy that has created marginal opportunities for immigrants and heightened hardships for African Americans and Puerto Ricans (Abu-Lughod 1999, 206). In valorizing immigrant economic incorporation and investments, neoliberal urbanism diverts attention from the uneven inclusion of Asians and Latinos that speaks to much more complex experiences of heightened class divisions and racial and ethnic tensions (Smith 2002, 437).

Neoliberal urban policies were reinvigorated in response to a confluence of post-1970s demographic and economic restructurings and are evidenced by devolution, deregulation, and privatization, which have facilitated an upward redistribution of resources and a return to Gilded Age–era inequality (Newman and Ashton 2004; Duggan 2003; Phillips-Fein 2013). This neoliberal period is marked by state retrenchment of interventions that mediated the material conditions of urban inequality in housing and labor conditions. One aspect of neoliberal urbanism is the remaking of urban spaces for the affluent, which is distinguished by a high level of corporatization and state involvement through planning and land-use tools of zoning and eminent domain (J. M. Thomas 1994; Smith 2002; Hackworth 2002; Brenner, Peck, and Theodore 2005).

A neoliberal urban agenda was advanced by Mayor Bloomberg through a corporate approach to governance that consolidated the interests and agenda of a ruling elite in an administration defined by technocracy, meritocracy, and professionalism. In his book on New York City as a luxury city, Julian Brash (2011, 5) defined neoliberal governance as "entrepreneurialism" that "prioritizes the stimulation of corporate investment and real estate development and entails speculative and activist governmental means to attain this goal." As a CEO mayor, Bloomberg, who is a billionaire and accepts one dollar per year for his mayoral salary, exemplifies a neoliberal governance approach and priorities. Inheriting leadership in the immediate aftermath of the 9/11 tragedies, Bloomberg has steered the city through a sustained period of urban development and population growth that has also been marked by heightening race and class inequality.

One of Bloomberg's closest advisers, Dan Doctoroff, a fellow billionaire who made his fortune in investment banking and private equity investment, served as deputy mayor for economic development and rebuilding and over-saw more than forty city agencies and corporations, including the New York City Economic Development Corporation, the Department of City Plan-ning, and the Department of Small Business Services, for the same one-dollar annual salary from 2002 to 2007. Doctoroff helped to solidify and implement a corporatist governance approach to urban education, poverty reduction, economic development, and city service delivery and elevated urban planning and land-use tools to achieve private market confidence and investments in New York City.

Doctoroff headed NYC 2012 prior to joining the Bloomberg admin-istration, and even though the NYC 2012 Olympic bid failed, it served as the organizing principle or "blueprint" for the administration's development vision of a revitalized New York City (Robbins and McIntire 2004). In his article "No Small Plans: The Rebirth of Economic Development in New York City," Doctoroff (2006) laid out the Bloomberg administration's ambi-tious real estate–driven economic development strategy, encompassing all five boroughs and representing a massive restructuring of the city's built environment.[15] The urban renewal vision to make the city more livable and business friendly and to diversify its economy was centered on upscale com-mercial and retail development, recreational open spaces and sports sta-diums, and luxury housing and hotels. This reconfiguration of the built environment prominently featured the rezoning and redevelopment of the city's neglected and contaminated industrial waterfront at key neighborhood sites, including Hudson Yards in Manhattan, Greenpoint and Williamsburg in Brooklyn, and Long Island City and Flushing in Queens. The Manhatta-nization of the outer boroughs is exemplified by megadevelopment proposals such as Forest Ratner City's controversial $4 billion Atlantic Yards project, which involved eminent domain to assemble a twenty-two-acre site for a mixed-use retail and commercial development that included a sports and entertainment arena, mixed-income housing, and a hotel that, according to critics, will overwhelm surrounding Brooklyn brownstone neighborhoods (Adcock 2007).

Reminiscent of the scale and top-down planning style of Robert Moses during the urban renewal initiatives of the 1950s and 1960s, rezoning, eminent domain, and public subsidies to incentivize private-sector devel-opment are now essential and ubiquitous tools of city building (Fainstein 2005). The primary strategy for this property-led revitalization is the city's land-use tool of zoning through contextual zonings, upzonings, and downzonings (Barbarnel 2004; Moody 2007, 215). With the 1916 New

York City Zoning Ordinance, the city was the first municipality in the country to adopt comprehensive and citywide zoning regulations. The ordinance established basic land-use types (e.g., residential, manufacturing, and commercial) and building setback and height criteria, which were expanded and revised in 1961. Since then, the city's zoning text has been largely updated in a piecemeal fashion—neighborhood by neighborhood—representing a cumulative sea change in land use and the cityscape. During Bloomberg's twelve-year mayoralty, the New York City Department of City Planning has completed 119 rezonings covering nearly 40 percent of New York City's total built area—more rezonings than the previous six administrations combined.

Central to a neoliberal urban agenda is the active role of the state to incentivize and lubricate private capital through city plans and land-use tools. A primary vehicle for promoting public-private partnerships is urban development corporations (Fainstein 2001).[16] Functioning like private firms, these quasi-public entities retain governmental powers, such as access to resources, tax credits, and exercising eminent domain, and are exempted from public-sector accountability and transparency measures, including community participation, public hearings, and the preparation of reports that account for activities (Fainstein 2001; Moody 2007; Fitch 1993).

The New York City Economic Development Corporation (NYCEDC), formed in 1991 by restructuring the city's Public Development Corporation, is the lead agency "charged with leveraging the City's assets to drive growth, create jobs and improve quality of life" (Rivera 2012). The NYCEDC functions as a quasi-public nonprofit organization with a mayoral-appointed president. The organization is the key agency that hands out tax exemptions and subsidies to private corporations as a job-creation strategy and maintains a heavy presence in Sunset Park with major city-owned waterfront properties, including Bush Terminal and the Brooklyn Army Terminal. Because its operations are largely outside of city procurement procedures, the NYCEDC is subject to minimal oversight.

Under the Bloomberg administration, the NYCEDC has emerged as a powerhouse in pushing forward the mayor's transformative and aggressive development agenda (Angotti 2008b; Brash 2011). The most recent example of the extensive overlap between Bloomberg economic development officials and corporate real estate executives is NYCEDC president Seth Pinksy, who announced in July 2013 that he is stepping down to join RXR Realty as executive vice president (Geiger 2013c).

For much of his tenure as city comptroller, John Liu has been a vocal critic of the NYCEDC's lack of transparency and accountability as well as numerous incidences of conflicts of interest. Since taking office in 2009, Liu has shed light "on the black hole that has been EDC"; he uncovered that the NYCEDC had withheld $125 million generated by city property lease payments and sales (Chen and Barbero 2010) and brokered a "secret deal" representing the worst land deal since the sale of Manhattan island for $24 (McShane 2013). Decrying the NYCEDC's violation of "its fiduciary responsibility to act in the best interests of our taxpayers," Comptroller Liu criticized the city's revision of an agreement with the Marriott Marquis to shorten its lease period to 2017, when Marriott will have the opportunity to purchase its Times Square property for $20 million, representing a tenth of its current fair market value (Liu 2013). Opting not to wait until 2017, Host Hotels and Resorts (owner of numerous Marriott-operated hotels) purchased the Times Square site, whose fair market value is estimated to be upwards of $200 million, for a mere $19.9 million from the NYCEDC in December 2013 (Clarke 2013).

In 2012, New York state attorney general Eric Schneiderman conducted an investigation in which the NYCEDC and two local development corporations—Flushing Willets Point Corona Local Development Corporation and the Coney Island Development Corporation, both established to coordinate Bloomberg legacy mega-development initiatives (Willets Point in Queens and Coney Island in Brooklyn)—were found to be in violation of the Not-for-Profit Corporations Law (Anuta 2012; Rivera 2012). The attorney general's investigation described how the NYCEDC directed both local development corporations to engage in such activities as ghostwriting op-eds, lobbying City Council members, preparing testimony, and organizing transportation to public hearings in order to "foster the appearance of independent 'grassroots' support for the Projects in the local community."[17] Upon the attorney general's findings, Comptroller Liu (2012a) demanded reform of the NYCEDC's "law-breaking" culture and called for public access to the organization finances through the Comptroller's Checkbook NYC website.[18]

Public agencies such as the Department of City Planning that are charged with serving the public interest in land-use planning ultimately acquiesced to the NYCEDC in promoting cityscapes that accommodate private development (Fainstein 2001; Moody 2007). As a function of the state, "planning is one of the many social technologies of power available to the ruling elites, and has primarily been used to support the power and privileges of dominant classes and cultures" (Sandercock 2003, 2). The intertwining of corporate leadership and urban governance was evident in Dan Doctoroff's departure in December 2007 to assume the position of president for the financial and media conglomeration Bloomberg L.P., founded by Mayor Bloomberg (Cardwell and Bagli 2007). The Bloomberg administration's request to retain Doctoroff as an unpaid adviser on key urban development initiatives, including PlaNYC 2030, Moynihan Station, and Queens West and Hudson Yards, passed muster with the city's Conflict of Interest Board (McGeehan and Rivera 2008).

Zoning has been instrumental in the Bloomberg administration's aggressive urban planning strategies for meeting the spatial needs and placemaking of a postindustrial city (Lander and Wolf-Powers 2004). The Bloomberg administration has overseen an unprecedented number of rezonings to leverage commercial value through the upzoning of "blighted" and underutilized areas, including 368 blocks of Jamaica, Queens, and in other cases preserving neighborhood quality and character by downzoning or granting landmark status to majority white middle-class suburban-like neighborhoods in the outer boroughs of Queens, Brooklyn, and Staten Island (Lieberman 2004; Murphy 2006b; Santucci 2007). The progrowth position is rationalized in part by the need to accommodate a projected population increase of one million new New Yorkers by 2030—an increase comparable to the population of several major U.S. metropolitan areas such as San Jose, California, or Austin, Texas.[19]

The scale of gentrification as an urban strategy has escalated from individual hipsters and artists colonizing a depressed neighborhood to corporate invasion led by public subsidies for a heightened level of globalization and privatization in many local neighborhoods (Smith 2002). Asian immigrant neighborhoods are a prime example of "globalization and a dominant neoliberal policy agenda that together are contributing to a vast restructuring of urban space" (Newman and Ashton 2004, 1169). Neoliberal urbanism is marked by a massive restructuring of established immigrant neighborhoods such as Flushing, Queens, where Asian capital has advanced from small individual investors to major real estate corporations and development firms that are able to mobilize international finance capital for local urban initiatives. Several development projects demonstrate Flushing's integral link to New York City's regional economy as a center for international capital and tourism and the synergistic interests of the city's governmental and private developers to transform Flushing's immigrant neighborhood.

The NYCEDC's 2004 Downtown Flushing Framework, which staff members are careful to point out resulted from "an organic planning process," delineates three central planning initiatives (Fink 2011). The first is to reconnect and renew downtown with high-quality development initiatives such as the Flushing Commons project, approved for a five-acre municipal parking lot in the center of downtown Flushing. The $850 million development project features three sixteen-story towers of luxury residential condominiums and a hotel or office space, nearly 300,000 square feet of "American-style" corporate retailers, and a small town plaza.[20] The second is to revitalize Flushing's waterfront, which the NYCEDC has identified as the "strongest potential unifying element" to connect downtown Flushing to surrounding new developments in Willets Point and Flushing Meadows Corona Park. The third is to transform Willets Point, which according to the latest plan proposed by the NYCEDC and the Queens Development Group LLC (a partnership of Related Companies and New York Mets baseball team owner Sterling Equities) will entail 1.4 million square feet of entertainment and retail space in what will be Queens' largest shopping mall plus a two hundred–room hotel in the first phase, called Willets West. More mixed residential and commercial development is planned in a second phase, with the construction of the promised affordable housing not to begin until 2025.[21] Community activists are outraged that the affordable housing component, which was essential to their support in 2008, has been pushed back and have protested the lack of a guarantee that the affordable housing will ever be built (Bartlett 2013).

A central actor in Flushing's transformative developments is Taiwanese-born Michael Lee, owner and founder of the F&T Group, an international development company whose corporate motto is "Global Vision for Local Development."[22] The F&T Group is the parent company of TDC Development LLC, which the NYCEDC partnered with the Rockefeller Development Corporation to develop Flushing Commons. TDC Development LLC is also a key property owner of waterfront lots that will be instrumental in shaping Flushing's future.

A sign of future Flushing waterfront redevelopment is Sky View Parc—a fortresslike luxury living complex located at the central intersection of Roosevelt Avenue and College Point Boulevard. Developed on a former Con Edison brownfield in 2008, the fourteen-acre development includes Sky View Center, a shopping mall that occupies three stories with big-box retailers such as Target's and Bed, Bath & Beyond. Above the mall, a private garden oasis and open space with tennis courts and a playground is anchored by three luxury condominium towers with 832 units. Although situated directly across the street from Bland Houses, one of Flushing's two New York City Housing Authority public housing developments, there are no design elements or streetscape features that integrate these two residential complexes.

In fact, residential Sky View Parc exemplifies an urban gated community with no connection to the surrounding neighborhood. Sky View Parc has been troubled by poor sales and management, and in 2010 nearly 80 prospective buyers filed a lawsuit to recoup their deposits (Bernstein 2011). As capital markets have rebounded, plans to construct an additional 800 luxury residential condominium units in three new towers are proceeding (Trapasso 2014).

Sky View Parc residents have a prime view directly across the contaminated Flushing River to Willets Point. The area, also known as the Iron Triangle, is currently a squalid industrial enclave lacking basic infrastructure, including a sewage system and paved roads. Despite city neglect, approximately 255 auto-related businesses and small machine shops—many immigrant-owned and -operated have thrived for decades because businesses are in the process of relocation (Angotti and Romalewski 2006). To assemble the sixty-one-acre development site, the city threatened to exercise its power of eminent domain (as the state did in the Atlantic Yards project in Brooklyn). Thirty-two (of fifty-one) New York City Council members signed a letter calling the city's plan "deeply flawed" and warned that the opportunity for public accountability "has been dangerously absent" (Santos 2008a; Lauinger 2008). In addition to the imminent displacement of small businesses and seventeen hundred jobs, the abuse of city zoning and eminent domain powers and the actions of quasi-public organizations such as the NYCEDC in the interest of private capital and profit are of central concern.

Neoliberal urbanism means that the public interest goal of city planning is increasingly at the service of private development, as city policies and agencies are integral to designating blighted areas and using zoning, urban renewal, historic landmark designation, and public resources to facilitate private investments (Moody 2007, 234). As Brenner, Peck, and Theodore (2005, 12) argue, "The overarching goal of such neoliberal urban policy experiments is to mobilize city space as an arena for market-oriented economic growth and elite consumption practices, while at the same time securing order and control amongst 'underclass' populations."

From proposals to develop the country's largest urban amusement and entertainment area in Coney Island, preserve newly gentrified and affluent wealthy enclaves such as the East Village, facilitate Columbia University institutional expansion in West Harlem, and create an "airport village" in Jamaica, Queens, New York City is being reconfigured to be livable and sustainable for the wealthy and elite. Advancing this development vision has entailed city planning and decision-making processes whereby public accountability is notably and "dangerously absent" (Monserrate et al. 2008).

Conclusion

By reviewing current political economic trends and conditions, this theoretical framework highlights the need to revise enclave and ethnoburb theorizations of immigrant Asian neighborhoods that emphasize ethnic identity, resources, and solidarity. The experience of Asian urbanism includes increasing numbers of multiracial, multiethnic neighborhood formations. Sunset Park is a paradigmatic global neighborhood, and in the following chapters I investigate how a study of Sunset Park advances a theoretical framework of immigrant urbanization that (1) situates immigrant community studies and placemaking in a postindustrial political economic context, (2) focuses on emergent immigrant urban growth coalitions and how they shape urbanization and land-use politics, (3) examines the opportunities and challenges for immigrant civic engagement and the mobilization of Latino and Asian common interests, and (4) analyzes how neoliberal economic development and neighborhood revitalization strategies impact local gentrification and placemaking.

2

Making Sunset Park

Settlement, Decline, and Transformation

S unset Park's evolution from a white ethnic industrial waterfront neighborhood to its decline during the fiscal crisis of the late 1960s and the
1970s, marked by white flight and controversial urban renewal tactics, and its remaking in the 1980s as a multiethnic, multiracial neighborhood is an account of economic restructuring, modern urban planning, and
mass international migration. In documenting the making of Sunset Park,
this chapter establishes that post-1970s urban development trajectories have
resulted in a paradigmatic shift of immigrant spatial formations as enclaves,
barrios, or ethnoburbs to global neighborhoods. Although Sunset Park's
evolution tells a compelling story of successive immigrant waves and neighborhood renewal, the making of Sunset Park is most important for insight
into the changing urban political economy and the centrality of urban
development policies and institutions in shaping New York City's local eth-
nogeography. This chapter documents how the dynamics of race, immigration, and economic restructuring have structured Sunset Park's spatial and
social landscape and established the context for ongoing debate and struggle
over neighborhood definition, land use, and community development.

Industrial Port Economy

Sunset Park's waterfront location and proximity to the New Amsterdam
village at the tip of lower Manhattan made the area among the first in
Brooklyn to be settled by the Dutch in the 1600s (Sunset Park Restoration

Committee 1979; Ment and Donovan 1980). With African slave labor, Dutch and Huguenot families established farmsteads along Brooklyn's waterfront and harvested cash crops, such as tobacco and grain. By 1855, Brooklyn evolved from a prospering village to become the nation's third-largest city, and in 1898, the year New York City was formed by unifying five counties, Sunset Park's waterfront was already an integral part of the emergent regional port economy.[1]

As water access was critical for transportation and industry, Sunset Park's waterfront was a prime site for development. Drawn by plentiful employment opportunities along an industrializing waterfront, Irish, Scandinavian (particularly Norwegians and Finns), Polish, and Italian immigrants settled in Sunset Park in successive waves beginning in the early 1800s. Institutions built by these immigrants—including St. Michael's Church (with its distinctive egg-shaped dome), Our Lady of Perpetual Help, the Norwegian Lutheran Deaconesses' Home and Hospital (now the Lutheran Medical Center), and the Finnish Housing Cooperatives—are standing testimonials to the rich community life of this early period. Numerous neighborhood streets have been renamed to honor their contributions, such as Our Lady of Czestochowa Street/24th Street and Finlandia Street/40th Street.

The nineteenth-century potato famine in Ireland facilitated a massive migration of Irish laborers beginning in the 1840s, which provided a seemingly endless source of unskilled workers who helped build the infrastructure of a growing urban metropolis. Making inroads often by replacing black workers, Irish immigrants took on numerous high-risk and labor-intensive jobs (e.g., as sandhogs or underground construction workers) and were integral in building New York City's defining skyscrapers, bridges, tunnels, and extensive subway network.[2] The contributions of Irish labor are evident in many parts of Sunset Park (Ment and Donovan 1980, 54). The Irish excavated the Gowanus Creek to construct a canal that allowed barges to access industrializing sections of Brooklyn. They helped build the neighborhood's industrial structures, piers, housing stock, churches, and public transportation, first by laying tracks for horsecar lines, next by constructing the elevated steam railroads, and finally by constructing the subway system, including the 4th Avenue Brooklyn-Manhattan Transit (BMT) line that runs through Sunset Park.[3] Until a few years ago, the United Irish Foundation, a neighborhood organization housed in a small storefront, provided social service assistance to the remaining Irish residents of Sunset Park.

Although the earliest clustering of Polish immigrants was centered in the Brooklyn neighborhoods of Williamsburg and Greenpoint in the 1870s, Polish immigrants also settled in Sunset Park and continue to make up a sizable share of the neighborhood's white population. Polish immigrants worked as gravediggers and landscape and maintenance workers in Greenwood Cemetery and as factory workers for Ansonia Clock Company north of Sunset Park until the factory closed in the 1930s.[4] In the late 1890s, Polish immigrants in Sunset Park founded Our Lady of Czestochowa—a Catholic church that started in a small house purchased by local congregants, who raised funds to build the present church in 1904. Ment and Donovan's (1980) documentation of community life in Sunset Park described numerous Polish meat markets and grocery stores along 3rd Avenue.

During the 1880s, Sunset Park and neighboring Red Hook contained the largest concentration of Norwegians east of Minneapolis (Winnick 1990; Mauk 1997). In contrast to the Norwegian population in the Midwest who farmed, Norwegian immigrants in New York and along the Northeast coast worked in the maritime trades (Mauk 1997; Binder and Reimers 1995). Dislocated from their shipbuilding occupations when steam power replaced sailing vessels, seamen from Norway's southern coastal counties, who were highly dependent on the shipping industry, emigrated in search of employment in Brooklyn's growing port economy (Mauk 1997, 9). The ensuing "maritime chain migration" fueled the establishment of Brooklyn's Norwegian community (Mauk 1997, 14), and as late as the 1940s, Norwegians were still concentrated in maritime-related jobs as shipbuilders, dockworkers, and sailors (Ment and Donovan 1980, 63).

The newspaper *Nordisk Tidende* (Norse News) was established in 1891, and the office for the newspaper was located in Sunset Park for several years. Later called the *Norway Times,* with its headquarters in Manhattan, the weekly paper, which covered Brooklyn's Norwegian community, folded in 2008, leaving only one remaining published Norwegian newspaper in North America, the *Norwegian American Weekly.*[5] Known as Lapskaus Boulevard, Sunset Park's 8th Avenue between 45th and 60th Streets (now the center of its Chinese community) served as the main Norwegian commercial thoroughfare. The last remaining Scandinavian shop, Signy's Imports, eventually closed its doors in May 2004 long after neighboring shops had transformed into Chinese bakeries, meat markets, and grocery stores (Anon. 2007b). Complete with photographs, the Scandinavian East Coast Museum website documents how Sunset Park had been a key residential and economic center for the Norwegian population.[6]

A number of Lutheran churches built in the mid-nineteenth century remain active today, although the congregations served are now Chinese and Latino. For example, the Second Evangelical Free Church on 52nd Street, established by the Norwegians, provided space for Reverend Samuel Wong's

Chinese Promise Baptist Church throughout the 1990s.[7] These churches continue to serve as key community institutions, and in the case of Trinity Lutheran Church, located "in the heart of Sunset Park," the church is actively engaged in political mobilization and social justice actions. Led by Reverend Samuel Cruz, who "expresses and lives out a gospel that addresses real social issues and engages racial, gender, sexual and class oppressions,"[8] Trinity Lutheran Church was recently described as a "house of justice" by UPROSE executive director Elizabeth Yeampierre.[9] In addition to hosting events such as a African American–Latino dialogue with prominent activist and public intellectual Dr. Cornel West in December 2012 and a Good Friday service on New York City's controversial Stop and Frisk policy on March 29, 2013, during which Reverend Cruz depicted Sunset Park as the modern-day city of Nazareth, Trinity Lutheran Church is also involved with monitoring the lending practices of local banks.

An enduring legacy of Sunset Park's Norwegian roots is the Norwegian Lutheran Deaconesses' Home and Hospital, now the Lutheran Medical Center (LMC). Established in 1889, the hospital quickly expanded beyond the health care needs of the Norwegian community to provide vital social services to all neighborhood residents. The LMC is central to Sunset Park's evolution, particularly in mediating its transition from a working-class white ethnic neighborhood to a largely poor Latino barrio (Winnick 1990; Ment and Donovan 1980). In 1969, the LMC lost a battle to prevent the relocation of the Fort Greene meatpacking plant to a former shipyard and drydock site on Sunset Park's waterfront.[10] The LMC had considered the Bethlehem Steel Company shipyard for the construction of a new and larger hospital. This defeat, however, gave the LMC tremendous leverage to exact important concessions from the city. The city agreed to facilitate the LMC's acquisition of the nearby American Machine and Foundry Company building and four acres of land for $1, priority access to urban renewal funds to improve conditions in the surrounding industrial area, and a $40,000 city grant to conduct a study to amend zoning regulations that would permit a small residential zone (necessary for the future development of senior housing and a nursing home) on the industrial waterfront (Fischer 1973).

The LMC had considered a move to neighboring Bay Ridge, but relocation to an affluent area would have made the hospital ineligible for millions of dollars in federal antipoverty funding through the 1964 Economic Opportunity Act.[11] Sunset Park's status as a poor immigrant neighborhood has continued to present the LMC with an opportunity to expand its institutional programs and extensive neighborhood infrastructure. The LMC has successfully adapted its provision of health and social services according to federal antipoverty policy priorities over the decades in community development and community health centers (1970s), cultural competency (1980s), and, most recently, President Barack Obama's Promise Neighborhood Initiative (2010s).

The LMC is sensitive about its reputation and involvement in Sunset Park development. Despite its innovative practices in culturally competent health care provision to diverse immigrant groups (Hartocollis 2004; Confessore 2006b), public complaints of poor treatment are not uncommon. In a May 2005 community board meeting, a longtime member proclaimed, "The staff is heartless, they don't care, and they don't pay attention. LMC comes to the board to be granted whatever is needed. It's Lutheran's turn to give back to the community."[12] The LMC's controversial role in shaping neighborhood transition and community development will be examined in a later section in this chapter.

In contrast to their shipbuilding Scandinavian compatriots, Finnish immigrants settling in Sunset Park worked primarily in the building trades as skilled craftsmen and laborers and as tailors, mechanics, and small business owners (Ment and Donovan 1980, 66). The Finnish community concentrated in the northeastern section near the park in an area they called Pukin Maki (Goat Hill) that became known simply as Finntown. Local ethnic institutions included the Imatra—a Finnish Aid Society that provided housing and employment information to new immigrants—and the Brooklyn Socialist Club meeting hall on 40th Street near 8th Avenue (Ment and Donovan 1980, 68). Their collective self-help activities included the construction of one- and two-family homes and, most notably, New York's first cooperative apartment house—a common housing type in Finland.

In 1924, a cooperative housing exhibition sponsored by the Russell Sage Foundation included a representative of the Finnish Cooperative Trading Association and the executive secretary of the Cooperative League of America, who both spoke of the successful efforts of "a colony of Finns in Brooklyn who built ten apartment houses" (Anon. 1924). In 1916, sixteen families contributed $500 each to purchase a lot on 43rd Street between 8th and 9th Avenues in Sunset Park and built a four-story apartment building. Upon its completion, the families paid a modest monthly maintenance fee. The building was named Alku I (Beginning I), and in the ensuing years, twenty additional housing cooperatives were established nearby (Ment and Donovan 1980, 67–68). These buildings housed subsequent generations of Finnish Americans; however, the presence of this population in Sunset Park has diminished greatly (Cohen 1996a).

The development of South Brooklyn's waterfront was critical for relieving congestion along Manhattan's piers, which was necessary for the expansion of New York City's port economy. Brooklyn's natural advantages in wide and deep channels could accommodate the increasing numbers of large steamships. Seizing the opportunity to mitigate port congestion, Irving T. Bush commenced the construction of Bush Terminal in the late 1890s.[13] By the time of its completion in 1912, Bush Terminal occupied a 250-acre site that covered nearly two miles of Sunset Park's shoreline from 28th to 51st Streets and from 3rd Avenue to the Upper New York Bay.

Formerly a desolate "waste of pebbly beach" called Ambrose Park, Bush Terminal was unprecedented in size and form. Consisting of a complex of 8 piers, 118 brick warehouses that provided twenty-five million cubic feet of storage space, and factory lofts in more than a dozen industrial structures, Bush Terminal's facilities were linked by twenty-one miles of railway track "meandering through the terminal's cobbled streets" (Anon. 1918). Bush Terminal symbolized a "port of the future" where the varied needs of industrial manufacturers and commercial shippers could be met in one location (Gallagher 1908; Bush 1916) and quickly became a prototype for industrial park development (Anon. 1908; Anon. 1909).[14]

Employing tens of thousands in manufacturing- and shipping-related industries, Bush Terminal was New York City's largest and busiest commercial and industrial facility (Anon. 1918; Ment and Donovan 1980). Early references to an "industrial colony" later became formalized on the side of a twelve-story factory building, which proclaimed in huge painted letters "A Great Industrial City Within a City" (Anon. 1910; Stern 1961; Sunset Park Restoration Committee 1979). Raw materials were shipped to manufacturing firms, which produced goods that were moved by boxcars and floated across New York Harbor to New Jersey and then transported by trucks and railroads for distribution throughout the country (Ment and Donovan 1980). Sunset Park's Bush Terminal gave Brooklyn a "commanding position in New York City's port economy." In addition to its commercial prominence, Bush Terminal was requisitioned by the U.S. War Department during World War I to meet wartime production and shipping needs (Anon. 1918).

As World War I drew to an end, Sunset Park's waterfront expanded to include the Brooklyn Army Terminal (BAT) designed by legendary architect Cass Gilbert, who had also designed the famous Woolworth Building and the U.S. Customs House. Opened in 1919, BAT—a fifty-seven acre site consisting of piers, two of the world's largest warehouses (large enough to hold material and supplies to load twelve 8,000-ton ships), railroad yards, administration buildings, and mechanical facilities, including a power plant—served as a central embarkation point for soldiers and provisions during World War II and the Korean War (Shephard 1919; Anon. 1945). At the height of World War II, BAT employed ten thousand civilians and handled nearly 80 percent of the supplies and troops involved in the war effort (Winnick 1990).

As New York City's industrial pulse, Sunset Park's waterfront was a key center of industrial production and transnational trade (Freeman 2000; Stern 1961). During this time, Brooklyn's waterfront was the main entry point for imported goods to the United States, and in 1960 Brooklyn handled two-fifths of all shipping traffic in the region (Abu-Lughod 1999, 190). Moreover, 60 percent of the dollar value of all cargo handled in the Port of New York passed through Brooklyn's piers (Stern 1961). Compared to Manhattan piers, which accommodated lighter cargo and passenger ships, at Brooklyn piers more labor-intensive cargo, such as from banana boats, was unloaded (Mello 2002). In addition to the Bethlehem Steel Shipyard and the American Machine & Foundry Company, which employed sixteen hundred workers to produce bowling alley equipment and vending machines, numerous industrial firms—such as Topps Chewing Gum, Colgate-Palmolive-Peet, and American Can Company—as well as hundreds of small machine shops, repair shops, trucking companies, and waterfront suppliers provided a steady flow of blue-collar manufacturing and longshoring jobs in Sunset Park.

While Norwegians specialized in shipbuilding and maintenance, the growing Italian immigrant population found work in the construction trades as bricklayers, masons, and, most notably, longshoremen and dockworkers involved in the backbreaking work of loading and unloading ships by distributing cargo into heavy sacks that were carried to warehouses or onto various transportation modes (Ment and Donovan 1980; Nelson 2001). Although Irish immigrants dominated New York City's port economy as dockworkers, the piers along the Brooklyn waterfront became a niche for Italian immigrants. Citing Charles Barnes's 1915 Russell Sage Foundation–funded study of New York City's waterfront laborers, Bruce Nelson (2001, 22) writes, "Brooklyn, especially, became an Italian stronghold. 'When you came down to the Bush [Terminal],' Barnes wrote of the port's largest concentration of shipping, 'probably two-thirds of the men . . . are Italians, and of course, conditions are a little worse.'"

In an early form of day laboring, Italian longshoremen assembled each morning at a shape-up, where foremen selected their crews for the day (Nelson 2001; Valenzuela 2003). This casual form of hiring favored the stevedores and labor contractors and ultimately the employers by generating a labor surplus. The constant fear of replacement helped to maintain a highly productive and disciplined workforce. Italian immigrants mobilized to improve work conditions and actively participated in the nationwide strike in 1919 that paralyzed New York City's port economy for nearly a month (Nelson 2001). One of the worst incidences of violence occurred early one morning near the Bush Terminal when one thousand Italian longshoremen attacked a group of approximately two hundred men who had just been picked by the foreman and were making their way onto the pier (Anon. 1919). One hundred reserve policemen were utilized to contain the rioting. All of those arrested were Italian men who lived in Sunset Park or neighboring South Brooklyn areas.

The 1924 National Origins Act ended mass immigration from southern and eastern Europe. The effect was that "the major sources of immigration for New York City for the previous thirty years suddenly were virtually shut off" (Binder and Reimers 1995, 152). Tight labor market conditions necessitated a greater reliance on internal surplus labor, namely Puerto Ricans, who were granted U.S. citizenship by the 1917 Jones Act, and southern blacks (Briggs 1989; Grosfugel 1999; Laurentz 1980).[15] Industrial cities such as Chicago and New York City were prime destinations for these racialized/colonial migrants, and the movement of rural southern blacks to northern cities in the Great Migration provided a vital replacement workforce (Osofsky 1963; Abu-Lughod 1999; Grosfugel 1999). During this period, Puerto Ricans and African Americans were able to make inroads in industries that once excluded them, although they experienced lower wages and poorer conditions. While it was not until the 1950s that large numbers of Puerto Ricans migrated to the United States, the employment of Puerto Rican and African American women in labor-intensive industry sectors such as New York City's garment industry commenced in the 1920s (Laurentz 1980, 105). These opportunities were limited, and as Binder and Reimers (1995, 169) note, blacks and Puerto Ricans "became a ghettoized population laboring in unskilled jobs."

During the 1940s, World War II brought a high level of industrial production back to Sunset Park's waterfront, albeit for a brief period. As Winnick (1990, 87) describes, "Bush Terminal and every plant in the Industrial Zone were strained to full capacity, most on a round-the-clock schedule" to meet war-related demands. The wartime economic boom, however, was not sustainable, and Ment and Donovan (1980, 73) note that "once the war ended, this activity ceased almost immediately, and hundreds of jobs were lost." A short decade later, technological advances, namely in cargo containerization, gave the competitive edge to huge modern facilities developed in Port Newark, New Jersey. Often referred to as longshoremen's coffins, huge containers greatly reduced the number of dockworkers necessary to unload cargo (Nelson 2001). A report prepared by the New York City Council's Committee on Waterfronts noted that as a result of containerization, a team of seventeen stevedores or longshoremen was able to unload five hundred tons of cargo in an hour, in contrast to the precontainerization amount of forty tons.[16]

Early signs of the structural shift in the industrial composition of the United States were evident in Sunset Park's waterfront (Bluestone and Harrison 1982; Yago et al. 1984; Sassen 1990). As a consequence of technology and a declining competitive edge for manufacturing in the Northeast, U.S. corporations relocated domestically to areas with lower production and labor costs and then increasingly relocated overseas to newly established export-processing zones in the Caribbean and other parts of the world. After fifty-two years of operation at the Bush Terminal, Norton Lilly & Co., one of the nation's oldest shipping establishments representing seven steamship companies, decided to relocate its terminal operations to Port Newark (Anon. 1957). A few years later, the U.S. Department of Defense offered more than half a million square feet of unused space in the Brooklyn Army Terminal warehouse buildings for commercial lease as office or storage space (Anon. 1961). By the late 1960s, key manufacturing firms—including Bethlehem Steel and the American Machine and Foundry Company—abandoned Bush Terminal. These losses were compounded by the closure of the Brooklyn Army Terminal in 1968, and the eight Bush Terminal piers, which were so vital to New York City's port economy by accommodating large ocean freighters, were closed in 1969. Nearly one thousand longshoremen and manufacturing workers, including tool and die makers, subsequently lost their jobs (Clark 1968; Anon. 1969a; Anon. 1969b).

Although the direction of international trade shifted from a transatlantic to an emergent Pacific Rim flow, which facilitated the rapid expansion of West Coast ports such as California's Los Angeles and Long Beach ports, government policies and actions were also culpable in the demise of New York City's industrial port economy. Long before neoliberalism became a popular catchall phrase for government actions that serve private-sector interests, scholars have documented and theorized about state participation in an urban growth machine driven by a real estate logic of economic growth and development (Logan and Molotch 1987; Fitch 1993). Global market conditions made industrial development increasingly unsustainable, but the city's elite—including real estate developers, elected officials, urban planners, and their partners—helped foment the death sentence for New York City's manufacturing industries and related neighborhood economies. As early as 1929, the Regional Plan Association issued a "Regional Plan of New York and Its Environs," which laid out a vision of New York City with an expanded central business district and eliminated the city's numerous urban

manufacturing districts that exemplified the city's non-Fordist manufacturing production mode (Fitch 1993; Schwartz 1993). Robert Moses essentially
carried out this early vision of an automobile-centric region.

As with many New York City neighborhoods during the 1940s, Moses's
capital infrastructure projects set the stage for residential displacement and
neighborhood destruction (Caro 1974). A key agent in Sunset Park's decline
was the construction in 1941 of the Gowanus Expressway, which replaced
an old elevated subway line. Despite community opposition and pleas to
locate the expressway one block west on 2nd Avenue, the 5.7-mile Gowanus
Expressway connecting the Brooklyn-Battery Tunnel with South Brooklyn
(and eventually the Verrazano-Narrows Bridge) was routed through Sunset
Park along 3rd Avenue—a commercial stretch that had served as the heart
of the neighborhood because of its Irish and Italian residential concentration
(Caro 1974; Ment and Donovan 1980). Approximately one hundred stores
were closed and thirteen hundred families were relocated, and every building on the east side of 3rd Avenue between 39th and 63rd Streets was torn
down to make way for the Gowanus Expressway (Caro 1974, 522).

The process of displacement and destruction occurred again in the late
1950s as the elevated Gowanus Expressway was widened from four to six
lanes to accommodate additional traffic.[17] The expressway, now ninety-four
feet wide, cast a dark shadow on 3rd Avenue and transformed it into a dark-
ened ten-lane surface road. Carrying a daily traffic volume of two hundred
thousand vehicles, including freight trucks and commuters,[18] the Gowanus
Expressway created a physical barrier that essentially severed the waterfront
from the rest of Sunset Park upland and prompted the decline of the surrounding area, marked by concentrated levels of Latino poverty (Sullivan
1993). While the expressway has scarred the neighborhood landscape and
presents a daily life-threatening hazard to pedestrians who dare to cross the
multiple-lane 3rd Avenue, it is also credited with extending the viability of
industrial activity on Sunset Park's waterfront (see Chapter 6).

Public investments in highway construction coupled with postwar federal
programs such as low-interest home mortgage loans to veterans facilitated the
rapid out-migration of whites to nearby suburbanizing areas, including Long
Island, Staten Island, and Westchester County (Abu-Lughod 1999; Jackson 1987). Ment and Donovan (1980, 74) state that "over and over again, a
serviceman from Sunset Park returned to his crowded home neighborhood,
married the girl next door and took her to live in one of the large suburban
developments being built farther out on Long Island." With the extensive
network of highways reshaping the city's landscape, trucks replaced rail and
water transportation in moving goods and products throughout the United

States. These urban development trends contributed to the decline of Sunset Park's industrial and waterfront activity because its location near the harbor and railways ceased to be a competitive advantage as manufacturing became increasingly decentralized and outsourced.

The Latinization of Sunset Park

Although a small number of Puerto Ricans lived in South Brooklyn since the 1920s and worked on the docks and in the factories (Sullivan 1993), Sunset Park was a relatively new neighborhood compared to the pre–World War II Puerto Rican colonias, which were firmly established in Manhattan's Lower East Side and East Harlem, and the East Tremont and Morrisannia neighborhoods in the Bronx (Sanchez Korrol 1983; Haslip-Viera 1996). Puerto Rican migration to New York City was precipitated by economic dislocation at home. The heightened postwar mobility of U.S. capital led to investments in Caribbean export-processing zones and the outsourcing of industrial production as a strategy for lowering labor costs (Sassen 1988; Whalen 2002). Whalen (2002, 47) argues that "US companies could now manufacture goods in Puerto Rico tax-free and then 'export' these goods to the States without having to pay 'import' duties." U.S. political and economic interventions, however, led to the collapse of the agricultural island economy in the 1950s, which facilitated a mass exodus of displaced rural workers (Whalen 2002; Sanchez Korrol 2005). Facing severe racial discrimination, Puerto Ricans found work in labor-intensive manufacturing jobs in the garment, paper box, and plastic products industries and also worked in service jobs as cooks, dishwashers, busboys, messengers, elevator operators, custodians, and building superintendents (Kihss 1953a, 1953b; Haslip-Viera 1996, 16).

Movement to Brooklyn from established colonias in Manhattan was an outcome of residential displacement due to massive urban renewal projects in the Puerto Rican neighborhoods of East Harlem and Lower East Side (Muniz 1998; Aponte-Parés 1998; Abu-Lughod 1999). According to Anderson (1964, 64–65), blacks and Puerto Ricans made up an overwhelming two-thirds majority of those displaced, leading to references that urban renewal was a "Negro removal" or "Negro clearance" program.[19] Describing the significant displacement of recently arrived Puerto Ricans, a 1955 *New York Times* article reported that several new public housing and commercial construction projects in Manhattan would force the removal of twelve thousand families, among whom the overwhelming majority were black and Puerto Rican families (Ennis 1955). Puerto Rican displacement in Manhattan is evident in their declining numbers, despite a continuing in-migration from the island through the 1970s. In 1960 Manhattan's Puerto Rican population numbered 225,639, and by 1990 this number fell 31 percent to 154,978 (Aponte-Parés 1998).

Local industries and the widening of the Gowanus Expressway provided employment opportunities for Puerto Ricans settling in Sunset Park in the 1950s and 1960s. The reception was hostile, and local unions actively excluded Puerto Rican workers. In the late 1950s, the Brooklyn Army Terminal and the International Longshoremen Association were accused of discriminatory hiring practices. According to a study conducted by the Urban League, the ongoing practice of the shape-up served as an "instrument of racial and individual discrimination, not only for the Negro and Puerto Rican workers, but for white longshoremen who are not favorites" (Nevard 1959). And when they did get work, Puerto Rican and black dockworkers were relegated to the most dangerous and undesirable jobs (Nelson 2001). Puerto Rican women were integrated as an indispensable labor source for downgraded manufacturing in Sunset Park's garment factories (Ment and Donovan 1980; Whalen 2002). Puerto Rican labor was "crucial to salvaging New York industries that depended on inexpensive labor," such as the production of artificial flowers, toys, brushes, and millinery in addition to apparel production (Anon. 1954; Abu-Lughod 1999, 206). A fair number were self-employed and established small ethnic-specific businesses, such as bodegas, formacias, and botanicas, in Sunset Park (Ment and Donovan 1980; Sanchez Korrol 2005).

Unlike earlier immigrants who arrived in a period of significant industrial and urban expansion, Puerto Ricans occupied a marginal economic position that steadily worsened. The closing of the Brooklyn Army Terminal and the Bush Terminal piers during the late 1960s marked the deindustrialization of Sunset Park's local economy and foreshadowed New York state's "industrial infrastructural collapse" (Yago et al. 1984, 29).[20] The contraction of New York City's manufacturing employment was significant in all its major industries, including apparel, textile, furniture, paper, fabricated metal, leather, and lumber (Yago et al. 1984). The resulting Puerto Rican joblessness reached alarming levels, and the community consequences were dire (Sullivan 1993; Lissner 1969). As a prominent Sunset Park community activist lamented, "It was the decline of this industrial area that really caused the destruction of our residential community."[21]

The influx of Puerto Ricans coupled with a shrinking employment base facilitated Sunset Park's racial transformation as white ethnic groups fled to surrounding suburbs (Winnick 1990; Sullivan 1993). This seismic demographic shift is evident in the decennial census (Table 2.1).

TABLE 2.1   SIX DECADES OF RACIAL TRANSFORMATION IN SUNSET PARK[a]

	Population Number						Racial Composition						Demographic Change by Decade				
	1960	1970	1980	1990	2000	2010[b]	1960	1970	1980	1990	2000	2010	1960–1970	1970–1980	1980–1990	1990–2000	2000–2010
Total Population	90,070	86,278	78,181	84,147	102,644	109,973	100%	100%	100%	100%	100%	100%	-4.2%	-9%	8%	22%	7%
Non-Hispanic white	81,952	65,341	31,794	22,091	14,628	12,355	91%	76%	41%	26%	14%	11%	-20%	-51%	-31%	-34%	-16%
Latino/Hispanic	7,916	20,730	40,430	45,948	55,585	52,530	9%	24%	52%	55%	54%	48%	162%	95%	14%	21%	-5%
Asian[c]	—	—	3,615	12,971	26,175	41,013	—	—	5%	15%	26%	37%	—	—	259%	102%	57%
Black/African American	202	207	1,284	2,625	2,599	2,447	0.2%	0.2%	2%	3%	3%	2%	2%	520%	104%	-1%	-6%
Multi-Race[d]	—	—	—	—	2,827	1,156	—	—	—	—	3%	91%	—	—	—	—	-59%
Other	—	—	1,058	512	830	472	—	—	1%	1%	1%	0.4%	—	—	-52%	62%	-43%

[a] Sunset Park is defined by 26 census tracts - 2, 18, 20, 22, 72, 74, 76, 78, 80, 82, 84, 86, 88, 90, 92, 94, 96, 98, 100, 101, 102, 104, 106, 108, 118, 122.

[b] The 2010 census was disputed by Mayor Michael Bloomberg for a severe undercount that was most pronounced in New York City's minority neighborhoods (Roberts 2011).

[c] For the 1980 and 1990 censuses I used the Asian and Pacific Islander category, and for the 2000 and 2010 censuses I used Asian alone.

[d] Multi-Race is a new 2000 category.

Source: U.S. census data for 1960, 1970, 1980, 1990, 2000, and 2010 retrieved from Queens College Social Explorer.

In 1959 Sunset Park's population stood at 106,508, with a small non-white population of only 8 percent. Ten years later Sunset Park lost nearly 10,000 residents, and, more important, the racial shift in residential composition was apparent—the Latino population increased by 161 percent and numbered more than 20,000, representing nearly a quarter of neighborhood residents. Clearly, the 1960s marked the onset of Sunset Park's Latinization. In the following decade, deindustrialization coupled with racial transformation took its toll, and Sunset Park's population continued to decline. Most significantly, the white population shrank by nearly half during the 1970s, from more than 75,000 to 41,000, while the Latino population again doubled its numbers. The dramatic decline in the white population continued throughout the 1980s, 1990s, and 2000s, accompanied by steady growth in the Latino population.

As previously noted, postwar federal home mortgage assistance programs through the Federal Housing Administration (FHA) and the Veterans Administration in addition to the numerous transportation development projects, including the 1964 completion of the Verrazano-Narrows Bridge connecting Brooklyn to Staten Island, provided the means for whites to escape transitioning inner-city neighborhoods (Ment and Donovan 1980; Oliver and Shapiro 1995). To address the resulting disinvestment and poverty in urban communities, the Economic Opportunity Act of 1964—the centerpiece of President Lyndon B. Johnson's declaration of the War on Poverty—enabled the federal government to designate certain places as poverty areas. In 1966 Sunset Park was carved out of South Brooklyn and its boundaries formally established by this designation.[22] Sunset Park's decline from a vibrant industrial working-class neighborhood was evident in a city-sponsored study that found that the number of welfare cases increased sharply in Brooklyn relative to the city overall, especially in the neighborhoods of East New York, Bushwick, Crown Heights, and Sunset Park (Burks 1972).

These conditions created a ripe opportunity for real estate blockbusting. The federal poverty-area designation coupled with the continuing influx of Puerto Ricans heightened fears among Sunset Park's white population. This sentiment was expressed by a local business owner in a *New York Times* interview: "People saw Hispanics moving in and so they moved out. They were afraid of another Bronx" (Maitland 1978). Unscrupulous real estate brokers sought to exploit these fears and offered white homeowners cash for their homes. In a panic about neighborhood change, Sunset Park homeowners sold low, many for a mere $5,000 (Blumenthal 1972). These realtors then colluded with the FHA, Dun & Bradstreet (a national credit rating firm), and Eastern Service Corporation (a Long Island–based mortgage company) to sell these houses to low-income Puerto Ricans, who financed their $20,000 home purchases with FHA-guaranteed mortgages.[23] The new homeowners would soon find that their mortgage payments exceeded their rental income and their ability to pay, and many subsequently abandoned their homes and foreclosed on their mortgages. By the late 1970s, two hundred properties and forty apartment buildings were abandoned, and Sunset Park represented a "dying neighborhood, another sad victim of urban blight" (Winnick 1991).

The impact of blockbusting tactics in Sunset Park was relatively minor compared to the wholesale devastation and abandonment of other communities such as East New York, where "up to 200 real estate firms worked overtime to turn East New York from white to black" (Thabit 2003, 1). Nevertheless, systematic disinvestment in Sunset Park was facilitated in part by federal policies and misconduct. The waning presence of white ethnics was evident in boarded-up storefronts on the commercial avenues. Dilapidated vacant buildings and deteriorating piers in the closed or underutilized Bush Terminal and Brooklyn Army Terminal symbolized the massive industrial job loss. Although some warehouses, bakeries, and garment factories remained, these firms represented only a shadow of an earlier period of economic vitality.

The Lutheran Medical Center's Tradition of Community Development

Two factors stemmed complete racial turnover and economic devastation in Sunset Park. The first factor is the dominant presence of the LMC and its opportunistic fund-raising strategies that included the formation of a nonprofit community corporation, spurred by the availability of antipoverty funding, that promoted comprehensive approaches to neighborhood health and incorporated community organizing. The second factor (not so readily separate from the interests of the LMC, since a key individual promoting the institution's community development activities was Robert Walsh, vice president of community relations for nearly thirty years, and his wife, Alice, both longtime Sunset Park resident homeowners) is the white homeowners of the distinctive brownstones that make up a sizable share of the local housing stock.

The LMC's revitalization activities helped stem the economic and political abandonment of Sunset Park. During the 1970s, the LMC built a modern new hospital by renovating a factory, five hundred thousand square feet in size, that had been abandoned by the American Machine and Foundry Company. The factory was located on the dilapidated waterfront, and it was in the interest of the LMC to clean up and stabilize the area (Wylde 2005). Sunset Park's federal poverty designation made the neighborhood eligible for numerous public funding opportunities. From 1967 to 1969, the LMC received nearly $4 million in federal funds, and "larger amounts were in sight" (Winnick 1990, 103). The War on Poverty's Office of Economic Opportunity defined health broadly, and federal funding required grass-roots organizing and the "maximum feasible participation" of neighborhood residents (Sardell 1988, 55). These sentiments were echoed by LMC president George Adams: "Our point of view is that we have no reason to exist other than taking care of our neighbors. We will continue to do what our neighbors need for us to do" (Cerne 1995, 50).

In the 1970s, the LMC maximized access to public funds by spinning off a nonprofit community development organization, Sunset Park Redevelopment Committee (SPRC). The LMC and the SPRC then focused on securing "every federal, state, and City subsidy within reach" to achieve their highest priority of restoring a homeownership base (Winnick 1990, 104–109). Designation in the late 1970s as a Neighborhood Stabilization Area gave Sunset Park priority access to housing rehabilitation and federal community development funds. Kathryn S. Wylde, currently the CEO and president of the Partnership for New York City, was an LMC community relations staff member and assumed leadership of the Sunset Park Redevelopment Committee.[24] She figured prominently in the LMC's efforts to stabilize the waterfront neighborhood section by renovating abandoned homes and offering them for resale to low- and middle-income families (Wylde 2005). Wylde's affiliation with the LMC continues, and until recently she held the chairperson position on the Board of Trustees.

In addition to public funding, the SPRC received grants from the Ford Foundation and the newly formed Local Support Initiatives Corporation for housing rehabilitation and neighborhood preservation.[25] Despite extensive public and private resources, the SPRC produced paltry results. During its nearly twenty-year existence, it rehabilitated twenty FHA-held houses but was only able to resell fewer than ten and also managed approximately six hundred housing units that received Section 8 certificates (Winnick 1990). Fiscal mismanagement and related litigation led to the SPRC's decline in 1987, but in 2000 the SPRC was revived as a weatherization program, with two hundred clients.[26] The LMC, however, continues to have a strong record in subsidized housing development, particularly for seniors.[27]

Sunset Park's mixed housing stock includes brownstones, an important neighborhood amenity that also helped stem the area's decline. In the mid-1970s, homeowners who purchased and restored their brownstones formed the Sunset Park Restoration Committee and "worked to attract potential homeowners." Toward this effort, the Sunset Park Restoration Committee successfully petitioned to have much of Sunset Park between 4th and 7th Avenues and 38th and 64th Streets listed in the Federal Register of Historic Places in September 1988.[28] This designation, however, does not provide for the strict controls or enforceable protections regarding building demolition or alterations that the New York City Landmarks Preservation Commission requires for designation.[29] Nevertheless, the federal application process is relatively simple and was eagerly sought by the Sunset Park Restoration Committee to "welcome" gentrification so that Sunset Park can develop as "Park Slope South" (Winnick 1990, 169). Other activities to promote the neighborhood included a film financed by Anchor Savings Bank, where Kathryn Wylde had moved to after working for the SPRC to serve as the bank's urban affairs officer. A companion booklet and pictorial history titled *Sunset Park: A Time Remembered,* which includes an introduction by Alice Walsh, was funded by the Brooklyn Educational and Cultural Alliance.

In addition to celebrating historic landmarks and Sunset Park's immigrant past, the Sunset Park Restoration Committee conducted walking tours to highlight the neighborhood's brownstones. For example, the *New York Times* publicized an "out of the ordinary house tour" of Brooklyn brownstones in Sunset Park that featured eight recently purchased brownstones for less than $40,000 in various stages of renovation (Anon. 1979). The close ties between the Sunset Park Restoration Committee and the LMC are apparent. In 1981, the Sunset Park House and Garden Tour sponsored by the committee met at the Marien Heim Senior Citizen Apartments—the original site of the LMC that was redeveloped as one of the hospital's numerous senior housing complexes. Before the tour, guests were treated to snacks and entertainment, including the fifteen-minute promotional film about Sunset Park (Anon. 1981a).

The Sunset Park Restoration Committee sought to anchor the neighborhood by asserting a connection with Brownstone Brooklyn rather than with the neighborhood's new majority Puerto Rican population. Through neighborhood boosterism and participation in events such as the annual Brooklyn Brownstone Fair, the Sunset Park Restoration Committee promoted Sunset Park as the newest source of brownstone bargains, a desirable alternative to expensive historic brownstones in neighboring Park Slope (Bonavoglia 1977). The Puerto Rican community perceived the Sunset Park Restoration Committee "as a gentrifying agent" (Muniz 1998, 15) and was excluded from the organization's materials and activities. Except for a sentence that noted "a substantial influx of Puerto Ricans, as well as other

Spanish-speaking people," there is no acknowledgment in the Sunset Park Restoration Committee's monograph of the role and contributions of Puerto Ricans in the making of Sunset Park (Sunset Park Restoration Committee 1979). A deep mistrust about the organization's activities and community development objectives was prevalent among Puerto Rican community members and leaders.[30]

Although the Sunset Park Restoration Committee did not last long enough to harness the trickle-down effects of New York City's overheated real estate market of the 1990s, the gentrification process is indeed reshaping neighborhood life. But unlike historic processes, the renewal of Sunset Park's housing and real estate market is driven in part by a new urban growth coalition that consists of ethnic banks and immigrant realtors and developers (see Chapter 4). The unfinished work of the Sunset Park Restoration Committee is now being spearheaded by the recently formed Sunset Park Landmarks Committee, whose mission is to "preserve Sunset Park's historic architectural character and *sense of place*" (my emphasis).[31] Racial struggles about neighborhood quality and change remain an undercurrent, but the contestation is much more complex in the current market context, and increasing diversity poses new challenges for community definition and building.

Reacting to the immigrant-driven growth and development that is remaking Sunset Park's built environment through new construction, additional floors to building heights, and illegal basement apartments, community members have resurrected an effort to preserve the neighborhood's primary housing stock of two-story limestone rowhouses. As member Darlene Vecchino was quoted in a *New York Daily News* article, the Sunset Park Landmarks Committee's mission is to protect buildings from people and developers who do not "understand the history of the neighborhood or respect the architecture" (Morales 2013). In addition to neighborhood walking tours, the Sunset Park Landmarks Committee's mission is being advanced by a grant and technical assistance from a citywide preservation organization, the Historic Districts Council (HDC). The HDC selected Sunset Park as one of its 2013 "Six to Celebrate" neighborhoods because of its "elegantly-detailed rowhouses constructed for middle- and working-class families at the turn of the twentieth century" (Historic Districts Council 2013). Moreover, City Council member Sara Gonzalez honored three members of the Sunset Park Landmarks Committee, including Vecchino for community leadership and contributions as part of her 2013 Women's History Month celebration (Stumpf 2013). These accolades and resources add momentum to the committee's effort to gain New York City landmark district designation, which would confer strict guidelines on architectural preservation.[32] According to Vecchino, "There are 10 to 12 blocks that haven't been disturbed by development and *we want to freeze them in time and preserve them just like buildings in Brooklyn Heights and Park Slope*" (Morales 2013, my emphasis).

"Sunset Park/the Barrio/the Chinatown/People with Lesser Means Who Live on Higher Ground"

Federal immigration policies regulate the ebb and flow of human migration to the United States and continue to dramatically reshape the urban demography.[33] Key immigration acts—including the Hart-Celler Act of 1965, the Immigration and Reform Control Act of 1986, the Immigration Act of 1990, and the Antiterrorism and Effective Death Penalty Act of 1996—and the ongoing debate on immigration reform, especially in the aftermath of 9/11, reverberate in the making of New York City's neighborhood fabric. Standing out among American cities in the sheer volume and diversity of newcomers, New York City, the quintessential immigrant city, has long transitioned to a majority nonwhite population. The Hart-Celler Act repealed the racist quotas of the National Origins Act of 1924 and enacted family reunification and skill preferences as the main admission criteria for immigrating to the United States.[34] An unintended consequence of the Hart-Celler Act was the massive influx of immigrants from Asia, Latin America, and the Caribbean (Hing 1993).

From 1881 to 1920, 23.5 million people migrated to the United States (Saenz, Morales, and Ayala 2004, 215). An overwhelming majority (88 percent) were from Europe, with Italy (4 million) and the former Soviet Union (3 million) sending the largest numbers. Although the post-1965 period witnessed a comparable volume of renewed international migration, a mere 14 percent of immigrants who settled in the United States from 1971 to 2002 were European. In contrast to the last great immigration wave, while no one region dominated, newcomers largely came from developing Third World countries. Approximately a third of the immigrants to the United States since the early 1970s are from Asian countries, while 11 percent are from the Caribbean and 36 percent are from Latin America, with Mexico accounting for more than two-thirds (67 percent) of Latino immigration to the United States. During this period of renewed immigration, five states— California, New York, Texas, Florida, and Illinois—received the majority of the newcomers. An annual average of 110,000 immigrants settled in New York City during the 1990s, which New York City Department of City

Planning's Population Division director Joseph Salvo contends "mitigated catastrophic population losses" and helped prevent the city's devolution into another Detroit (Bernstein 2005).

With Sunset Park offering a vast affordable housing stock, convenient public transportation access, and weakened resistance to newcomers, Asian and Latino immigrants made the neighborhood their home starting in the early 1980s. Table 2.1 documents racial composition and change in Sunset Park for the past six decades. Since the late 1970s, the numbers and population share of non-Hispanic whites have declined steadily, and by 2010, non-Hispanic whites represented only one in ten Sunset Park residents. By 1980, Latinos made up the majority population in Sunset Park, and Asians marked their small but growing presence at 5 percent. During the next decade the Asian population more than doubled, and this dramatic growth continued through the 1990s and 2000s. By 2010 at 37 percent of the population, Sunset Park's Asian population, which is overwhelmingly Chinese now, constitutes the neighborhood's single-largest ethnic group.

Once predominantly Puerto Rican, Sunset Park's Latino population diversified with the influx of Dominicans followed by Ecuadorians and, most significantly, Mexicans (Table 2.2). The Immigration Reform and Control Act of 1986 was a key factor in the growth of the Dominican and Mexican populations—the two largest groups to seek legalization under the act (Smith 1996; Durand, Massey, and Zenteno 2001). By proving continuous residence in the United States since January 1, 1982, or employment as seasonal agricultural workers, approximately 125,700 immigrants in New York City received amnesty. Dominicans represented the largest group of amnestied individuals at 11,900, followed by Mexicans at 9,300 (New York City Department of City Planning 1996). The Immigration Act of 1990, which was the most significant modification to U.S. immigration policy since the Hart-Celler Act, contained provisions for these formerly undocumented immigrants to sponsor their spouses and minor children. The cumulative impact of these two immigration policies was instrumental in the notable increase in New York City's Latino immigrant populations and their subsequent concentration in neighborhoods such as Sunset Park.

Since the 1970s, the top source country of new immigration to New York City has been the Dominican Republic. Although the geographic center of Dominican New York City is Washington Heights, also known as Quisqueya Heights (Pressar 1995, 24), some Dominicans have chosen to settle in Sunset Park, and since the 1990s, Dominicans represent 14 percent of the neighborhood's majority Latino population. Dominican immigrants

TABLE 2.2 SUNSET PARK RACIAL-ETHNIC COMPOSITION AND CHANGE, 1990–2010

	Population Number			Population Change		Population Share		
	1990	2000	2010	1990–2000	2000–2010	1990	2000	2010
Asian Ethnic Groups	**12,971**	**26,175**	**41,013**	**102%**	**57%**	**100%**	**100%**	**100%**
Chinese	10,420	22,504	37,328	116%	66%	80%	86%	91%
South Asian	1,238	1,503	1,116	21%	-26%	10%	6%	3%
Filipino	664	627	524	-6%	-16%	5%	2%	1%
Vietnamese	408	513	468	26%	-9%	3%	2%	1%
Pakastani	—	240	342	—	43%	1%	1%	1%
Korean	180	123	139	-32%	13%	1%	0.5%	0.3%
Other Asian[a]	61	665	1,096	990%	65%	0.5%	3%	3%
Latino Ethnic Groups	**45,948**	**55,585**	**52,530**	**21%**	**-5%**	**100%**	**100%**	**100%**
Puerto Rican	31,041	22,443	13,614	-28%	-39%	68%	40%	26%
Mexican	3,085	10,582	18,713	243%	77%	7%	19%	36%
Dominican	5,765	7,823	7,599	36%	-3%	13%	14%	14%
Central American[b]	2,718	2,796	3,529	3%	26%	6%	5%	7%
Ecuadorian	2,257	2,767	4,051	23%	46%	5%	5%	8%
Colombian	1,088	980	851	-10%	-13%	2%	2%	2%
Peruvian	494	337	449	-32%	33%	1%	1%	1%
Other Latino[c]	3,219	7,857	3,724	144%	-53%	7%	14%	7%

[a] Other Asian includes Thais, Malaysians, and Pacific Islanders.

[b] Central American includes Central American, Costa Rican, Guatemalan, Honduran, Nicaraguan, Panamanian, Salvadoran, and other Central American.

[c] Other Latino includes Cuban, Argentinean, Bolivian, Chilean, Paraguayan, Uruguayan, Venezuelan, other South American, and other Hispanic.

Source: U.S. census data for 1990, 2000, and 2010 retrieved from Queens College Social Explorer.

came with greater class resources than Puerto Ricans in the 1950s and 1960s and, as a result, have higher rates of business and homeownership (Winnick 1990; Muniz 1998).[35] Small storefront businesses are a common niche for Latinos, and by the 1980s, more than eight thousand bodegas were established in New York City (Howe 1986). A source of tension between Puerto Ricans and Dominicans is centered on the transitioning ownership of these small businesses; in many neighborhoods, including Washington Heights and Sunset Park, Dominicans began to take over bodegas once owned by Puerto Ricans (Brooklyn Historical Society 1989; Howe 1986; Pressar 1995). In addition to this economic niche, Dominicans also pursued other forms of self-employment, such as driving livery cabs.[36]

Dominican immigrant success is tempered by experiences such as those of Sunset Park's Ortiz family, portrayed in an acclaimed 2001 independent documentary titled *My American Girls*.[37] The film featured the Ortiz family's struggle with working poverty, an impoverished neighborhood context, second-generation identity conflicts, social problems that arose from absent parents because of long work hours, and transnational ties maintained through frequent trips home and the social obligations entailed in these visits. Increasingly, the dearth of affordable homeownership opportunities has propelled many Dominicans and Puerto Ricans to leave New York City for small, struggling industrial cities where homeownership is still obtainable (Kugel 2006; Maya 2005).

While the presence of Dominican and Mexican communities in Sunset Park was established in the early 1980s, the Mexican growth trajectory has since dwarfed that of Dominicans (see Table 2.2). Consistent with citywide trends, Mexicans are the fastest-growing Latino group, nearly doubling and tripling their numbers through the 1990s and 2000s. Numbering more than 18,000, Mexicans have now surpassed Puerto Ricans as Sunset Park's largest Latino group. This figure, however, understates the actual size of the Mexican population. Official estimates of undocumented Mexicans in New York City range from 250,000 to 300,000.[38] Underscoring this observation, the LMC found in a 2005 survey of Mexican immigrants that 82 percent of the respondents are undocumented (McNees et al. 2005).

Most Mexican New Yorkers are from the Mixteca region of Mexico, with a majority coming from the states of Puebla, Guerrero, and Oaxaca (Negrete 2013; Smith 1996; McNees et al. 2005). As one of New York City's largest Mexican neighborhoods, 5th Avenue near the park is resplendent with Mexican flags that decorate the awnings of numerous storefront businesses—such as bakeries, music stores, travel agencies, and restaurants—that serve the local population. These small businesses revived and diversified the discount chain stores that dominated 5th Avenue. Built by their Irish and Italian congregations, local Catholic churches such as St. Agatha's Roman Catholic Church, St. Michael's, and Our Lady of Perpetual Help are now an integral part of Mexican community life and provide a base for the provision of social services, immigrant assistance, and legal advocacy as well as cultural preservation. Because of the Catholic Church's conservative and hierarchical leadership, Leticia Alanis has tried to persuade La Unión members to worship at St. Jacobi Evangelical Lutheran Church with progressive and neighborhood-based pastors, but her suggestion has been met with great resistance (Alanis 2013). Nevertheless, new immigrant populations have revived the centrality of churches in Sunset Park's community life and brought new vitality to 4th Avenue, known informally as the avenue of churches.[39]

Sunset Park's growing Mexican presence is also evidenced by an expanding migrant civil society that consists of nonprofit membership-based organizations such as La Unión, which formed to engage the people of the global South in community building and advocating for immigrant rights.[40] Initially a project of the Fifth Avenue Committee, a community development corporation headed by Michelle de la Uz whose deep roots in Sunset Park date back to her community liaison position with Congresswoman Nydia Velázquez, La Unión incorporated as a nonprofit organization in 2011. Since then, La Unión has been searching for a permanent space in Sunset Park's overheated real estate market (see Chapter 4). Through her relationship with Kathy Hopkins, senior vice president of community-based programs at the LMC, La Unión shares a small office space located in one of the family health centers. Heeding the priority concerns of La Unión's membership, the organization focuses on immigration reform, youth activism and leadership, education access and retention, and urban farming as key social justice action and policy areas.

Sunset Park's emergent Mexican population has reshaped the local political landscape by helping to elect the first Mexican American to the New York City Council. In 1989, a U.S. Supreme Court decision found that the all-powerful eight-member New York City Board of Estimates discriminated against minority groups by violating the constitutional principle of one person, one vote. As a result of this decision, the Board of Estimates was dismantled, and the number of districts in the New York City Council was expanded from thirty-five to fifty-one in order to better represent the city's diverse racial and ethnic composition (Macchiarola and Diaz 1993). Created as a Hispanic-majority district, City Council District 38, which is largely made up of Sunset Park, has been represented by lifelong resident

Sara Gonzalez, a Puerto Rican woman who founded a now-defunct youth organization and served as the chair of Community Board 7.

Gonzalez's eleven-year tenure was controversial because of her weak legislative and attendance record. In the 2013 Democratic primary, Carlos Menchaca, a young gay Mexican American community organizer, challenged Gonzalez and opened a campaign office in the heart of Sunset Park on 5th Avenue between 44th and 45th Streets.[41] Trained as an urban planner and formerly employed by the Brooklyn Borough president and New York City Council Speaker, Menchaca was motivated to run as a result of the government's failure to respond in the immediate aftermath of Superstorm Sandy. He was heavily involved in relief work in neighboring Red Hook and was instructed by residents that "you must stay to run for City Council and fight for us" (Menchaca 2013).

Gonzalez's absence at an August 2013 candidates forum at the Trinity Lutheran Church underscored simmering criticism of her lack of accountability and effectiveness as a community leader.[42] Nevertheless, as an incumbent, she was a formidable opponent with endorsements from the political establishment, including the mayor and the New York City Council Speaker; local immigrant leaders, such as Paul Mak of the Brooklyn Chinese American Association; and numerous Chinese business owners.[43] Stating a commitment to "building bridges" among Sunset Park's diverse communities and advocating for access and transparency in policy making, Menchaca ran a grassroots campaign and received the coveted *New York Times* endorsement. As one local newspaper's headline proclaimed, his resounding victory on primary day, with 57.6 percent of the votes, was a "Men-shocka" (Musumeci 2013). Gonzalez was the only incumbent candidate for the New York City Council who was defeated on September 10, 2013.

The fact that the first Mexican American member to the New York City Council was elected from Sunset Park's District 38 and will replace a longtime Puerto Rican representative speaks volumes about the community's shifting Latino composition. More important, Menchaca's election is significant because he is a part of a new contingent that *New York Daily News* columnist and *Democracy Now!* host Juan Gonzalez has declared as possibly constituting the most progressive government in New York City in fifty years (Gonzalez 2013). Just as Bill de Blasio's victory is a repudiation of Mayor Bloomberg's governance, which exacerbated "a tale of two cities," Menchaca's victory rejects Sunset Park's political status quo and raises the possibility for accountable and transformative leadership and community building.

Sunset Park's renewed immigrant presence contributes to its significance as a local site of worker organizing. Sunset Park's prominence was evident in the National Day of Action for Immigrant Rights on May Day 2006. Promoting "a day without immigrants," immigrant rights organizers throughout the country advocated a boycott of work and shopping to demonstrate the magnitude of immigrant contributions to the local and national economy. New York City activists organized the formation of a human chain at 12:16 P.M. to mark the passage on December 16, 2005, of the Border Protection, Anti-Terrorism and Illegal Immigrant Act, sponsored by Wisconsin representative Jim Sensenbrenner and New York representative Peter King. The act provides for the construction of a fence along the U.S.-Mexican border, new visa restrictions, increased border patrol, and expedited deportation proceedings and also criminalizes undocumented immigrants by making their presence in the United States a felony.[44] Sunset Park was one of eight New York City neighborhoods that participated in the formation of a human chain to express solidarity in the demand for the legalization of eleven million undocumented immigrants nationwide.

As Raza Youth Collective founder Citlalli Negrete recalled, her family knew that the National Day of Action for Immigrant Rights was "something extremely important" (Negrete 2013). Negrete is a twenty-four-year-old Chicana born and raised in Sunset Park. Her parents moved to the neighborhood in 1986 and owned a small Mexican deli/grocery store on 51st Street between 5th and 6th Avenues until 1999, when they sold their business because of competition from the growing number of similar establishments. Negrete remembered La Unión organizers instructing the Latino community not to go to school or work. While Negrete and her family participated in the larger action in Manhattan's Union Square, she remembered hearing that many Sunset Park Latino businesses closed down as owners and workers participated in the human chain. Even though Negrete's parents are naturalized citizens, they were motivated to advocate on behalf of many family members and friends who are undocumented immigrants.

One of the earliest (and largest) post-1965 immigrant groups to settle in Sunset Park is the Chinese. The emergence of ethnic settlements outside historic enclaves was due to an aging and overcrowded housing stock and the importance of public transportation networks (Binder and Reimers 1995). For example, the 1903 construction of the Williamsburg Bridge was a factor in the so-called Jewish passover from the Lower East Side to new community formations in North Brooklyn (Berger 2003). In a similar mode, the BMT N subway line provides a direct link from the Canal Street station in Manhattan Chinatown to Sunset Park's 8th Avenue.[45] Poor subway services, however, have contributed to the establishment of informal commuter vans that help sustain the intensive, spatial connections between work, residence, and community life for New York City's Chinese populations in Sunset Park and Manhattan's Chinatown (Sengupta 1996).

As late as the mid-1980s, only a few thousand Chinese lived in Sunset Park, clustered around several city blocks surrounding 8th Avenue with about twenty or so Asian-owned businesses (Charles 1994).[46] However, by the end of that decade, the number of Chinese had nearly tripled and accounted for 15 percent of Sunset Park's total population (see Table 2.1). Similar to Manhattan's Chinatown, Sunset Park's Chinese population consists mostly of new immigrants with limited or no English-language ability and a high rate of working poverty due to their concentration in low-wage employment niches (Zhou 2001; Hum 2002a). More than half of Sunset Park's Chinese working population is employed in food services, garment production, and personal services such as nail and beauty salons (see Chapter 3). These shared qualities were highlighted in the Asian American Legal Defense and Education Fund's successful 1997 defense of Congressional District 12's constitutionality and boundaries, which unite Sunset Park and Manhattan's Chinatown as a "community of interest" (Hicks 1997; Levy 1997).[47]

The dramatic growth in Sunset Park's Asian population took off in the 1990s, driven by two trends—the expansion of the Fujianese population, many of whom are undocumented, and the infusion of overseas Chinese capital (McCarthy 2002). June 6, 2013 marks, twenty years since the grounding of an old freighter named *Golden Venture* on the shores of Rockaway Beach with 286 Chinese abroad, nearly all from Fujian Province. The vivid media images of Chinese men huddled in blankets on the Far Rockaways in Queens brought stark awareness to an extensive international network of human smugglers and an emergent population of Chinese desperate to leave China.[48] The 1993 *Golden Venture* grounding also marked the mass detention of undocumented immigrants as federal immigration policy. After the decision to detain *Golden Venture* passengers in jails and detention facilities in New Jersey and Pennsylvania, "the practice took root" (Keefe 2013). Among the 286 mostly Chinese male passengers, 10 drowned trying to swim to shore, some were deported, some received asylum, and a large number were detained for more than three years. Upon their pardon by President Bill Clinton in 1997, these men joined the 11 million undocumented immigrants in the United States (Bernstein 2006b). Recent news coverage found that a full two decades after the incident, 20 *Golden Venture* immigrants remain in limbo without legal status (NPR Staff 2012; Argento 2013).

Peter Kwong (1997) in his book *Forbidden Workers* argues that corporate demands for ever cheaper sources of labor and free trade agreements, which eliminate tariffs and regulations and eases the flow of capital across national borders, promote waves of undocumented immigration. Upon its emergence from thirty years of political isolation in the 1980s, China lifted bans on emigration, unleashing a "fever of going abroad" (Liang 2001, 679). Once (re)started, the escalation of social and economic dislocations resulting from China's transition to a market economy dictated by a politically oppressive regime and its complicit support of human smuggling helped to create a vast internal floating population that continues to exert tremendous pressures for out-migration (Kwong 1997; Sassen 1988; Liang 2001; Rosenthal 2000).

The shift in the regional origin of the Chinese migrant population is reflected in the lingua franca of community retailers and institutions, including local churches. Reverend Samuel Wong founded the Chinese Promise Baptist Church in Sunset Park in 1983. After thirty years, he has finally secured a permanent home on 41st Street outside the historic core of Sunset Park's Chinese population, anchoring that population's current northern expansion. To commemorate the church's new building and thirtieth anniversary, Reverend Wong's dedication service included a special publication of photographs, testimonials, and a timeline of the church's history. The significance of the Fujianese population was noted in 1994, when Mandarin translation was provided for all church activities, and then again in 2004, when Mandarin replaced Cantonese for all church activities. Over the span of its thirty years in Sunset Park, Reverend Wong's once Cantonese church congregation is now 90 percent Fujianese.

In addition to affirming family reunification admissions criteria, the 1990 Immigration Act placed a premium on skills preferences that escalated the transnational movement of Chinese capital and people, particularly those with human and financial capital, to the United States (Rosen, Wieler, and Pereira 2005). As Ong and Patraporn (2006, 184) observe, "These Asian immigrants arrive ready to ride the wave of the new economy contributing their skills, knowledge and dollars in the United States." This divergent influx of people and investments helped fuel Sunset Park's economic renewal. Numerous news accounts in the 1990s lauded Sunset Park's immigrant-driven neighborhood revitalization and specifically Chinese home and business ownership as agents for economic renewal and stabilization (Oser 1996; Browning 1994; Howe 1987). Chinese investors purchased these dilapidated storefronts, transforming Sunset Park's streetscape and local economy. Immigrant renewal is premised on economic niches defined by the formation of businesses in low-entry barrier sectors such as restaurants, grocery stores, and garment factories, whose profitability depends on reestablishing sweatshop conditions (see Chapter 3). The formation of ethnic banks helped to underwrite investment in Sunset Park, and as part of a nascent emergent immigrant growth coalition, ethnic banks are a key actor in real estate development and speculation (see Chapter 4).

As one of New York City's most diverse neighborhoods, Sunset Park includes among its Pan-Latino and Chinese population a visible and growing Arab American and Muslim population. Although the Fatih Camii Mosque (Conqueror's Mosque) was established by the United American Muslim Association in a former theater building on 8th Avenue when the commercial avenue was still referred to as "Little Scandinavia," a visible Muslim community did not emerge in Sunset Park until the 1990s (Dodds 2013). New York City's Arab American community is largely centered in neighboring Bay Ridge; however, relatively less expensive rents led to the establishment of numerous institutions, including mosques, community centers, catering halls, and the Al Noor School (a K–12 private educational institution) in Sunset Park (Cristillo 2004). Founded in 2001 a few months after the 9/11 tragedies, the Arab American Association of New York established an office in northern Bay Ridge bordering Sunset Park.[49] Sunset Park resident and community activist Linda Sansour serves as the executive director and was recently featured in a *New York Times* video and news article on new immigrant enclaves (Semple 2013).[50] Sunset Park's Muslim population consists of Arab Americans of modest socioeconomic means and a small Pakistani community.

As the neighborhood site of the federal Metropolitan Detention Center (MDC), Sunset Park holds particular significance in the post-9/11 treatment of Arab and Muslim Americans (see Chapter 1). Despite community protests that Sunset Park was once again a "dumping ground," the federal prison, which has a maximum security unit, was constructed on 29th Street and 3rd Avenue in 1993.[51] As community activist David Galarza (2005) noted, "It's a symbol of what can happen if you exercise your right to free speech." Through several months of 2002, weekly protests organized by human and immigrant rights organizations took place outside the facility to call attention to the detainment of eighty-four Arab and South Asian immigrants without cause and the subsequent hardships on their families and communities (Ruiz 2002). Referred to as Brooklyn's "Abu Ghraib," Sunset Park's MDC became the subject of a 2003 Department of Justice investigation, which found widespread abuses of immigrant detainees (Moses 2004; Bernstein 2004a, 2004c; Cohler-Esses 2005).[52]

In 2001, four prominent New York City political leaders were jailed at the MDC for trespassing on military property in protest of the U.S. Navy's bombing of the Puerto Rican island of Vieques. Serving sentences of between forty and ninety days were the so-called Vieques Four—Roberto

Ramirez, chairman of the Bronx Democratic Party; then–City Council member Adolfo Carrión Jr., who lost his bid for mayor in 2013; New York state assemblyman Jose Rivera; and Reverend Al Sharpton. Several rallies were held outside, including one with the mayor of Vieques and another when Reverend Sharpton was released from prison and proceeded to lead the protestors to the nearby 3rd Avenue site, where four members of the Pena-Herrera family were killed by a drunken police officer (Hicks 2001; Ingrassia 2001).

The making of Sunset Park is embedded in a narrative of contested terrains, as the transition from a neighborhood of working-class white ethnics to a hyperdiverse immigrant Latino-Asian mix was a confluence of the complex processes of international migration, economic restructuring, and urban renewal. The resurrected Sunset Park Landmarks Committee shares the call to protect Sunset Park, but local activists seek to protect immigrant neighborhood spaces and the rights of the working poor rather than the neighborhood's architecture, view corridors, or historic landmarks (see Chapter 5). Moreover, Sunset Park's "sense of place" is dynamic and continually being defined and contested. In the tradition of business-oriented Chinatown placemaking, the Brooklyn Chinese American Association recently announced China's donation of a pagoda-style "Friendship Arch" to formally mark the arrival of Sunset Park's Little Fuzhou, as the arch will be placed on the southern end of 8th Avenue between 64th and 65th Streets (Lutz 2013). Illustrative of an immigrant growth coalition strategy, Ritz Realty owner Denny Chen hopes that the arch will spur city officials to rezone the surrounding area from manufacturing to commercial uses so that "booming businesses and immigrant capital will follow" (Chen 2013).

The annual Puerto Rican Day Parade exposes the differential racialization of Sunset Park's public spaces. For the past eight years, El Grito de Sunset Park has organized a neighborhood gathering after the annual Puerto Rican Day Parade on Manhattan's 5th Avenue to monitor and protest police brutality and aggression.[53] As noted by organizers, "It is our community and our right to freely assemble and reclaim that which is ours, Sunset Park."[54] In anticipation of the postparade celebration, Community Board 7 forwarded a New York City Police Department 72nd Precinct notice reminding the public that as revelers "celebrate their heritage by driving in cars with their music playing and flags waving," the police will exercise "Zero-Tolerance" for "quality of life" violations, including "grilling on the sidewalk with BBQ grills."[55] Overzealous regulation and enforcement of "quality of life" standards, however, substantiate community claims that police actions "dehumanize, demonize, and criminalize our expressions of unity and strength."[56]

Conclusion

The history of Sunset Park documents the making of an immigrant global neighborhood by describing how the changing urban economy, evidenced by the rise and fall of an industrial waterfront and related urban policies, facilitated divergent fates for Latinos and Asians relative to earlier European immigrant groups. For decades, Sunset Park provided modest housing for working-class New Yorkers employed in manufacturing- and maritime-related industries on the waterfront. Rather than a natural process of ethnic succession, the racial transformation of Sunset Park was an outcome of the interrelated dynamics of economic decline, federal housing policies that favored white homeownership and encouraged disinvestment in transitioning neighborhoods, and urban renewal activities that destroyed neighborhoods in the service of highway construction and suburbanization.

The "concrete, localized" forms and processes of globalization are evident in Sunset Park's multitiered economic landscape and its racially differentiated immigrant composition, including a substantive undocumented population (Sassen 2000b, 80). Immigrant neighborhoods are no longer easily labeled as Chinese enclaves or Latino barrios, and Sunset Park's hyperdiverse demography and class-stratified neighborhood economy exemplifies critical new challenges to community building and development. As in the past, land-use decisions and policies continue to shape Sunset Park's economic fate, but now the challenge is a neoliberal development agenda for waterfront revitalization. Environmental justice and community control of development remain prominent themes of Sunset Park's evolution. The making of Sunset Park is instructive, because it is these immigrant global neighborhoods that will determine the future of our multiracial democracy.

3

The Working Poverty of
Neighborhood Revitalization

Industrial Sweatshops and Street Vendors

S
unset Park is frequently lauded as an exemplar of immigrant-driven
neighborhood revitalization.[1] The Center for an Urban Future's (2007)
report "A World of Opportunity" celebrates immigrant entrepreneurialism and documents how small business enterprises established by hardwork-
ing immigrant groups have generated new economic vibrancy in many New
York City neighborhoods. Although acclaimed for their rejuvenating qualities, immigrant economies provide insight into the bifurcated nature of New
York City's neighborhood economic renewal. In addition to the concentration of retailers along Sunset Park's main commercial avenues, immigrant
small businesses are often part of a dynamic informal economy characterized by sweatshop conditions in food and garment production; new services,
including transportation vans that link the city's three Chinatowns; and the
reemergence of street vendors. Sunset Park was once integral to the city's
non-Fordist industrialism and extensive port economy, and the revitalization of the neighborhood economy's is embedded in an economic restructuring that has facilitated the growth of informal and formal economic sectors
which thrive on immigrant labor.

This chapter focuses on two historic immigrant sectors—garment production and street vending—and examines how the prevalence of informality is integral to New York City's postindustrial economy. The chapter
begins with an overview of Sunset Park's industry and occupational sectors to underscore the city's dramatic and nearly complete shift to a highly
bifurcated service economy. This data analysis substantiates the dominance

of immigrant clusters in the downgraded manufacturing, food-related, and health care service industries.

Sunset Park is distinguished by a vibrant Chinese and Latino immigrant economy anchored in retail, food-related and garment production, expanding health and social service sectors, and a revitalizing waterfront. The economic decline of the 1970s, marked by a largely abandoned industrial waterfront, was partially abated by the influx of post-1965 immigration (see Chapter 2). Asian and Latino immigrants with financial and human capital purchased or rented dilapidated commercial storefronts and established numerous small businesses that catered to growing and captive ethnic markets. While immigrant small businesses continue to be a dynamic force and have expanded beyond typical retail and service niches to include construction, auto repair, and home improvement, work conditions remain embedded in informality, poor wages, and weak enforcement of labor standards. The entrepreneurial efforts of Asian and Latino immigrants helped revitalize Sunset Park, but it is a revitalization premised on extensive immigrant working poverty (Sassen 1991).

Despite decades of deindustrialization, Sunset Park remains one of New York City's few remaining industrial production sites. Place-based economic development policies such as the New York State Empire Zones and New York City's Industrial Business Zones seek to retain manufacturing firms and employment (see Chapter 6). Although a compelling rationale to sustain and grow the manufacturing sector draws from its historic incorporation of low-skill workers and immigrants, particularly those lacking English-language proficiency, Sunset Park's downgraded garment sector illustrates how the economic fate of immigrant New Yorkers is now shaped by a lowered floor on employment practices and standards and also by weakened unions. Moreover, reindustrialization strategies premised on niche manufacturing to meet the consumption needs of New York City's elite (in artisanal foods, designer fashions, and customized furniture) has so far failed to mitigate immigrant marginalization and working poverty. Finally, in examining Sunset Park's controversial policy approach to street vendors, this chapter concludes by discussing the spatial and social justice implications in regulating the informal economy and public spaces (e.g., sidewalks).

Labor Market Segmentation: Sunset Park's Industry and Occupational Clusters

Sunset Park's neighborhood economy mirrored the national and regional shift from manufacturing to services; however, the local waterfront remains a key industrial site for New York City. Affirming Sunset Park as one of the city's industrial manufacturing hubs, the New York City Economic Development Corporation (NYCEDC) recently designated the neighborhood as a "sustainable urban industrial district" (New York City Economic Development Corporation 2009). Calculation of a location quotient substantiates Sunset Park's specialization in industrial manufacturing–related sectors relative to the city's economy as a whole.[2] Table 3.1 presents the results of a location quotient analysis that compares Sunset Park's industry composition to New York City and identifies those industries where Sunset Park retains a greater share of workers relative to the city.

The findings of this analysis affirm that Sunset Park's industrial waterfront remains anchored in manufacturing, wholesale trades, and construction. The location quotient ratios for these industries—in particular manufacturing—all exceed 1.0, indicating a higher presence in Sunset Park relative to the city overall. Despite the sharp decline in manufacturing citywide, Sunset Park clearly remains a key site for industrial- and maritime-related sectors. However, as this chapter will discuss, these sectors are no longer high wage or unionized, as Sunset Park's remaining manufacturing sector is largely based on garment production.

Sunset Park industry clusters also include health care and social assistance. The concentration of health-related services is a direct outcome of the Lutheran Medical Center's (LMC) major presence in Sunset Park and its steady expansion to meet the multiple health and family service needs of the neighborhood's diverse immigrant populations. The LMC is frequently cited as the largest employer in the neighborhood, and the high location quotient for health care and social assistance substantiates the LMC's continuing centrality in the economic fate of Sunset Park (see Chapter 2). While a concentration of health services employment is related to the LMC's role as a regional hospital, the location quotient for social assistance also underscores the high level of need for social services among Sunset Park's neighborhood population.

Sunset Park's institutional landscape includes several multiservice agencies, such as the Center for Family Life, the Brooklyn Chinese-American Association, and the Chinese American Planning Council.[3] Neighborhood institutions are particularly important in mediating access to social services, health care, child care, and vital information ranging from immigration to voter registration. The presence and density of comprehensive social assistance organizations, which are viewed as "resource brokers," is often a sign of neighborhood poverty (Small 2006). Their density in Sunset Park has led some community leaders, including Reverend Juan Carlos Ruiz of St. Jacobi

TABLE 3.1   SUNSET PARK NEIGHBORHOOD ECONOMY
EMPLOYMENT SECTORS

| | 2010 | | |
Industry	Sunset Park	New York City	Location Quotient
Total Employment	36,021	3,055,663	—
Manufacturing	3,874	77,025	**4.3**
Wholesale trade	3,537	129,178	**2.3**
Construction	2,630	109,649	**2.0**
Health care and social assistance	8,446	573,682	**1.2**
Retail trade	3,702	299,977	**1.0**
Other services	1,273	143,746	0.8
Administrative and waste services	1,194	182,801	0.6
Transportation and warehousing	622	101,659	0.5
Accommodation and food services	1,458	255,918	0.5
Finance and insurance	1,264	306,044	0.4
Utilities	50	15,830	0.3
Professional and technical services	971	313,168	0.3
Real estate and rental and leasing	353	117,102	0.3
Educational services	276	139,860	0.2
Information	212	150,132	0.1
Arts, entertainment, and recreation	29	67,125	0.0
Management of companies and enterprises	D[a]	61,527	—
Agriculture and mining	D	294	—
Unclassified	248	10,946	1.9

[a] D is suppressed data and refers to a small number of firms in order to protect confidentiality.
Source: New York State Department of Labor, Quarterly Census of Employment and Wages, 2nd quarter, 2010.

Evangelical Lutheran Church, to observe an extensive "nonprofit industrial complex" premised on institutional and professional service providers reliant on government funds (J. C. Ruiz 2013). While government-funded service providers are a source of essential programs for a working-poor immigrant population, these providers tend to promote a top-down and paternalistic leadership approach based on community need and dependency.

Sunset Park's neighborhood economy is also defined by immigrant penetration in new sectors, such as construction supplies, ground transportation, home improvement, and auto repair. The expansion of these immigrant niches indicates a dynamic and diverse ethnic economy that is tied to regional markets supporting New York City's construction and development industries. One of the earliest bus companies to provide inexpensive regional shuttle service between Chinatowns in New York City, Boston, and Philadelphia is Fung Wah Bus, which was established in 1996 to provide a van service for workers commuting between Manhattan's Chinatown and Brooklyn's Sunset Park. The notable presence of Chinese businesses along Sunset Park's waterfront included a Fung Wah Bus depot and garage. Typical for immigrant niches characterized by hypercompetition, dangerous cost-cutting strategies have resulted in numerous accidents, as bargain travel has become quite risky (Luo 2004; Abel and Green 2006; Daniel 2006). In April 2013, the U.S. Department of Transportation revoked Fung Wah Bus's license to operate because of poor safety and maintenance practices that posed an "imminent hazard" (Anon. 2013c). Table 3.1 indicates that Sunset Park's notable employment clusters include retail trade, which is consistent with the prominence of Chinese and Latino immigrant small business enterprises, and administrative and waste services, indicating the concentration of garbage processing uses along the industrial waterfront (see Chapter 6).

Table 3.2 compares the occupational composition and average 2010 wages for service-sector employment in Sunset Park and New York City. The service sector generates nearly 60 percent of New York City's employment base, and its bimodal quality is evident in the employment categories and average earnings. For New York City overall, the largest share of service employment at 21 percent is professional, scientific, and technical service jobs, with average 2010 earnings of approximately $100,000. Following professional and technical service jobs is a clustering of low-wage food service ($23,419) and social assistance ($28,111) jobs. Closer to the citywide service-sector average earnings are administrative and support services ($43,298) and ambulatory health care ($45,190) jobs. Rounding out New York City's largest service employment sectors is educational services, with an average 2010 wage of $53,362.

Sunset Park's social service employment sector does not reflect the same bimodal pattern, and it is notable that the average 2010 earnings for service employment in the community, at $27,261, is significantly lower than the New York City average of $45,358 (see Table 3.2). This earnings disparity is due to the prevalence of low-wage service jobs in Sunset Park. While New York City's service sector has a greater share of high-skill, high-pay jobs in professional, scientific, and technical services, it is notable that even for comparable service employment categories, a significant earnings differential persists, with Sunset Park employees earning less than the city average. An important example are food services and drinking places that make up approximately 11 percent of the employment base for Sunset Park and New York City, but this category is marked by an $8,000 wage disparity.

TABLE 3.2 EMPLOYMENT DISTRIBUTION AND AVERAGE WAGES IN SERVICE SECTORS FOR SUNSET PARK AND NEW YORK CITY, 2010

Services	Sunset Park			New York City		
	Employed	Percent	2010 Wage	Employed	Percent	2010 Wage
Total Employment	**13,662**	**100%**	**$27,261**	**1,459,968**	**100%**	**$45,358**
Social assistance	3,455	25%	$26,592	163,350	11%	$28,111
Ambulatory health care	2,679	20%	$47,495	179,174	12%	$45,190
Nursing and residential care	2,312	17%	$31,078	76,798	5%	$37,942
Food services and drinking places	1,458	11%	$15,063	212,097	15%	$23,419
Administrative and support services	1,194	9%	$25,285	178,088	12%	$43,298
Professional, scientific, technical services	971	7%	$31,261	311,967	21%	$100,677
Religious civic and grant making	485	4%	$32,386	68,942	5%	$53,164
Personal and laundry services	434	3%	$23,246	45,535	3%	$27,119
Repair and maintenance	345	3%	$31,079	13,379	1%	$32,825
Educational services	276	2%	$26,689	139,789	10%	$53,362
Amusement, recreation, and gambling	29	0.2%	$15,313	21,594	1%	$23,903
Performing arts and spectator sports	15	0.1%	31,280	33,382	2%	$90,115
Private households	9	0.1%	$17,626	15,873	1%	$30,523

Source: New York State Department of Labor, Quarterly Census of Employment and Wages, 2nd quarter, 2010.

Sunset Park is one of the last remaining industrial centers in New York City, and the location quotients analysis confirm the neighborhood's concentration in several key industrial sectors.[4] Nevertheless, the trends of the past decade or so indicate continued deindustrialization and a shift to services employment. Table 3.3 compares 1990 and 2010 economic data for Sunset Park and finds that the number of manufacturing firms and workers has steadily declined in the past two decades. Even as late as 1990, manufacturing generated nearly 40 percent of Sunset Park's employment base. By 2010, only one in ten (11 percent) of Sunset Park workers were employed in manufacturing industries. The relative share of manufacturing businesses also dropped from 20 percent to only 9 percent of Sunset Park firms. Correspondingly, the average manufacturing firm size shrank the greatest in the past two decades.

Employment in the service sector steadily increased to replace manufacturing as the largest employment source and represents 38 percent of Sunset Park's workforce. Notably, the sector that grew the most was finance, insurance, and real estate (FIRE), with a 2010 average income of $59,067—well above the annual average neighborhood earnings of $40,060. The FIRE sector includes real estate firms and financial institutions such as ethnic banks, which are discussed in Chapter 4.

Signs of economic hardship are evident in the comparison of inflation-adjusted average earnings in 1990 and 2010. In the largest 2010 employment sector, the real value of average annual earnings for service-sector employment fell nearly $13,000, from $38,956 (in 2010 dollars) to $26,288. Clearly, the wage quality of Sunset Park service jobs has eroded. Among Sunset Park's top four industry sectors, real annual earnings also fell in wholesale trade. The 1990 and 2010 comparisons of private-sector employment indicates an increased base of low-wage earners in services and a significant wage gap in emergent sectors, such as the FIRE sector.

The labor market niches of Asian and Latino residents in Sunset Park reflect their concentration in jobs that are typically defined by low wages, high turnover, and lack of mobility opportunities and benefits. Table 3.4 locates the top occupations and industries for Sunset Park and New York City's Asian and Latino labor force. Several observations are driven home by this table—one is the prevalence of typical immigrant employment niches in janitorial services, garment manufacturing, food services, home health aides, and retail. These are also the occupations and industries that make up much of the unregulated work in New York City, defined as work that systematically violates basic labor laws and standards (Bernhardt, McGarth, and DeFilippis 2007).

TABLE 3.3 COMPOSITION AND PATTERNS OF PRIVATE-SECTOR EMPLOYMENT IN SUNSET PARK, 1990–2010

Employment Sectors	1990				CPI Adjusted Wage 2010	2010				Average Wage	1990–2010 Growth		Average Firm Size	
	Firms	Workers	% Firms	% Workers		Firms[a]	Workers	% Firms	% Workers		Firms	Workers	1990	2010
Total	1,718	23,015	100%	100%	$33,752	3,192	36,021	100%	100%	$40,060	86%	57%	13	11
Manufacturing	344	8,733	20%	39%	$29,813	285	3,874	9%	11%	$33,710	-17%	-56%	25	14
Services	299	4,808	17%	21%	$38,956	1,005	13,647	31%	38%	$26,288	236%	184%	16	14
Wholesale trade	216	2,878	13%	13%	$37,511	417	3,537	13%	10%	$34,432	93%	23%	13	8
Retail trade	411	2,463	24%	11%	$30,552	600	3,702	19%	10%	$37,603	46%	50%	6	6
Construction	198	1,562	12%	7%	$41,917	307	2,630	10%	7%	$52,267	55%	68%	8	9
Transportation, warehousing	78	1,400	5%	6%	$31,405	86	622	3%	2%	$26,192	10%	-56%	18	7
FIRE[b]	103	376	6%	2%	$33,272	243	1,829	8%	5%	$59,067	136%	386%	4	8
Agriculture and mining	5	17	0.3%	0.1%	$24,218	D	D	D	D	—	—	—	—	—
Utilities	—	—	—	—	—	10	50	0.3%	0.1%	$127,667	100%	194%	3	5
Unclassified	64	247	4%	1%	$19,453	239	248	7%	1%	$19,601	273%	0.4%	4	1

[a] The total does not add up because for some subindustry sectors the numbers of workers were small and noted as D.
[b] Fire, insurance, and real estate.
Source: New York State Department of Labor, 1990 ES-202 and Quarterly Census of Employment and Wages, 2nd quarter, 2010.

TABLE 3.4   TOP OCCUPATION SECTORS FOR ASIAN AND LATINO WORKERS IN SUNSET PARK AND NEW YORK CITY, 1990, 2000, AND 2010

1990 Occupation	Sunset Park Latinos	Employment Share	1990 Occupation	New York City Latinos	Employment Share
Sewing machine operators	1,004	4%	Janitors and cleaners	44,047	5%
Janitors and cleaners	834	3%	Sewing machine operators	29,706	3%
Cooks	827	3%	Cashiers	28,438	3%
Assemblers	779	3%	Secretaries	27,671	3%
Cashiers	697	3%	Nursing aides, orderlies, and attendants	26,712	3%
Top five occupations	4,141	16%	Top five occupations	156,574	18%
Total Employed	25,207	100%	Labor force	875,983	100%

1990 Occupation	Sunset Park Asians	Employment Share	1990 Occupation	New York City Asians	Employment Share
Sewing machine operators	1,278	14%	Sewing machine operators	22,624	7%
Cooks	733	8%	Cooks	15,734	5%
Waiters and waitresses	342	4%	Supervisors and proprietors, sales	12,261	4%
Cashiers	291	3%	Cashiers	11,304	4%
Supervisors and proprietors, sales	266	3%	Managers and administrators, N.E.C.[a]	10,380	3%
Top five occupations	2,910	32%	Top five occupations	72,303	23%
Labor force	9,218	100%	Labor force	318,205	100%

2000 Occupation	Sunset Park Latinos	Employment Share	2000 Occupation	New York City Latinos	Employment Share
Janitors and building cleaners	1,833	5%	Janitors and building cleaners	52,150	5%
Sewing machine operators	1,470	4%	Cashiers	40,367	4%
Driver/sales workers and truck drivers	1,238	4%	Nursing, psychiatric, home health aides	40,325	4%
Nursing, psychiatric, home health aides	1,035	3%	Retail salespersons	33,342	3%
Cashiers	987	3%	Secretaries and administrative assistants	31,092	3%
Top five occupations	6,563	20%	Top five occupations	197,276	18%
Total employed	33,640	100%	Total employed	1,088,917	100%

(continued)

TABLE 3.4 (*Continued*)

2000 Occupation	Sunset Park Asians	Employment Share	2000 Occupation	New York City Asians	Employment Share
Sewing machine operators	2,514	14%	Sewing machine operators	23,682	5%
Cooks	1,039	6%	Cashiers	17,862	4%
Chefs and head cooks	915	5%	Retail salespersons	13,228	3%
Cashiers	757	4%	First-line supervisors/ managers, retail sales	12,912	3%
Driver/sales workers and truck drivers	671	4%	Cooks	12,635	3%
Top five occupations	5,896	34%	Top five occupations	80,319	17%
Total employed	17,410	100%	Total Employed	476,130	100%

2010 Occupation	Sunset Park Latinos	Employment Share	2010 Occupation	New York City Latinos	Employment Share
Janitors and building cleaners	1,692	5%	Janitors and building cleaners	48,030	5%
Construction laborers	1,604	5%	Nursing, psychiatric, home health aides	32,777	4%
Cooks	1,148	3%	Maids and housekeeping cleaners	31,346	3%
Driver/sales workers and truck drivers	1,092	3%	Cashiers	30,022	3%
Maids and housekeeping cleaners	1,002	3%	Child care workers	26,483	3%
Top five occupations	6,538	19%	Top five occupations	168,658	18%
Total employed	34,547	100%	Total employed	931,948	100%

2010 Occupation	Sunset Park Asians	Employment Share	2010 Occupation	New York City Asians	Employment Share
Chefs and head cooks	2,245	10%	Cashiers	18,360	4%
Waiters and waitresses	1,498	7%	Accountants and auditors	16,032	3%
Sewing machine operators	1,226	6%	Retail salespersons	14,147	3%
Cashiers	1,199	5%	Taxi drivers and chauffeurs	12,170	3%
Food preparation workers	1,128	5%	Waiters and waitresses	11,562	2%
Top five occupations	7,296	33%	Top five occupations	72,271	15%
Total employed	22,090	100%	Total employed	486,098	100%

[a] According to the U.S. Bureau of Labor Statistics, N.E.C means Not Elsewhere Classified. See the U.S. Bureau of Labor Statistics website (http://www.bls.gov/ocsm/comuseocsm.htm) for further explanation.
Source: 1990 and 2000, Public Use Microsample Data; 2006-2010, American Community Survey, U.S. census.

One particularly egregious practice that received national attention was Wal-Mart's routine of locking janitors—many of whom are undocumented Mexican immigrants—in the store during their night shift (Greenhouse 2004a). Not only is this practice illegal, but it poses a dire safety hazard. In 2004, several Latino janitors approached La Unión de la Communidad Latina (now known as La Unión), a Sunset Park–based social, economic, and cultural rights advocacy group, because they had also been locked in by their employers during the night shift. La Unión found thirty-six supermarkets in Brooklyn, Queens, and the Bronx routinely engaged in this practice (Greenhouse 2004b). The group organized protests in front of several supermarkets and successfully pressured the New York City Council to pass legislation that imposed penalties on employers who locked in their employees. Citlalli Negrete, a twenty-four-year-old Chicana born and raised in Sunset Park, remembers participating with her parents in a La Unión protest at a MET supermarket on Smith and Baltic Streets (in nearby Cobble Hill) "because the market was locking in Mexican workers" (Negrete 2013). Intro 629A was signed into law by Mayor Michael Bloomberg in October 2005, and supporting materials for the bill recalled the tragedy of the 1911 Triangle Shirtwaist Factory fire, when 146 young Jewish and Italian garment workers lost their lives—many jumping to their deaths because exit doors were locked by the employer to prevent worker theft and the entry of union organizers (New York City Council 2005).[5]

A second observation is the persistence of racially segmented labor niches over time. Table 3.4 shows similar occupational categories for 1990, 2000, and 2010, indicating enduring racially segmented labor market niches for Asian and Latino workers. A final observation is the relatively high concentration of Sunset Park Asians in particular low-wage sectors. The top five listed occupations, which includes sewing machine operators, account for one-third of Asian workers in Sunset Park in 1990, 2000, and 2010. The composite profile of the Sunset Park neighborhood economy based on these data sources underscores the concentration of low-wage occupational niches in downgraded manufacturing and service sectors, namely in food services, janitorial services, and health care.

Shape-up sites remain an integral feature of Sunset Park's local economy. No longer defined by longshoremen gathering at the waterfront piers, Sunset Park's day labor force now consists of numerous undocumented Chinese, Mexican, South American, and Central American immigrants congregating near the Home Depot and key neighborhood transportation nodes, including under the Gowanus Expressway along 3rd Avenue, most headed for construction sites (Kwong 1997; Greenhouse 2003). Longtime

Sunset Park residents Lelia Johnson and Fragrance Chen note the daily presence of Chinese and Mexican day laborers starting as early as 6 A.M.[6] A study of day labor in New York City confirmed that in contrast to the national experience, New York City's day laboring population is racially diverse and includes Chinese and Asian Indians (Valenzuela and Melendez 2003). Sunset Park's day laboring sites are frequented by a diversity of racial and ethnic groups—Mexicans, Chinese, Ecuadorians, Salvadorans, and East Europeans (Turnovsky 2003). The significant presence of Asian day laborers in New York City is further substantiated by photojournalist Michael Kamber's (2001) essay on Sikh day laborers in Richmond Hill in Queens and the daily congregation of Asian immigrants on downtown Flushing street corners.

The Anatomy of New York City's Garment Industry

New York City is a world fashion capital, and until a decade or so ago the city served as a significant production site for U.S. apparel manufacturing, particularly in women's outerwear—a broad category of women's clothing that includes dresses, shirts, pants, suits, and coats. Since styles in women's apparel change frequently, the agglomeration of designers, manufacturers, and garment factories is necessary to accommodate the fashion cycles (Hum 2003; Fiscal Policy Institute 2003). Despite the steady decline of manufacturing jobs starting in the late 1960s, the mass influx of Asian and Latino immigrants enabled New York City to hold on to several manufacturing industries, including the garment industry (Johnson 1998; Levitan 1998). Cheap imports and production outsourcing, however, created conditions of fierce competition, as reflected in the comment of a local Sunset Park manufacturer who noted that "We're dying a slow death."[7] New York City was able to retain a segment of garment production because of several competitive advantages, including its stature as a fashion and design center, its proximity to customers and suppliers, the agglomeration effects of innovation and flexibility, and access to a skilled and low-wage workforce.[8]

Employment statistics underscore the steady hemorrhaging of manufacturing employment in past decades from 533,429 jobs, representing 20 percent of New York City workers, in 1975 to 76,383 manufacturing jobs, representing 3 percent of workers, by 2010. Three sectors continue to anchor the city's diminished manufacturing base: apparel production, which remains the largest with 1,266 firms and 16,513 jobs, followed by food manufacturing (977 firms and 13,918 jobs) and printing and related activities (735 firms and 6,494 jobs).[9]

New York City's garment industry was geographically concentrated in two Manhattan neighborhoods—the Midtown Garment Center and Chinatown. The Midtown Garment Center, located between 6th and 9th Avenues from 35th to 41st Streets, remains the largest production center, with more than eight hundred garment manufacturing firms. In the 1970s, Manhattan's Chinatown emerged as a garment-production center as new Chinese immigrants exploited marginal entrepreneurial opportunities presented by the low barriers to setting up a garment factory. Requiring minimal skills and no English, this manufacturing sector became a key employer for immigrant Chinese women (Kwong 1987). Beginning in the late 1980s, garment production spread out to immigrant neighborhoods in Brooklyn and Queens, often to avoid Manhattan's dominant union presence and rising commercial real estate rents (Howe 1987; Yarrow 1991). Although the garment industry is still centralized in Manhattan, the expanding corporate real estate market and neighborhood rezoning and rebranding efforts continue to dislocate garment manufacturers and subcontractors.[10] In fact, the Fashion Center Business Improvement District has embarked on an initiative to rebrand the Midtown Garment Center to reflect its new creative economy sectors, including high-tech start-ups and architecture and design firms (Yost 2012; Daily 2012).

Once a national production center for fashion-sensitive women's outerwear, Manhattan Chinatown's garment industry is now so diminished that its remaining firms employ approximately eight hundred workers in a handful of buildings with a total of seventy-one thousand square feet of manufacturing space. In 2000, Manhattan Chinatown still represented a key industrial cluster, with four hundred firms employing eleven thousand workers (Table 3.5). While the number of apparel firms and workers continued to decline citywide, the drop between 2000 and 2005 was particularly acute in Chinatown. This uneven decline is striking, as immigrant clusters in the outer boroughs—namely Brooklyn's Sunset Park—has now surpassed Chinatown in terms of the number of garment firms and workers. According to the 2010 data, the Midtown Garment Center remains the city's densest apparel manufacturing site. However, the relatively high wages and the significant earnings differential in Midtown Garment Center apparel manufacturing suggests the prominence of nonproduction employment.

During the late 1970s, the incorporation of thousands of immigrant Chinese women in an industrial labor force expanded and transformed Chinatown's economy. The garment industry anchored Chinatown's immigrant economy by providing an avenue for small business formation in garment contracting, and its labor force generated demand for retail, professional

TABLE 3.5   RATE OF DECLINE IN NEW YORK CITY'S APPAREL MANUFACTURING SPATIAL CLUSTERS, 2000-2010

	2000					2005				
	Firms	% Mfg. Firms	Employees	% Mfg. Employees	Avg. Wages	Firms	% Mfg. Firms	Employees	% Mfg. Employees	Avg. Wages
New York City Private Sector Total	209,079	—	3,071,920	—	$53,589	217,740	—	2,953,458	—	$59,849
All Manufacturing	10,024	5%	176,399	6%	$33,065	7,191	3%	114,578	4%	$43,699
Apparel Manufacturing	3,325	33%	60,538	34%	$24,774	1,824	25%	29,153	25%	$39,459
Apparel Manufacturing Clusters[a]										
Midtown Garment Center	891	27%	15,006	25%	$42,123	593	33%	10,138	35%	$57,052
Greater Midtown Garment Center[b]	304	9%	3,028	5%	$36,005	187	10%	1,838	6%	$45,027
Manhattan Chinatown	407	12%	11,245	19%	$10,600	130	7%	2,587	9%	$11,384
Sunset Park	272	8%	4,677	8%	$11,538	155	8%	2,313	8%	$13,532
Long Island City/Hunters Point	146	4%	2,981	5%	$29,006	86	5%	1,660	6%	$44,512
Ridgewood/Glendale	116	3%	2,773	5%	$17,507	51	3%	827	3%	$17,911

(continued)

TABLE 3.5 (*Continued*)

	2010				Firms		Employment	
	Firms	% Mfg. Firms	Employees	% Mfg. Employees	Avg. Wages	2000-2005 Change	2005-2010 Change	2000-2005 Change	2005-2010 Change
New York City Private Sector Total	238,288	—	3,052,953	—	$71,970	4%	9%	-4%	3%
All Manufacturing	6,269	3%	76,811	3%	$47,317	-28%	-13%	-35%	-33%
Apparel Manufacturing	1,270	20%	17,201	22%	$45,245	-45%	-30%	-52%	-41%
Apparel Manufacturing Clusters[a]									
Midtown Garment Center	454	36%	6,654	39%	$62,339	-33%	-23%	-32%	-34%
Greater Midtown Garment Center[b]	132	10%	1,014	6%	$48,761	-38%	-29%	-39%	-45%
Manhattan Chinatown	74	6%	836	5%	$15,034	-68%	-43%	-77%	-68%
Sunset Park	113	9%	1,332	8%	$14,480	-43%	-27%	-51%	-42%
Long Island City/Hunters Point	52	4%	689	4%	$27,394	-41%	-40%	-44%	-58%
Ridgewood/Glendale	23	2%	262	2%	$19,057	-56%	-55%	-70%	-68%

[a] Zip codes of apparel manufacturing clusters: Midtown Garment Center, 10018; Greater Midtown Garment Center District, 10001; Manhattan Chinatown, 10002, 10013, and 10038; Sunset Park, 11220 and 11232; Long Island City/Hunters Point, 11101; and Ridgewood/Glendale, 11385.
[b] The Greater Midtown Garment Center zip code is 10001 and is referred to as the Fur-Flower District.
Source: New York State Department of Labor, 2000, 2005; Quarterly Census of Employment and Wages, 2nd quarter, 2010.

services, and personal services. Women's labor force participation was integral to the industrial working-class composition and identity of Manhattan's Chinatown. The prevalence of garment sweatshops and working poverty provided fertile ground for union activism, namely by UNITE's Local 23-25, the establishment of worker centers such as the Chinese Staff and Workers' Association, and other progressive organizations that advocate for immigrant and worker rights. The evolution of Chinatown's industrial economy advanced a multitiered institutional structure that was once dominated by traditional family associations but now consists of nonprofit organizations, social service agencies, and advocacy groups, representing a vibrant migrant civil society.

Women's labor force participation and earnings are integral to a family-based strategy for economic survival (Bao 2002; Chin 2005). Women's labor enabled working-class Chinese families to move to outer borough neighborhoods, often connected to Manhattan's Chinatown via public transportation lines. The N subway line travels from Canal Street in Chinatown through South Brooklyn neighborhoods, starting with Sunset Park's 8th Avenue station (the first station that emerges from underground and is easily recognized by immigrants because of the "blue sky") and connecting a network of growing Chinese populations in Dyker Heights and Bensonhurst. The shared economic, educational, and social qualities of Manhattan Chinatown and Sunset Park residents have led civic leaders to describe the neighborhoods as constituting a "community of interest" for the purposes of political redistricting (Hum 2002b).

Access to a cheap labor force and the relative ease of entry into the labor-intensive end of garment manufacturing provided an important base of business ownership for many immigrant subcontractors. In addition to cheaper commercial rents, the prevalence of a largely nonunionized workforce was a draw to subcontractors (Chen 2000; Curan 2002). Virtually all of Sunset Park's garment firms are nonunionized.[11] Many workers and their advocates, however, claim that the ability of the garment workers' union, UNITE, to effectively advocate has been greatly diminished in the context of global production such that there is virtually no difference in the work conditions in a union versus a nonunion shop (Freeman 2000, 273).[12] Sunset Park's garment industry illustrates the positioning of immigrant neighborhoods in the spatial geography of global production, as Asian and Latino immigrant women labor under substandard work conditions in competition with their counterparts in China, Bangladesh, Mexico, and the Dominican Republic.

Key community advocates blame the 9/11 tragedies and the subsequent inadequate state response for delivering the death knell to Chinatown's industry, already weakened by global deregulation and free trade policies such as NAFTA and by the expiration of the Multi-Fiber Agreements, which imposed quotas on U.S. apparel imports. As Patrick Murphy of the NYCEDC noted, these conditions coalesced into a "perfect storm" (Murphy 2010). Located approximately ten blocks from Ground Zero, Chinatown was immediately impacted by 9/11. A lockdown followed by a frozen zone limited vehicular and pedestrian access to Lower Manhattan neighborhoods, and the intermittent loss of telephone and electricity for several months essentially halted normal commercial activities. The 9/11 impact on Chinatown's economy and in particular its garment industry was immediate and devastating. According to an internal UNITE document, mega retail chains that dominate the garment industry cancelled orders to Lower Manhattan shops because of concerns about timely shipping from an area with limited roadway access.[13] As noted in a Fiscal Policy Institute (2001, 2) study on the disproportionate impact of 9/11 on New York City's immigrant low-wage labor force, "The industry hardest hit by reduced work volume is apparel manufacturing which has much of its production based in Chinatown." In 2000, approximately eleven thousand of New York City's sixty thousand garment workers (representing 19 percent of the apparel workforce) worked in factories in Manhattan's Chinatown (see Table 3.5). A few years later, Chinatown's garment workforce shrank by more than three-quarters (77 percent), and by 2010, about eight hundred workers were employed in a mere seventy-four garment shops that make up Chinatown's garment industry.

The extensive manufacturing infrastructure, including Bush Terminal and the Brooklyn Army Terminal, helped Sunset Park retain a manufacturing base, but industrial production transitioned to downgraded nondurable manufacturing namely in garment production (Lii 1995). Eclipsing Chinatown as a key site for the immigrant garment industry, Sunset Park now represents the largest cluster of garment-production firms outside of Manhattan's Midtown Garment Center. The New York State Department of Labor's Apparel Industry Task Force updates a weekly list of registered garment manufacturers and contractors, and data retrieved on July 24, 2012, indicated a total of 198 garment manufacturers and subcontractors in Sunset Park, compared to 77 in Manhattan Chinatown.[14] Sunset Park's garment shops are clustered in a handful of industrial buildings along the waterfront—many in buildings owned by Industry City Associates, which is actively engaged in remaking industrial Sunset Park as part of a creative artisan and high-technology hub (see Chapter 6)—and along several upland streets, creating a corridor of low-rise warehouses and garages converted into factory use. By providing relatively inexpensive industrial space, easy access to regional transportation networks, and a largely nonunionized labor supply, Sunset Park and its immigrant subcontractors and laborers serve as a critical link in the globalized process of garment manufacturing.

Each of New York City's geographically clustered garment centers serves distinct production niches and consumer markets (Fiscal Policy Institute 2003). Manhattan's Midtown Garment Center overlaps with the Fashion District, where showrooms and high-end couture designer production is located. Chinatown specialized in moderate- to low-priced women's sportswear, and small contractors, mainly cut-and-sew shops, dominated. Sunset Park's garment industry is similarly concentrated in this production niche, whose primary competitive advantage is quick turnaround. According to an industry expert, Sunset Park's garment industry is focused on orders that need to be filled within two to three weeks, as opposed to six weeks if produced in China.[15] This production work includes fashion knock-offs for retailers such as Rainbow Shops, Sears, and Joyce Leslie (Chen 2010). In August 2010, I visited two Sunset Park garment subcontractors with Lana Cheung, education director for UNITE Local 23-25, who arranged the meetings. Dennis Lee's 353 Fashion Inc. produced evening gowns, and New Kiko Fashion manufactured women's blouses. Both owners relocated to Sunset Park as a result of displacement from Manhattan's Chinatown, and they expressed concerns that labor-intensive production processes may no longer be viable in New York City. Diminishing and irregular manufacturing orders made it especially difficult to retain a skilled workforce, as immigrant women opt for steadier work in hospitality and home health care sectors. Along the industrial waterfront, companies such the American Fleece Association and M. Franabar Inc. are less tied to a volatile and hypercompetitive fashion industry and continue to manufacture clothing such as Girl Scouts uniforms, employing a largely Latina workforce.

Informalization is a strategy that creates marginal opportunities for risk-taking immigrants with access to a cheap coethnic labor force to provide a pliable and economically competitive option for local manufacturers in the face of globalization. These subcontracting arrangements essentially pass on accountability for poor labor conditions to immigrant employers. The factors of fashion sensitivity and quick turnaround will continue to provide a need for sewers and their employers to serve the New York City fashion industry but under conditions of invisibility and labor exploitation as workers with few options (namely undocumented workers) continue to labor in an industry in which union and industry advocates, such as the Garment Industry Development Corporation, have essentially been gutted.

The distinct niches of New York City's garment clusters are evident in the significant differential in average 2010 annual wages of $64,678 for apparel manufacturing employees in the Midtown Garment Center, compared to Sunset Park's $11,957 and Chinatown's $11,651 (see Table 3.5).

Downgraded manufacturing conditions are a prominent aspect of Sunset Park's garment industry (Bao 2002; Hum 2003). Garment production relies heavily on subcontracting whereby immigrant workers ultimately bear the brunt of common cost-cutting business practices that violate basic labor and health standards (Bernhardt, McGarth, and DeFilippis 2007). Characteristic low-road strategies in the garment industry are the prevalence of wage theft and employer intimidation and threats.[16] Two public hearings sponsored by the New York State Subcommittee on Sweatshops during the late 1990s collected testimonials from workers, community leaders, and industry representatives on the prevalence of a sweatshop economy in Sunset Park.[17] Among the most serious violations are wage withholding; dangerous conditions, including blocked exits and lack of ventilation; and long workdays with no overtime pay (Greenhouse 2001; Bernhardt, McGarth, and DeFilippis 2007). Current investigations and lawsuits filed against garment subcontractors and manufacturers producing for retailers and labels—including Macy's, Gap, DKNY, and Victoria's Secret—confirm that violations of the Fair Labor Standards Act remain common in immigrant garment clusters (Sussman 2011; Greenhouse 2008). In some cases, accused employers resort to intimidation tactics and threats of physical violence in an effort to silence employees and the community groups that assist and advocate for garment workers (Greenhouse 2008; Hum 2003; Port 2001). A recent walk through Sunset Park revealed several garment shops located in converted garages, which is clearly in violation of workplace fire and safety standards (Figure 3.1).

Institutional responses to Sunset Park's largely unregulated garment industry tend to be short-lived, such as Community Board 7's Apparel Industry Task Force and the Kings County Apparel Association.[18] Assemblyman Felix Ortiz represents Sunset Park at the New York State Assembly and chaired the Sub-Committee on Sweatshops; however, the committee has not been active for years.[19] In a historic demonstration, Assemblyman Ortiz, Congresswoman Velazquez, and UNITE's Vice President Edgar Romney led a march of Sunset Park garment workers and their families to protest poor work conditions and wages (Figure 3.2). UNITE opened the Garment Workers Center in 1997, but it closed just one year later because of funding issues and the departure of a key staff member, Dan Yun Feng, who had made significant inroads building solidarity among Sunset Park's Asian and Latina garment workers (Sandberg 1997). The closure of the Sunset

Figure 3.1   A Chinese radio program and the whir of sewing machines are audible from this Sunset Park garment factory on 64th Street, May 2010. (*Photo taken by Tarry Hum.*)

Park Garment Workers Center represented a significant void in sustained union organizing in New York City's second-largest apparel manufacturing cluster and marked UNITE's growing irrelevance in mobilizing immigrant garment workers (Kwong and Lum 1988; Kwong 2002). The Chinese and Staff Workers Association (CSWA) opened a satellite office in Sunset Park in 1995 to counter the proliferation of sweatshop conditions and continues to be a key organizing force in the neighborhood (see Chapter 5).

Founded in 1979, the CSWA is one of the country's oldest nonprofit worker centers and has an established and extensive track record in organizing immigrant Chinese workers and building successful cross-racial collaborations for economic justice in diverse immigrant neighborhoods (Kwong 1994). The CSWA does not adhere to an advocacy model of organizing, nor does it provide social services. Rather, the CSWA views immigrants and workers as "agents for change" and is frequently noted for direct and militant actions in the three industry sectors where its membership is most concentrated—construction, restaurants, and garment factories.[20] The CSWA has successfully seeded new organizations, including the National Mobilization Against Sweatshops and the 318 Restaurant Workers' Union.[21] Based on the strong linkages that bind immigrant workplaces and neighborhoods, the CSWA focuses on workplace

Figure 3.2   Sunset Park Garments Worker rally, including Assemblyman Felix Ortiz, UNITE's Edgar Romney, and Congresswoman Nydia Velázquez, June 1995. (*Photo by Mike Dabin,* New York Daily News.)

issues, affordable housing, and community development. The CSWA frequently partners with civil rights organizations, such as the Asian American Legal Defense and Education Fund, to litigate cases of wage theft, discriminatory hiring and subcontracting practices, immigrant rights, and neighborhood gentrification and displacement (see Chapter 5).

While the catastrophic events of 9/11 dealt a fatal blow to the garment industry in Manhattan's Chinatown, its demise should also be problematized through the lens of city economic development policies and the planning objectives of local community elites. Formed as a subsidiary of New York state's Empire State Development Corporation, the Lower Manhattan Development Corporation (LMDC) had among its primary tasks overseeing the development of the World Trade Center memorial site and the planning and revitalization of Lower Manhattan. Consisting of gubernatorial and mayoral appointees largely representing real estate and corporate interests, the LMDC was charged with overseeing a total of $3.4 billion in federal community development block grants. The wealthiest downtown neighborhoods, such as TriBeCa and the Financial District, received a majority share of rebuilding allocations, in contrast to the area's low-income immigrant and communities of color, namely Chinatown and the Lower East Side.[22]

Recognizing that virtually all of the marginal garment contracting shops did not survive the 9/11 economic fallout, key industry actors collaborated on a proposal to develop the NY Fashion Space—modeled after Brooklyn's successful nonprofit Greenpoint Manufacturing and Design Center—as a last-ditch effort to preserve a much leaner Chinatown garment industry by providing and maintaining a stable supply of affordable manufacturing space. UNITE, the Garment Industry Development Corporation, and the New York Industrial Retention Network sought $25 million from the LMDC to acquire and renovate approximately one hundred thousand square feet to sustain Chinatown's specialized niche in quick-turnaround and small-production orders. While industry advocates believed that an infusion of money and public support could save a much-diminished but viable garment cluster, the proposal was summarily dismissed, and to date the LMDC has taken no official action on this funding request (Chen 2010).

Post-9/11 planning and rebuilding in Chinatown marked a concerted effort to remake a paradigmatic immigrant working-class neighborhood to better serve Lower Manhattan's position as an epicenter of global finance and the consummate entrepreneurial world city. The LMDC's objective for Chinatown revitalization was clearly articulated in a 2003 request for proposals "to encourage changes in the Chinatown community that would promote tourism."[23] This imperative to grow New York City's tourist economy materialized in supplemental sanitation and regulatory services to rid Chinatown of filth, dirt, and vice—historically symbolized by opium dens and now embodied by the informal trade in designer knock-offs. According to a 2006 Committee on Homeland Security staff report, the LMDC committed $176 million to Chinatown of which a tiny 4 percent was dedicated to economic development, with most of the funds to support a Clean Streets program overseen by the New York City Department of Small Business Services and the newly formed Chinatown Partnership Local Development Corporation. Post-9/11 strategies to rebuild Chinatown's economy focused on criminalizing its informal economy and spending $7 million to sanitize local streets.[24]

In October 2009, fashion designers, retailers, union representatives and members, and local elected officials gathered to launch the Save the Garment Center Trade Association and called for policy action to retain garment production in a rapidly transforming Midtown Center.[25] Once the largest site of garment production in the United States, New York City continues to pride itself on being the fashion capital of the world, despite the steady decline of its local manufacturing base. Designated a special district in the late 1980s to protect the garment industry, the Midtown Garment

Center is widely recognized as a planning failure, as office and retail development has remade the area into an extension of Times Square. Essential to New York City's status as a world fashion capital, however, is the retention of local garment manufacturing capacity in sample making, small runs, and inventory replacement. Moreover, advocates claim that the spatial clustering of industry actors is critical for quality control, innovation and creativity, and retention of a sense of place.

Since the effort to save garment production in New York City is focused on the Midtown Garment Center, the network of immigrant manufacturing clusters integral to the local industry is not part of the fashion rebranding. At its height in the 1980s, Manhattan's Chinatown was a key production site, with approximately five hundred garment shops and a workforce of twenty thousand. Today, Chinatown's garment industry has essentially vanished. Although a handful of factories struggle to survive in a small area currently undergoing a rezoning study, the future is written in neighboring gentrified streets noted for high-end retail and condominium buildings. While the demise of manufacturing in the United States is attributed to globalization and the emergence of vast exploitable labor in industrializing Asia and the Caribbean, New York City local racial politics, land-use planning and zoning policies, and a post-9/11 development agenda are key factors in the anatomy of the city's declining garment industry. Moreover, at this critical juncture when momentum has gathered to save some garment production to support the city's fashion industry, it is significant to note that immigrant labor is marginalized in industrial retention strategies as historic production clusters are remade to serve a creative economy.

Sunset Park's garment industry is relatively stable for now. The 2012 New York State Quarterly Census of Employment and Wages enumerated more than one hundred garment factories employing 1,124 workers, which is comparable to the 2010 data indicated in Table 3.5. However, sweatshop conditions are the norm for the sizable numbers of Asian and Latino women who continue to labor in local factories. Although greatly diminished, garment production still represents New York City's largest manufacturing sector in terms of firm number and workforce size. While industry stakeholders, including designers, agree that retention of some garment-production capacity is necessary to support the city's fashion industry, there are no initiatives or resources to improve or strengthen Sunset Park's garment sector or to retrain immigrant workers. Deeming Sunset Park a niche for cheap products and cheap labor (despite many Sunset Park factories producing for Midtown Garment Center manufacturers), industry stakeholders argue that capital (including political capital) should be targeted to saving the Midtown

Garment Center. While Manhattan's Chinatown is remade as a tourist destination and center for Pacific Rim capital, the NYCEDC's vision for Sunset Park as a "sustainable urban industrial district" favors remaking the vast industrial infrastructure to accommodate new niche manufacturing— defined as customized, highly detailed, and high-quality "Made in Brooklyn" branded products that fulfill the consumptive desires of New York City's elite (Sadovi 2013). Despite the policy discourse that manufacturing is an entry point for immigrant workers and entrepreneurs, the NYCEDC and industry stakeholders have clearly stated their disinterest in supporting Sunset Park's immigrant-dominated garment industry.

What remains of New York City's garment industry is being refashioned as a "service" component to the city's creative economy. In other words, the rationale for the retention of manufacturing capacity is framed as providing an essential service to New York City's fashion industry (McCormick et al. 2012). Historic production sites such as Chinatown and Sunset Park no longer have a place in this refashioned landscape, and in fact, Chinatown's historic role in supporting New York City's apparel industry has been erased, as exemplified by a 2011 map of apparel production sites, produced by the Design Trust for Public Space, that does not name Chinatown.[26] Current efforts to retain garment-production capacity in the fashion capital of the world are now led by the Council of Fashion Designers of America, the Design Trust for Public Space, and the Municipal Arts Society and are solely focused on the Midtown Garment Center.[27] Postindustrial New York City involves remaking Manhattan's Chinatown from a dense working-class neighborhood into a tourist destination and headquarters for Pacific Rim capital. The LMDC's selective funding decisions helped to legitimate the Chinatown community elite's embrace of a neoliberal development vision and agenda.

In Sunset Park's "sustainable urban industrial district," real estate pressures and marketing strategies for the neighborhood's "industrial artists' colony" will surely drive out remaining garment shops located on the waterfront (Stein 2009). Industry City Associates owns several industrial buildings in Bush Terminal that currently house 41 of Sunset Park's 198 garment shops, representing one-fifth of the local garment industry.[28] Industry City Associates is engaged in a "non-traditional approach" to draw tenants for its significant inventory of industrial space and is actively marketing to artists and other small, specialized, crafts-based manufacturers (Turcotte 2009).

Jamestown Properties, owner and developer of Chelsea Market (formerly a Nabisco factory), has purchased a controlling share of Industry City (Geiger 2013a). Andrew Kimball, who was appointed by Mayor Bloomberg in

2005 to head up the Brooklyn Navy Yard, has joined Jamestown Properties as director of innovation and global initiatives and chief executive of Industry City (Geiger 2013d). Kimball led the transformation of the Brooklyn Navy Yard into a vibrant complex of modern manufacturers, including designers and artists, small craft manufacturers, and Steiner Studios (a self-described film "production factory")[29] housed in renovated buildings on a three hundred–acre waterfront site. The news of Kimball's leadership role in Industry City has raised hopes and expectations that Sunset Park will have its "Navy Yard moment" (Geiger 2013b).

Sunset Park's emergent status in New York City's creative economy was recently advanced by its inclusion in a September 2012 Brooklyn-wide artist studio tour, with several artists located in the city-owned Brooklyn Army Terminal (Croghan 2011). The NYCEDC recently issued a Request for Proposals to disburse up to $8 million from the City Council Small Manufacturing Investment Fund to reactivate these spaces by subdividing and renovating large, vacant, privately held industrial floor plates to accommodate the spatial needs of niche manufacturers and "modern" industrial firms.[30] These trends, augmented by a city economic development policy discourse of sustainability and modernization, further the invisibility of immigrant workers and the varied informal economic sectors that are integral in supporting a postindustrial urban economy.

Plaza del Mercado Unido: Locating Street Vendors in an Immigrant Marketplace

Sunset Park's upland area includes the commercial heart of the neighborhood centered on two distinct and vibrant avenues—5th Avenue, with numerous immigrant small businesses serving the community's Pan-Latino population, and 8th Avenue, frequently referred to as Brooklyn's Chinatown. While there is no official enumeration of immigrant-owned businesses, New York State Department of Labor data confirms that the number of businesses and jobs created in immigrant neighborhoods greatly outpaced New York City overall (Center for an Urban Future 2007, 11). In a study of New York City neighborhoods with the greatest growth in business establishments and workforce size between 1994 and 2004, Sunset Park ranked second only to Flushing in Queens (Center for an Urban Future 2007, 12). Informalization shapes Sunset Park's commercial landscapes, as brick-and-mortar businesses often include growing numbers of informal microbusinesses, evident in the subdivision of storefronts to accommodate numerous individual shops, many in spaces no larger than the dimensions of a street food cart.

Another prominent feature of small businesses in immigrant neighborhoods is stoop-line vendors who rent sidewalk space from commercial tenants in brick-and-mortar storefronts (Gaber 1994). Stoop-line vendors frequently pay exorbitant rents and rarely have licenses.

Sunset Park's main commercial avenues also host numerous street vendors. Many sell specialized foods, reflecting Sunset Park's diverse demography—piragua vendors offering vibrant-colored Puerto Rican shaved ice treats, women with ice coolers or shopping carts selling tamales and roasted corncobs on 5th Avenue, and vendors of taro cakes and stinky tofu on 8th Avenue. Many vendors on both avenues also sell all types of general merchandise, including batteries, DVDs, underwear, and socks. Some vendors have carts, while others simply lay out their wares on the sidewalk. For these immigrants, street vending is a form of self-employment of last resort (Street Vendors Project 2006).[31] While Sunset Park's street food is increasingly noted by New York City's hipster food scene bloggers and journalists,[32] food vendors serve an essential need of a low-income neighborhood by providing fresh, affordable meals for workers and their families, especially for those living in cramped living quarters or without kitchens.

Immigrant vendors are an enduring and quintessential feature of New York City streetscapes. The city's long history of street vending is exemplified by Lower East Side peddlers (Bluestone 1991). Perceived as unfair competitors to brick-and-mortar businesses because street vendors do not pay rent, overhead, or sales taxes while generating street congestion and downgrading neighborhood quality, state regulation of street vendors to protect public welfare and safety dates back to the 1800s (Bluestone 1991). According to a 2006 study by the Urban Justice Center's Street Vendors Project, there are approximately 12,557 street vendors in New York City, of which approximately half are unlicensed because of a cap on the number of vending licenses and permits instituted three decades ago.[33] Street vending remains heavily regulated, and a study by the New York City Independent Budget Office (2010) finds that the numerous regulations and laws governing street vending are confusing and costly. No fewer than ten city agencies are involved with some aspect of regulation and oversight of street vending, and the New York Police Department's Peddler Squad is responsible for enforcement of street-vending laws.

A favored Bloomberg administration place-based economic development tool is the establishment of Business Improvement Districts (BIDs). BIDs are defined as geographic areas where property owners pay an additional tax assessment that is collected by the city and returned to the BIDs to supplement city services such as street cleaning and maintenance, public safety, and marketing and neighborhood branding through banners and uniform signage, beautification, and landscaping.[34] BIDs vary in size and scope, ranging from neighborhood BIDs such as Sunset Park's 5th Avenue BID to the Grand Central Partnership, which represents some of the city's largest property owners and real estate developers. The wide spectrum of BIDs is reflected in their annual operating budgets, which range from $53,000 to more than $11 million (Gross 2005). As private nonprofit entities, BIDs are governed by a Board of Directors that consists of commercial property owners; public officials, including the mayor, the borough president, and the local city council member; and commercial tenants and residents. However, a majority of the board must be commercial property owners.

The emphasis on private-public partnerships and quasi-public organizations to supplement government services and promote business-friendly environments is a central feature of Mayor Bloomberg's neoliberal governance approach (Brash 2011). BIDs consolidate real estate concerns and formalize property owners' ability to exercise control over public street maintenance, commercial center identity (branding) and aesthetics (uniform signage), programming, and public relations. Moreover, property owners typically pass on the additional tax assessment to their commercial tenants in increased rents, potentially displacing small businesses. Large BIDs such as the Grand Central Partnership and the Bryant Park Corporation are quite powerful and drive business development and investment in the area. BIDs have existed in New York City since the early 1980s, but it was during the Bloomberg administration that BIDs were established in every borough, and their numbers increased by a third, from forty-four to sixty-seven BIDs, including the highly controversial Manhattan Chinatown BID in 2011.[35] BIDS represent the interests of commercial property owners, so it not surprising that BIDs have an antagonistic relationship with street vendors.

At the nexus of public streets, street vending is an exemplar of economic informality in advanced urban economies. BIDs are vocal advocates for restoring social order on public streets and frequently criminalize street vendors in an effort to eliminate their presence. As noted on the Bryant Park Corporation website, a BID is "a private entity [that] takes over the management of a public space" (Harris 2010). Sunset Park's 5th Avenue BID has had a long and contentious relationship with the numerous Latino street vendors who sell their goods in front of BID members' property and storefronts. Community Board 7 claims that street vendors continue to be problematic for 5th Avenue, and the growing presence of "illegal" street vendors on 6th and 8th Avenues has resulted in increased complaints to the community board (Laufer 2013a). In response, Community Board 7's statement of needs clearly upholds the goal of "a stronger, coordinated effort between City agencies to rid 5th Avenue of illegal vendors" (New York City Department of City Planning 2013, 176).

In 2007, the 5th Avenue BID proposed an experimental grassroots solution that called for the formation of a special vending district, La Plaza del Mercado Unido, to respond to the concerns and needs of both brick-and-mortar businesses and street vendors.[36] Prepared by longtime Sunset Park resident and 5th Avenue BID founder Tony Giordano,[37] the proposal for La Plaza represented a departure in antagonistic BID and street vendor relations in that the 5th Avenue BID formally acknowledged that street vendors are not marginal to the local economy but in fact contribute to a "market synergism" by providing complimentary products and expanding the customer base and foot traffic (Gaber 1994, 399). The 5th Avenue BID found that Sunset Park's street vendors are largely neighborhood residents and provide an essential service to the local working-poor Latino population.[38]

The specific provisions of the Plaza del Mercado Unido proposal called for the removal of street vendors on 5th Avenue, creating a vending-free zone on the heavily trafficked main commercial avenue. Street vendors selected by a lottery system would be provided a special Sunset Park Vending Permit to locate on a limited number of spots on the side streets along 5th Avenue from 38th to 64th Streets. The benefits to street vendors would be the opportunity to join the BID for a nominal fee and access social services and technical assistance provided by local institutions, such as the Brooklyn Public Library, the Brooklyn Economic Development Corporation, and the Center for Family Life. Recognizing a continuum in the form of immigrant self-employment, including "survivalist entrepreneurs" (Valenzuela 2001), Sunset Park's 5th Avenue BID sought to centralize community resources to assist in the formalization of neighborhood street vendors.

The BID leadership convinced their members to collaborate with the street vendors by pointing out the potential expansion of BID resources (due to an increase in members and fees) and, more important, in marketing Sunset Park as a "unique" destination to tap into Brooklyn's world-renown reputation for hipster taste-making in street vending and food carts (Zukin 2010). By enforcing the exclusion of street vendors on 5th Avenue and restricting them to the side streets with "colorful umbrellas," Plaza del Mercado Unido reconciles the interests of Sunset Park's two merchant communities and creates a unique shopping environment. Moreover, Sunset Park's property and business owners will have the satisfaction of "knowing they took a very courageous step in doing the *morally right* thing" (Sunset Park 5th Avenue BID 2007, 11, my emphasis). The BID proposal to establish a

Sunset Park Vending District was supported by Community Board 7, local nonprofit organizations, small business assistance centers (including Accion New York), economic development institutions, and all Sunset Park elected representatives, including Congresswoman Nydia Velázquez, ranking member of the House Committee on Small Business (Anon. 2012b).

Sunset Park 5th Avenue BID's Plaza del Mercado Unido proposal was formalized by City Council member Sara Gonzalez into two bills, Intro 846 in 2008 and Intro 36 in 2010, to amend New York City's administrative code in establishing a Sunset Park Vending District. Intro 846 and several other bills proposing reform of New York City's street vendor laws were aired on November 14, 2008, at a public hearing held jointly by the City Council Committees on Consumer Affairs and Immigration. Intro 846 was never brought to a vote, and with new cosponsors—including City Council members Diana Reyna (chair, New York City Council Small Business Committee), Peter Koo of Flushing, and Brad Lander of neighboring Park Slope—Gonzalez reintroduced the Sunset Park Vending District bill in 2010 as Intro 36. Since Sunset Park vendors are largely unlicensed, the testimonies of the neighborhood's street vendors underscore that their participation in the Plaza del Mercado Unido proposal was based on the promise of permits. The public hearing transcript notes Mr. Alarcon's translated testimony as stating that "It's been over 20 years that we haven't gotten any permits for our carts. So it's just not for us but the entire vendor community that we can have these permits" (New York City Council 2008, 130).

A key provision of the proposed Sunset Park Vending District is to prohibit vending at all times on 5th Avenue between 38th and 64th Streets. Violators would be charged with a misdemeanor and required to pay penalties and/or face a prison sentence of up to three months (New York City Council 2010, 6). The Sunset Park 5th Avenue BID claim that street vendors are not legally permitted to locate on this commercial avenue is not entirely accurate.[39] A review of the New York City administrative code general vendors' rules, which include a list of restricted streets, finds that Brooklyn's 5th Avenue is only restricted from 44th to 59th Streets on Thursdays to Saturdays from 10 A.M. to 7 P.M. (New York City Council 2013a). Intros 846 and 36 would extend the restricted area and completely exclude street vendors at all times on Sunset Park's 5th Avenue.

Both the NYC BID Managers Association and the Street Vendors Project rejected the bill's neighborhood proposed solution but for different reasons. Barbara Randall, president of the Fashion Center BID and member of the NYC BID Managers Association, testified about the "destabilizing" economic effects of "illegal" street vendors. With respect to the Sunset Park

Vending District proposal, she argued that "any proposed law that attempts to benefit a single neighborhood at the cost of the nearby districts is ill advised" (New York City Council 2008, 145). Randall's description of street vendors as illegal is a common way to criminalize street vendors, and her testimony did not deviate from the BID narrative of street vendors as unfair competitors who degrade the business environment and quality of public space.

Despite the participation of the Street Vendors Project in early planning meetings,[40] project members objected to Intro 846 because it introduces the possibility of "separate vending regulations in each neighborhood throughout the city" and adds to the current complex overregulation of street vendors (New York City Council 2008, 132). Objections voiced at the November 2008 public hearing and at a May 2009 City Hall rally included advocates' incredulity about possible common interests between BIDs and street vendors, especially since BIDs "have always tried to take away our rights."[41] The bills would allow the Sunset Park 5th Avenue BID to exclude all street vendors from a major public sidewalk at all times. Even though 5th Avenue is a busy public marketplace for Sunset Park's Pan-Latino immigrant population, street vendors would be banned from this public space. Moreover, the number of legal vending spots along designated side streets is limited to eighty: forty for general vending and forty for food vending. The appeal of the Plaza del Mercado Unido proposal for Sunset Park's immigrant vendors was an opportunity to secure a legal permit through a random lottery. However, new applicants are listed last, as preference will be given in order to disabled veterans, disabled persons, veterans, and persons currently on the city's waiting list for a license or permit for one of the eighty designated vending locations (New York City Council 2010, 3).

The proposal for Plaza del Mercado Unido represents a modicum of improvement in a policy discourse that tends to criminalize street vendors as illegal and unfair competitors and depicts immigrant vendors in particular as reproducing Third World practices and economic conditions that degrade neighborhood quality.[42] While Sunset Park's 5th Avenue BID acknowledges that street vendors are an integral part of the local economy and can advance Sunset Park as a tourist destination, the Plaza del Mercado Unido proposal legitimates their marginalization by erasing the presence of street vendors on 5th Avenue and relegating them to the side streets. The Sunset Park Vending District would further privatize public space by extending the BID's reach in determining designated vending locations and the type of vendor for each legal spot. Essentially, the Sunset Park Vending District allows the 5th Avenue BID to impose a local regulatory apparatus that requires vendors to agree to the terms and goals of private property owners. As a demonstration project, Intro 36 would formally extend the reach of a local BID to regulate and govern a main public commercial street. Even though this approach fails to achieve necessary and democratic reform of the myriad regulatory rules that govern street vending, City Council member Sara Gonzalez stated an intention to reintroduce the Sunset Park Vending District bill after "revisions to make it a little more workable and avoid legal challenges."[43]

Conclusion

Sunset Park's neighborhood revitalization is often cited as an example of the transformative qualities of immigrant capital and market-driven economic change. While immigrant economic activity helped revitalize Sunset Park, immigrants are heavily concentrated in marginal retail, service, and downgraded manufacturing sectors. Sunset Park's revitalization was driven in part by the expansion of an unregulated economy whereby basic fair labor standards are consistently violated. The valorization of immigrant economies as examples of entrepreneurialism and ethnic-based strategies for economic incorporation and mobility is countered by an indisputable reality embedded in widespread economic hardship and exploitation. Undoubtedly, the influx of post-1965 Asian and Latino immigrant labor renewed Sunset Park's neighborhood economy, but it is a renewal that reflects widening race and class divides.

4
Immigrant Growth Coalitions and Neighborhood Change

The Role of Ethnic Banks

A prominent but understudied aspect of neoliberal urbanization is an emergent Asian immigrant growth coalition that consists of ethnic banks, realtors, property owners, contractors, and developers. Established by racial minorities in the United States, ethnic banks are distinct from foreign or transnational banks because they formed to remedy the financial exclusion of coethnic compatriots.[1] Logan and Molotch's (1987) theorization of place-based elites and their treatment of the city as a growth machine for wealth accumulation is applicable to post-1965 Asian immigrants who have mobilized financial, human, and social capital to advance an active development agenda and facilitate new "transnational space(s) for the circulation of capital" (Sassen 1988, 1). The infusion of immigrant capital in a progrowth urban environment is transforming the process of neighborhood change in New York City's working-class communities. Global capital in Manhattan real estate developments is long-standing and well documented (Fainstein 2001). China's emergence as a world economic power is evident in extensive investments in U.S. real estate and corporations, including iconic developments such as the China Center—two hundred thousand square foot occupying six floors—to serve as "a gateway for international business and cultural exchange" in the nearly completed One World Trade Center (Bagli 2008b). Urban theorist Neil Smith (2002, 441), however, argued that a "hallmark of the latest phase of gentrification" is the reach of global capital throughout the urban landscape, including the local neighborhood level.

Immigrants are frequently credited with aiding New York City's recovery from fiscal crisis of the mid-1970s through high rates of labor force participation and entrepreneurial startups. According to the putative urban revitalization narrative, immigrants stabilized disinvested neighborhoods by purchasing discounted residential and commercial real estate and establishing numerous mom-and-pop small businesses (Muller 1993; Center for an Urban Future 2007). Since the late 1980s, the scale of immigrant capital investments has accelerated, as evidenced by the emergence of an immigrant growth coalition, or place entrepreneurs (Light 2002; Ley 2010).[2] The influx of Asian capital is in part an outcome of U.S. policies, notably the extensive deregulation in the 1980s of the banking industry as well as the increasing emphasis on skill and investor preferences in federal immigration policy. The consequences for local community dynamics were significant—heightened class bifurcation among the Asian immigrant population (Cheng and Yang 1998) and an intraethnic gentrification process that is "densely connected into the circuits of global capital and cultural circulation" (Smith 2002, 427).

Sunset Park's transition from a multiethnic white neighborhood to a majority Puerto Rican neighborhood during the 1960s and 1970s told a familiar urban tale of capital disinvestment, redlining, and discriminatory banking practices (see Chapter 2). Designated a federal poverty area, Sunset Park was devastated by the systemic disinvestments that destroyed numerous minority New York City communities (Wilder 2000; Thabit 2003; Caskey 1994). The lack of fair capital access hindered viable homeownership and small business formation (Squires and Kubrin 2005; Immergluck 2004; Halpern 1995). An extensive brownstone housing stock and its proximity to affluent neighborhoods such as Park Slope and Bay Ridge helped stem Sunset Park's wholesale abandonment. This marginalized neighborhood, however, mustered little resistance to the influx in the 1980s of new Asian and Latino immigrants seeking affordable housing, including homeownership opportunities, that initiated a dramatic demographic transformation.

Broad-based banking deregulation in the 1980s during the Ronald Reagan era of laissez-faire economics contributed to a more competitive environment as banks became highly mobile and geographic boundaries no longer limited their scope of operations. During this period, the rules that governed the formation and entry of new banks and their financial activities were greatly eased (Strahan 2003). For example, the 1982 Garn–St. Germain Depository Institutions Act permitted savings banks to engage in activities that were limited to commercial banks, such as issuing credit cards and making nonresidential real estate and commercial loans. This act also amended the Bank Holding Company Act to allow bank holding companies to acquire failed banks and thrifts, regardless of state boundaries (Krugman 2009; Stiroh and Strahan 2003). Moreover, legislation governing federal banks, such as the International Banking Acts of 1978 and 1981, bolstered New York City's role in global finance by liberalizing the entry of foreign banks into the U.S. retail banking market (Lin 1998).

The conditions leading up to the 2008 global financial crisis were further advanced during the Clinton administration with the passage of key deregulation acts that "forever altered American banking" (Matasar and Heiney 2002, viii). These acts are the 1994 Riegle-Neal Interstate Banking and Branching Efficiency Act and the 1999 Gramm-Leach-Bliley Financial Services Modernization Act, which repealed major provisions of the Depression-era Glass-Steagall Act of 1933. Texas senator Phil Gramm, one of three Republican sponsors of the 1999 act, was quoted in the *New York Times* extolling the demise of government regulation: "In this era of economic prosperity, we have decided that freedom is the answer" (Labaton 1999).

Despite high poverty rates, immigrant neighborhoods are typically not without the presence of capital in the form of formal banks, informal institutions, and fringe financial venues that help facilitate the substantial outflow of remittances to family members and hometown communities.[3] While there is significant interest in immigrants and access to financial capital, the research has largely focused on consumer financial services and predatory lending.[4] With the exception of the research by Li et al. (2001, 2002) and Dymski et al. (2010) on Chinese ethnic banks in Los Angeles, there is little research on the role of ethnic banks in facilitating immigrant financial incorporation or community development. This void is especially notable for New York City.

This chapter investigates Sunset Park's growing presence of ethnic banks and the paradox of persistent Asian and Latino poverty amid relatively high volumes of capital represented by the numerous banks in the neighborhood.[5] Based on a detailed analysis of Home Mortgage Disclosure Act (HMDA) data, Community Reinvestment Act (CRA) reports, and in-depth interviews with bank executives and other community stakeholders, this chapter finds that in contrast to a dominant theme in the current research that ethnic banks act as financial institutions with a community service orientation (Li et al. 2001, 2002), ethnic banks are largely not agents of immigrant asset building. Rather than promoting first-time home mortgages, ethnic banks concentrate their lending in commercial real estate loans, including market-rate condominium developments, and as a result promote capital investments that fuel real estate speculation and gentrification in immigrant working-class neighborhoods.[6] Moreover, even in the context of weakened CRA requirements, ethnic banks fare poorly in their community reinvestment activities.

Prevailing arguments of ethnic solidarity assert that ethnic institutions, including banks, know their community needs best and act to mitigate immigrant financial exclusion. The presence of major Chinese ethnic banks—along with an extensive base of realtors, property owners, and developers—is transforming the scale, aesthetics, and economics of immigrant neighborhoods not by the promotion of individual homeownership but by extensive investments in commercial real estate development. This chapter describes how ethnic institutions advance neighborhood change and uneven development and, more important, underscores the need for improved definitions of the underbanked and for policy strategies to remediate financial inequality in immigrant neighborhoods.

Immigrant Financial Access

A review of the current research on Chinese ethnic banks establishes several dominant themes premised on the social and cultural nature of financial institutional practices. Established to counter financial exclusion due to discrimination and linguistic and cultural barriers, ethnic banks serve as a "key facilitator for capital circulation" by establishing ethnic businesses, expanding the spatial boundaries of residential communities, and promoting opportunities for immigrant homeownership (Li et al. 2002, 779). Researchers argue that two factors—largely based on the experience of Los Angeles County—drive the dynamism of the Chinese ethnic banking sector: (1) globalization and financial deregulation, which facilitated the influx of offshore or transnational capital, and (2) the accumulation of local social capital in dense community and ethnic-specific networks, creating information sources on individual creditworthiness typically not available to mainstream banks. As Li et al. (2001, 1929) argue, "intimate knowledge of community financial patterns, trust, and business and social networks enables minority bankers to take on more credit risk and, in effect, become more highly leveraged than they could otherwise be."

Ethnic banks are instrumental in the formation and development of Asian settlement and entrepreneurial patterns. Dymski and Mohanty (1999, 365) describe how "a key element in Asians' transition from ethnic enclave to ethnoburb is a powerful Asian banking sector—not informal small-scale lenders, but formal institutions with large-scale financial resources." The importance of ethnic banks was substantiated in Zonta's (2004) study of mortgage lending in Los Angeles County, which found that Asian-owned banks have a high propensity for lending to Asian applicants. This is heightened in enclave areas because of access to informal informational sources, underscoring Dymski and Mohanty's (1999, 364) argument for the comparative advantages of ethnic banks: "Ethnobanks may resolve information asymmetries differently than other lenders, using informal information rooted in extensive business interrelations based on reputation ('face'). In addition, ethnobanks' locational proximity may provide extra insights into their core loan customers' prospects; indeed, the very presence of an ethnic banking network may reduce transaction costs and have spillovers enhancing overall business prospects."

Ethnic banks occupy a niche that differentiates them from mainstream banks, and this niche is based on a community service orientation, an emphasis on relationship banking, and a specialization in international banking. As Li et al. (2001, 1934) contend, "In common with non-Asian ethnic banks, but in contrast to large mainstream banks, Chinese American bankers insist on the importance of enduring relationships with communities they serve, and believe their institutions to be vital in local economic growth and social well-being." So central is the mission of community service that ethnic banks, according to Dymski, Li, and their colleagues, will pursue it at the expense of profit levels (Dymski et al. 2010). Researchers argue that ethnic banks rely on social capital and cultural understanding rather than "balance-sheet criteria" to make lending decisions (Li et al. 2001, 1934)—for example, making mortgages without checking credit histories because they know that Chinese borrowers would never default. And "this cultural understanding *has made single-family housing mortgage lending a safe business* for many Chinese American banks" (Li et al. 2001, 1935, my emphasis). Based on their comparative advantages of localized knowledge, language access, ethnic social capital, and informal networks, ethnic banks are well positioned to capture the largely unbanked immigrant market (Li et al. 2002; Zonta 2004).

The demographic forecasts for the United States portend an increase in the numbers and scope of ethnic banking (Shanmuganathan, Stone, and Foss 2004). This literature underscores the tremendous market potential and increasing competition between mainstream and ethnic banks to meet the financial needs of numerous underbanked and unbanked population groups. While globalization trends and deregulation policies figure prominently in facilitating demographic transitions and the growth of ethnic banks, the research agenda continues to focus on the social nature of ethnic banks and how cultural and social values shape the allocation of money, credit, and routine banking practices (Dymski et al. 2010; Pollard 2004; Zonta 2004; Li et al. 2001, 2002).

The research of Kwong (1987, 2009) and Lin (1998), in their analyses of Manhattan Chinatown's enclave economy as a center of sweatshops and overseas foreign investment, is notable. Both authors discuss the influx of transnational Asian capital and the growth in the numbers and sizes of ethnic banks. They argue that ethnic banks fuel real estate speculation and commercial development, ultimately making Chinatown less viable as a neighborhood for working-class immigrants.[7] This dualism—apparent in the parallel realties of prosperity and poverty, formal and informal economies—also defines Sunset Park's neighborhood economy and multitiered banking sector, which includes conventional lenders (both ethnic and mainstream banks) as well as fringe bankers.

An Overview of Ethnic Banks in New York City

More than two hundred transnational foreign banks have branches, agencies, or representative offices or own U.S. commercial banks or investment companies in New York City.[8] The number of ethnic banks also increased significantly during the 1980s in major immigrant gateway cities such as Los Angeles and New York. More recently, ethnic banks have established a strong presence in the financial landscape of southern cities such as Houston and Atlanta. Asian ethnic banks represent one of the most dynamic sectors of the banking industry (Fredrickson 2004). Driven by expanding markets, especially by the recent influx of Fuzhounese immigrants, ethnic banks in New York City have multiplied to meet the retail service needs of this new demographic base (Fredrickson 2003; Chan 2002).

The compositional landscape of ethnic banks is dynamic and constantly changing. The saturation of West Coast markets has contributed to the expansion of California-based ethnic banks to East Coast cities such as New York City, Boston, and Philadelphia (Kranz 2004). The establishment of local branches of Cathay Bank and the United Commercial Bank (UCB)[9] in New York City illustrates this pattern. Cathay Bank and UCB represented the two largest Asian American–owned banks in the United States, each with assets that exceeded $10 billion in 2007. While the majority of Cathay Bank and UCB branches are located throughout California, New York City represents a second concentrated market.[10] Both banks have also established an international presence with branches and/or representative offices in China and Taiwan. In 2007, UCB advanced the integration of Chinese financial markets by acquiring a bank in Shanghai and became the first Chinese

American bank to offer banking services in China (Iritani 2007). UCB vice president Ernest Fung noted that this acquisition helps facilitate global trade transactions and business development (particularly small- and medium-sized ethnic businesses) in the United States and China (Fung 2008).

One way that California-based Chinese banks have expanded in the Northeast is through the acquisition of small, locally established, ethnic-owned banks, and in several notable cases these acquisitions have been of troubled ethnic banks charged with fraudulent practices.[11] The acute level of competitiveness among ethnic banks was exemplified in an aggressive bidding war between Cathay Bank and UCB in 2005 to acquire the locally Chinese-owned Great Eastern Bank.[12] Cathay Bank, prevailed and this acquisition represented the second troubled New York–based Chinese ethnic bank that Cathay had acquired in recent years. A year later, Cathay Bank made headway into Chicago by acquiring New Asia Bank, with three local branch locations. In 2007 Cathay Bank acquired United Heritage Bank, establishing the bank's presence in New Jersey (Cathay Bank 2013). UCB pursued its expansion on the East Coast with the January 2007 acquisition of the Chinese American Bank, one of the earliest New York City ethnic banks (established in 1972) whose lending activities primarily consisted of small loans to Manhattan Chinatown businesses (Lin 1998, 95).

Incidences of misconduct involving embezzlement and illegal transfers to real estate development or other business ventures have marred the reputation of New York City Asian ethnic banks and in some cases have precipitated their acquisition. These incidences also raise important questions about the depth of social capital and community trust in ethnic-based financial institutions. In 1985, Golden Pacific National Bank, headquartered in Manhattan's Chinatown with branches in Queens, was acquired by HSBC after federal regulators ordered its closure upon learning that the bank diverted funds by setting up false certificates of deposits, referred to as "yellow certificates" (Kerr 1985; Bennett 1985a, 1985b, 1985c). In 1999, Golden City Commercial Bank, with branches in Manhattan's Chinatown and in Queens, was acquired by Cathay Bank when founder Jack Liu was charged in a 135-count indictment alleging grand larceny, forgery, perjury, and criminal solicitation (Ross 1999; El-Faizy and Becker 1999). Before its acquisition by Cathay Bank, Great Eastern Bank was also colored by an extensive and troubled history of misconduct by a former bank president and members of the board of directors, resulting in the 2002 conviction of the former bank president Joseph Liu[13] and three former bank directors for scheming to divert $1 million of the bank's assets to a real estate company co-owned by the defendants (Allen 2001; Shifrel 2001; Claffey 2002).[14]

Abacus Federal Savings Bank has also engaged in questionable banking activities. In 2003, six bank employees—including a bank vice president and a branch manager—were charged with embezzlement and conspiracy to defraud bank customers of at least $10 million.[15] This incident resulted in several days of mayhem as thousands of depositors rushed to the Manhattan Chinatown branches to retrieve their savings, causing a Depression-style run on the bank (Retsinas 2003a, 2003b; Buettner 2012). In 2012, Abacus Federal Savings Bank and eleven bank employees were served with an indictment based on an investigation by New York City district attorney's office that found the bank had "participated in a systematic and pervasive mortgage fraud scheme" between May 2005 and February 2010.[16] In addition to residential mortgage fraud, the bank is charged with securities fraud, grand larceny, conspiracy, and falsifying business records (Rodriguez 2012). Despite Manhattan's Wall Street being the epicenter of the 2008 subprime mortgage meltdown, which catalyzed a global financial crisis and an economic recession, New York district attorney Cyrus Vance noted that the Abacus Federal Savings Bank investigation resulted in his office's first bank indictment since 1991 (Buettner 2012; Bennett 2013).

First American International Bank (FAIB) was founded in Sunset Park as a community development bank and is certified by the U.S. Department of Treasury as a community development financial institution (CDFI). A CDFI is defined as "a specialized financial institution that works in market niches that are underserved by traditional financial institutions" (Community Development Financial Institutions Fund 2013). Certification as a CDFI qualifies FAIB for various programs that provide monetary awards as incentives to expand lending, investment, and service activities in underserved and/or economically distressed areas. For six years, FAIB received a Bank Enterprise Award totaling more than $4 million with very little to show in terms of community development investments in Sunset Park.[17] The bank's questionable community service record was compounded by the issuance of a Federal Deposit Insurance Corporation (FDIC) cease and desist order in August 2007 for unsafe and unsound banking practices.[18] The FDIC order delineates FAIB's international money laundering practices in violation of the Bank Secrecy Act (also known as the Currency and Foreign Transactions Reporting Act) and U.S. Department of Treasury Office of Foreign Assets Control regulations.

The dynamism of the ethnic bank landscape is further shaped by bank failures. A notable failure is UCB, which was ranked as the second-largest Asian-owned bank in the country before its collapse. The demise of UCB, which was seized by the FDIC and sold to East West Bancorp, Inc., in

2009, was due to "substantial concentrations in commercial real estate lending and acquisition, construction and development loans" (Federal Deposit Insurance Corporation 2009). According to the FDIC, "alleged fraud" and "unsafe and unsound banking practices" by UCB senior executives were also factors in the failure of the overleveraged bank. A few years earlier, UCB had received nearly $300 million in federal assistance through the Troubled Assets Relief Program (TARP). Ultimately, UCB's failure cost the public an estimated $1.4 billion (Reckard 2009). As a result of the sale, East West Bank emerged as not only the largest Asian American bank but also the largest bank based in southern California. By 2013, East West Bank was listed among the top fifty U.S. banks based on total assets (Benoit 2013).

Ethnic banks that serve Latinos are also a part of the economic landscape of immigrant neighborhoods; however, there are significant differences in history, scale, and mission. The market potential of the Latino community is evident in the demographic trends that highlight Latinos as the fastest-growing population group, attributable to a high birthrate and immigration flows. Although trends indicate a rising disposable income, the Latino population remains a largely unbanked group (Shanmuganathan, Stone, and Foss 2004; Wisniewski 2005). The potential to harvest this huge market has launched multimillion-dollar advertising campaigns by mainstream banks and other corporations to attract Latino deposits and consumer spending (Kramer 2002). One of the earliest ethnic banks established to address the systemic financial exclusion of Latinos was Ponce de Leon Federal Savings and Loan Association. Founder Enrique Campos del Toro sought to replicate the First Federal Savings and Loan Association, which he established in San Juan, to help remedy the substandard housing conditions of Puerto Ricans in New York City (Anon. 1960).

The number of Latino financial institutions increased with the 1961 change in the New York state banking law that permitted foreign and out-of-state banks to establish full-service branches instead of licensed agencies that were limited to a few transactions, such as letters of credit. Shortly after, one of Puerto Rico's largest banks, Banco de Ponce, quickly moved to close its licensed agency in Manhattan and open a bank branch in the Bronx, "where other banks had feared to tread" (Cole 1970a). Puerto Rico's two other large banks—Banco Popular and Banco Credito—followed and established bank branches in neighborhoods with large and growing Latino populations, including East Harlem (also known as El Barrio or Spanish Harlem) and Williamsburg, Brooklyn.

Many contemporary themes in the ethnic bank literature resonate in the mainstream media coverage of these early ethnic banks (Cole 1970a, 1970b).

Utilizing alternative ways to ascertain individual creditworthiness, Banco de Ponce, Banco Popular, and Banco Credito became profitable by extending credit to a growing Spanish-speaking Puerto Rican population that was largely excluded by mainstream banks. In 1989, Banco de Ponce agreed to merge with its prime rival, Banco Popular, Puerto Rico's largest bank (Bradsher 1989). Building on a public service mission, the merger promised to place a Banco Popular branch serving Puerto Ricans as well as the emergent immigrant Caribbean and Central and South American populations on "every neighborhood street corner" (Bradsher 1989).

Since the 1978 sale of Banco Credito, Latino banks in New York City include Banco Popular, Ponce de Leon Federal Bank (formerly Ponce de Leon Federal Savings and Loan Association), and Doral Bank.[19] With ninety-five branches in six states, Banco Popular, which rebranded as Popular Community Bank in 2010, is among the top fifty banks in the nation in terms of assets (Benoit 2013; Crosman 2012). An example of its marketing strategies includes a recent five-year agreement to be the exclusive bank sponsor of the New York Mets baseball team, which entitles the bank to advertise and set up ATMs in Shea Stadium (Sandomir 2005). While much smaller in total assets and deposits, Ponce de Leon Federal Bank promotes itself as "A Bank with Community Spirit" and remains headquartered in the Bronx, with nine local branches in the Bronx, Queens, and Brooklyn as well as in Union City, New Jersey. Established in 1999 to serve New York City's underserved Hispanic community, Doral Bank is a bank subsidiary owned by Doral Financial Corporation, the largest residential mortgage lender in Puerto Rico. In contrast to Chinese-owned ethnic banks, Latino ethnic banks in New York City are typically large banks with headquarters based in Puerto Rico (Rohter 1985).

Despite the presence of a diverse institutional banking landscape consisting of the biggest banks in the industry—including JP Morgan Chase, union banks such as Amalgamated Bank, and community and ethnic banks—Latino Sunset Park residents are severely underbanked. A history of redlining and racial discrimination is compounded by a diverse population that includes undocumented immigrants as well as those who have limited experience with formal banking institutions and practices. According to Leticia Alanis of La Unión, Mexican immigrants in Sunset Park come from a rural background with no familiarity or prior experience with institutional financial services (Alanis 2013). Alanis also noted a complete lack of regard by banks for this sizable segment of Sunset Park's population. She recounted her own experiences at Amalgamated Bank and noted that it was only in the past year that the bank, which was founded in 1923 by immigrant garment workers, had hired a Latino employee in the Sunset Park branch. Alanis observed that banks overall are "not welcoming" and can do a much better job in financial literacy, education, and outreach to the Latino community. Sunset Park's extensive underserved and low-income market is punctuated by the recent branch establishment of the Nobel Peace Prize–winning Grameen Bank, which promotes microfinancing and small lending circles as sources of start-up capital.

Ethnic Banks and Neighborhood Change in Sunset Park

The past two decades have been marked by a dramatic increase in the presence and density of Chinese banks in Sunset Park. In 1997, Sunset Park's banking infrastructure consisted of seven banks, which included two Chinese banks (Abacus Federal Savings Bank and Chinatrust Bank), with total deposits of $428 million. Since then, several Chinese ethnic banks with headquarters in Manhattan's Chinatown or California have opened a branch office along Sunset Park's 8th Avenue Chinatown commercial corridor. In addition, Chinese-owned FAIB was established in Sunset Park in 1999 and proceeded in rapid succession to open three branches in Manhattan's Chinatown and four branches in Queens, making FAIB one of the financial industry's fastest-growing banks.[20]

Sunset Park's highly stratified financial infrastructure now includes ethnic and nonethnic regional, national, and transnational banks (Table 4.1) as well as numerous check cashing outlets and wire transfer centers that facilitate remittances and access to cash for Sunset Park's large underbanked population.[21] Since 1997, the total number of bank branches in Sunset Park has more than doubled from seven to nineteen in 2012. During this period, Chinese banks increased fourfold from two to eight, serving an Asian population of approximately forty thousand, and now represent a significant share of local bank branches. The bank density for Sunset Park's Asian population is thus one bank per five thousand individuals, which is comparable to the bank density of Manhattan financial centers.[22] Notwithstanding the dominant presence of banks, a large segment of Sunset Park's population remains underbanked—in other words, the population lacks access to financial capital (Fredrickson 2006; Weiner 2007).

In 2012, the total deposits in Sunset Park banks was approximately $1.2 billion, with more than a quarter (29 percent or $351 million) held in Chinese banks. Sunset Park is an important depository resource for locally established ethnic banks, especially FAIB, as 11 percent of FAIB's total New York City deposits are based in its Sunset Park branches. Moreover, in terms of the distribution of deposits among Sunset Park's nineteen banks, FAIB's

TABLE 4.1   BANKS WITH BRANCHES IN SUNSET PARK, JUNE 30, 2012

Bank Name and Sunset Park (SP) Location	Date Established	Headquarters	Date SP Branch Established	Total NYC Deposits ($000)[a]	Sunset Park Deposits ($000)	% NYC Deposits Sunset Park	Deposit Share Sunset Park
Chinese Banks (Inc. Transnational Banks)							
Abacus Federal Savings Bank 5518 8th Avenue	11/29/1984	6 Bowery New York, NY, 10013	9/9/1993	$187,734	$29,824	16%	2%
First American International Bank 5503 8th Avenue 5902 8th Avenue	11/15/1999	5503 8th Avenue Brooklyn, NY 11220	11/15/1999 1/15/2004	$445,402	$129,333	29%	11%
Chinatown Federal Savings Bank 5512 8th Avenue	4/27/1984	107-109 Bowery Street New York, NY 10002	2/27/2007	$127,961	$16,909	13%	1%
Cathay Bank 5402 8th Avenue	4/19/1962	777 North Broadway Street Los Angeles, CA 90012	6/27/2002	$632,332	$54,076	9%	4%
Chinatrust Bank USA 5413 8th Avenue	4/27/1965	22939 Hawthorne Blvd. Torrance, CA 90505	11/18/1993	$281,761	$49,639	18%	4%
East West Bank 5801 8th Avenue	1/1/1972	135 N. Robles Avenue Pasadena, CA 91101	11/6/2009[b]	$478,438	$51,614	11%	4%
Industrial and Commercial Bank of China USA, NA 5714 8th Avenue	2/14/1983	202 Canal Street New York, NY 10013	3/21/2007	$190,554	$20,097	11%	2%
Regional Bank							
Alma Bank[c] 140 58th Avenue	9/12/2007	28-31 31st Street Astoria, NY 11102	5/7/2010	$644,133	$27,238	4%	2%

(continued)

TABLE 4.1 (Continued)

Bank Name and Sunset Park (SP) Location	Date Established	Headquarters	Date SP Branch Established	Total NYC Deposits ($000)[a]	Sunset Park Deposits ($000)	% NYC Deposits Sunset Park	Deposit Share Sunset Park
National Bank							
Amalgamated Bank 4502 Fifth Avenue	4/14/1923	275 7th Avenue New York, NY 10001	8/11/2008	$2,255,005	$27,501	1%	2%
Transnational Banks							
Banco Popular North America 5216 5th Avenue	1/1/1920	7 West 51st Street New York, NY 10019	12/4/1970	$2,635,978	$44,215	2%	4%
HSBC Bank USA 5515 8th Avenue 6102-6106 8th Avenue	6/1/1812	One HSBC Center Buffalo, NY 14203	3/30/1998 7/23/2007	$51,079,184	$147,430	0.3%	12%
Capital One, NA 5001 5th Avenue	5/22/1933	1680 Capital One Drive Mclean, VA 22102	5/4/2009	$12,276,876	$13,079	0.1%	1%
Citibank, National Association 5324 5th Avenue	6/16/1812	399 Park Avenue New York, NY 10022	6/16/1812	$51,153,118	$161,867	0.3%	13%
JP Morgan Chase Bank 5101 4th Avenue 5423 8th Avenue 5323 5th Avenue	1/1/1824	1111 Polaris Parkway Columbus, OH 43240	5/18/1912 10/23/2006 9/25/2008	$357,431,530	$286,532	0.1%	24%
TD Bank, National Association 987 4th Avenue	1/1/1852	2035 Limestone Road Wilmington, DE 19808	5/31/2008[a]	$12,225,237	$154,923	1%	13%

[a] Total NYC Deposits represents the total sum of deposits in New York City bank branches. Sunset Park deposits represents the total sum of deposits in Sunset Park bank branches.
[b] Date acquired.
[d] Took over Sunset Park's Banking Development District in 2010.
Source: Federal Deposit Insurance Corporation, http://www2.fdic.gov/idasp/main.asp

market share is competitive with larger mainstream banks with world name recognition, such as JP Morgan Chase, Citibank, HSBC, and TD Bank (see Table 4.1). We will see, however, that Sunset Park deposits are not matched by reinvestments in community development. By way of comparison, the total deposits of its affluent neighbor, Park Slope, is more than $1.7 billion, even though Sunset Park is a mixed industrial, commercial, and residential neighborhood. Moreover, Sunset Park's deposits are significantly dwarfed by the size of deposits in Manhattan's Chinatown ($11.7 billion) and Flushing in Queens ($6 billion), which are clearly centers of transnational Asian capital.[23]

The concentration of ethnic banks in Sunset Park suggests that they are active lenders. The HMDA data tells a more nuanced story of ethnic banks and home mortgage lending, especially in comparing loan originations before and after the 2008 financial crisis. Overall, ethnic banks are not the primary sources of home mortgage loans for Asians who purchased new homes in Sunset Park. While small thrifts or savings banks such as Abacus Federal Savings Bank do make a fair number of home mortgages, providing loans for home ownership is clearly not the primary activity of ethnic banks. An examination of HMDA data for an eleven-year period (2000–2011) highlights several important patterns in the Sunset Park housing finance market. First, an annual average of 741 home loans was originated in Sunset Park, largely for new home purchases or refinancing (Table 4.2). With interest rates dipping to a historic low in the summer of 2003 (Deane 2003), lending activity in Sunset Park reflected the refinancing boom as loan activity reached a high of 1,231 originations, with 60 percent of this loan activity in refinancing. This general pattern was disrupted by the 2008 financial crisis, which resulted in a significant drop in overall home lending as total loan originations declined from an average of 863 in the pre-2008 crisis years to 372 in the recessionary period, defined as 2009 to 2011.[24]

Second, the demographic transformation of Sunset Park is evident in the racial composition of new home buyers. While home lending activity in Sunset Park typically involves an Asian, Latino, or non-Hispanic white applicant, Asians dominate as home purchasers, and this is particularly acute in the aftermath of the 2008 financial crisis (see Table 4.2). In the pre-2008 crisis period, 49 percent of loans originated for the new purchase of a one- to four-family home went to Asian borrowers, while 21 percent were obtained by Latino and 17 percent by non-Hispanic white home buyers. This trend changed dramatically in the post-2008 recession, with Latinos being most impacted. While the number of mortgages originated to Asian home buyers dropped a negligible 6 percent, from an average of 179 to 169 originated loans, Latinos went from an average of 78 loans in the

TABLE 4.2   TOTAL HOME LOAN ORIGINATIONS IN SUNSET PARK, 2000-2011

	2000	2001	2002	2003	2004	2005	2006	2007	2008	2009	2010	2011	11-Year Average	2000–2008 Average	Percent Loans Precrisis	2009–2011 Average	Percent Loans Postcrisis	Change before/after 2008
Total Originations	591	800	959	1,231	972	1,024	883	755	555	451	314	352	741	863	100%	372	100%	-132%
Loan Types																		
Home Purchase	318	332	305	391	393	447	369	386	334	237	186	222	327	364	42%	215	58%	-69%
Home Improvement	77	56	61	37	55	62	81	39	24	7	5	8	43	55	6%	7	2%	-720%
Refinance	155	354	509	733	452	445	354	265	148	181	101	98	316	379	44%	127	34%	-200%
Multifamily	41	58	84	70	72	70	79	65	49	26	22	24	55	65	8%	24	6%	-172%
Applicant Race																		
Asian	148	242	233	362	243	297	230	297	299	270	174	192	249	261	30%	212	57%	-23%
Latino	168	221	260	347	318	341	302	189	86	43	40	47	197	248	29%	43	12%	-472%
Non-Hispanic white	106	140	192	270	193	184	159	125	78	77	56	66	137	161	19%	66	18%	-142%
Black	21	17	20	43	32	43	29	22	9	7	6	3	21	26	3%	5	1%	-392%
Other	13	18	15	28	7	3	11	2	1	1	3	2	9	11	1%	2	1%	-444%
No Info	135	162	239	181	179	156	152	120	82	53	35	42	128	156	18%	43	12%	-261%
Total 1-4 Family Home Purchase																		
Asian	130	171	128	188	173	204	151	230	237	195	148	163	177	179	49%	169	78%	-6%
Latino	97	78	76	87	78	117	88	59	21	4	8	8	60	78	21%	7	3%	-1068%
Non-Hispanic white	54	51	64	68	73	78	67	59	43	24	16	37	53	62	17%	26	12%	-141%
Black	11	8	7	18	11	14	16	13	5	1	1	2	9	11	3%	1	1%	-758%
Other	4	4	2	11	1	1	5	4	1	1	2	2	3	4	1%	2	1%	-120%
No Info	22	20	28	19	57	33	42	21	27	12	11	10	25	30	8%	11	5%	-172%

Source: Federal Financial Institutions Examination Council, 2000-2011 Raw Home Mortgage Disclosure Act (HMDA) data.

pre-2008 crisis period to fewer than 10. While the share of home mortgages to non-Hispanic whites also dropped, their relative share of total new home mortgages precrisis (17 percent) and postcrisis (12 percent) did not change significantly. In contrast, 78 percent of home mortgages in the recession period were originated for Asian home buyers and only 3 percent for Latinos compared, to 21 percent before the crisis. If these patterns continue, the race and class composition of Sunset Park will surely be affected.

The significant drop-off in home lending to non-Hispanic whites in the years immediately following the 2008 crisis may be temporary. The 2011 HMDA shows a slight uptick in mortgages to non-Hispanic whites purchasing homes in Sunset Park. A resumption of their home purchases is consistent with Brooklyn's development trajectory that portends an influx of more affluent residents, especially as Sunset Park is once again promoted as an affordable extension of Brownstone Brooklyn. A March 2013 *New York Times* article, "Brooklyn's New Gentrification Frontiers," features Sunset Park as a possible site for prospective home buyers who may need to "hunt deeper in Brooklyn" because they are priced out of established hipster neighborhoods, such as Park Slope and Williamsburg (Higgins 2013).

Consistent with citywide lending patterns, ethnic banks are not the primary sources of home mortgage loans for Asians who purchased new homes in Sunset Park, despite their concentrated and growing institutional presence.[25] If all Chinese banks (including transnational banks) that originated home mortgages in Sunset Park were accounted for, the average number of loans made annually by these ethnic institutions during the eleven-year period of 2000–2011 represents a mere sixty loans, or 34 percent of all loans originated to Asian borrowers for a home purchase (Table 4.3). Prior to 2008, the average was significantly lower at forty loans, representing 22 percent of total home loans to Asian borrowers. The 2008 financial crisis created an opportunity for ethnic banks. The withdrawal of mainstream banking institutions resulted in a handful of ethnic banks originating home mortgage loans for Asian buyers in Sunset Park. Abacus Federal Savings Bank was joined by FAIB, Cathay Bank, and East West Bank, and their post-2008 loans maintained a steady number of Asian home buyers, while lending to Latinos in particular virtually ceased.

The post-2008 financial crisis underscores the lack of capital access for Latinos. The withdrawal of mainstream banks, however, may not be totally responsible for the precipitous drop in Latino home loans, because these institutions were never primary sources of capital. Rather, the analysis of HMDA data finds that subprime lenders were key sources of home mortgage capital for Latinos. For several years, Greenpoint Mortgage Funding

TABLE 4.3   HOME MORTGAGE LENDING FOR ONE- TO FOUR-FAMILY UNITS BY ETHNIC BANKS FOR ASIAN HOMEBUYERS IN SUNSET PARK, 2000-2011

Bank	2000	2001	2002	2003	2004	2005	2006	2007	2008	2009	2010	2011	2000-2011 Average	Precrisis Average	Postcrisis Average
Total Loans	130	171	128	188	173	204	151	230	237	195	148	163	177	179	169
Abacus Federal Savings Bank	26	37	27	45	20	21	8	23	32	74	35	1	29	27	37
First American International Bank	—	—	1	9	12	7	3	8	39	71	30	5	19	11	35
Chinatown Federal Savings Bank	1	4	—	4	—	—	—	1	6	1	—	—	3	3	1
Chinatrust Bank	—	—	—	—	—	—	—	—	—	—	1	3	2	—	2
United Orient Bank	—	1	—	—	1	—	—	1	2	—	—	—	1	1	—
Bank of China	4	—	1	—	—	1	1	—	2	—	—	1	2	2	1
Asia Bank, National Association	—	—	—	—	—	1	—	—	—	—	—	—	1	1	—
The Chinese American Bank	—	—	—	—	—	1	—	—	—	—	—	—	1	1	—
Cathay Bank	—	—	—	—	—	—	2	—	2	—	37	48	22	2	43
Bank of East Asia	—	—	—	—	—	—	2	1	—	—	—	1	1	2	1
Global Bank	—	—	—	—	—	—	—	—	2	1	1	—	1	2	1
East West Bank	—	—	—	—	—	—	—	—	—	—	1	43	22	—	22
Summit Mortgage Bankers, Inc.	—	—	—	—	—	—	21	36	48	16	—	10	26	35	13
Total Lending by Ethnic Banks	31 24%	42 25%	29 23%	58 31%	33 19%	30 15%	16 11%	34 15%	85 36%	147 75%	105 71%	112 69%	60 34%	40 22%	121 72%
Total Lending by Summit Mortgage Bankers	—	—	—	—	—	—	14%	16%	20%	8%	—	6%	15%	20%	8%
Total Lending by Nonethnic Banks	99 76%	129 75%	99 77%	130 69%	140 81%	174 85%	135 89%	160 70%	104 44%	32 16%	43 29%	41 25%	107 61%	130 73%	39 23%

Source: 2000–2011 Home Mortgage Disclosure Act (HMDA) Raw Data, http://www.ffiec.gov/hmda/hmdaproducts.htm.

originated the highest number of home loans to Latinos. Greenpoint Mortgage Funding specializes in low-documentation (Alternative A) mortgages, which are subprime fixed-rate loans for people who lack traditional credit information and/or have problematic credit histories. In varying years, the top lenders for Latinos have included independent mortgage companies that are regulated by the U.S. Department of Housing and Urban Development. A survey of the top lenders to Latinos indicates a heavy reliance on subprime mortgages as an avenue for homeownership. Banco Popular did not originate any home mortgage loans to Latinos purchasing a home in Sunset Park during this period. This underscores the significant community need for fair and responsive capital access.

Contrary to the literature of ethnic banks, those banks are averse to risk, and this is affirmed by high denial rates among Asian applicants for home purchase loans. Compared to mainstream banks, which encouraged customers to apply for a loan even if there is only a "slice of hope," ethnic banks readily discouraged applications and told Asian customers "don't even think about it" if they lacked the resources for a downpayment or necessary documentation or if their needs could not be met by a standard fifteen-year mortgage.[26] Even in the immediate aftermath of the 2008 financial crisis when ethnic banks faced little competition from mainstream banks, the denial rate for Asian applicants for home loans increased.[27] In contrast to the ethnic bank literature that emphasizes relationship banking, which enables ethnic institutions to take on more credit risk, ethnic banks appear quite risk averse and will invest resources and time to screen applicants (Yu 2005). The limited mortgage lending activity of most ethnic banks in the post-2008 period when mainstream banks were no longer competitors substantiate that ethnic banks exert relatively little effort to promote Asian homeownership.

Notwithstanding the post-2008 uptick in home mortgages and the role of small thrift institutions such as Abacus Federal Savings Bank, homeownership is not the primary lending activity of Chinese banks. Although the lending practices of Abacus Federal Savings Bank are consistent with the ethnic bank literature's argument that ethnic institutions help facilitate enclave expansion and immigrant homeownership, a more compelling story is the relative absence of ethnic banks as lenders to Asians purchasing a new home in Sunset Park. While ethnic banks may not be key actors in promoting homeownership in immigrant neighborhoods, they are deeply engaged in underwriting neighborhood commercial real estate development, especially in market-rate luxury condominiums, as illustrated in Figure 4.1. Table 4.4 looks at the loan portfolios of New York City's Chinese banks and finds that with few exceptions, their real estate loans are concentrated in commercial

Figure 4.1   Residential and commercial condominium development financed by Cathay Bank on 7th Avenue and 58th Street, June 2007. (*Photo taken by Tarry Hum.*)

real estate, construction, and land development.[28] Although this loan portfolio data is not disaggregated by census tract and thus it is not possible to determine the specific volume of commercial real estate loans in Sunset Park, a neighborhood census shows numerous development projects financed by ethnic banks—including FAIB, East West Bank, and Bank of China—involve large-scale commercial developments and new condominium complexes.[29]

Several notable examples include the 420 43rd Street development, which generated community uproar about overdevelopment and was the catalyst for the 2009 rezoning struggle (see Chapter 5).[30] This market-rate residential condominium complex, with thirty-one units, was financed with a $5 million loan by FAIB. Another example is the local development company Hang Seng Capital Group LLC, whose office is based in its twenty-seven-unit residential condominium building that was capitalized by a UCB $8.2 million mortgage in 2008 that was subsequently assumed by East West Bank in 2010. Ethnic banks do not lend exclusively to Asian developers. A major new addition to Sunset Park's commercial 8th Avenue is a twenty-two thousand–square foot food mall and supermarket that occupies a city

TABLE 4.4   LOAN PORTFOLIO FOR SELECT BANKS, JUNE 30, 2012

	East West Bank		Cathay Bank		Chinatrust Bank		First American International Bank		Abacus Bank		HSBC Bank USA	
	($000s)	Dist.	($000s)	Dist.	($000s)	Dist.	($000s)	Dist.	($000s)	Dist.	($000s)	Dist.
Total Loans and Leases	**$14,386,959**	**100%**	**$7,044,182**	**100%**	**$969,147**	**100%**	**$394,388**	**100%**	**$147,453**	**100%**	**$56,562,704**	**100%**
Real Estate Loans	$9,763,687	68%	$5,081,791	72%	$843,971	87%	$383,692	97%	$147,089	100%	$26,553,133	47%
Construction and land development	$684,165	7%	$274,465	5%	$13,056	2%	$55,525	14%	$0	0%	$926,723	3%
Commercial real estate	$4,661,523	48%	$3,102,990	61%	$561,233	66%	$184,278	48%	$71,412	49%	$6,104,295	23%
Multifamily residential real estate	$1,636,804	17%	$406,951	8%	$112,384	13%	$19,091	5%	$11,476	8%	$1,372,182	5%
1- to 4-unit family residential	$2,721,489	28%	$1,277,690	25%	$157,298	19%	$124,798	33%	$64,201	44%	$18,148,481	68%
Real estate loans foreign offices	$59,706	1%	$19,695	0%	$0	0%	$0	0%	$0	0%	$1,452	0%
Commercial and Industrial Loans	$4,027,467	28%	$1,887,940	27%	$64,566	7%	$10,134	3%	$58	0%	$18,025,468	32%
Individual Loans	$540,093	4%	$10,161	0.1%	$594	0.1%	$562	0.1%	$306	0%	$1,617,938	3%
Credit cards	$716	0.1%	$0	0%	$0	0%	$175	31%	$306	100%	$864,823	53%
Other revolving credit plans	$2,326	0.4%	$0	0%	$0	0%	$383	68%	$0	0%	$190,395	12%
Automobile loans	$2,230	0.4%	$5	0.05%	$0	0%	$2	0.4%	$0	0%	$24,350	2%
Other individual loans	$534,821	99%	$10,156	100%	$594	100%	$2	0.4%	$0	0%	$538,370	33%
Total Other Loans and Leases	$55,712	0.4%	$64,290	0.9%	$60,016	6%	$0	0%	$0	0%	$10,196,104	18%

Source: Federal Deposit Insurance Corporation, http://www2.fdic.gov/idasp/main.asp. This URL links to FDIC's bank institutions database, where one can enter a bank's name for further links to information about bank assets and liabilities.

block. Longtime *Village Voice* food writer Robert Sietsema (2009) claimed, "I haven't seen an Asian grocery this big anywhere in the five boroughs." The Fei Long Market opened in 2009 and marks the center of Sunset Park's Little Fuzhou. The developer is 6301 8th Avenue LLC, whose owners are John Giuffre and his nephew, attorney John Iacono. The Giuffre family owns several automotive dealerships and Sunset Park properties and received a $13,239,590 mortgage from the Bank of China to develop the Fei Long Market.[31] Describing the Fei Long Market as "his project," Ritz Realty owner Denny Chen was hired by the developers to secure Chinese tenants and food vendors. For the majority of Chinese banks (including the CDFI-certified FAIB), addressing the financial exclusion of Asian immigrants by promoting homeownership is not their primary lending activity. Moreover, despite the claim that ethnic banks serve the financial needs of low-income immigrant populations to "help them have access to capital and funds on an individual basis" (Yau 2013), Table 4.4 documents the minuscule share of individual lending in credit cards and personal loans.

The growth of Chinese banks in Sunset Park is supported by the active engagement of multiple immigrant growth coalition actors, including realtors, developers, property owners, and building-related professionals such as engineers and architects. A survey of permit applications filed with the New York City Department of Buildings (DoB) provides ample evidence of the high volume of ongoing and proposed new developments in Sunset Park (Table 4.5). A total of seventy-five permit applications (in the three major categories of demolition, major alteration, and new building) were filed for Sunset Park properties in the first six months of 2008.[32] An overwhelming majority (71 percent) of these permit applications involved a Chinese owner or developer.[33] Most of the permits filed were for a major alteration that typically involved the expansion of a two-story, two-family home to a three-unit or larger multifamily building by adding on floors or legalizing a basement apartment. A full 40 percent of permit applications were filed by limited liability corporations (LLCs), representing a partnership of individuals or nonresident owners (i.e., property owners who listed a home address outside of Sunset Park and in some cases in another state). Numerous LLCs were formed to profit from the renovation and resale or management of a single property, as indicated by their names that refer simply to the property address (e.g., 420 43rd Street LLC, 713 43rd Street LLC, and 320 57th Street LLC). Rather than individual owners, the presence of investors in the form of LLCs is remaking Sunset Park's residential landscape.

Ethnic banks are active in Sunset Park's building boom not only through the underwriting of commercial real estate development but also as property

TABLE 4.5   NEW YORK CITY DEPARTMENT OF BUILDINGS PERMITS FILED, 1/2008 TO 6/2008

	Total Permit Applications	Full Demolition	Major Alteration	New Building
Community Board 7	82	19	40	23
Sunset Park	61	13	34	14
Chinese owner/developer	42	9	24	9
Community Board 12	108	29	40	39
Sunset Park	14	6	8	0
Chinese owner/developer	11	4	7	0
TOTAL SUNSET PARK	75	19	42	14
Chinese owner/developer	53	13	31	9
% Chinese owner/developer	71%	68%	74%	64%
% LLC or Nonresident owner	40%	54%	26%	67%

Source: New York City Department of Buildings (n.d.).

owners and investors. Both Abacus Federal Savings Bank and FAIB have filed for DoB permits to develop Sunset Park properties. Abacus Federal Savings Bank through its affiliate, VJHC Development Corporation, filed a permit application to develop a new market-rate condominium development.[34] FAIB purchased and renovated a former factory into a five-story commercial building that includes offices for a community-based organization, a day care facility, and a medical office.[35]

Information about ethnic banks' investments are not readily accessible to the public. The case of 135 Bowery Street made transparent the role of ethnic banks as real estate speculators and developers, often in collusion with local elected officials. The three-and-a-half-story Federal-style row house building on 135 Bowery Street in Manhattan Chinatown dates back to the early 1800s (Amateau 2011). City Council member Margaret Chin initially supported historic landmark status for the building, which had earlier received designation approval from the New York City Landmarks Preservation Commission. Claiming that Chinatown's post-9/11 economic recovery needed a boost, Chin changed her mind, permitting the FAIB to proceed with its plan to demolish the building and develop a seven-story commercial building. In a typical speculative action, FAIB decided not to develop 135 Bowery Street after demolishing the building and instead decided to sell the vacant lot. FAIB listed the property with Massey Knakal Realty Services (n.d.) as a "prime development opportunity" for $8.5 million. FAIB paid $2 million for the vacant building in 2007.

Integral to the branding and marketing of Sunset Park is an extensive development infrastructure that includes numerous realtors and real estate agencies.[36] Property ownership and redevelopment is a lucrative entrepreneurial niche and is preferable to labor-intensive and marginal endeavors, such as restaurant ownership (Kwong and Miscevic 2005, 323). A notable Sunset Park example is Danny Choi, who was featured in a 1994 *Wall Street Journal* article on the emergence of a Chinatown "satellite" in Sunset Park (Browning 1994). Choi has since sold his Ocean Seafood Palace restaurant and is now involved with a real estate development company.[37] Others like Choi include garment factory owners such as John Lam, CEO and president of the Lam Group. During the 1970s and 1980s, Lam owned fifteen garment factories in Manhattan's Chinatown that employed up to two thousand people. In pursuit of "Chinatown's 'Mountain of Gold,'"[38] Lam diversified into real estate by purchasing numerous buildings in Chinatown and cofounding a local ethnic community bank, Eastbank, which later evolved and formed a bank holding company—Evergreen Holdings, LLC. In the late 1990s John Lam founded the Lam Group, which specializes in the ownership, development, and management of franchised hotels. The corporation's extensive real estate portfolio includes two million square feet of residential, retail, and office development in New York, New Jersey, and Pennsylvania.[39]

Ethnic Banks and Fair Lending Practices

The themes of exclusion and cultural knowledge resonate in the narratives of local ethnic bankers, who emphasize that the formation of their financial institutions serves to meet a perceived void in banking services in immigrant neighborhoods. Abacus Federal Savings Bank CEO Thomas Sung recalled his experience in seeking a loan to purchase a burned-out building near Seward Park in Manhattan's Chinatown in the mid-1960s. Sung went to the major banking institution in Chinatown at the time, the Manhattan Savings Bank, but was informed that he had to go to the uptown branch to apply for a loan.[40] His reaction was "you'll take our money but you won't lend in the community," and he abandoned his career as a real estate developer and proceeded to establish the Abacus Federal Savings Bank to help remedy the financial exclusion of the Chinese community (Sung 2005). These experiences endow ethnic banks with an informational advantage on the particular challenges to financial access for immigrant populations. As the Abacus Federal Savings Bank website claimed, "We Speak Your Language!" and "We understand your special needs as a minority and an immigrant. Our knowledge of your culture and practice will make your banking experience a pleasure and we will help you integrating [sic] into American society smoothly; we speak your language."[41]

The cultural nature of financial practices was further elaborated by Mr. Patrick Yau, executive vice president of FAIB. Yau used the analogy of another cultural product—food—to describe the unique advantages of ethnic banks in understanding cultural habits and customers' ethnic specific concerns (Yau 2005). Consequently, Yau noted that if you want to serve Hispanics, you have to prepare the types of food that Hispanics eat and prefer. Cultural insights are a form of social capital that supposedly provide ethnic banks with a competitive advantage over mainstream banks in serving an immigrant population that typically lacks English-language proficiency, a credit history, and trust with formal banking institutions in their home country as well as in the United States.

Mainstream banks are successfully competing with ethnic banks to meet specialized retail services and products by hiring multilingual staff, including bank executives; developing multilingual promotional materials, advertisements, and ATM machines; offering seven-day banking to accommodate work schedules and limited checking accounts; and even consulting feng shui experts (Kranz 2004; Collins 2005b). There was tremendous fanfare about the opening of a new Commerce Bank branch in the heart of Manhattan's Chinatown, because the bank responded to an outstanding community need by incorporating seventy-five hundred safe deposit boxes in the building's design—the largest number of safe deposit boxes in any bank serving the Asian population (Collins 2005b). Former Abacus Federal Savings Bank loan officer Emily Yu, a loan officer for Washington Mutual Bank, corroborated Sunset Park housing advocate Lisa Nicolle-Grist's observation of the increasing sophistication among immigrants in their use of the Internet to research and compare bank products and interest rates (Yu 2005; Nicolle-Grist 2005). These developments will surely continue to erode the informational advantage of ethnic banks.

The objective of serving the Asian population is evident in the nearly exclusive outreach and lending to Asians by Chinese ethnic banks. As noted, the social capital literature emphasizes ethnic banks' alternative informational channels on individual creditworthiness and deeper insights on immigrant employment conditions (e.g., lack of earnings documentation) that give these banks a competitive edge in facilitating immigrant access to capital. Interviews with CEOs and loan officers suggest that ethnic banks invest more time in screening and filtering applicants during an initial consultation phase, with the net effect that many potential applicants are discouraged from ever submitting a loan application.

The ethnic-centered definition of community employed by ethnic banks raises serious concerns for two reasons. First, a majority of U.S. ethnic banks

are large banks and should be subject to antidiscriminatory lending regulations, as is the case for all mainstream banks. Second, ethnic banks—both
small and large—are frequently located in immigrant neighborhoods, many
of which have undergone dramatic demographic shifts resulting in multiethnic, multiracial populations, especially in New York City. These demographic realities coupled with the rapid growth trajectory of ethnic banks
will push the issue of when ethnic banks' sole focus on their ethnic populations constitutes discriminatory lending practices.

In recent years, large West Coast banks—including Cathay Bank and
UCB—have been targeted for their discriminatory lending practices (Reckard 2003). Several advocacy organizations—including the Greenlining
Institute, the Mexican American Political Association, the Black Business
Association, and the Council of Asian American Business Association—
have organized to protest Cathay Bank's refusal to make home loans to
African Americans and serve the credit needs of the Latino and Filipino
populations and its failure to recruit Latinos and African Americans to top
management positions and the Board of Directors (Connell and Muir 1993).
These concerns are now immediate to New York City with Cathay Bank's
rapid expansion. The December 12, 2005, issue of Inner City Press/Fair
Finance Watch's online newsletter included an update on Cathay Bank's
acquisition of Great Eastern Bank and inquired about the Needs to Improve
rating on its CRA Service Test, to which Cathay Bank answered, "Cathay
is currently working on a marketing plan to better reach persons of Latino
heritage in the communities Cathay serves" (Anon. n.d.-c).

Predatory Equity and Housing Stratification

The massive influx of capital and its central role in facilitating a hyperfre-
netic, speculative real estate and housing market is one of the most significant and impactful ways that everyday life in Sunset Park is shaped by the
macroprocesses of globalization and neoliberal governance. The local housing market is highly stratified, with conditions reminiscent of the global
South coexisting side by side (oftentimes literally) with new luxury condominiums and majestic brownstones. Amina Ali has lived in Sunset Park for
twelve years (Ali 2013a, 2013b). She moved to the neighborhood in 2001
because of its affordability. Ali lived in a rent-stabilized apartment, but over
the years services declined while the rent kept increasing. Tenants "had to
fight to get heat," and when they protested, her landlord would call the
police to file a complaint. Ali moved to another building temporarily but
was unable to find an affordable and decent apartment, and ultimately she

was "pushed out" of the neighborhood. By February 2012 when she vacated her apartment in a six-unit building, all of her neighbors were gone. According to Ali, who is Puerto Rican and Syrian, her landlord preferred to rent to non-Hispanic whites.

Ali's experience with steadily increasing rents while maintenance was neglected and basic services such as heat were withheld is a standard landlord tactic to remove tenants in anticipation of making building improvements in order to rent to higher-income tenants. The erosion of tenant rights and rental affordability for low- and middle-income households is endemic to New York City's housing market, which is largely a rental market. According to the 2007–2011 American Community Survey, 68 percent of New York City's three million occupied housing units are rental units. Despite Sunset Park's reputation as a source of affordable homeownership, the overwhelming majority of neighborhood residents are renters, as indicated by the census finding that 78 percent of occupied housing units are occupied by renters.[42] More than half (56 percent) of New York City tenants pays 30 percent or more of their income for rent.[43] The official definition of affordability established by the U.S. Department of Housing and Urban Development states that housing affordability is defined by 30 percent or less of annual household income spent on rent. Based on this generally accepted affordability measure, "families who pay more than 30 percent of their income for housing are considered cost burdened and may have difficulty affording necessities such as food, clothing, transportation and medical care."[44]

The prevalence of a rent burden is augmented by eroding tenant protections. Reverend Vanessa Cardinale, associate pastor at the Trinity Lutheran Church, noted that informal rental agreements between landlords and tenants are becoming more commonplace, especially among immigrants (Cardinale 2013). Through the church congregation, which includes a growing number of Ecuadorians, she has learned of numerous incidences of tenant evictions without any advance notice, including evictions of families with young children. Informal rental agreements in which tenants do not have anything in writing makes them extremely vulnerable to displacement and homelessness.

For the past two years, tenants of three buildings formerly owned by an individual on the list of worst landlords issued by Mayor Bill de Blasio when he was New York City Public Advocate, have been on a rent strike to protest inhumane conditions, such as the lack of hot water and heat in the winter, a leaky roof, and faulty wiring resulting in frequent electrical outages. Occupy Sunset Park and Trinity Lutheran Church's La Casita de Communal Sunset Park have actively worked with and advised the rent strikers in direct actions to demand accountability and building improvements. Occupy Sunset Park cofounder and lifelong resident Dennis Flores was arrested for intervening in an altercation between a building superintendent and an elderly female rent striker. Flores was interviewed on the *Democracy Now!* commemoration of the Occupy movement's one-year anniversary and spoke about the deplorable conditions that typify low-income housing for Chinese and Latino Sunset Park residents.[45]

In addition to regular protests in front of the three adjacent buildings, direct actions in July 2012 included the Sidewalk Sleep-In and People's Inspection and an occupation (i.e., sit-in) of Assemblyman Felix Ortiz's office (Occupy Wall Street 2012). As of June 2013, Occupy Sunset Park and tenant activism has resulted in material improvements, such as some structural repairs and the removal of asbestos from the decrepit basements by city agencies. Moreover, New York City's Department of Housing Preservation and Development has exercised receivership and sold the buildings to a new owner. In the meantime, the rent strikers continue to organize with Occupy Sunset Park and the Urban Homesteading Assistance Board—a nonprofit organization that provide advice on tenant ownership and cooperatives. While the option of forming a housing cooperative is being considered, this proposal, according to Occupy Sunset Park activist Ian Horst, has moved to the "back burner" because some residents don't want to "rock the boat," since 46th Street tenants include undocumented immigrants and drug dealers (Horst 2013). While tenant activism and organizing may not result in collective ownership, the ultimate goal for the 46th Street rent strikers was to assert and actualize the more fundamental human right to a safe and decent place to live.

The high demand for affordable housing, especially among an immigrant population, has contributed to the growing numbers of single-room occupancy (SRO) units. Sunset Park landlords, both investors and individual owners, capitalize on this pent-up housing demand by subdividing their buildings into numerous single rooms with one shared kitchen and bath. According to Ritz Realty owner Denny Chen, the average monthly rent for an SRO in Sunset Park is $600 to $700, which even he conceded is "not inexpensive" (D. Chen 2013). SRO units provide affordable housing for a highly mobile immigrant population, including a large male workforce as well as poor working families that can only afford to live in an SRO unit or a basement apartment despite overcrowded and unsafe conditions. Relative to a citywide poverty rate of 21 percent, a full third (33 percent) of Asians have incomes below the poverty threshold, which is the highest among Sunset Park's Latino (28 percent) and non-Hispanic white (11 percent) residents.[46]

Rather than approach SRO units as an outcome of the dire need for affordable housing, official stakeholders such as Community Board 7 tend to criminalize this practice by framing SRO units as "illegally converted apartments" that require greater enforcement of housing regulations and standards (see Chapter 5).[47] In March 2013, Community Board 7 and the Concerned Citizens of Greenwood Heights convened a meeting with numerous city agencies, including the Department of Housing Preservation and Development, the Department of Buildings, the Fire Department, and the mayor's Illegal Occupancy Task Force. Even the best-intentioned Sunset Park residents complain about diminished neighborhood quality as "10 refrigerators are moved into" two-family homes and lament how new immigrants do not share the same desire for "a nice and clean neighborhood" (Johnson 2013). For others such as Ian Horst, a relative newcomer who purchased a home eight years ago and is an active member of Occupy Sunset Park, SRO units evoke moral concerns about economic justice rather than the mere enforcement of housing codes and a neighborhood social order.

Sunset Park's stratified housing market is defined by a dearth of housing that is affordable to an immigrant working-poor population in the midst of speculative real estate investments by banks, developers, LLCs, and individual investors. This stratification is evident in the countless number of new market-rate residential and commercial condominium buildings reshaping Sunset Park's built environment. Sunset Park resident Fragrance Chen described the "crazy housing market" whereby property sales transactions for modest two-family homes whose market value can exceed $1 million are frequently in cash. Chen remarked that the fierce competition among potential buyers appear "as if they're giving housing away for free" (F. Chen 2013). Chen and her husband have been unsuccessful in their effort to purchase a home in Sunset Park, and as way of explanation, she pointed out the obvious outcome of competing bids from an all cash buyer versus a young family who needs a mortgage. Despite her sixteen years in the neighborhood and her leadership in the Chinese congregation at St. Jacobi Church, Chen and her husband have decided to resume their house search in New Jersey.

Policy Strategies for Community Capital? Community Reinvestment Act and Banking Development Districts

The CRA was enacted in 1977 to address banks' discriminatory practices and requires the four federal financial supervisory agencies to assess banks' records of meeting the credit needs of local communities, particularly low- and moderate-income neighborhoods (Marsico 2005). CRA ratings include

"Outstanding," "Satisfactory," "Needs to Improve," and "Substantial Non-compliance," and a 1990 amendment required CRA ratings to be made public. CRA evaluations are conducted every few years, and the ratings are taken into consideration in five types of regulatory actions: (1) obtaining or changing a bank charter, (2) obtaining FDIC insurance, (3) establishment of a new domestic branch, (4) relocation of a main office or branch, and (5) merger, consolidation, or acquisition of bank assets or liabilities (Seidman 2005, 211).

Based on the 1995 CRA regulations, the assessment methods employed by federal bank examiners vary depending on bank size and type.[48] Large banks are evaluated according to three components: (1) *lending* in terms of the total number and dollar amount of home mortgage, small business/small farms, and community development loans as well as geographic distribution of loans, especially to low- and moderate-income areas, and borrower characteristics; (2) *service* in retail banking and community development services; and (3) *investment* in terms of the dollar amount of loans, grants, and donations as well as innovative financing for community development (Seidman 2005, 187). Since the primary focus of CRA enforcement is large banks, the criteria are significantly streamlined or weakened in the evaluation of small banks. Small banks are evaluated based on a five-part lending test: (1) loan to deposit ratio, (2) share of loans in assessment area, (3) loan penetration among individuals of different income levels, (4) loan penetration among businesses of different sizes, and (5) geographic distribution of loans in the assessment area.

Since implementation of the CRA, legislative modifications and amendments have significantly weakened CRA provisions over time. One change that affects ethnic banks is the expansion of the small bank category to include a new intermediate small bank category defined as banks with assets of $250 million to $1 billion regardless of whether the small- and intermediate-sized banks are owned by a bank holding company with assets of $1 billion or more (Tucker 2006). This new designation applies to banks regulated by the Board of Governors of the Federal Reserve System, the Office of the Comptroller of the Currency, and the FDIC, while those regulated by the Office of Thrift Supervision of the intermediate size remain in an expanded small bank category. The CRA revision reduces the regulatory burden for intermediate or midsized banks that previously had to comply with the rules and regulations for large banks. For example, FAIB's rapid growth would have elevated it to a large bank, but the 2005 change means that it is now considered an intermediate small bank. No longer subject to the three-part lending, investment, and service test, intermediate banks report on the five-point lending criteria like small banks and a community development test that combines community development loans, investments, and services into one test. This change also means that small ethnic banks are greatly relieved of the "burden" of demonstrating even minimal community outreach.[49]

A review of the most recent CRA evaluations and ratings of Chinese banks in Sunset Park underscores a consistently mixed record of community reinvestment (Table 4.6). Two banks—Abacus Federal Savings Bank and Chinatown Federal Savings Bank—received an outstanding rating. Since Abacus Federal Savings Bank and Chinatown Federal Savings Bank are small thrift associations, their CRA review was premised largely on the simple calculation of a loan to deposit ratio. Even so, Abacus Federal Savings Bank's outstanding rating is tempered by its recent history of mismanagement and the 2012 New York City district attorney's indictment of residential mortgage fraud. Cathay Bank's low satisfactory ratings in New York state are very troubling, particularly in light of the bank's aggressive Northeast expansion and its failure to improve service and community lending practices. Cathay Bank received an overall satisfactory rating in 2007 and 2011 but continued to receive a low satisfactory rating in the community investment and service tests in New York state.[50] While this may be perceived as an improvement since Cathay Bank received a low satisfactory rating in all three categories of lending, investment, and service in 2007, it is evident that the bank has failed to redress the assessment that "The bank exhibits *a poor record of serving the credit needs of the most economically disadvantaged* in the bank's New York AA within low-income tracts, to low-income individuals, and very small businesses consistent with safe and sound banking practices" (Federal Deposit Insurance Corporation 2007a, 73).

In light of FAIB's numerous designations—including membership in the Community Development Bankers Association, certification by the Department of Treasury as a Community Development Financial Institution, and designation as an approved lender of Small Business Administration guaranty loans and an authorized seller-servicer of Fannie Mae mortgages—FAIB's mere satisfactory CRA rating and 2007 New York State Banking Department order to cease and desist underscores serious concerns regarding its banking practices. Another example of FAIB's poor community service pertains to its Credit Education and Assistance Program. Collaborating with local social service providers, FAIB conducts financial literacy workshops on basic banking services, personal credit, and housing mortgages to help incorporate new immigrants into the financial mainstream. However, the former Brooklyn director of the Chinese American Planning Council commented that the workshop promoted FAIB services

TABLE 4.6   COMMUNITY REINVESTMENT ACT RATINGS OF CHINESE BANKS WITH SUNSET PARK BRANCHES

Agency	Exam Date	Bank Name	CRA Rating	Asset Size ($000)[a]	Exam Method
OTS[b]	5/4/2009	Abacus Federal Savings Bank	Outstanding	$239,578	Small bank
FDIC	1/1/2013	First American International Bank	Satisfactory	$529,380	Intermediate small bank
OTS	4/6/2009	Chinatown Federal Savings Bank	Outstanding	$178,386	Small bank
OCC	4/26/2006	The Bank of East Asia (USA), NA	Satisfactory	$693,861	Intermediate small bank
FDIC	4/1/2013	Chinatrust Bank	Satisfactory	$1,456,398	Large bank
FDIC	3/1/2011	Cathay Bank	Satisfactory	$11,237,605	Large bank
FED	10/25/2010	East West Bank	Satisfactory	$21,136,598	Large bank

[a] Asset size at the time of CRA review.
[b] OTS = Office of Thrift Supervision; FDIC = Federal Deposit Insurance Corporation; OCC = Office of the Comptroller of the Currency; FED = Federal Reserve.
Source: Federal Deposit Insurance Corporation, FDIC, http://www2.fdic.gov/idasp/main.asp. This URL links to the FDIC's bank institutions database, where one can enter a bank's name for further links to information about the bank, including CRA ratings.

and products and served as a marketing opportunity for the bank rather than a workshop on outstanding financial needs and barriers to fair credit in the community (Xie 2006).

In contrast to other minority-owned banks in the United States, the mixed CRA records of Chinese banks corroborates a 2004 study that found that banks owned by Asian and Pacific Islanders "were not addressing the needs of their communities in a manner that would distinguish them from non-minority banks" (Matasar and Pavelka 2004, 52). In other words, Asian banks were least robust and impressive in meeting CRA obligations. This review of HMDA data and CRA evaluations provides ample evidence that counter the ethnic bank literature's emphasis on community orientation and service (Li et al. 2001).

Much discussion on capital access and investment is based on the African American experience of redlining and disinvestment, with policy remedies aimed at establishing market institutions in underserved low-income neighborhoods. New York state's program to establish banking development districts (BDDs) in underbanked neighborhoods is a prime example of this type of policy response. Defined as an underserved neighborhood, Sunset Park is the site of two BDDs—one established along the industrial waterfront and a second for the residential upland section bounded to the north by 36th Street, Ft. Hamilton Parkway to the east, 52nd Street to the south, and 5th Avenue to the west (New York State Banking Department 2010, 37). Although FAIB had contemplated a BDD application submission for this section of Sunset Park (Yau 2005), Amalgamated Bank was awarded BDD designation in early 2008.

Established to motivate banks to open branches in underserved neighborhoods, banks in a designated BDD are capitalized with up to $25 million of state funds and $10 million of municipal funds (New York State Banking Department 2010, 11). This public capitalization at below-market rates serves as an incentive for banks to meet outstanding local credit needs through reduced market-rate loans for homeownership and small business development and also through financial literacy programs (Colangelo 2003; Dunaief 2004). The application process to designate a neighborhood area as a BDD requires a collaboration between a state-chartered commercial bank, trust company, or national bank and a local governmental entity (e.g., borough president's office). In addition to the public capitalization, BDD incentives include real property tax exemptions and favorable CRA consideration.

In 2000, Community Capital Bank's application to designate Sunset Park's industrial waterfront area as a BDD was successful, and the bank opened a branch in the Brooklyn Army Terminal that was capitalized with

$10 million in state funds and $5 million in city funds (Dunaief 2004).
The bank's CEO and president Charles Koehler described the approval of
Community Capital Bank's application as a "slam dunk" because Community Capital Bank replaced JP Morgan Chase, which "had abandoned
the neighborhood" (Koehler 2005). Specializing in business loans to the
numerous firms along the industrial waterfront, Community Capital Bank
established important ties with local economic development organizations,
such as the Southwest Brooklyn Industrial Development Corporation and
the Brooklyn Economic Development Corporation (Mr. Koehler served as
chairperson of the Brooklyn Economic Development Corporation's Board
of Directors). In 2006, Carver Bancorp, Inc., the holding company for
Carver Federal Savings Bank—a pioneering ethnic bank established more
than fifty years ago and currently the nation's largest African American–
and Caribbean American–operated bank—acquired Community Capital
Bank and its BDD.[51] Four short years later, Alma Bank's application to
take over Sunset Park's BDD was approved by the New York State Banking
Department.[52]

Sunset Park's second BDD is administered by Amalgamated Bank,
which prides itself on being America's labor bank and, according to its
website, "the only majority owned union bank in the United States."[53]
Amalgamated Bank now has a total of four BDDs throughout New York
City, and its goals for Sunset Park's BDD focuses on affordable banking
products and services and community development initiatives to preserve
and develop affordable housing. As a union-owned bank, Amalgamated
Bank proposes to tap into "our union relationships" and collaborate with
local community organizations on job creation, training, and retention
initiatives.[54] While these are important goals that constitute meaningful
strategies to address the capital needs of a low-income neighborhood, it
remains unclear how the New York State Banking Department will measure accountability and success.

Conversations with New York State Banking Department BDD directors noted that the criteria for measuring performance outcomes are not
stated as part of the legal code or regulations—New York Banking Law
Section 96-d—that created and governs BDDs (Delehanty 2005; Soadwa
2008). Rather, BDD banks are required to submit annual reports that serve
as the basis for an internal review of performance goals in terms of job creation, small business loans, and home mortgages. The annual reports are
not part of the public record, and the performance measures of success are
not explicitly defined on the New York State Banking Department website.
The investment of public funds requires a transparent review process and

a set of clear measures to evaluate the policy impacts in creating avenues for financial capital in underbanked neighborhoods. The New York State Department of Banking should establish clear criteria for measuring outcomes in improvements to capital access among the underserved in designated BDDs.

Conclusion

The confluence of economic and political restructurings in Asia and the United States contributed to a significant increase in the presence of ethnic banks in immigrant gateway cities such as Los Angeles and New York City. Geopolitical and economic developments in Asia—such as the 1997 return of the British colony Hong Kong to China, the deregulation of the U.S. banking industry, and a significant bifurcated migrant flow in terms of human and financial capital—contributed to the establishment and expansion of ethnic banks, particularly Chinese ethnic banks, in the United States. The ethnic banks' literature to date emphasizes social capital and cultural solidarity in mediating the practices of ethnic banks to facilitate greater access to capital and investments in immigrant neighborhood development. A thorough investigation of the lending practices of ethnic banks in Sunset Park, however, finds that ethnic banks are significant in promoting neighborhood development based on their relationships with realtors and developers in forging an immigrant growth coalition.

Immigrant growth coalition alliances are reinforced by overlapping organizational membership. For example, FAIB's Patrick Yau and Cathay Bank's Pin Tai serve as members of the Board of Directors of the Chinatown Partnership. The Chinatown Partnership is headed by Wellington Chen (formerly of TDC Development LLC, based in Flushing, Queens) and was instrumental in pushing through a controversial Business Improvement District in Manhattan's Chinatown. Ethnic banks are transforming immigrant neighborhoods not by their promotion of immigrant homeownership but by their extensive investments in commercial real estate and gentrification driven by global capital (Smith 2002).

The presence of ethnic banks sharpens intraethnic class divides in working-poor Sunset Park with competing agendas for neighborhood land use with respect to affordable housing and the banks' meager reinvestments in community-based organizations and development activities. Moreover, the ethnic-specific orientation of these banks even among large banks such as Cathay Bank reproduces a racially stratified Sunset Park by continuing to exclude the neighborhood's significant underbanked Latino population.[55]

This pattern has only become more acute in the post-2008 crisis context, as capital access was diminished by the withdrawal of mainstream banks from mortgage lending. Disinvestments in the 1960s and 1970s were visible in Sunset Park's deteriorating landscape and infrastructure. However, the mere presence of financial institutions does not translate to greater capital access or economic justice. Ethnic banks are a prominent part of the revitalized economic landscape, but new and old forms of inequality persist in Sunset Park.

5

Gentrifying Sunset Park

Community Boards, City Planning, and a Migrant Civil Society

N ew York City mayor Michael Bloomberg's administration has initiated an unprecedented number of rezonings that cumulatively represent a dramatic reconfiguration of land use in the city. Community boards serve as a conduit for public review and oversight of the development process. The decentralization of municipal governance through community boards as venues for citizen inclusion and voice has a long history in New York City (Rogers 1990). Evolving from early citizen planning councils of the 1950s, New York City's political landscape includes fifty-nine community boards that serve an official, albeit advisory, role on city service delivery, land-use and zoning, and budgetary matters (Marcuse 1990). Mediating the local and daily lived consequences of economic restructuring, demographic and racial shifts, and progrowth urban policies has increasingly dominated the work of New York City's community boards.

By the time of Sunset Park's designation as a federal poverty area in the late 1960s, its transition to a majority-poor Puerto Rican neighborhood was well under way. Its housing stock, however, included a sizable brownstone belt that helped sustain a small but stable population of white homeowners during a period of neighborhood decline and the revitalization of the 1980s that was driven by a massive immigration from the Dominican Republic, China, and Mexico (see Chapter 2). As one of New York City's most racially and ethnically diverse neighborhoods, Sunset Park is once again at a crossroads as gentrification pressures intensify because of two market trends. Young white professionals and creative-class members who can no longer afford neighboring Park Slope are settling in once-dilapidated areas near Greenwood Cemetery and redefining geographic boundaries by forming new neighborhoods (e.g., Greenwood Heights and South Park Slope) in the northern section of Sunset Park. A second gentrifying force is mobilized by an immigrant growth coalition that consists of Chinese developers, realtors, and ethnic banks in the development of luxury condominium projects throughout the neighborhood (see Chapter 4). The working-poor Puerto Ricans who did not abandon the neighborhood and the immigrant groups who helped revitalize its local economy are increasingly at risk of displacement because of real estate speculation and rising housing costs in Sunset Park.

Everyday concerns about new development, illegal construction activity, and out-of-scale and out-of-context land uses are voiced at community board meetings. Concerns about the physical environment and development consequences—such as traffic congestion, infrastructure strain, overcrowded housing, and degradation of neighborhood life—barely disguise the intense anxiety about the volume of new immigration and the shifting social demography of local neighborhoods.[1] This chapter documents escalating racial tensions stemming from transformative neighborhood change and growth and investigates Brooklyn's Community Board 7, which represents the neighborhoods of Sunset Park, Windsor Terrace, South Park Slope, and Greenwood Heights as a "pivotal" public arena that facilitates cross-racial dialogue and engages stakeholders, including immigrant groups, in neighborhood planning and policy decisions (Sanjek 1998, 2000). Since concerns fueling dissension and potential conflict center on land-use and development initiatives, community boards are the noted political sphere where grievances are aired and public debate becomes framed or crystallized around particular concerns and issues. While community boards legitimate citizen participation in policy-making processes and local governance, Sunset Park's experience underscore that community boards do not necessarily engage all stakeholders in meaningful or sustained ways and are limited in advancing race and ethnic relations in a complex and challenging socioeconomic context.

Participating in land-use and development reviews may be the most significant and lasting way that community boards shape their local neighborhoods (Pecorella 1989). As a body of politically appointed individuals, community boards are often extensions of the political agenda of borough presidents and city council members. This chapter documents how community boards often lack autonomy and grassroots accountability and fail to promote the inclusion of disenfranchised community members, such as immigrants. Community boards often function as a form of symbolic inclusion and are rarely able to affect progressive redistributive outcomes. This chapter discusses how city planning practices, including rezoning, continue to serve as a terrain for race and class contestation regarding the right to define neighborhood space and identity and to exercise claims for economic justice and equity in urban development (J. M. Thomas 1994). The key institutions that engage multiple publics and advance community capacity to participate in technical planning and land-use debates are not community boards but rather grassroots community-based organizations. These often informal organizations are integral to promoting a migrant civic society that provides a venue in which marginalized immigrant stakeholders have a voice in urban governance and decision-making (Theodore and Martin 2007). The emergence of a migrant civil society in Sunset Park provided the critical public space to advance an analysis of local power relationships and forge a Latino-Chinese alliance to counter shared conditions of economic and social inequality.

New York City's Community Boards and Participatory Planning

In her seminal book *The Death and Life of American Cities,* Jane Jacobs (1961, 121) formulated three neighborhood typologies—street, district, and city level—and proposed that the district level was most effective for self-governance because it mediated between the powerless street-based neighborhoods and the all-powerful city. The political infrastructure of New York City includes fifty-nine district-level community boards—the most decentralized or local body of urban governance. As district-level entities, community boards are seen as venues for formalizing local everyday concerns and elevating these issues to the city level for political action and/or policy formulations. Evolving from community planning councils of the 1950s, community boards became a part of municipal government through a 1975 New York City Charter provision that formalized citizen participation in the public review of land-use and zoning amendments. Community boards review development proposals, and their decisions to reject or support zoning changes are an official and procedural part of the city's Uniform Land Use Review Procedure (ULURP) along with the City Planning Commission, borough presidents, and the City Council. Subsequent revisions to the New York City Charter expanded the powers of community boards to engage in proactive, comprehensive neighborhood planning through the 197-a provision.

The geographic boundaries of community boards are coterminous with service agency districts such as sanitation, police, and fire. The population encompassed by community boards ranges from 100,000 to 250,000 residents, and several community boards—among them Queens Community Board 7, which includes Flushing—have now reached the upper population limit, which is comparable to the size of numerous small U.S. cities such as Portland, Maine and Irvine, California. Each community board consists of up to 50 unpaid members who serve staggered two-year terms and are appointed by the borough president, with half nominated by the City Council member(s). A minimal paid staff of a district manager and office assistant(s) provide clerical and administrative support.

Although advisory and largely reactive, community boards represent a local body politic whose jurisdiction is fairly broad and includes land-use planning and zoning issues, monitoring municipal services delivery, and conveying local priorities in the city expense and capital budgets (Pecorella 1989). Marcuse (1990, 155) noted that although these "voices of local democracy" have no real influence, the dynamic conditions of the real estate market particularly in the past decades has meant that community boards "attained a real power through no doing of their own, but simply because events on their turf were suddenly of real importance to someone else." An illustration of their importance is indicated in the *New York Times* article "Local Boards Now Crucial to the Process of Change," published just four years after the 1975 New York City Charter revision that expanded the role and influence of community boards in land-use and planning processes (Shaman 1979).

As a politically appointed body, the community board is constrained in its ability to act independently. This important limitation was illustrated in two highly publicized incidences involving the removal of community board members who opposed the development agendas of elected officials. In the spring of 2007, Brooklyn borough president Marty Markowitz removed nine Community Board 6 members for their outspoken opposition to the Atlantic Yards project, a megadevelopment project by Forest Ratner City for downtown Brooklyn that includes the completed Barclays Center, home of the Brooklyn Nets basketball team, formerly the New Jersey Nets (Newman 2007). A similar action was taken by former Bronx borough president Aldofo Carrión when Community Board 4 members opposed the Yankee Stadium redevelopment.[2] Carrión's rationalization of his refusal to reappoint these community board members provides a fairly transparent statement on the function of community boards, according to one New York City elected official: "My very clear expectation is that these appointees are there to carry out a vision for the borough president and the leadership of this borough, and that's simply what I expect" (Kappstatter 2006).

Community boards are also criticized for their parochial interests, emotional reactions, and lack of technical expertise (Rogers 1990). Nevertheless, as the official "voice of the people,"[3] community boards are integral to urban planning processes and city governance, and there are current initiatives to improve community boards as well as expand their influence. Notably, as a candidate for Manhattan borough president, Scott Stringer conducted a 2005 study to substantiate the urgency for community board reform.[4] Among his findings was the lack of uniform criteria for member appointments, long-term vacancies, conflicts of interest, funding (mis)use, and uneven performance and accountability. Upon his election, Stringer initiated a series of changes for Manhattan's twelve community boards, including the establishment of a review board to facilitate merit-based appointments and the professionalization of community boards through a community planning fellowship program that assigns a New York City–area graduate student to provide technical assistance.[5] Progressive planning advocates have spearheaded the Campaign for Community-Based Planning to advance recommendations for further revision of the New York City Charter, provide professional planning and technical support, and diversify community board membership in order to facilitate inclusive and democratic participation in land-use review and decision making (Angotti 2010; Stringer 2010).[6]

Negotiating Neighborhood Change

Recent research on immigrant incorporation has established that the waning presence of neighborhood-based mainstream political organizations has been filled by multiple and varied civic and nonprofit institutions, including labor and advocacy groups, worker centers, and social service organizations (Wong 2006; Jones-Correa 1998). Increasingly, the nonprofit sector is key to materializing a political voice and the civic engagement of immigrants, including those who are undocumented. Political actions and protests around immigrant and workers' rights illustrate the success of local organizations in mobilizing a migrant civic society.[7]

A migrant civil society that consists of neighborhood-level nonprofit and grassroots organizations—including social service agencies, community development corporations, ethnic associations and advocacy groups, labor and worker centers, religious institutions, and civic associations—provides critical pathways to immigrant incorporation (Theodore and Martin 2007). Studies document the provision of culturally sensitive social services and assistance, especially for linguistic minorities (Cordero-Guzman 2005; Hess, McGowan, and Botsko 2003). Zhou et al. (2000, 8) argue that social relations based on family and friendship are often disrupted during migration, and ethnic-based nonprofit organizations provide "an important physical site for new immigrants to re-orient themselves, to interact with members of their own group, new and old, and to re-build social networks and a sense of community." The restructuring of production arrangements in low-skill labor markets centers on informal small businesses and practices such as subcontracting, which has hastened the decline of traditional unions and organizing strategies. Increasingly, neighborhoods rather than workplaces have become key sites for mobilizing immigrant workers whose ethnic, racial, or religious identities are reinforced by concentrated residence in enclave neighborhoods (Fine 2006; Ness 2005).

As critical intermediary organizations, nonprofit groups are vital in mediating access to resources, representation, and relationships between immigrant populations and civil society at large (Lamphere 1992). The social organization of immigrant communities has been described as "institutionally complete" because of the density of nonprofit and civic organizations that provide direct human services, promote business formations, mediate ethnic labor markets, and serve as venues for cultural activities—all of which helps to sustain ethnic-based solidarity and bonding social capital (Breton 1964; Aldrich and Waldinger 1990). However, the institutional landscape of immigrant communities is increasingly marked by interorganizational and intraorganizational divergences in terms of generation, political orientation, and the polarizing class positions of a professional-managerial leadership staff and a largely low-income constituent base (Kwong 1987; Espiritu and Ong 1994). As the negotiating site for reparations to make amends for historic and contemporary racial and social inequality, Reagan-era policies of federal devolution and privatization have increasingly shifted this responsibility to local and state governments (Marwell 2004; Espiritu and Ong 1994). Since established nonprofit institutions are reliant on government allocations and seek to foster ties with local elected officials to maintain service contracts, these elite organizations in particular are less likely to engage in community protest or uphold oppositional positions because of their vulnerability to fiscal discipline (Hackworth 2007; Marwell 2004).

The demographic restructuring of local neighborhoods coincided with a revitalized period of economic growth and capital influx, evidenced by the dominant presence of ethnic banks, realtors, and developers in Sunset Park (see Chapter 4). As a primary actor in facilitating the changing neighborhood economy and character, Asian immigrant capital has racialized local tension and reactions to urban growth. Sunset Park illustrates how the "ecology of civic engagement"[8] is increasingly complex as new actors, including

Asian developers and property owners, complicate relations of race and class. Common in diverse urban neighborhoods with significant immigrant populations, racial tensions and conflicts express deep anxiety about immigrant settlement, perceived differences in immigrant experiences and aspirations, housing development patterns, and changes in the local neighborhood economy. Research on the concerns of longtime residents in North American communities undergoing demographic transformations have documented (1) fear of exclusion and displacement; (2) threat of engulfment, "invasion" or "takeover"; (3) threat of loss of the neighborhood way of life, that is, its character, heritage, and traditions; (4) transformation of the physical environment, including public spaces and amenities in terms of out-of-scale noncontextual development and obstruction of views; and (5) concerns that immigrants are not good neighbors because of cultural differences in housing styles, land-use practices, and strategies for affordable homeownership (Mitchell 1993; Harwood and Myers 2002; Harwood 2005; Smith 1995; Li 1994; Li 2005; Luk 2005; Saito 1998). Clearly, the daily life of local neighborhoods is fraught with escalating tensions about immigrants and how their presence is transforming neighborhood places.

The Politics of Rezoning and Equitable Development

Land-use policies and controls such as urban renewal designations and zoning ordinances are tools that shape the public production of space, including patterns of residential racial segregation (Yiftachel 1998; J. M. Thomas 1994). Contemporary community development struggles continue to illustrate how city planning tools help configure the spatial arrangements of race and class marginalization. In the early spring of 2007, an as-of-right development proposal for a twelve-story residential project in Sunset Park stirred community uproar about yet another example of noncontextual development on a residential block of two- and three-story row houses, which includes a landmarked historic building housing Community Board 7 and New York City Police Department processing and administrative functions (Zraick 2007). New York City's 1961 zoning ordinance designated much of the city's residential areas, including Sunset Park, an R6 zone, which is a fairly permissive medium density designation with no explicit height restrictions. The proposed condominium project would rise more than one hundred feet, obstructing the view from Sunset Park past another local landmark—St. Michael Church's egg-shaped dome—toward the upper New York Harbor.[9]

The fact that the developer and contractor were Chinese further infused overdevelopment concerns, with racialized comments made about a "Chinese

invasion," transnational real estate investments as a form of money laundering, and fear of neighborhood degradation as new owners will inevitably
subdivide their condominium units and rent to numerous undocumented
immigrants.[10] To defeat this proposed project, a community coalition consisting largely of longtime white homeowners and Latino residents (tenants and
homeowners) quickly formed and named themselves the Sunset Park Alliance
of Neighbors (SPAN). SPAN proceeded to gather hundreds of signatures on
a petition calling for zoning protections from "irresponsible" developers. A
recently formed civic association, Concerned Citizens of Greenwood Heights,
was consulted on "guerilla tactics" to monitor the development site and harass
the contractor and developer at the first suspicion of illegal work activity.[11]

A planned march and rally at the development site by SPAN, however,
was preempted by an agreement negotiated by City Council member Sara
Gonzalez with the developer Michael Wong of 420 42 Street Realty LLC in
which Mr. Wong agreed to reduce the height of the proposed project, stating
his desire to foster good neighbor relations in light of future development
prospects (Brownstoner 2007; Real Deal Staff 2007). A few weeks later at
a Sunset Park town hall meeting on March 27, 2007, that was attended by
Mayor Bloomberg and New York City Department of City Planning (DCP)
director and City Planning Commission chair Amanda Burden, the city
announced an expedited contextual rezoning study for Sunset Park with an
end-of-the-year completion deadline (Robert 2007).

The victory in reducing the building size was tempered by the splinter-
ing of SPAN into two factions. The white homeowners regrouped as the
Sunset Park Alliance for Rezoning (SPARZ) and were singularly focused on
downzoning Sunset Park's side streets to protect the "architectural integrity"
of the dominant housing stock of two- and three-story row houses and the
"unique panoramic views" of the New York skyline from the twenty-four-
acre Sunset Park. The second faction retained the organizational name of
SPAN, whose leadership now consisted of Latino activists, including union
organizer David Galarza, one-time opponent of Gonzalez. The cause of the
split was ostensibly over the language used in the public acknowledgment
of Gonzalez's role in brokering a compromise with Wong. However, the
division between longtime white homeowners and Latino residents reflects
fundamental and irreconcilable differences in neighborhood history and
positioning as well as short- and long-term goals for the rezoning of Sunset
Park. SPARZ sought to work with the neighborhood's political power base,
including elected officials and Community Board 7, as the group's objectives
can be met by the narrow rezoning parameters as proposed by the DCP to
protect the historic built environment. On the other hand, SPAN sought to

mobilize a broad-based participatory dialogue on equity in urban planning processes and development policies.

Gonzalez, a former chairperson of Community Board 7, was elected in a 2002 special nonpartisan election after the conviction of Angel Rodriguez, Sunset Park's first Latino City Council member, on charges that he tried to extort developer Gregory O'Connell for $1.5 million in cash and real estate property in exchange for an endorsement of a multimillion-dollar conversion of a Red Hook waterfront warehouse for a Fairway supermarket.[12] Created as a result of the 1991 New York City Charter revision to expand the number of city council districts from thirty-five to fifty-one to ensure the fair representation of the city's sizable Latino and African American populations, Sunset Park's City Council District 38 was drawn to be a Hispanic-majority district. Because of term limits that resulted in a massive 2009 turnover in elected representatives,[13] Gonzalez was poised to be the most senior member of the New York City Council, and despite controversy about her leadership and effectiveness,[14] she could certainly have been an influential New York City legislator.

Gonzalez hired the Pratt Center for Community Development to conduct a parallel study to the DCP's Sunset Park rezoning study. Founded in the 1960s by advocacy and activist planners, the Pratt Center has established a strong record of providing technical assistance that "empowers low- and moderate-income communities in New York to plan for and realize their futures" (Pratt Institute n.d.). Based on three public meetings cosponsored by Community Board 7 in November and October 2007 (including one meeting that served as a primer on zoning), the Pratt Center prepared a report, "Sunset Park Voices in the Rezoning Process," that proposed a "balanced zoning" plan (Pratt Center for Community Development 2007). Despite that the top community concern of residential displacement was repeatedly expressed at various public meetings, Pratt's report supported the upzoning of Sunset Park's 4th and 7th Avenues from R6 to R7A with voluntary inclusionary zoning. Along the side streets, Pratt recommended a contextual zone of R6B to protect the housing stock and harbor views. During the Pratt Center planning study period, executive director Brad Lander announced his candidacy for the New York City Council to represent neighboring District 39 (which encompasses neighborhoods to the north, including Park Slope and four blocks in Sunset Park) (Appelbaum 2007).

In response to the DCP's commencement of a Sunset Park rezoning study, several Chinese local property owners, developers, realtors, and other business owners formed the Eighth Avenue Improvement Association (EAIA) to advance their agenda for Sunset Park's growth and "improvement."[15] The EAIA also collected signatures, but their petition protested any downzoning of Sunset Park. As developers vested in rising property values and maximizing opportunities for residential and commercial development, the EAIA pushed a progrowth agenda premised in part on Mayor Bloomberg's population projection increase of 1 million new New Yorkers by 2030.[16] At numerous public meetings, EAIA founder and representative Denny Chen, owner of Ritz Realty, claimed that an additional ten thousand Chinese will settle in Sunset Park in the near future. The EAIA's progrowth rationale is to meet the resulting housing and community service demands.[17] Despite the current development pressures, they reasoned that a contextual zone was not necessary because the market would protect Sunset Park's coveted brownstones, since it was cost prohibitive to replace this housing stock with multifamily buildings. Sunset Park's improvement would be in the destruction of the lesser-valued housing for new condominium developments that would attract an upgraded class of residents.[18] Despite that the fair market value of a one-bedroom condominium unit is $430,000 and clearly out of reach of Sunset Park's working-poor majority,[19] the EAIA appealed for ethnic solidarity and community support in reaping the mutual benefits of the anticipated Chinese population growth that would result in an expanding market for housing development, consumer products and services, and religious salvation.[20] While segments of the Chinese community remain doubtful that this development trajectory would trickle down gains for the working-poor majority, the EAIA found a receptive ear among Community Board 7 members.

Contextual Zoning: Protect Neighborhood Character and Waterfront Views

In a piecemeal fashion, the Bloomberg administration is rewriting the 1961 zoning regulations to advance a progrowth agenda for a postindustrial New York City through an unprecedented number of rezonings. A key rezoning principle is to stimulate and accommodate development in "underutilized" areas along commercial avenues and near transportation nodes (through upzonings) while preserving the unique or historic residential character (through downzoning or contextual zoning) of New York City's largely white middle- and upper-middle-class neighborhoods.[21] As New York City planning commissioner Amanda Burden rationalized, "We needed to channel growth directed to areas that can handle it. At the same time, we have to preserve our neighborhoods because they are *the city's crown jewels.*"[22]

This zoning approach provides a convenient logic for reconciling the demands of two potentially opposing Sunset Park factions: white homeowners' desire to protect the neighborhood's architectural fabric and waterfront views and the Chinese immigrant growth coalition's intent to maximize market opportunities for commercial and residential development. These objectives are consistent with the Bloomberg administration's rezoning strategy, because contextualizing residential zoning to conform to the existing character of the largely two- and three-story row houses on Sunset Park's side streets will satisfy homeowners, while upzoning commercial avenues will accommodate new developments and concentrate growth in Sunset Park's existing Chinese commercial and residential sections. And this was essentially the "balanced zoning plan" presented by the Pratt Center in February 2008 and reiterated in the rezoning proposed by the DCP a month later at a special March Community Board 7 meeting.[23]

The DCP viewed the objective of Sunset Park's rezoning within the narrowest framework as requested by the minority but vocal electoral base of white homeowners and Community Board 7, which is to protect the physical form, waterfront views, and architectural quality of a predominantly low-rise neighborhood. The DCP's proposed rezoning establishes contextual zoning with explicit height limits for all of Sunset Park's rezoning study area with the exception of 8th Avenue (Sunset Park's Chinese commercial center). Residential side streets are rezoned to R6B, and other major avenues—4th and 7th Avenues—are rezoned to R7A, a contextual zone that caps building heights at eighty feet. On 8th Avenue, a proposed C2-4 overlay district would reduce the depth of commercial establishments along the side streets to one hundred feet; however, the zoning remains R6, essentially retaining the status quo.

Utilizing 8th Avenue as the boundary for Sunset Park's rezoning study area effectively disenfranchises the Chinese community. While 8th Avenue serves as the geographic boundary between two community boards—Community Boards 7 and 12—the delineation of administrative boundaries does not necessarily cohere with neighborhood definitions. A study conducted by the Asian American Legal Defense and Education Fund on neighborhood boundaries found that Chinese residents define Sunset Park's boundary much farther east than 8th Avenue (Hum 2002b). Despite this technicality having been brought to the attention of the DCP and Community Board 7 at the start of the rezoning study, both chose to neglect this inconvenient fact. As a commercial core, 8th Avenue represents Brooklyn's Chinatown, and by retaining its permissive R6 designation with no explicit height limits, the rezoning succeeds in pushing development pressures and containing new projects (i.e., the Chinese "invasion") to the Chinese-concentrated part of Sunset Park.

The subtext of Sunset Park's rezoning reflects a deep nativist anxiety about the decline of a particular social order and neighborhood character.

As Leland Saito (1998, 38) describes in his 1998 study of California's Monterey Park, "'Development' became a code word for Chinese immigrants, and nativist sentiments became politically respectable behind the cover of defending the community against uncontrolled development." Post-1965 immigration had transformed Sunset Park's local streetscapes and community life. White homeowners who hung on to their Sunset Park residences through the fiscal crisis of the 1970s and related urban disinvestments and the relocation of working-poor Puerto Ricans now had to contend with the influx of racialized immigrants and the "externalities" of immigrant-driven neighborhood growth and change (Smith 1995). Forming an easy alliance with these longtime white homeowners, young white "pioneers" priced out of gentrified Brooklyn neighborhoods added their angst and vocal opposition to overdevelopment that threatened the residential charm and waterfront views of their newly adopted neighborhood.[24] The urgency to stem further development was palpable as Community Board 7 members appealed for a speedy adoption of the DCP's rezoning plan, despite its shortcomings, before the "vultures" completely destroyed Sunset Park.

The New York City Charter includes a provision that community boards should cooperate "with respect to matters of common concern" (City of New York 2004, 315). Since Sunset Park's Chinese community is split in Community Boards 7 and 12, the DCP could have convened a special planning committee to undertake a comprehensive study of the 8th Avenue corridor. However, the DCP, City Council member Gonzalez, and Community Board 7 failed to heed the concerns raised by Chinese community leaders in July 2007. Comprehensiveness and respect for neighborhood boundaries essential to a meaningful discussion on community development fell by the wayside in the interest of an expedited rezoning to reassert Sunset Park's white demographic—which consists of a longtime homeowner electoral base as well as new gentrifiers drawn to the neighborhood for its affordable homeownership, waterfront location, and views—and to tip the scale of power in favor of Chinese developers and community power brokers, such as the Brooklyn Chinese American Association, because an agreement could be drawn that appeased concerns of a neighborhood takeover by Chinese immigrants through demarcating an area of growth outside of Sunset Park's contextual zone.

¡Basta Ya! Sunset Rise Up

Rejecting the DCP and the Pratt Center's proposal for an expedited contextual rezoning, SPAN and the Chinese Staff and Workers' Association (CSWA) viewed overdevelopment as being symptomatic of broader trends and challenges in sustaining immigrant working-class neighborhoods. By forming the Protect Sunset Park Committee, SPAN and the CSWA sought to build an alliance with community stakeholders and advocates for poor immigrants, including local religious institutions and the South Brooklyn Legal Services. Recognition that the influx of capital and urban planning actions have failed to benefit poor communities of color formed the basis of a shared ideological perspective that race and class disparities persist in institutional relationships and policy formulation. As Sunset Park resident and SPAN activist Ivette Cabrera noted in a video titled *¡Basta Ya! Sunset Rise Up* (Shao et al. 2010) documenting the rezoning struggle, "We love the community enough to say 'basta ya.'"[25]

In the 1986 landmark legal case *Chinese Staff and Workers' Association et al., Appellants, v. City of New York et al., Respondents,* the New York Court of Appeals upheld the argument by the CSWA and the Asian American Legal Defense and Education Fund that the city review of potential development impacts employed a limited definition of the "environment."[26] Citing the likelihood that a proposed luxury housing development would fundamentally alter Manhattan Chinatown's neighborhood characteristics, including population composition, the court agreed that agency review must consider the potential displacement of residents and businesses in determining the environmental effects of proposed projects.

Formed in response to current development pressures in Sunset Park, SPAN does not have the institutional history of the CSWA, but collectively SPAN consists of longtime Puerto Rican neighborhood residents, religious leaders, and environmental justice, civil rights, and union activists. Although Latino and Asian coalitions are not new to Sunset Park, they tend to be issue-oriented and episodic.[27] Nevertheless, Sunset Park's vibrant migrant civil society of community organizations, workers' centers, churches, and faith-based organizations facilitated the critical "free spaces" necessary for forming collective identities and "shared analyses of sociopolitical problems" (Theodore and Martin 2007, 271). Sunset Park's Latino and Chinese community leadership recognized the potential strength of their coalition in refocusing the zoning debate on the lack of procedural equity that reinforced the marginalization of Sunset Park's majority low-income immigrant population (Maantay 2002). The shared experiences of working and shelter poverty,[28] exclusion from established political venues including the community board, and the prospect of residential displacement formed the basis for a Latino-Asian coalition. SPAN leader David Galarza expressed this sense of linked fates at the March 2008 DCP presentation held at Community Board 7. In response to the exclusion of 8th Avenue from the proposed contextual zone, Galarza claimed that the DCP's plan was unjust because it marginalized the Chinese community, and as a result all of Sunset Park's working-class populations were similarly marginalized. Galarza called for a moratorium on development until an 8th Avenue planning study was completed.

Since remediation by tweaking or modifying the DCP's proposed contextual rezoning was limited, the Protect Sunset Park Coalition pressed for a comprehensive and inclusive planning process that would address systematic inequities that have long shaped neighborhood quality and life chances for working-poor Latinos and Chinese in Sunset Park. A key goal of the Latino-Asian coalition is to build community capacity to engage and participate in neighborhood planning that preserves Sunset Park as a multiracial immigrant working-class neighborhood. Through grassroots mobilization and the facilitation of a bilingual planning summit to hear community views on Sunset Park's present and future conditions, SPAN and the CSWA outreached to constituents and members who lack voice on the community board.[29] SPAN and Voices of the Everyday People, a Harlem-based group that filed a lawsuit to stop the rezoning of 125th Street in Manhattan, extended their shared antidisplacement struggles to protest the exclusion of Manhattan's Chinatown from the DCP's Lower East Side–East Village rezoning by participating in a CSWA direct action to disrupt a May 2008 Community Board 3 meeting.[30] By rejecting the narrow parameters of DCP rezoning initiatives and the complicity of community boards in immigrant exclusion, the Protect Sunset Park Coalition encouraged a more democratic planning process for equity in agenda setting that challenges the economic and political biases of neoliberal city planning practices. This Latino-Asian alliance developed a set of demands for an inclusive and comprehensive approach to neighborhood planning by setting realistic income guidelines for mandatory inclusionary housing provisions; locating potential development sites, such as underutilized manufacturing zones and the air rights over the N subway tracks for neighborhood expansion; and pointing out Community Board 7's significant representational gap.

The Empty Promise of Affordable Housing

The current period of sustained economic growth and real estate development has deepened New York City's affordable housing crisis. The share of New Yorkers who spend more than 30 percent of their income on housing costs continues to rise (Fernandez 2007). References to a new gilded age due to the heightening divide between the rich and poor have become commonplace (Uchitelle 2007). While the nation copes with the fallout from the most recent subprime mortgage crisis, New York City's real estate market remains insulated and fairly robust (Spinola 2008). Mayor Bloomberg's 2007 housing marketplace plan to construct or preserve 165,000 affordable housing units by 2013 relies in part on voluntary inclusionary zoning, despite producing meager results in Manhattan, New York City's strongest real estate market.[31] Two concerns with privately incentivized affordable housing construction through inclusionary zoning remain outstanding. First, resources for affordable housing are tied to density bonuses that further real estate development and direct and indirect displacement. Second, affordability income categories are not affordable to a majority of New Yorkers. These limitations have led progressive planners and community activists to critique affordable housing as a "trojan horse" for development projects.[32] For example, much ado was made about Mayor Bloomberg's kiss with ACORN director Bertha Lewis, who threw her political support behind the highly controversial Forest City Ratner Companies' $4 billion Atlantic Yards project upon negotiating a Memorandum of Understanding that delineated the provision of affordable housing, job hiring practices, and workforce development.[33] The ensuing debate and critiques about ACORN's support for Forest City Ratner's megadevelopment proposal lodged by accountable development groups such as Develop Don't Destroy Brooklyn and No Land Grab highlighted race and class divisions in assessing development costs and benefits (Confessore 2006a; Lewis 2006).

Upon learning of the Sunset Park rezoning study, several key community-based human service providers and advocacy organizations spearheaded the Affordable Housing Working Group to ensure that the interests of their constituents—working-poor Latino and Asian immigrants—were represented in the planning process and product. The Center for Family Life and Neighbors Helping Neighbors assumed leadership of the working group—which included the Fifth Avenue Committee, a community development corporation founded by former Pratt Center director Brad Lander—and commenced meetings in the late summer of 2007 to share information about rezoning politics and process and research strategies to protect and promote affordable housing development. Initially, the Affordable Housing Working Group worked under the umbrella of SPAN. However, in light of the acrimony between SPAN and SPARZ, Community Board 7, and Gonzalez, the Affordable Housing Working Group quickly disassociated itself, stating a desire to work cooperatively with the community board and Gonzalez, and began to hold meetings at Community Board 7 (Fitzgerald 2007). The Affordable Housing Working Group distributed meeting announcements and summaries to an email list of one hundred individuals, including members of the Protect Sunset Park Coalition, and met monthly to discuss and debate inclusionary zoning, special district designation to protect tenants from harassment, and other zoning measures to preserve and advocate for affordable housing.

The Affordable Housing Working Group arrived at two zoning recommendations that would protect Sunset Park's low-scale neighborhood quality and create incentives for affordable housing: (1) the side streets of Sunset Park should be rezoned to R6B, and (2) the avenues of Sunset Park should be rezoned to R6A with a *mandatory* inclusionary zoning provision. The R6A zoning represented a reduction in the as-of-right development rights and, coupled with mandatory inclusionary zoning, would have created meaningful pressures for developers to produce affordable housing. The group's interest in collaborating with Community Board 7 and Gonzalez to expedite a contextual rezoning for Sunset Park, however, may have moderated the group's potential resistance to the DCP and Pratt's proposed rezoning that called for the upzoning of Sunset Park's avenues. At the March monthly community board meeting, Community Board 7 chair Randy Peers and Neighbors Helping Neighbors executive director Julia Fitzgerald engaged in a heated exchange about rezoning and affordable housing. Peers underscored the urgency to implement a contextual zone because "his people are suffering" as a result of unabated new development throughout Sunset Park.[34] Peers warned that he did not want the downzoning to be delayed as a consequence of community demands for affordable housing.[35] A week later at the DCP presentation, Fitzgerald expressed relief with the DCP's proposed rezoning, which she felt "could have been a lot worst" (Fitzgerald 2008). Even though Sunset Park's avenues are upzoned to R7A with voluntary inclusionary zoning and 8th Avenue is completely excluded from any consideration, the Affordable Housing Working Group was able to make peace with this proposal.[36]

Despite its ardent advocacy for a contextual rezoning as a tool to protect Sunset Park and incentivize affordable housing, Community Board 7 conceded that the voluntary inclusionary zoning provision resulted in no community benefit. In the Statement of Needs, District Manager Jeremy Laufer wrote, "We realize zoning is not a great tool for promoting affordability, as the building size bonus allowed on 4th and 7th Avenues in previous rezoning has resulted in *zero additional affordable units in our community*" (New York City Department of City Planning 2013, 185, my emphasis). Housing production is occurring in Sunset Park primarily through the development of market-rate condominiums and/or the addition of units built above typical two-family row houses—the kind of development that sparked the community uproar and demand for a rezoning solution. Rezoning has not solved the problem of overdevelopment either, and Community Board 7 continues to battle projects perceived to be out of context and nonconforming to neighborhood scale. Currently, Community Board 7 is reviewing an as-of-right development on 429 43rd Street. The property sales and development trajectory are typical of real estate transactions in Sunset Park and are part of the gentrifying forces that will transform not only the built environment but, more important, the neighborhood class composition.

In August 2012 after five decades of ownership by the Schoenhardt family, their three-story two-family limestone home was sold to Spring Hill Realty LLC, represented by owner Andy Leung, for $710,000.[37] Two months later Mr. Leung filed for permits with the New York City Department of Buildings (DoB) for a "vertical enlargement" to add a story and renovate the two-family into a four-family home. Based on the New York State Department of State's Corporations and Businesses database, Spring Hill Realty LLC was established on May 9, 2012. The address given for the limited liability corporation was on East 40th Street in Manhattan's Murray Hill neighborhood. A quick review of the census data for Spring Hill Realty LLC's zip code indicates an affluent neighborhood with a median income of $107,200 and an overwhelmingly non-Hispanic white (75 percent) residential population.

Since construction began in March 2013, neighbors called 311[38] and filed two complaints in March and May pertaining to vibrations, banging, shaking, and claims that the construction caused damage, including one complainant's claim that the construction caused cabinets "to fall off wall."[39] Both complaints were summarily dismissed by the DoB. Neighbors and community members are outraged by this out-of-context development, which is located in the proposed Sunset Park landmark district and is less than one block from the twenty-four-acre park. However, this development and a dozen more on neighboring streets are all permissible under the 2009 hard-fought rezoning. Community Board 7 endorsed the rationale that without a contextual rezoning, there were no limits to building heights in an R6 zone. According to New York City zoning rules, building heights are determined by two factors: floor area ratio and property lot size. And given typical urban residential lot sizes, building heights in Sunset Park are generally limited. Nevertheless, the DCP pushed its proposal while being fully aware that a contextual rezoning cannot stop or contain development but in fact may facilitate further growth and developments (Angotti 2009). According to a local reporter's coverage of a May 2009 community meeting on rezoning Sunset Park, DCP Brooklyn director Purnima Kapur's explanation that a contextual zone R6B would cap building heights at five stories in order to preserve the neighborhood's row house character *"was greeted with applause"* (Egeln 2009, my emphasis). It is notable that SPAN, the CSWA, and the Chinese and Latino protestors who were accused of "spread[ing] misinformation about the rezoning" were correct after all in their objection to a DCP rezoning proposal that "would bring more condos, higher rents and greater displacement."[40]

Since it is apparent the rezoning is ineffective in preventing new development, stricter tools to protect Sunset Park—such as securing New York City historic landmark designation—are being sought. According to Community Board 7, concerns with the new developments do not pertain to zoning rules per se. Rather, the Landmark Committee is concerned that by adding one or two stories, developers are "popping off cornices and building out the back," which is destroying the integrity of the buildings (Laufer 2013a). After months of informal advisement and collaboration, Community Board 7 officially voted in June 2013 to endorse the efforts of the Sunset Park Landmark Committee. Of utmost concern to Community Board 7 and committee members is the destructive impact of Asian development on the aesthetics of Sunset Park's built environment rather than the frenzied levels of capital investment and city rezoning and economic development policies that create the conditions for single-room occupancy units, basement apartments, and overdevelopment as well as make homeownership an impossible American Dream for most New Yorkers (see Chapter 4).

Transformative and Redistributive Populism

On a local geographic scale, the Protect Sunset Park Coalition and the Affordable Housing Working Group illustrate critical differences in the strategies and goals of two broader social movements for equity in the neoliberal city—Right to the City and One City, One Future: Making Growth Work for All New Yorkers. While both movements focus on economic justice, they differ in strategies for mobilization and goals for changes in political economic practices. The Right to the City movement questions fundamental principles of a capitalist society such as the concept of individual rights, which in a capitalist context is tied to individual property rights (Smith 2002). According to David Harvey (2003), a right to the city does not mean the right of access to what exists but a right to change and transform the city. He elaborated that a right to the city "is not merely a right of access to what the property speculators and state planners define, but an active right to make the city different, to shape it more in accord with our heart's desire, and to re-make ourselves thereby in a different image" (941). As Harvey indicates, the right to the city is premised on collective rights such as those advocated for by the transformative social movements of the 1950s and 1960s civil rights, women, and student movements.

The Right to the City movement is a form of transformative populism, as an objective is to change everyday people's consciousness and power dynamics (Kennedy, Tilly, and Gaston 1990, 306–307). By bringing together working-class Chinese and Latinos to demand inclusion in the planning process, challenge political jurisdictional boundaries that fragment and marginalize, and assert a right to remain in their neighborhood, the Protect Sunset Park Coalition integrates an analysis of structural racism in its community empowerment strategies. An example of this activism is the production of the 2010 video *¡Basta Ya! Sunset Rise Up*. The film was a collective effort by Sunset Park residents and activists Lida Shao, May Lin, and Rebecca Giordano. Media production is key to mobilizing youths, and lifelong Sunset Park resident Giordano worked with United Puerto Rican Organization of Sunset Park (UPROSE) youths to produce videos about the environmental conditions in industrial Sunset Park.[41] Translated into three languages with Spanish and Chinese subtitles, *¡Basta Ya! Sunset Rise Up* documents Sunset Park's multiracial immigrant population and how market-driven real estate development and city policies such as rezoning are threatening the ability of working-class people to remain in the neighborhood.

Local high school students affiliated with the Center for Family Life and the youth programs of the Chinese American Planning Council (CPC) were involved in the production of the video. May Lin was a youth director at the CPC and engaged her twenty-member youth group in the video's production. Lin's pedagogic approach to working with the youths was purposefully political to help them develop critical thinking skills and viewpoints about the politics of Sunset Park's development and improvement. The "opaque" politics of social service–based organizations led Lin to feel that her overtly political education work and engagement of local youths in Sunset Park antigentrification activism was "subversive" (Lin 2013).

Consisting of interviews with community stakeholders and footage of neighborhood protests and contentious Community Board 7 meetings, the video gives voice to longtime residents and provides vital information, including a multilingual explanation of how zoning works and the city's rationale for rezoning Sunset Park. The video begins with several lines from "The Manifesto" signed by "Publius" and penned by one of Lin's CPC youths, David Au, a lifelong Sunset Park resident, in which he describes Sunset Park's multiracial landscapes as "suffering from a disease, the disease of gentrification and displacement." "The Manifesto" was also posted on a Save Sunset Park blog created by Lin's CPC youth group.[42] Writing about the neighborhood's working class-residents, Au describes the goal of the youth blog initiative:

> Save Sunset Park stands to unite these individuals to collectively reclaim control of our homes and businesses. We're here to empower the poor and underprivileged, to give a voice to those that others would allow to go unheard. We will not sit idly by while our livelihood is being taken away from us, nor will we watch our rents outpace our paychecks with foolish indifference.[43]

The production of *¡Basta Ya! Sunset Rise Up* and other media venues, including the Save Sunset Park blog, engaged local youths and reflects a particular form of representation and placemaking that is rooted in a racial and political economic perspective. Working on a documentary of Sunset Park's rezoning struggle catalyzed changes in everyday people's consciousness to see the neighborhood as a working-class Chinese-Latino Chinatown/barrio. Au's "The Manifesto" exemplified transformative populism as he insightfully pointed out the shared concern of Sunset Park's diverse immigrant populations:

> Those are the symptoms, but what could be the cure? Awareness is a start, and inter-communal dialogue is good progress. *Gentrification is a problem that transcends ethnic, cultural and religious boundaries because our homes literally share common ground.* Only a united front, forged from our collective talents and resources, can stand any chance against the fast approaching forces of displacement.[44]

Au and his family continue to reside in Sunset Park, and he recently graduated from Brooklyn College and holds a part-time job. Au is seeking ways to remain engaged in community-based arts, and he expressed an interest in participating in La Unión's mural project. While May Lin's leadership in the CPC youth program was critical in cultivating youth consciousness and activism, it is equally important to build and sustain youth leadership and community engagement through multifaceted opportunities.

SPAN activists also challenged local power structures by mobilizing grassroots initiatives related to food justice, prison and criminal justice reform, and solidifying alliances with other Sunset Park–based immigrant organizations such as La Unión. These initiatives included forming a people's kitchen named Rice and Dreams and raising funds to build a chicken coop and purchase chickens for La Unión's urban farm, Granja Los Colibries (see the Conclusion). In addition to these ongoing initiatives, SPAN organized the People's Transportation Project (PTP), modeled after a similar initiative in Manhattan's El Barrio (Dunn 2009). For a year, PTP activists were located at two subway stations at 36th and 45th Streets and used donated or purchased MetroCards to give a free ride to neighborhood passengers. Since New Yorkers are dependent on a complex network of public transit, subways are a critical public space that brings together neighborhood people. In fact, aspiring New York City politicians typically stand at key subway nodes to meet and greet commuters on their way to work. Similarly, the PTP saw this activity as an outreach strategy and used the opportunity (between Metro-Card swipes) to talk with everyday people about neighborhood issues and events. Twelve-year Sunset Park resident and former SPAN activist Amina Ali (2013) described her involvement in the PTP as the most fun she ever had. In addition to speaking with subway riders, the PTP set up an information table to publicize Sunset Park actions, including the protest of a proposed generator plant on the waterfront.

Transformative populism in Sunset Park directly addressed conditions of racial inequality and sought to cultivate a community consciousness about the neighborhood's positionality in New York City's landscape of power. In contrast, redistributive populism tends to "suppress non-class differences" such as race (Kennedy 1996). In the Sunset Park rezoning struggle, the actions of the Affordable Housing Working Group exemplified how a strategy of redistributive populism neglected the differential racialization of Sunset Park stakeholders. The primary objective of the Affordable Housing Working Group was to preserve or create affordable housing in Sunset Park, but this goal was neutralized from any consideration of the racial dynamics of community board representation and developing capacity among working-poor people of color to plan and control their neighborhood spaces.

Redistributive populism defines many New York City initiatives to address urban inequality. The May 31, 2008, People's Summit for Accountable Development, organized by the Fifth Avenue Committee, started off by inviting elected officials to sign a pledge to uphold Accountable Development Principles.[45] This "rising tide lifts all boats" approach to economic justice depends on organizational leaders, elected officials, and other community elites to secure a fairer reallocation of the residual benefits of state-supported gentrification. One City, One Future: Making Growth Work for All New Yorkers was a coalition of progressive organizations, including New York University's Brennan Justice Center, Jobs for Justice, and the Pratt Center for Community Development as well as community development corporations, civic organizations, labor unions, and policy groups.[46] The most recent iteration of this citywide progressive alliance is spearheaded by City University of New York (CUNY) distinguished professor John Mollenkopf and City Council member Brad Lander in their "Toward a 21st Century City for All" initiative.[47] The website "Toward a 21st Century City for All" provides a compilation of more than thirty papers to illuminate and promote policy ideas on a range of critical urban challenges, including economic development and education, to help inform and shape the political discourse of the 2013 electoral season during which New Yorkers will elect key citywide officials, including the mayor, the comptroller, the public advocate, and nearly half (twenty-three of fifty-one seats) of the New York City Council. The May 2013 CUNY Graduate Center event to launch the initiative was moderated by Michael Powell of the *New York Times* and did not include a person of color on the five-member panel. While race remains central to shaping the lives of New Yorkers and their neighborhoods' positionality in a city landscape of deepening social and economic polarizations, the need for a substantive and engaged examination of the complex and persistent significance of immigration, race, and urban development remains outstanding.

Community Board Limitations

Community boards are severely limited in providing a shared public space to mediate conflicts related to neighborhood change and to advocate a planning agenda that advances the concerns and needs of working-poor Asians and Latinos. Like many New York City community boards, Community Board 7 is marked by an acute representational gap. The distinct demographic composition of Sunset Park and Windsor Terrace—neighborhoods represented by Community Board 7—has become even more pronounced with the formalization of South Park Slope and Greenwood Heights—carved from Community Board 7's northern section closest to affluent and predominately white Park Slope. The creation of Greenwood Heights, a formerly dilapidated area west of the renowned Greenwood Cemetery, illustrates how real estate agents participate in the social production of space. As place entrepreneurs, they create real estate value and speculation in part through marketing imagined associations with desirable places. Fillmore

Real Estate vice president Sal Cappi (2008) takes credit for creating Greenwood Heights in 1988 out of a "no-man's-land" to market new townhouse
developments (Huege 2006). According to Mr. Cappi (2008), "No one
knew what to call it, it was too far south at the time to be considered South
Slope, and it really wasn't Sunset Park, so as a marketing strategy I came
up with the name Greenwood Heights, a play on Brooklyn Heights, for the
name of the development. We hung up huge banners trumpeting 'Greenwood Heights' along 6th Ave, and ran ads in the Times under that heading.
Soon after, homeowners who were selling their properties in the same neighborhood, listed their homes for sale as being in Greenwood Heights, and a
newly named community was born."

The practice of delineating neighborhood spaces and constructing new
identities and neighborhood names is noted in Community Board 7's (2013,
171) Statement of Needs: "Recently, other community identities have gained
popularity and become more established including Greenwood Heights,
South Park Slope and East Windsor Terrace."

New residents priced out of gentrified New York City neighborhoods
found affordable homeownership in Greenwood Heights. Seeking to protect
the qualities that drew them to the area, neighbors formed the Concerned
Citizens of Greenwood Heights (CCGH) to protest the growing numbers of
noncontextual and out-of-scale development (Brashear and Holwin 2005).
In a well-publicized case that established the protection of views as a key
zoning principle, the CCGH successfully stopped a proposed as-of-right
condominium development at the site of the former National Produce Warehouse. The CCGH claimed that the seventy-foot-high project would block
the sight line or view between two historic monuments—a statue of the
Roman goddess of wisdom, Minerva, on Battle Hill in Greenwood Cemetery
and the Statue of Liberty in upper New York Harbor (Collins 2005a; Buiso
2007). The opposition to this project was framed on the primacy of view
protections, historic preservation, and a low-density neighborhood quality.
The leaders of Greenwood Heights and South Park Slope's antidevelopment
battles assumed leadership roles on Community Board 7 and helped frame
Sunset Park's rezoning struggle.[48]

Sunset Park organizations, including Community Board 7, are supportive of community-based planning and have endorsed the Campaign for
Community-Based Planning. While zoning tools should be developed in the
context of comprehensive planning, this did not take place in Sunset Park.
Community Board 7's approach to community planning has been deliber-
ately piecemeal in the preparation of a 197-a for the industrial waterfront
(see Chapter 6) and in the successful rezonings of Greenwood Heights and

South Park Slope.[49] While the capacity of community boards to engage in community planning is hampered by a lack of resources, including funding and technical expertise, the willful marginalization of a working-poor immigrant population also factors in as a reason for their absence in community board planning agendas. Community Board 7's planning initiatives have largely ignored Sunset Park's majority Latino and Asian working poor. Community Board 7 has seized on zoning as a defensive tool to protect against "development that disrespects the scale and charm of the neighborhoods" (Brooklyn Borough President 2005). For Community Board 7, the goals of rezoning are framed around responsible and contextual development that protects Sunset Park's built environment, harbor views, and historic significance. Resistance to addressing Sunset Park's complex relationship with race, immigration, and neighborhood change was exemplified by a Community Board 7 member's derisive response to a community leader's concerns about racial equity and community planning, which this community board member dismissed as "waving the Latino flag."[50]

Conclusion

Sunset Park is a dynamic immigrant neighborhood facing the challenges of community building under local conditions of globalization. The collusion of an immigrant growth coalition and corporatized city planning practices promotes market land values and escalates the threat of displacement. In this political economic context, a vibrant migrant civil society consisting of grassroots and nonprofit organizations is critical to cultivating the leadership and invented public spaces for comprehensive and inclusive neighborhood planning and development. Community-based grassroots organizations provide vital resources for mobilizing immigrant incorporation and actions for social and economic justice.

Sunset Park demonstrates the multiple intersections of race and class and the complex task of democratizing urban planning and local governance. Sunset Park is defined by stark class divisions among its Asian stakeholders. Asian developers and property owners sought racial solidarity with the majority working poor to support progrowth activities. Recognizing common class interests between Asians and Latinos, two community-based nonprofit organizations built an alliance to protect Sunset Park as an affordable and sustainable working-class neighborhood. Since the overwhelming majority of Sunset Park's Asian and Latino immigrant populations are not property owners, the rezoning objectives were not framed around preserving neighborhood quality and waterfront vistas. The CSWA and SPAN engaged in political action to push the community board discussion and agenda toward inclusion and equitable planning practices and outcomes.

A 1974 *New York Times* article on community boards noted that "perhaps the best argument for the boards' existence is that they provide a point of view in planning decisions that might not otherwise be expressed" (Selver 1974). In this regard, New York City's approach to decentralizing urban governance is successful because community boards have become integral to the land-use and development review process. However, community boards as the official structure for citizen participation in planning and local governance represent a form of "bureaucratic enfranchisement" (Fainstein and Fainstein 1982, 12), as members are appointed by elected officials and deemed "city officers."[51] Although the New York City Council electoral representative for Sunset Park is Latino, community boards typically reflect the New York City electorate, which remains a largely embattled white middle class. Racial disparity is chronic, and even in diverse immigrant neighborhoods, community boards are defined by acute underrepresentation of the population majority.

Since community boards remain "the only official form of neighborhood-level governance,"[52] critical review and reform of these local institutions are imperative to democratic practices and citizen engagement. Equally important to community board reforms for accountability, professionalism, transparency, and representation, global cities with large immigrant populations need to support and engage a vibrant migrant civil society consisting of community-based nonprofit organizations. These organizations can create opportunities and support for immigrant integration and mobilization and can also broaden urban planning agendas to advance redistributive economic justice and fairness in diverse neighborhoods. In Sunset Park, activist nonprofit organizations invented the necessary public space to air grievances and "challenge the status quo in the hope of larger societal change" (Miraftab 2004, 1).

In the spirit of the Occupy movement, many of the same progressive community activists—such as David Galarza and CSWA members, including Wendy Cheung and Josephine Lee—have mobilized Occupy Sunset Park, which regularly held meetings in the park and now holds meetings at St. Jacobi Church. In June 2012, Trinity Lutheran Church established a nonprofit community center, La Casita Communal de Sunset Park, that serves as gallery and performance space for local artists and musicians and as a community space for events. In reaching out to Sunset Park's 99 percent, many Occupy Sunset Park and La Casita events and materials are translated into multiple languages—English, Spanish, and Chinese and in some cases in Arabic as well. In addition to citywide labor and community actions, Occupy Sunset Park has provided leadership and advisement to a group of Latino tenants engaged in a protracted battle over dangerous and substandard conditions in three buildings on 46th Street (see Chapter 4).[53] In creating alternative spaces, these community-based grassroots organizations engaged in collective action and cross-racial alliances to tackle substantive issues of equity, neighborhood planning and decision-making power, and immigrant rights to the city.

6

Power Plants, Sex Shops, Industrial Zones, and Open Space

The Politics of a Sustainable Working Waterfront

ommunities of color, including immigrant Latino and Asian neighborhoods, continue to be disproportionately burdened by environmental pollutants and toxic facilities. Workplace hazards, former industrial sites (i.e., brownfields), highways, and major thoroughfares pose numerous environmental risks that are common to Asian immigrant neighborhoods (Sze 2007). Historically, urban renewal and highway construction have split and divided Asian neighborhoods, diminished their land area and housing stock, and compromised environmental quality. Notable examples include Seattle's International District and Boston's Chinatown (Lai, Leong, and Wu 2000). While Manhattan Chinatown's Canal Street is not a designated highway, Canal Street is a major regional thoroughfare that connects Lower Manhattan to New Jersey (via the Holland Tunnel) and Brooklyn (via the Manhattan Bridge) and brings heavy volumes of vehicular traffic, including diesel trucks, through a dense mixed-use commercial and residential neighborhood. Location near highways or major thoroughfares adds to traffic noise, pollution, and congestion as well as increased risks of traffic injuries and respiratory ailments, among other health problems.

Heightened health risks such as asthma in environmentally burdened neighborhoods in the Bronx and Manhattan's Harlem are well documented (Perez-Pena 2003; Fernandez 2006; New York University 2006). Research on the environmental conditions of working-poor Asian neighborhoods are comparatively few, but important case studies include the Tufts

University–Boston Chinatown research collaborations to document health burdens and environmental justice activism (Brugge, Leong, and Law 2003; Brugge et al. 2010) and the Vietnamese American community's mobilization in the New Orleans Versailles neighborhood to protest and shut down a landfill for post–Hurricane Katrina debris (Eaton 2006).[1] In Sunset Park, two local community organizations collaborated on a 2007 survey of health issues and found high incidences of asthma due to the prevalence of substandard rental housing conditions, including rodent and vermin infestations and mold.[2] Moreover, the waterfront concentration of power plants compounded by the heavily trafficked Gowanus Expressway, which slices the neighborhood along 3rd Avenue, emits tons of "invisible" particulate matter, compromising air quality and public health (Brugge 2013).

In addition to tackling the relationship between substandard housing, toxic facilities, highways, and chronic health problems in low-income communities, Asian American stakeholders and community planners must also address environmental resiliency and just sustainability because our neighborhoods are vulnerable. For example, New York City's three Chinatowns—Flushing, Sunset Park, and Chinatown–Lower East Side—are waterfront neighborhoods with high numbers of brownfields and are at risk of flooding because of rising sea levels and storm surges.[3] Superstorm Sandy resulted in devastation to numerous low-lying neighborhoods, including Manhattan's Chinatown, and exposed New York City's extreme vulnerability (Reynolds 2012). Climate change is a present-day reality, and subsequently it is imperative to apply an environmental justice framework to the study of Asian immigrant neighborhoods; community development practices and strategies must integrate principles of sustainability, equity, and resilience.

After decades of abandonment and disinvestment, New York City's industrial waterfront is stirring back to life, as waterfront reclamation and revitalization are central factors in the city's economic development agenda. Envisioning a more livable city, Mayor Michael Bloomberg, City Planning Commission chair and director of the Department of City Planning (DCP) Amanda Burden, and the New York City Economic Development Corporation (NYCEDC) have advanced plans for waterfront parks, luxury residential towers, cruise ship terminals, high-end retail, and high–value-added production to replace the obsolete industrial infrastructure that defines much of New York City's 520-mile waterfront. The city's award-winning Vision 2020 comprehensive waterfront plan designates the "blue network" surrounding the city as the sixth borough and proposes a blueprint to protect the city from rising sea levels due to climate change and reconnect New

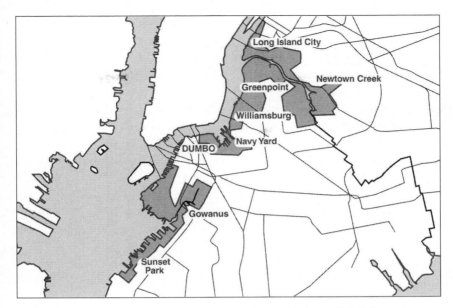

Map 6.1 Brooklyn-Queens waterfront, Mayor's Special Initiative on Rebuilding and Resilience.

Yorkers to a revitalized and transformed waterfront.[4] From Manhattan's Hudson Yards to Staten Island's old Navy Homeport to North Brooklyn's Greenpoint and Williamsburg to Queens' Long Island City and the Bronx's Hunts Point neighborhoods, waterfront rezoning and private developers are transforming the industrial urban spaces that had sustained generations of workers and preparing for their reuse as sites for recreation, high-rise luxury development, and tourism.

Sunset Park's waterfront stretches for two miles from the Gowanus Canal, a federal Superfund site,[5] to the 65th Street Rail Yard and is central to Brooklyn's historic working waterfront, which begins at Newton Creek and encompasses the neighborhoods of Williamsburg, Greenpoint, Brooklyn Heights, Carroll Gardens, Gowanus, and Red Hook (Map 6.1).[6] The industrial waterfront has always been intricately linked to Sunset Park's economic fate. In 2007, the National Trust for Historic Preservation named Brooklyn's industrial waterfront one of the nation's eleven most endangered historic places.[7] Sunset Park is one of the largest remaining industrial centers in New York City. This chapter examines the politics of Sunset Park's manufacturing future and the gentrifying effects of waterfront redevelopment.

Increasing market interest and gentrification pressures are evident in realtor schemes to brand Sunset Park as "New York's next hot neighborhood" by marketing its industrial lofts as an artists' colony and renaming the neighborhood DUGO (Down Under Gowanus Overpass) (Hess 2006; Stein 2009; Polsky 2012). Integral to Sunset Park's potent hipster draw is the waterfront and its spectacular and panoramic views of Lower Manhattan and the New York Harbor. Former New York City planning commissioner and Yale University professor Alex Garvin's 2006 strategic land-use plan, titled "Visions for New York City: Housing and the Public Realm," identified Sunset Park as one of five possible "waterfront development opportunities" for mixed-use development featuring artist live/work lofts and design lofts.[8] Major property owners such as Industry City Associates are actively marketing Bush Terminal artist lofts and Sunset Park's industrial waterfront as alternatives to pricey DUMBO and Williamsburg for a range of creative workers and entrepreneurs (Turcotte 2009). Industry City Associates' efforts to rebrand Sunset Park's industrial waterfront is assisted by an artists' blog that issued the following call:

Attention Artists!
Looking for affordable studio space?
The next up and coming cool neighborhood in NYC?
The Next Big Art Scene emerging from this economic recession?
Well . . . here it is try Industry City in Brooklyn, NYC.[9]

Will Sunset Park's waterfront renaissance portend a shared fate with numerous New York City neighborhoods that had once served as centers for immigrant working-class life in mixed-use industrial neighborhoods such as Manhattan's Lower East Side, Queens' Long Island City, and Brooklyn's Red Hook and Gowanus neighborhoods? Once sites of New York City's spatially dispersed, non-Fordist production infrastructure (Freeman 2000), these neighborhoods now symbolize postindustrial gentrification as waterfronts are remade by luxury condos, large retailers such as IKEA and Fairway Supermarket, and parkland (Curran and Hanson 2005; Smith and DeFilippis 1999). While Sunset Park's maritime and manufacturing roots are currently protected by city initiatives and zoning designations that recognize an industrial cluster remaining at the core of the local economy, this chapter examines how the prospects for Sunset Park's waterfront redevelopment in a postindustrial urban economy will be decided in part on the success of environmental justice and sustainable development discourses and actions to shift from noxious threats to countering a neoliberal development vision for industrial waterfront revitalization.

This chapter documents the city's industrial retention policies and examines how New York City's high real estate premiums may mean that the future of local industrial production is defined by the spatial demands of high value-added artisanal and niche manufacturers serving nearby affluent consumer markets (Voien 2012b). With residents having endured decades of environmental abuses and noxious uses along the waterfront, community protests and actions have evolved to engage urban planning experts and practices in participatory planning and environmental policy decision making. While demands for brownfield remediation and equitable access to open green space are central to Sunset Park's environmental justice agenda and goals, the challenge remains how to ensure that waterfront improvements do not lead to transformative gentrification and displacement.

Although Superstorm Sandy questioned the safety and sensibility of Mayor Bloomberg's waterfront redevelopment plans, he has vowed to build smarter and better (Salazar 2013). At the June 2013 briefing for his administration's comprehensive post-Sandy rebuilding plan, released as *A Stronger, More Resilient New York,* Bloomberg proclaimed, "As New Yorkers, we will not and cannot abandon our waterfront. We must protect it, not retreat from it."[10] As in the past when Sunset Park's industrial waterfront was central to the evolution of a working-class neighborhood, a revitalized and resilient waterfront will be essential to shaping the postindustrial and post-Sandy future of Latino-Asian Sunset Park.

As a waterfront neighborhood and designated Significant Maritime and Industrial Area (SMIA), Sunset Park is vulnerable to storm surges and flooding, which is exacerbated by its concentration of noxious uses. Numerous planning studies—including Community Board 7's 197-a plan "New Connections/New Opportunities" (Community Board 7 2011) and the NYCEDC's "Sunset Park Waterfront Vision Plan," which designates Sunset Park as a "sustainable urban industrial district" (New York City Economic Development Corporation 2009)—elaborate a planning vision of a revitalized waterfront that integrates the upland community by creating connectors for waterfront access and redevelops underutilized city-owned parcels and an extensive industrial infrastructure for job generation. Employing a comprehensive definition of sustainability inclusive of environmental improvement, economic development, and equity (including procedural, geographic, and social equity), this chapter examines the relationship of Sunset Park's "sustainable urban industrial district" to its working-poor immigrant Latino and Asian populations.

A History of Environmental Injustice

Since the relocation of the Fort Greene Meat Packing Distribution Plant to a city-owned site formerly occupied by Bethlehem Steel's shipyard in the late 1960s, Sunset Park has borne a disproportionate share of New York City's noxious land uses.[11] The migration of Puerto Ricans—many of whom were displaced by urban renewal initiatives in other neighborhoods—led to the "allegation that Sunset Park was being used as a dumping ground" for poor people and poor environmental uses (Winnick 1990, 92). New York City's 1992 comprehensive waterfront plan designated SMIAs to support land use related to industrial working waterfronts, including toxic uses such as power plants and waste transfer stations. The city's six SMIAs are all located in storm-surge zones and primarily residentially dense low-income communities of color. At an April 2013 meeting, environmental justice leader and United Puerto Rican Organization of Sunset Park (UPROSE) executive director Elizabeth Yeampierre warned that unregulated chemicals on Sunset Park's waterfront could potentially create a superfund situation, exposing all residents to extreme health risks.[12] Community Board 7 underscores the waterfront's vulnerability to environmental disaster by noting that "many of our waterfront facilities are sensitive sites containing power plants and transformers, garbage and sewer facilities, fuel and chemical storage and biological agents" (New York City Department of City Planning 2013, 179).

Manufacturing zones permit a wide range of nonindustrial but toxic uses, including sludge treatment plants, waste transfer stations, incinerators, power plants, and pornography shops. Moreover, heavy highway and truck traffic has created "a major asthma and lead poisoning corridor" in Sunset Park, as "thousands of tons of garbage [are trucked] in and out of our community every day" (New York City Department of City Planning 2013, 178). The following section elaborates on three current environmental burdens—power plants, waste transfer stations, and sex shops—that compromise daily neighborhood health and conditions for Sunset Park's immigrant Latino-Asian population.

Power Plants

Sunset Park is overburdened by power and electrical generators that produce electricity for the New York City metropolitan region (Sze 2007). The waterfront infrastructure includes two gas turbine generators operated by the New York Power Authority, the largest state-owned electrical utility.

These generators produce 79.9 megawatts of electricity, just eking by the 80-megawatt threshold that would have triggered a full environmental impact review under Article X of the New York State Public Service Law.[13] The Con Edison Greenwood area substation has four diesel-powered electric generators that provide citywide service and is also located on Sunset Park's waterfront. The U.S. Power Generating Company (USPowerGen) operates two Sunset Park facilities. USPowerGen's Gowanus Generating Station, consisting of thirty-two combustion turbine units that generate 560 mega-watts, is situated across four barges in Gowanus Bay and is one of the world's largest floating generating stations. USPowerGen's smaller Narrows Gener-ating Station is made up of sixteen combustion turbine units on two floating power barges and generates 276 megawatts.

Proposals to expand this infrastructure include USPowerGen's South Pier Improvement Project, which will not only update the Gowanus Gen-erating Station (in operation since the 1970s) but will also add approxi-mately 100 megawatts of greener energy by installing a modern, cleaner combustion turbine (US Power Generating Company 2008). According to USPowerGen, the new turbine with built-in green designs and technologies will allow the older turbines to be operated less frequently, thereby reducing their overall emissions and environmental impacts.[14] Although the South Pier Improvement Project is consistent with Mayor Bloomberg's PlaNYC 2030 to promote clean energy sources, much of the waterfront power plant infrastructure is clustered less than one mile from the neighborhood's heav-ily used Sunset Park and dense residential streets. Sunset Park's electrical generation capacity at 950 megawatts represents approximately 10 percent of New York City's total capacity. Since Sunset Park's peak demand is only 125 megawatts, the concentration of power plants underscores the disparate environmental and health impacts on "a community already suffering from many adverse environmental influences."[15]

In 2006 as a community benefit, the New York Power Authority con-structed a $1 million concrete-reinforced, brick-faced, twelve-foot-high wall to improve street aesthetics (i.e., hide the power plant along 3rd Avenue and 23rd Street).[16] Community leader David Galarza immediately criticized Community Board 7 for failure in leadership, since the "wall of shame" will do nothing to protect community health.[17] Despite the waterfront density of power and electrical infrastructure that provides service region-wide, Sunset Park remains vulnerable to blackouts during periods of high demand. In fact, Southwest Brooklyn experienced the greatest number of blackouts in New York City during the summer of 2008 (Egeln 2008b; Santos 2008b). Even though the community bears a disproportionate share of power-generating facilities and related environmental and health consequences, their concentration does not translate to adequate service for neighborhood residents.

Processing New York City's Garbage

New York City residents, businesses, and visitors generate more than thirty-two thousand tons of garbage daily. Until 2001, the New York City Department of Sanitation (DSNY) collected thirteen thousand tons of primarily residential trash and trucked their loads to nine municipal marine transfer stations (MTS) as well as numerous privately owned waste transfer stations scattered throughout the city for processing and transport to the municipal-owned landfill—Fresh Kills on Staten Island (Sze 2007, 113). Sunset Park's Hamilton Marine Transfer Station contains a decommissioned municipal incinerator that burned seven hundred tons of city garbage daily from 1963 to 1981 and was one of the nine municipal MTS sites where DSNY trucks tipped their loads of solid waste onto barges headed for Fresh Kills—an open dump covering twenty-two hundred acres (Anon. 1981b; City Planning Commission 2005; Sze 2007). As the largest landfill in the world, Fresh Kills was noted as one of two man-made structures—the other being China's Great Wall—that can be seen by the naked eye from space (Adinyayev et al. 2002). In March 2001, Mayor Rudolph Giuliani closed the landfill as political payback for the strong support of Staten Island voters—the only New York City borough with a white majority. The closure of Fresh Kills forced the city to come up with alternative waste management solutions, which mostly focused on exporting our garbage to other states.

Even though Sunset Park successfully fought a 1993 proposal for a one hundred–acre sludge treatment plant along the waterfront, its garbage infrastructure included the "temporary" storage of freight containers used to transport sewage sludge for loading onto barges headed west (J. Thomas 1994). Sunset Park's southern border at 65th Street is also the site of one of New York City's fourteen sewage treatment plants—the Owls Head Water Pollution Control Plant, where controlling for odors and potential health risks is a constant neighborhood concern.[18]

Sunset Park shoulders more than its fair share of sanitation infrastructure. As a central site for processing and transporting the city's solid waste, its infrastructure includes the Hamilton Avenue Marine Transfer Station, the IESI commercial waste station, the SIMS recycling facility, and a DSNY garage for garbage trucks that serves two community districts. The IESI solid waste transfer station illustrates Sunset Park's central role in processing the city's garbage. A daily average of 950 tons of solid waste collected from four Brooklyn community districts winds up at Sunset Park's IESI solid waste transfer station. The waste is transported to disposal locations by trailer trucks that travel along 50th Street to the Gowanus Expressway and then onto Interstate Highway I-278 heading for landfills in Pennsylvania and upstate New York (City of New York Department of Sanitation 2011).

Adding to the daily heavy volume of truck traffic and diesel fumes is Lafarge North America, the world's largest cement producer, that developed a 6.8-acre storage and shipping terminal at its longtime location on Sunset Park's 25th Street pier (New York City Economic Development Corporation 2005b). The facility serves as a distribution point for cement and cementitious materials transported by barge from Lafarge's Ravena cement plant near Albany, New York, and then by truck via surface roads to construction sites throughout the New York City metropolitan area, including large-scale projects located in Lower Manhattan and Hudson Yards.

Sex Industry

During the 1970s, Times Square was the "King of Midtown Pornography," and the area was notorious for peep shows, topless bars, X-rated video stores, prostitution, and drugs (Barry 1995). The remaking of Times Square necessitated an image of blight, disorder, and crime in order to rationalize its total destruction and redevelopment through urban renewal and private corporate investments (Reichl 1999). Mayor Rudolph Giuliani's Quality of Life campaigns, famously known for targeting squeegee men, sought to sanitize the Times Square area in preparation for a massive development project initiated by his predecessor, Mayor Edward Koch (Tierney n.d.). To facilitate the transformation of Times Square, the New York City Council amended the zoning laws to restrict the location and size of adult entertainment establishments in 1995. The city's adult-zoning resolution banned adult establishments from all but a small number of high-density commercial districts and largely restricted their location to manufacturing districts (Simon 1995, 190). In addition, adult establishments must be located five hundred feet from schools, day care centers, houses of worship, and residences and five hundred feet apart from other such establishments.[19] The zoning ordinance essentially forced "sex shops to switch neighborhoods," and many relocated to the outer boroughs' manufacturing zones, including Sunset Park's industrial waterfront (Long 2007).[20]

The 1995 zoning resolution contributed to a flourishing red-light district along Sunset Park's 3rd Avenue, where once only a few adult video stores and bars dotted the waterfront.[21] The presence of prostitutes became commonplace as the numbers of adult establishments, particularly topless lounges, increased (Allam 2005). To discourage adult establishments in the mixed-use and dense residential neighborhood, Chinese clergy once sought to seed the neighborhood with houses of worship (Cohen 1996b). A particularly egregious and horrific example of the lethal collusion of police misconduct, the presence of adult establishments, and a multilane surface road cutting through a residential neighborhood occurred in August 2001. Upon completing his shift, Joseph Gray, a fifteen-year veteran of the New York City Police Department at the local 72nd Precinct, began a twelve-hour drinking binge that was joined at various points by fellow officers. As Gray headed home, he sped through a red light and slammed his minivan into three pedestrians as they crossed 3rd Avenue at 46th Street. Twenty-four-year-old Maria Herrera, who was eight and a half months pregnant, was killed along with her four-year-old-son, Andy, and sixteen-year-old sister, Dilcia Peña (Jones and Flynn 2001). Gray's daylong drinking binge started with several beers in front of the station house and then moved to the topless bar, Wild Wild West, a few blocks away.[22]

Some argue that even without the city's zoning initiative, the prevalence of Internet pornography and a heated real estate market would have displaced sex shops from their midtown Manhattan location (Stern 1999). Even so, the Times Square Business Improvement District (BID) director praised the 1995 zoning change because "no neighborhood will ever again have to suffer the abuses that Times Square did."[23] However, city land-use policies helped reconfigure the urban landscape by dumping "unsavory" uses in less premium neighborhoods. Community Board 7 (2013) notes the "proliferation of adult entertainment establishments along 3rd Avenue" in its Statement of Needs, and a June 2013 article in the neighborhood newspaper *Home Reporter* on a proposed "adult toy store" documents the continuing struggle with adult entertainment businesses (Romano 2013).

Sunset Park's sex industry is, however, not limited to adult establishments along the waterfront. Community leaders note that an increasing number of Sunset Park's beauty salons on 8th Avenue offer massages and serve as storefronts for prostitution (Wong 2004; Lee 2000). In addition to beauty salons, the recent proliferation of spas and massage parlors in Manhattan Chinatown, Flushing, Sunset Park, and Bay Ridge has been covered by mainstream media, including the *New York Times* (Berger 2013a, 2013b). In July

2013, the New York City Police Department arrested nineteen immigrant Chinese and Korean massage parlor employees (fifteen of whom are women) and charged ten with prostitution or promoting prostitution. Because of their immigrant status, the Brooklyn District Attorney's Office plans to investigate whether the women are victims of sex trafficking. The arrests resulted from a police investigation of nineteen massage parlors in Bay Ridge and Dyker Heights—neighborhoods surrounding Sunset Park and located in South Brooklyn. The nineteen businesses, located in a six-block area, had late hours and advertised erotic services on the Internet (Berger 2013b).

A quick scan of a June 2013 issue of the *Sing Tao* newspaper, a major Chinese-language daily, resulted in several ads for massages by "pretty, young girls."[24] The advertisements included a telephone contact but no address to a brick-and-mortar establishment, because according to reporter James Lim (2013) of *World Journal* (another Chinese-language daily), the massages are provided in private apartments and houses in Sunset Park. Similar to what was described in a 2003 article titled "Globalization's Underside: Sex Trafficking in Brooklyn," which featured a Chinese brothel operating in a Sunset Park row house (Hoffman 2003), Lim (2013) stated that the typical arrangement in these ads consists of one or two women and a guard "who helps to bring customers" to a private residence.

New York City sex workers are largely invisible because they work indoors, and a 2005 study found that 40 percent are immigrant women "woven into most neighborhoods" (Urban Justice Center 2005, 3). Sunset Park's underground sex industry is based on immigrant women working indoors not only in private residences but also in restaurants and laundromats, which convert into dance halls or places for prostitution at night. Sunset Park resident and anthropologist Cynthia Ruiz is researching Latina sex workers in Sunset Park (Ruiz 2013). She described her recent fieldwork at a local restaurant, where men were seated at tables and a woman went to each table and allowed the men to grope her. She carried a jar to collect the men's tips for this service. Ruiz noted that the woman earned $30 on average for a half hour of work, which is significantly greater than average Sunset Park wages. In similarly dense working-class immigrant neighborhoods such as Jackson Heights and Corona in Queens, the distribution of "chica chica" cards advertise scantily clad women and dance halls. As an integral site of immigrant laborers, including significant populations of both Chinese and Mexican male workers, these neighborhoods are part of the global network of human smuggling and sex trafficking (Kwong 1997). The proliferation of a sex industry in its public and less visible forms in Sunset Park is an outcome not only of city zoning but also of the international trafficking of women (Raymond and Hughes 2001).

Organizing for Environmental Justice

The cumulative impact of these burdens contributed to a dismal environment that threatened public health and politicized many Sunset Park residents. As Clean Air Ambassador David Galarza described in his 2013 Earthjustice narrative,

> I grew up in the shadow of the Gowanus Expressway in Sunset Park, Brooklyn. The noisy, congested, soot-spewing highway physically cut us off from the rest of the neighborhood and no doubt created many generations of children and adults afflicted by asthma, other respiratory diseases and high concentrations of lead in the surrounding air and soil. Add a waste transfer station or two and a proposed sludge treatment plant on the waterfront and *Sunset Park had all the toxic ingredients needed to wage a war against environmental injustice.* (Galarza n.d., my emphasis)

As a neighborhood with a long and extensive history of environmental injustice, Sunset Park has cultivated a strong organizational infrastructure and leadership to engage in battle. This infrastructure includes UPROSE's Elizabeth Yeampierre and the New York City Environmental Justice Alliance's Eddie Bautista, dynamic Puerto Rican civil rights activists who are also a married couple and residents of Sunset Park. Few Sunset Park community-based organizations have an explicit commitment to environmental justice that is deeply rooted in the neighborhood's working-class, multiracial diversity. UPROSE is a notable exception. Under Yeampierre's leadership, UPROSE cultivates multiracial community engagement in deliberative democracy and political mobilization on issues of environmental and racial justice, sustainable development, and youth leadership.[25] UPROSE's commitment to neighborhood diversity is evident in its staff and membership, which includes Latinos, Asians, and Palestinians.

A frequent UPROSE partner during his fifteen-year tenure as the Brooklyn director of the Chinese American Planning Council (CPC), Chang Xie (2013) said that his motivation to collaborate with Yeampierre was due to his concern that the Chinese community is similarly impacted by environmental hazards and risks, "just like the Latino community." Xie described the health risks posed by the Gowanus Expressway, "which generates pollution and dust." All Sunset Park residents live with high volumes of truck traffic due to the industrial and warehouse waterfront. According to Xie, these substandard environmental conditions and public health hazards were "a constant topic" for the Sunset Park Health Council (SPHC) on which Xie continues to serve as a Board of Directors member. As president of the SPHC, Reverend Samuel Wong consistently raises concerns about the potential toxic impact of Sunset Park's industrial landscape on community health. Although the SPHC does not have the capacity to conduct research and is unaware of any formal studies that document Sunset Park's environmental burdens and rates of asthma and cancer, Xie noted that "the concern about the correlation of the neighborhood environment and the health issues in the community is constantly being raised. In fact, they have been raised all the years of my participation on the board."

In addition to shared concerns about Sunset Park's disproportionate environmental burdens, Xie and Yeampierre prioritize youth training and cultivating youth leadership, particularly in regard to environmental justice issues. Given the immigrant status, language barriers, and urgent survival issues of Chinese immigrants, Xie notes that they tend not to be involved with social justice campaigns. However, he argues that institutional leadership "needs to step up" to commit resources and build organizational relations that engage in "critical community education and outreach." Most important according to Xie is the need to educate and involve young people because they are in diverse environments in the public schools and other neighborhood spaces daily. Engaging youths and cultivating a consciousness about multiracial Sunset Park and environment justice means that "down the road, their actions and involvement will impact on the parents" (Xie 2013).

During his directorship, Xie collaborated with Yeampierre on funding proposals to promote community adoption of clean energy practices, such as hybrid buses. Xie attended numerous meetings to brainstorm ideas and strategies for community education and campaigns on issues, including clean air. Their shared commitment to multiracial youth leadership led to CPC attendance at UPROSE youth focus groups and organizational meetings. The CPC and UPROSE youths also participated in collaborative projects, such as video productions about the environmental conditions of Sunset Park (see Chapter 5). This cross-fertilization of youth activists is critical to building community in multiracial Sunset Park. Yeampierre frequently recounts the astonished expressions of Community Board 7 members when Asian and Latino youths from the CPC and UPROSE acknowledged each other in a friendly manner at a community meeting. This simple act visibly unnerved Community Board 7 members, because even a nascent multiracial youth alliance, according to Yeampierre, posed a threat to the status quo (Yeampierre 2006).

The Future of Manufacturing in Postindustrial New York

Described as the "last self-contained industrial ecosystem in New York City," Sunset Park serves a central role in anchoring and sustaining a manufacturing presence in the city (McGowan 1999). Sunset Park's historic prominence in industrial manufacturing, extensive rail and waterfront infrastructure, and location near key regional surface transportation nodes establishes it as the "last safe industrial neighborhood" in New York City (Bartolomeo 2004). U.S. manufacturing sectors, including New York City's concentrations in garment and printing, have greatly diminished and continue to decline in terms of the number of firms and the size of the workforce. Recognizing that industrial production remains an employment source for low-skill workers and immigrants, the Bloomberg administration initiated several programs to sustain manufacturing. These initiatives designate industrial zones and seek to modernize industrial spaces to support manufacturing that is viable and suited to urban markets. Mass production is long gone—modern manufacturing is based on small firms that produce artisanal and high value-added goods, engage in skilled craft production processes, and require proximity to elite consumer markets. Despite putative job-creation goals for a low-skill workforce, it is uncertain that New York City's modern manufacturing niches will incorporate large numbers of workers. Bloomberg's reindustrialization strategies build on branding New York City and meeting the demands of elite consumers for locally produced luxury items. Industrial policy is not so much about jobs retention or creation but instead promotes a form of niche production consistent with the gentrified landscape and elite consumption of an entrepreneurial city.

New York City has a long and ambivalent relationship with industrial manufacturing (Fitch 1993; Moody 2007). Segregating and removing industrial uses from Manhattan's central business districts were objectives of the 1916 zoning regulations adopted by New York City, the first municipality in the United States to adopt land-use rules (Maantay 2002). Since then, there have been periodic calls to amend the city's zoning regulations to shrink the landmass dedicated to manufacturing uses. During the 1960s, approximately 1.7 million industrial jobs were located on twenty thousand acres of land zoned for manufacturing. By the early 1990s industrial jobs dropped to less than half, even though the percentage of land zoned for industrial uses fell by only 5 percent. Critics argued that manufacturing zones essentially banked acres of land that could be better used for housing and commercial development (Wylde 2005; Armstrong and Lind 2005). Industrial retention advocates, on the other hand, contend that manufacturing is viable, provides employment opportunities for an immigrant labor force, and creates higher-paying jobs than services and retail (Friedman 2009).

Although industrial retention was not a priority economic development goal, Mayor Bloomberg announced with great fanfare the appointment of an industry czar and the creation of the Mayor's Office of Industrial and Manufacturing Businesses in 2005 (New York City Economic Development Corporation 2005a). Based on an NYCEDC-commissioned real estate study that found low vacancy rates in the city's manufacturing districts, Bloomberg (2005) issued the report "Protecting and Growing New York City's Industrial Job Base." The policy centerpiece was the designation of Industrial Business Zones (IBZs), which were largely intended to replace the 1978 city-designated in-place industrial parks. A priority task for the new industry czar was to negotiate specific IBZ street boundaries with property owners and other stakeholders. Periodic review of IBZ boundaries is mandated by the New York City administrative code, and an IBZ Boundary Commission consisting of elected officials and city agency representatives conducted a review in the summer of 2012.[26]

As a single point of coordination, the Mayor's Office of Industrial and Manufacturing Businesses consolidated information and access to varied city, state, and federal business assistance programs, including tax credits, tax exemptions, relocation grants, and energy savings programs. To promote a supportive and industry-friendly environment, the Mayor's Office of Industrial and Manufacturing Businesses coordinated the multiple city agencies (DSNY, Department of Transportation, etc.) that are involved in the operations and regulation of small businesses. Initially located in the New York City Department of Small Business Services, the Mayor's Office of Industrial and Manufacturing Businesses was recently subsumed by the NYCEDC.

The most significant purpose of IBZs is a no-rezoning guarantee in which the city promises to prohibit the rezoning of industrial land within these areas for residential use. In effect, the mayor's policy officiated the removal of industrial manufacturing from Manhattan, as all sixteen IBZs are located in Brooklyn, Queens, and the Bronx. Moreover, IBZs represent only a fraction of the city's areas zones for manufacturing.[27] In other words, a majority of the city's manufacturing zones are not protected by the city's promise not to rezone for residential or commercial uses. In addition to the IBZs, three Industrial Ombudsman Areas were defined—Manhattan's Midtown Garment Center, Brooklyn's Greenpoint-Williamsburg, and Howland Hook in Staten Island. While an Ombudsman Area designation provides support to neighborhood industrial businesses, these neighborhoods also do not benefit from the city's "ironclad commitment" to prohibit rezoning.[28]

A 1993 New York City DCP study found that Manhattan's Garment Center was the densest manufacturing employment area, with 676 manufacturing jobs per acre. The Garment Center had been designated a special zoning district in 1987 to help sustain the industry by requiring that half the space in manufacturing buildings be used for production-related purposes. However, as office towers saturated Midtown Manhattan, real estate investors and corporate tenants moved steadily into the Garment Center, and city policies accommodated this economic reality by permitting the conversion of industrial buildings into office uses (Bleyer 2007; Cardwell 2007; Bagli 1989; Prokesch 1993). For example, the Hudson Yards Special District incorporated several blocks within the Special Garment Center District for high-density commercial development.[29] While greatly diminished, the Midtown Garment Center remains a central manufacturing hub in New York City, but the Garment Center's exclusion from IBZ designation signaled the reclaiming of Manhattan's industrial land for "more promising uses" (Prokesch 1993). Today, the Midtown Garment Center is no longer listed as an IBZ Ombudsman Area on the NYCEDC website. Moreover, the Fashion Center BID is aggressively seeking to rebrand the former industrial production zone to reflect an emergent and diverse creative sector featuring fashion showrooms, hoteliers, visual arts and design firms, and architecture and high-tech firms (Pasquarelli 2012; Ohrstrom 2008).

Sunset Park's industrial waterfront makes up the bulk of the Southwest Brooklyn IBZ, which includes neighboring Red Hook and represents the city's largest IBZ.[30] Sunset Park's waterfront is also a New York State Empire Zone, providing a variety of state tax incentives for business establishment and expansion.[31] The city's industrial policy to "protect and grow" industrial businesses essentially centralized resources and services that were in place prior to the introduction of IBZs (Bloomberg 2005). Except for a one-time tax credit for industrial businesses relocating within New York City, IBZs as a tool to grow and retain industrial manufacturing is fairly limited, and much of the policy's teeth is solely premised on a city promise or "strong statement" to preserve industrial space by disallowing residential uses (Foggin 2006, 19). Since IBZs have no long-term legal protection, the next administration can simply change the zoning through the usual land-use review process (Pratt Center for Community Development 2008). Industrial advocates, including local elected officials, sought to codify IBZs as industrial employment districts that prohibit as-of-right nonindustrial uses, such as hotels and big-box retail in manufacturing zones. The New York City Council Resolution 141 of 2006 sought to do this by revising the city's zoning regulations to overlay industrial employment districts over IBZ boundaries (Lander 2006). But the Bloomberg administration resisted this more substantive "ironclad" mechanism to protect industrial "safe havens" (New York City Council 2006). As the assistant director of the Mayor's Office of Industrial and Manufacturing Businesses stated in his testimony at the September 19, 2006, New York City Council public hearing on Resolution 141,

> While we support the spirit of Resolution 141, we believe that IBZs will offer the same protection, as well as affording greater flexibility to make strategic land use decisions in particular areas of the City when required, to meet our overall best economic development interests. *We believe that it is premature to move toward more restrictive zoning measures.* (New York City Council 2006, 14, my emphasis)

New York City's desire for "greater flexibility" in IBZ land-use decisions has resulted in numerous nonindustrial developments in Sunset Park. The absence of an ironclad prohibition of nonindustrial uses has allowed several hotels to locate on Sunset Park's industrial waterfront. In addition to standard hotels, Sunset Park's "first and only luxury 4 star" and hip-hop–inspired hotel, Hotel BPM, opened in August 2012 and hopes to attract creative types drawn to the neighborhood's emergent music recording and artists' scene.[32] Rather than eliminating as-of-right hotel development, the Bloomberg administration considered a special permit requirement for large (rather than boutique) hotels in IBZs "to ensure the hotels meet the goals and intent of the zones" (New York City Small Business Services 2011).

The Mayor's Office of Industrial and Manufacturing Businesses is no longer headed by an industry czar and has been stripped of its prominence as an office of the mayor with a director and staff. The preservation of New York City's industrial zones and manufacturing sectors are now the province of an industrial desk at the NYCEDC's Center for Economic Transformation.[33] More important, Bloomberg's recent new initiatives to support industrial businesses have an overriding message that the NYCEDC is remaking industrial sites as places of innovation and creativity rather than places that support immigrant industrial workers and production, and this policy message has particular resonance for Sunset Park—one of the city's few remaining industrial centers. As stated in the 2009 Vision Plan for Sunset Park's waterfront, "Today, the main challenge is to figure out ways to adapt and re-use this antiquated industrial infrastructure, and develop Sunset Park into a *21st century model for diverse, dense and environmentally-sustainable industry*" (New York City Economic Development Corporation 2009, 6, my emphasis).

Based on New York City's competitive advantages of location, market size, and branding, the Bloomberg administration and the NYCEDC are banking on "modern" manufacturing industries such as specialty foods, customized furniture, and green manufacturing that are craft-based and high value added.[34] As noted in an April 2012 issue of *New York* magazine on Brooklyn's artisanal manufacturers, "This is not the Brooklyn on your map but a notional place consisting mainly of the western 'creative crescent' that arcs from Greenpoint south to Gowanus and runs on freelance design work and single-origin, crop-to-cup pour-over coffee."[35] Epitomizing Sunset Park's emergent role in Brooklyn's postindustrial manufacturing sector is the establishment of a new factory in the Brooklyn Army Terminal by the world-famous chocolatier Jacques Torres. Although preferred locations for creative commercial spaces with premium cache include Brooklyn's Williamsburg and DUMBO areas, Sunset Park's relatively cheap commercial rents are a compelling draw. In describing the selection of Sunset Park as the location for his modern, new factory, Jacques Torres stated, "You know, it's actually not a bad neighborhood. You can go there and not get shot" (Gray 2012).

To cultivate and promote an artisanal economy in Sunset Park, the Bloomberg administration has proposed two new initiatives to retrofit the physical industrial infrastructure. The first initiative is to modernize and create "right-sized" industrial spaces by subdividing large factory floor plates to accommodate small firms. Large factories met the spatial requirements of a past manufacturing era, and now the city needs to rehab dilapidated industrial buildings and carve out flexible smaller spaces for a "small-batch miniboom" (Kusisto 2012; see also Berger 2012; Wallace 2012). New York City has allocated $8 million to the City Council Small Manufacturing Investment Fund to renovate privately held vacant industrial spaces, which must also include a long-term restrictive covenant (New York City Small Business Services 2011). The second initiative is to provide funds to support small innovative food entrepreneurs. Based on a $10 million capitalization grant by Goldman Sachs, the NYCEDC and Goldman Sachs will provide loans and technical assistance to aspiring food entrepreneurs to grow their production capacity.

Notwithstanding Sunset Park's strategic status as a premier urban industrial district, the renovation and reuse of Federal Building #2 is illustrative of the NYCEDC's openness to use "innovative strategies" to expand "allowable non-residential uses," which may portend waterfront retail and commercial uses (New York City Economic Development Corporation 2009).[36] Once a vacant eight-story, 1.1 million-square-foot industrial building, Federal Building #2 was built in 1916 as a military warehouse. In 2006, the NYCEDC proposed a private-public partnership between the multinational development firm Time Equities and the Brooklyn Economic Development Corporation to develop a "Sunset Marketplace" of nearly 2 million square feet of light industrial, retail, and office space (New York City Economic Development Corporation 2007b). Despite IBZ designation and the Community Board 7 197-a plan, which prioritized industrial retention for the waterfront area, the Times Equities partnership promoted Sunset Marketplace as a "unique lifestyle retail development."[37] Advocates raised concerns that the partnership's proposal designated less than half of Federal Building #2's square footage for light manufacturing (Engquist and Sollars 2008; Egeln 2008a). This NYCEDC sponsored project would have introduced close to a million square feet of retail and office space in an industrial zone. Even though Times Equities invested more than $1 million for engineering and design studies, the collapse of the U.S. housing market and the related financial crisis in 2008 led to the firm's withdrawal from the project in early 2009 (Pincus 2009). Poor financing and market conditions killed the proposed transformative retail and commercial project rather than the city's "ironclad" commitment to industrial retention.

In reissuing a request for proposals to renovate and reuse Federal Building #2, the NYCEDC emphasized the creation of affordable industrial space and expanded light manufacturing uses to include technology and media start-ups and art studios. In 2011, the federal government transferred Federal Building #2 to NYCEDC, which then sold the building to Salmar Properties LLC for $10 million with a thirty-year deed restriction based on 85 percent of the building being used for light manufacturing and only 15 percent being used for retail space. Salmar Properties LLC has completed a $34 million renovation for a state-of-the-art industrial center, Liberty View Industrial Plaza, which the developer anticipates will create more than one thousand jobs (Kaysen 2012). The global real estate firm CBRE has developed a marketing campaign centered on a "Make It in Brooklyn" theme aimed at artisanal manufacturers and other creative production industries.[38]

Salmar Properties LLC is partnering with BrightFarms to construct the world's largest rooftop garden on one hundred thousand square feet of

Federal Building #2's rooftop space (Foderaro 2012). The multiacre hydroponic greenhouse is slated for construction in the spring of 2014 and is anticipated to produce one million pounds of produce—including tomatoes, lettuces, and herbs—annually (Foderaro 2012). BrightFarms locates near or on the properties of local supermarkets to reduce transportation costs and emissions. Once this commercial rooftop farm is operational, it will greatly expand New York City's urban agricultural farms and Brooklyn's local food scene.

Even as its premier urban industrial district, the Bloomberg administration was agnostic at best about industrial retention in Sunset Park. Despite the New York City's claim that IBZs would protect and preserve manufacturing jobs that are vital to low-skilled and immigrant New Yorkers, the policy essentially repackaged existing small business assistance programs. By refusing to codify and adopt advocates' proposals for industrial employment districts, the city sent a signal that it wanted the flexibility to sidetrack its promise not to rezone manufacturing areas. The NYCEDC seized the opportunity to modernize and subdivide New York City's industrial infrastructure to accommodate high value-added sectors in the creative economy, food production, media, and high technology—preferred industries of the Bloomberg administration that fit a rebranded luxury city (Brash 2011). The local urban growth machine—which includes property owners, developers, and realtors—is eager to advance Sunset Park's transformation to Brooklyn's vibrant industrial neighborhood with artisanal manufacturers and creative entrepreneurs (Kavanaugh 2012; Gray 2012; Stein 2009). The city's remaking of Sunset Park as a sustainable urban industrial district is consistent with waterfront transformation strategies in Williamsburg and Long Island City, particularly in terms of the deafening silence on employment opportunities for the local Latino and Asian immigrant workforce.

Immigrant entrepreneurs are lauded for their small businesses, which have sustained New York City's diverse economy and absorbed thousands of immigrant workers. However, economic development policies to advance the city's future, including a postmanufacturing future, make no reference to the numerous Chinese businesses located along the waterfront. May Chen, who retired as international vice president of UNITE HERE and manager of Local 23-25, has noted Mayor Bloomberg's lack of interest in preserving New York City's garment industry. About a decade or so ago, key industry stakeholders discussed a proposal to relocate Manhattan Chinatown's garment industry to the Brooklyn Army Terminal in Sunset Park. The ferry from the 58th Street pier to Lower Manhattan would make visits and quality control inspections by buyers and manufacturers very convenient. Chen (2010) said that Bloomberg rejected this proposal because he wanted high-value uses that would cater to "Wall Street commuters." Bloomberg's economic development policies, including his reindustrialization initiatives, do not consider how immigrant economies have anchored neighborhood revitalization and buffered the city during periods of economic decline.

"This Harbor Will Never Again Be the Epicenter of the World"

The Port of New York and New Jersey, which includes New York Harbor,[39] ranks as the largest container traffic center on the East Coast and the third largest in the nation, behind California's Long Angeles and Long Beach ports (U.S. Census Bureau 2012, 683). Consisting of numerous ports in New Jersey (Port Elizabeth, Port Newark, Port Jersey, and the Peninsula at Bayonne Harbor) and New York (Staten Island's reactivated Howland Hook Marine Terminal, now known as the New York Container Terminal, as well as Brooklyn's Red Hook Container Terminal, the Erie Basin Barge Port, and the South Brooklyn Marine Terminal [SBMT] in Sunset Park), the Port of New York and New Jersey is forecast to see a fourfold growth in international trade and cargo shipments from three million TEU (twenty-foot equivalent unit) to eleven million TEU by 2060 (Halcrow et al. 2005, 21).[40] The Port Authority of New York and New Jersey plans to expand port capacity to handle the record-setting cargo volume, which is largely the result of trade with Asia (Lipton 2004; McGeehan 2005). New channel construction in the Panama Canal will reduce shipping costs for supersize freight containers originating in Asia and traveling to the East Coast rather than the West Coast of the United States (Schwartz 2012; Babin 2012). Since New Jersey ports are reaching capacity, growth in New York City is possible, with much of it taking place on the Staten Island and Sunset Park waterfronts (Hawkins 2010; Genn 2005; Bagli 2006). Currently, Sunset Park's role in New York City's port economy centers on processing city garbage and importing luxury automobiles.

The largest volume of exports from the Port of New York and New Jersey are scrap or waste paper, scrap metal, wood pulp, and chemicals, described as "some of the grimiest remnants of modern-day life" (Anon. 2008d).[41] Much of the exported waste paper is consumed by China, the world's largest purchaser of recovered paper. According to Georgia Institute of Technology economists, the "U.S. alone accounted for 44% of all waste paper imported to China" (Zhuang, Ding, and Li 2008). Robert Fitch (1993, 259) stated that this port activity demonstrates "the poverty of post-industrial life in New York." While Americans import "everything from the sneakers on [our] feet to the food on [our] tables," we export waste products, scrap metal, and used automobiles. Sunset Park is a key site in this global network of processing garbage and recycled materials.

A legacy of the Bloomberg administration will be how it changed the way New York City handles the nearly twelve million tons of trash generated annually. The 2001 closure of the Fresh Kills landfill marked the first time that New York City did not bury or burn its garbage within the city's boundaries (Sze 2007, 112). Adopted in 2006, a modified ten-year Solid Waste Management Plan (SWMP) will export nearly all of New York City's garbage. Rather than continuing to rely on waste transfer stations clustered in the city's poor minority neighborhoods, the plan's two key recommendations involve (1) each borough handling its own waste and (2) switching from a truck-based garbage export system to a rail or barge-based export system. Mayor Bloomberg's SWMP adopted key principals of fair share or borough equity and truck traffic reduction based on the recommendations of a report prepared by a coalition of environmental justice organizations in consultation with the Consumer Policy Institute (Warren 2000). The passage of Bloomberg's SWMP was widely viewed as an environmental justice victory.[42] The SWMP redirects the city's daily twelve thousand tons of residential waste to local transfer stations in each borough, which would be responsible for handling their own trash, and employs railcars and barges rather than trucks to transport city garbage to landfills in upstate New York, Pennsylvania, Ohio, and Virginia (Murphy 2006a).

Sunset Park's Hamilton Marine Transfer Station (MTS) is part of the mayor's SWMP and is one of four MTSs that will be retrofitted to handle the city's waste. Toward the goal of equity in environmental burdens, Sunset Park will handle the residential trash generated by ten of Brooklyn's eighteen community districts, estimated at a total daily tonnage of more than 3,544 tons of garbage, as well as limited amounts of commercial waste.[43] Borough equity (fair share principle) as a goal was underscored by UPROSE's Elizabeth Yeampierre at a 2007 DSNY public hearing on the retrofitting of the Hamilton MTS. As Yeampierre warned, "We really believe that when the Mayor decided to push the Solid Waste Management Plan, we thought that it was a victory for the environmental justice community. How you treat the community will be a reflection of whether or not those promises are kept." Yeampierre proceeded to reiterate unresolved community concerns regarding the transfer station's capacity, truck traffic volume, and pollution emissions. Since Sunset Park is an overburdened neighborhood, Yeampierre noted, "This is an EJ community that accepted it [a retrofitted Hamilton MTS] in the interest of justice and fair play."[44]

A central fair-share component of New York City's SWMP entails the $240 million construction of the East 91st Street MTS located in the affluent Upper East Side neighborhood of Manhattan, currently the only borough without a marine transfer station. Even though the East 91st Street MTS would handle only a fraction of Manhattan's trash, community opposition (including nearly all local elected officials) has been relentless, as evidenced by seven lawsuits filed since 2006 (Taylor 2013). Coordinating much of the opposition is Residents for Sane Trash Solutions, founded by a lifelong resident and president of a boutique brokerage firm who is concerned about the project's impact on neighborhood property values (Kapalan 2013).[45]

Despite federal approvals, a lawsuit is pending before the New York State Supreme Court. Notably, Residents for Sane Trash Solutions claims that the proposed waste transfer station is located in Yorkville *and* East Harlem in an effort to align the Upper East Side neighborhood with the historic Puerto Rican community, which has shouldered a disproportionate share of environmental burdens similar to other low-income communities of color, including Sunset Park. This underhanded strategy elicited a written response by Melissa Mark-Viverito, a New York City Council member who represents East Harlem–El Barrio, titled "Taking on Our Fair Share of the City's Waste Burden." In her response, Mark-Viverito chides the organization for "exploiting East Harlem" and notes that seventy-nine East Harlem service organizations support the SWMP and East 91st Street waste transfer station because "by switching waste export from a truck-based to a barge-based approach, this marine transfer station would help clean the air in East Harlem" (Mark-Viverito 2012).

Sunset Park's deep natural harbor and proximity to the open ocean presents an opportunity for port expansion, and an NYCEDC-approved project for the SBMT further affirms Sunset Park's key role in the "multinational waste trade" (Sze 2007). For more than two decades after ceasing operations in 1985 as a container shipping port, Sunset Park's 110-acre SBMT, located between 29th and 39th Streets, served primarily as a tow pound for the New York City Police Department. Since the late 1980s, the 39th Street pier portion of the SBMT has housed a break-bulk stevedoring operation that represents the nation's third-largest entry point for cocoa beans (Yarrow 1991; Onishi 1994). The majority 88 acres of the SBMT has been reactivated for two NYCEDC projects that encapsulate Sunset Park's role in a port economy—first as a processing site for the city's recyclable waste and second as a major port for imported luxury automobiles.

To facilitate the recycling of twelve thousand tons of daily residential garbage produced by New Yorkers, the Bloomberg administration engaged the Sims Municipal Recycling—one of the country's largest scrap metal processors—to build a new state-of-the-art $45 million recycling plant on the SBMT.[46] Completed in December 2013, the Sunset Park Material Recovery Facility receives and processes *all* metal, glass, and plastic and a portion of mixed paper collected by the DSNY as part of New York City's residential curbside recycling program. Although 75 percent of this tonnage is transported by barge to Sunset Park, an additional twenty-eight DSNY collection trucks making twelve daily inbound and outbound trips is necessary. With the new recycling facility and planned reactivation of the Hamilton MTS, Sunset Park is clearly shouldering more than its fair share to improve the city's air quality and reduce the number of trucks used to transport trash in favor of barges, even if this means that daily citywide truck traffic will converge on neighborhood streets in order to unload waste at Sunset Park's waterfront facilities.

The reactivated SBMT will also be the site for an automobile-processing facility designated "America's Automotive Gateway."[47] In early November 2004, the NYCEDC entered an agreement with the Atlanta-based Axis Group Inc. to lease and develop a modern automobile-processing facility (New York City Economic Development Corporation 2007a). The Axis Group is a unit of Allied Holdings, which is a specialized trucking company and the largest transporter of new vehicles in the United States. The Axis Group is leasing seventy-four acres for twenty years with two five-year extensions to develop and operate an auto-processing facility to finish new imported cars destined for wholesale distribution. The company plans to use ocean vessels and rail barges to transport vehicles from the SBMT's general cargo marine terminal to New Jersey railheads and distribution centers. In addition to auto processing, the Axis Group plans to hire a general stevedore to market the facility for other types of maritime cargo.

To prepare the SBMT site for these new developments, the NYCEDC spent more than $80 million to reconstruct and rehabilitate several bulkheads, modernize rail connections to the 65th Street rail yard, and complete other essential infrastructure repairs (New York City Economic Development Corporation 2010). Despite NYCEDC fanfare about the revitalization of a working waterfront and related job creation, the actual numbers of new jobs are quite modest. For example, the NYCEDC initially projected that the Brooklyn Cruise Terminal in neighboring Red Hook would result in six hundred jobs through direct and indirect creation; however, only fifteen full-time jobs were ultimately created.[48] Based on this track record, there is much skepticism about the employment projections for Sunset Park's port-related developments. Congressman Jerrold Nadler, a longtime advocate of sustaining and expanding New York's port facilities, warned in a memo on the Axis Group project that "The job creation numbers are illusory. The real job creation numbers are probably about 15–20 new jobs, not the 300 EDC claims. Do not believe the numbers for job creation, like the cruise terminal the job numbers are illusory."[49]

Sunset Park's existing maritime-related infrastructure and assets, including a natural deep harbor, presents the potential to expand container port capacity and maintain the Port of New York and New Jersey's competitive position relative to two other Atlantic ports: Norfolk, Virginia, and Halifax, Nova Scotia. While there are currently no active container port facilities, the prospect of utilizing Sunset Park's deep harbor to accommodate a new container port is dependent on two controversial transportation projects—construction of a 5.5-mile cross-harbor freight tunnel underneath New York Harbor and the replacement of the Gowanus Expressway, a section of Interstate Highway 278 that provides key east-west linkages in a regional transportation network. A cross-harbor freight tunnel would provide a second Hudson River crossing that connects freight railroads in Jersey City, New Jersey, to Sunset Park and enable freight to access destinations east of the Hudson River by rail rather than by truck. For freight to cross the Hudson River by rail today, it must travel 140 miles north of New York City to a rail bridge crossing at Selkirk.

A cross-harbor freight tunnel would reduce overdependence on trucks, resulting in less traffic congestion and air pollution, and would improve the movement of goods in the region. However, the project would include construction of an intermodal rail yard (rail to truck transfer terminal) in Maspeth, Queens, that entails eminent domain and the displacement of numerous small industrial businesses as well as filling in two waterways—the Maspeth Creek and some of Newtown Creek. Surrounding communities have voiced strong objections to the cross-harbor freight tunnel, and although the NYCEDC completed a draft environmental impact statement in 2004, the project remains in the study phase.[50]

There has been much debate about a permanent solution to the Gowanus Expressway—a Robert Moses relic that severed neighborhood waterfront access, compromised environmental conditions by spewing particulate matter into the air, and carries two hundred thousand vehicles a day (see Chapter 2). While one of the replacement options includes a costly tunnel, the deteriorating Gowanus Expressway is currently undergoing redecking and rehabilitation to extend its useful life for another ten to fifteen years, and a permanent solution is not anticipated for years (New York State Department of Transportation 2006).[51]

Despite the Bloomberg administration's five-year effort to evict American Stevedoring and redevelop Piers 7–10 (adjacent to the Brooklyn Cruise Terminal) for a tourist-friendly complex with a marina, a beer garden, restaurants, and an art gallery, the Port Authority of New York and New Jersey decided not to sell the Brooklyn piers and in April 2008 extended American Stevedoring's lease for ten years (Bagli 2008a). Since American Stevedoring will continue to operate several cargo terminals in Red Hook, some community leaders expressed concern that the pressure to establish a container port at the larger Sunset Park site, as proposed in the 1999 strategic plan for the redevelopment of the Port of New York, is lessened (Wiley 2008a). The NYCEDC's developments on SBMT, such as the long-term lease with Axis Group for an automobile-processing facility, have been criticized by Congressman Nadler as "eliminating any hope for container facilities in the future." He laments that "it seems as if the City is not interested in these jobs or this industry."[52]

Greening Sunset Park

Typical of working-poor communities of color, Sunset Park has little public green space. Even with its namesake 24-acre park, Sunset Park has only 0.45 acres of open space per 1,000 residents, significantly below the borough average of 2 acres per 1,000 residents.[53] The lack of open space is an issue of environmental equity for the Sunset Park neighborhood. With the exception of the Brooklyn Army Terminal Pier 4 at 58th Street, there is no public access to Sunset Park's waterfront. Since the early 1990s, a park has been envisioned as part of a mixed-use maritime industrial waterfront. Sunset Park's waterfront, however, is dotted with brownfield sites as a result of industrial use and illegal dumping of construction and demolition debris as well as liquid wastes, such as oils, oil sludges, and wastewater.

Public funding for the remediation and redevelopment of Bush Terminal Piers 1–5 along 43rd to 51st Streets for a waterfront park was secured in 2006 (New York City Economic Development Corporation 2006). This area was used in the mid-1970s as a landfill for hazardous materials and is now classified as a Class 3 inactive hazardous waste disposal site. Even though residential housing is located within fifteen hundred feet of the brownfield site, the only public safety measure since the 1980s was a perimeter chain link fence.[54] The NYCEDC is coordinating this $36 million project, one of the largest brownfield remediation efforts in New York state's history. Work is currently under way, and the Bush Terminal Pier Park with panoramic waterfront views is expected to open in the spring of 2014. Because of a $2 million cost overrun in site remediation, the NYCEDC has scaled back on planned park amenities. This action is consistent with Sunset Park's history of environment injustice and was noted by Community Board 7. The city permitted the dumping of toxic materials in Sunset Park during the 1970s, and now "it is insulting that our playground, environmental center and active pier" have been taken out of the first phase of park development (Community Board 7 2013, 184).

Efforts to green Sunset Park's industrial waterfront also entail the neighborhood's inclusion in a statewide initiative to create a continuous eighteen-mile greenway for pedestrians and cyclists from Newton Creek in Greenpoint to the Shore Parkway Greenway in Bay Ridge. Much of this shoreline is currently inaccessible and underutilized. The plan to landscape and create a pedestrian path and bike lane along Brooklyn's waterfront is supported by New York state's Local Waterfront Revitalization Program and coordinated by the Brooklyn Waterfront Greenway Taskforce—a coalition of community groups, elected officials, and planning organizations, including the Regional Plan Association.

The Bush Terminal Pier Park and the Brooklyn Waterfront Greenway will contribute to remaking Sunset Park's industrial waterfront. As environmental justice victories, these developments remediate noxious uses and provide much-needed green space and waterfront access in a working-poor immigrant community. However, realtors are already anticipating the waterfront park's effects on property values and the potential momentum to rezone the industrial waterfront (or at least some sections) for "higher and better" uses. The antigentrification benefits of noxious uses were succinctly stated by a former Southwest Brooklyn Industrial Development Corporation director, who commented that uses such as the Gowanus Expressway protect industrial districts because they create such a toxic environment that no one would want to live there.[55] Yeampierre rejects this argument, stating that "What our communities are being told is that unless we live next to a waste transfer station or a power plant, we don't deserve to live there" (Yeampierre 2007).

UPROSE received a 2011 New York State Brownfield Opportunity Area (BOA) planning grant to develop a comprehensive remediation plan for the Sunset Park waterfront. The state's brownfield remediation program is driven by the potential reuse and redevelopment of dormant and polluted sites. According to the press release announcing the BOA grants, "The brownfield initiative provides a flexible framework for communities to *catalyze the redevelopment of strategic sites* and affected areas through a locally-driven process."[56] Neighborhood blueprints will identify strategies to restore environmental quality and facilitate the return of underutilized brownfield sites into "productive" and "catalytic" uses (New Partners for Community Revitalization 2007, 2). BOA implementation will test how UPROSE negotiates its role in mediating "environmental justice successes [that] have turned into gentrification opportunities" (Yeampierre 2007). As noxious uses give way to waterfront parks and pedestrian greenways that may facilitate employment and residential displacement, how the environmental justice movement translates principles of indigenous leadership, community control, and transformative populism into market-oriented economic development projects will be critical.

Resilience and Sustainability: Lessons from Superstorm Sandy

Superstorm Sandy hit the New York–New Jersey metro region on October 29, 2012, with devastating impact, including forty-eight deaths and $19 billion in environmental and property damage in New York City alone (Associated Press 2012; American Planning Association 2013). The city's most vulnerable communities are located along its waterfront and include many low-income communities of color (Furman Center for Real Estate and Urban Policy 2013). The newspaper coverage of public housing tenants in neighboring Red Hook and the Far Rockaways in Queens who were stranded for days with no water or electricity on high upper floors recounted their experiences of survival, which were particularly surreal. Even after the storm's one-year anniversary, hundreds of displaced residents and many small businesses had not returned to their homes or reopened (Cowan and Lander 2013; McGeehan and Palmer 2013). A report prepared by the Democrats of the House Committee on Small Business finds that the Small Business Administration approved fewer than one in four New York business applications for Superstorm Sandy assistance (Velázquez 2013).

The poorest New Yorkers were most dispossessed by the storm. Five months after Sandy, approximately 900 displaced households remained in forty-five area hotels paid for by the city (Navarro 2013c). The city was ordered by a state court judge to extend the program's May 31 expiration date as a result of a Legal Aid Society lawsuit (Legal Aid Society 2013). According to the *New York Times,* the city planned to appeal the decision saying that the housing assistance was not intended to continue "indefinitely" even though the city is slated to receive $1.8 billion in federal storm recovery aid with $9 million as housing subsidies (Navarro 2013b). In late September 2013, the Federal Emergency Management Agency stated that it would no longer reimburse the city for hotel rooms, and the remaining 300-plus evacuees were evicted (Dawsey 2013; Navarro 2013a). Many had no choice but to enter the city's homeless shelter system (Rose 2013).

Climate change and rising sea levels will affect all of New York City's 520-mile coastline, which wraps around the city's five boroughs; however, certain shorelines were hardest hit during Superstorm Sandy. Mayor Bloomberg's Special Initiative on Resilience and Rebuilding (SIRR) identified five areas most impacted by Superstorm Sandy, and the Brooklyn-Queens waterfront—which includes Sunset Park—is one of the most vulnerable areas. During Superstorm Sandy, Sunset Park experienced surge waters that overtopped the banks of the East River from 17th Street to 63rd Street and floodwater that pushed as far east as 3rd Avenue between 24th and 39th Streets (New York City Special Initiative for Rebuilding and Resiliency 2013).

In recognition of her expertise and leadership, which includes membership in several instrumental citywide environmental justice alliances such as Our Waterfront Neighborhoods, Yeampierre was appointed as a member of Mayor Bloomberg's Sustainability Advisory Board and as the first Latina chair of the U.S. Environmental Protection Agency's National Environmental Justice Advisory Council. Yeampierre's leadership elevates Sunset Park onto a national policy platform on environmental sustainability and racial justice. Sunset Park may be a national model, because as noted by Yeampierre, "We've been planning a long time, so resilience and sustainability are not new" (Yeampierre 2013b). To formalize resilience, defined as the ability to bounce back from a disaster as part of the organization's mission, Yeampierre launched the UPROSE Sunset Park Climate Justice Community Resiliency Center to "make resilience to climate change a priority in urban planning."[57] UPROSE's BOA has been folded into climate justice planning for Sunset Park (Yeampierre 2013b).

Post-Sandy rebuilding and planning for resilient communities continue to exemplify how sustainability as a policy approach tends to be an exclusive top-down process dominated by experts such as engineers, urban planners, scientists, and analysts in city government, in contrast to the mobilization for environmental justice, which is bottom up and grassroots but tends to be reactive (Agyeman 2005, 80). The mayor's SIRR was formed to coordinate planning efforts across the city, especially in the most storm-ravaged neighborhoods. One of the key SIRR tasks was to engage the public through town hall meetings to learn about experiences in the most impacted areas and to solicit input for a post-Sandy rebuilding agenda. Even with Yeampierre's prominent and multiple public leadership roles, SIRR did not plan a meeting in Sunset Park. Rather, there was one meeting for three neighborhoods held in Carroll Gardens (a gentrified, affluent, and largely non-Hispanic white community). The SIRR oversight is typical of the disregard that low-income communities of color continually endure, and Yeampierre demanded that SIRR cohost a meeting in Sunset Park (Yeampierre 2013b). At the April 24, 2013, meeting in Sunset Park's Trinity Lutheran Church, SIRR's Mark Ricks noted in his opening comments that Yeampierre has "unique skills," as she holds "official" capacities in both city and federal government and yet "operates outside the system to keep all accountable" by "holding our feet to the fire."[58]

The significance of Yeampierre's demand that the mayor's SIRR hold a town hall meeting in Sunset Park reflects that process is as essential to justice and equity as the final outcome or product. For environmental justice activists, meaningful participation (i.e., being at the table) in planning and decision making is critical. As Eddie Bautista of the New York City Environmental Justice Alliance frequently notes, "If you're not at the table, you're probably on the menu." Planning for sustainability and rebuilding a more resilient city require an inclusive and deliberative civic process of engagement, which begins with respecting the community enough to show up in their neighborhood space (Agyeman 2005, 89).

Yeampierre has a clear vision about a green economy agenda that would benefit Sunset Park as an working-poor immigrant waterfront neighborhood. Sunset Park prides itself as a neighborhood with a high rate of workers who walk to their place of employment. Yeampierre argues that new industries require fewer workers, so a green economy agenda must retrofit existing industrial businesses to be climate adaptive. For Sunset Park, sustainability and resilience mean job retention, economic growth, and environmental protection. Eddie Bautista argues that environmental justice communities "need both and insist on both."[59]

Despite Bloomberg's "visionary" PlaNYC 2030 and "great forward thinking" on environmental sustainability,[60] his administration is largely silent about sustainable economic development and job creation. Bloomberg's sustainability approach has yet to demonstrate a commitment to promoting a sustainable economy that is inclusive of immigrants and workers of color. Bloomberg's urban policies promote livable cities (e.g., New York City Bike Share program, whose repair center is based in Sunset Park) and public health reforms (e.g., initiatives to ban smoking and large soft drinks)—the kind of environmentalism that supports planning and building a luxury city. His economic development policies have failed the working-poor communities of color, as evidenced in the dramatic growth of income and wealth inequality in New York City under his watch. Moreover, Sunset Park's designation as a sustainable urban industrial district provides little in terms of policy resources and/or commitment to uplift the economic fortunes of all Sunset Park residents. Bloomberg's legacy highlights the convergence of neoliberalism and environmental sustainability.

Conclusion

Superstorm Sandy exposed Sunset Park's vulnerability to storm surges and environmental disaster due to the concentration of toxic uses on the waterfront. Sunset Park's waterfront remains a contested terrain—new artisanal industries and initiatives to rebrand Sunset Park coexist with its SMIA designation and noxious uses. Sunset Park's working-poor residents endure the environmental injustices while being marginalized by its remaking as a sustainable urban industrial district. Mayor Bloomberg may be "enlightened" about climate change, but the market imperative that defines his administration is evident in the proposal for a new "Seaport" neighborhood development on the East River, similar to Battery Park City, as part of his strategy for a "Stronger, More Resilient New York" (Yoneda 2013).

The rationale to preserve manufacturing and maritime employment frequently evokes a nostalgic narrative about stable blue-collar jobs that secure a stake in the American Dream.[61] There are no illusions that New York City industrial retention initiatives will re-create historic levels of industrial production and employment; however, according to one community advocate, the tension involved in defining a sustainable working waterfront and accommodating a diminished but specialized niche manufacturing sector has established in Sunset Park a contested "bantustan" (Wiley 2008b). New York City's economic sectors are highly polarized. Niche manufacturing and product imports (i.e., luxury items, including cars) coexist with Sunset Park's downgraded manufacturing and service sectors, which are dominated by immigrant small businesses and workers. Economic development leaders are aware of the concentrated presence of Sunset Park's immigrant small businesses but concede little knowledge about their numbers, sector concentration, market impact, size, and labor force conditions.[62] Immigrants are largely rendered invisible in the cityscape and official policy discourse on Sunset Park's sustainable urban industrial district. According to Creative

Real Estate Group founder Chris Havens, Sunset Park's mixed uses and diverse population are attractive to "cool 32-year-old" entrepreneurs who prefer funky neighborhoods with neighborhood amenities, such as the willingness of 8th Avenue Chinese restaurants to deliver lunch to the industrial waterfront (Havens 2010).[63] Sunset Park's polluted waterfront is indeed being reclaimed and tamed into a productive and beautiful space, but threats to community sustainability remain as noxious as ever.

Conclusion

On September 17, 2012, the first anniversary of the Occupy movement, activists reconvened at Zucotti Park near Wall Street—the site of a mass encampment for two months in 2011—before the New York City Police Department (NYPD) forcibly removed them, resulting in injuries and the arrest of a New York City Council member (Rodriguez 2011; Baker and Goldstein 2011). Representing the 99 percent, activists gathered to reaffirm a social movement that had mobilized to protest corporate dominance and malfeasance and to give voice to the voiceless. Occupy's first anniversary is also notable for the appearance of Occupy Sunset Park activists on the news program *Democracy Now!* Dennis Flores and Sara Lopez spoke about a two-year rent strike against a Sunset Park slumlord and the general conditions of inequality and injustice faced by the community's immigrant Chinese and Latino populations (Goodman and Gonzalez 2012). According to Occupy activist Ian Horst, Occupy Sunset Park is "legendary" in the Occupy movement because it is "the most plugged in with a neighborhood" (Horst 2013). An April 2012 news account reported that approximately twenty-five Sunset Park residents started to meet to "find common ground and plan a movement. *This was a different kind of occupation*" (Campbell 2012). For a year and a half, Occupy Sunset Park activists held weekly general assemblies in community and public spaces, including Sunset Park, Trinity Lutheran Church's La Casita, and St. Jacobi Church. Occupy Sunset Park's roots in activism on the everyday lived conditions of urban and racial inequality are deepened by their involvement in helping to create new forums and spaces for political discussion and actions, such as the nascent Sunset Park Unity Coalition.

As a strategic site of economic globalization, Sunset Park—with its racially diverse and class-stratified population and immigrant economies— offers important insights on the position and relationship of immigrant neighborhoods in an urban landscape defined by extreme economic and social polarizations. The making of Sunset Park as an immigrant global neighborhood is not the story of one New York City neighborhood. Sunset Park's narrative exemplifies local and concrete forms of globalization, neoliberal urban policies, and planning practices that promote gentrification and the consumptive desires of a luxury city and increasingly complex race and class contestations about neighborhood change and development trajectories. As a dense multiracial working-poor, immigrant neighborhood, Sunset Park is instructive on the possibilities for new types of community leadership as well as social and spatial practices that nurture cross-racial alliances and mobilizations.

As an academic urban planner, I find current theorizations of immigrant neighborhoods as enclaves or ethnoburbs limited in providing the conceptual depth or historic perspective necessary to facilitate effective tools and strategies to advance progressive actions for racial and economic justice and immigrants' right to the city. This study of Sunset Park points to potential research directions that help deepen our understanding of immigrant urbanization and help us strategize for new possibilities and challenges for transformative urban change. Sunset Park's neighborhood spaces and everyday lived experiences are finely differentiated by class, race and ethnicity, and immigrant identities and interests. This concluding chapter examines how Sunset Park creates space for its multiple publics and cultivates opportunities for transformative populism and innovative practices in community building. Sustaining progressive alliances and visionary leadership (especially among Sunset Park's youths) and expanding the capacity for crossing significant fault lines of poverty, racialization, space, and language remain monumental challenges.

Immigrant Entrepreneurialism and Global Capital

Through the lens of the African American urban experience, June Manning Thomas (1994) recounted how racial inequality is integral to the historic development of American cities and planning ideology and practices. As the national demography shifts to more complex patterns, urban planning remains instrumental in advancing racialized spatial landscapes and economic marginalization. Neoliberal urbanism and an immigrant narrative of entrepreneurialism and social capital are mutually reinforcing and help reify the free market and cultural dispositions (or lack thereof) in creating economic opportunity and upward trajectories. The concentration of Asian and Latino immigrants in economic enclaves, distinguished in part by the prevalence of unregulated business practices and poor employment conditions, did not concern Kathryn S. Wylde (2005), president and CEO of the New York City Partnership, because immigrant economies are evidence of a functioning free market.[1]

Immigrant businesses in Sunset Park were celebrated as the "seed of urban revival" (Sviridoff 1994), and the emphasis on the ethnic characteristics of family labor, social capital, and self-reliance is consistent with a neoliberal ideology that reifies self-employment as a symbol of the American Dream (Rath and Kloosterman 2000). Immigrants renewed Sunset Park's neighborhood economy through labor-intensive and downgraded manufacturing in garment production and a robust ethnic-based retail and service economy—much of which takes place as part of an extensive informal economy. Immigrant economic niches are integral to an advanced service economy in meeting the social reproduction needs of low-income populations and the consumptive needs of a cosmopolitan populace. The media and policy treatment of Sunset Park's extensive immigrant economies is an example of the valorization of immigrant entrepreneurialism to downplay the reproduction of racial and ethnic labor market segmentation and sharpened intraethnic class divisions embedded in persistent patterns of inequality in postindustrial cities.

The establishment of ethnic banks and their activities in restructuring the urban environment through the infusion of capital in the commercial development of immigrant neighborhoods are concrete examples of the localized processes that constitute economic globalization and transnationalism. Immigrant neighborhoods are increasingly contested terrains as emergent growth coalitions consisting of immigrant developers, realtors, property owners, and ethnic banks fuel real estate speculation, construct hotel and condominium developments, and intensify the threat of displacement for a majority working-poor population and the small businesses that support local consumption. The lending portfolios of Chinese ethnic banks in New York City are concentrated in real estate loans (for construction and land development and commercial real estate) rather than home mortgages or small business loans. Moreover, among minority-owned banks, Asian ethnic banks have the weakest track record in meeting Community Reinvestment Act obligations. With the rapid ascendance of China as the world economic power and the increasing density of transnational linkages between ethnic banks in the United States and China, the experiences and transformation of immigrant enclaves such as Manhattan Chinatown, Sunset Park, and Flushing portends the ways that Asian global capital will circulate in and restructure the political economy of local neighborhood spaces.

In response, Sunset Park incubates social justice projects that resist harsh and dehumanizing conditions through the formation of worker cooperatives. Worker cooperatives are democratically owned and operated businesses that help to transform low-paying labor-intensive immigrant niches through worker control, decision making, and profit sharing. Worker cooperatives advance democratic forms of immigrant entrepreneurialism. At a May 2013 ceremony, the Center for Family Life (CFL) Worker Cooperative Program received one of the first New York City Innovative Nonprofit Awards from the Mayor's Office of Economic Opportunity for its leadership and technical assistance in helping form several immigrant worker cooperatives in Sunset Park.

Sunset Park's immigrant workers are often concentrated in the informal economy in apparel production, domestic services, and the food industry (see Chapter 3). The post-2008 economic downturn heightened the marginal and exploitative conditions of these economic niches, contributing to high levels of neighborhood poverty and unemployment. The CFL's Adult Employment Program staff found that conventional job-readiness strategies such as résumé preparation, job search and interview techniques, basic computer skills, and English as a second language classes as well as arranging interviews with potential employers were increasingly unrealistic and ineffective. These conventional workforce development activities "require a certain skill set," but a significant segment of Sunset Park's immigrant population is undocumented, has limited or no English-language proficiency, and is typically described as "harder to employ."[2] The mismatch of the CFL's employment services, compounded by a deepening economic crisis, was among the factors that led to worker-controlled cooperatives.

The CFL's Vanessa Bransburg researched New York City–area worker cooperatives, including the UNITY Housecleaners Cooperative on Long Island and Las Senoras of St. Mary on Staten Island and decided to "take a shot," because there were "little barriers" to forming cooperatives. Bransburg found that Sunset Park immigrants were familiar with manufacturing cooperatives in the Dominican Republic and Mexico as well as alternative forms of financial access, such as credit unions. Moreover, several CFL clients were formerly members of cooperatives. According to Bransburg, some immigrants wanted to be entrepreneurs but desired the support of others and also wanted to work collectively. Because of cultural familiarity, cooperatives were "not shockingly different" to immigrants (Bransburg 2013). Elizabeth Yeampierre of UPROSE has often noted that cooperation and sustainable practices are "indigenous" to immigrant communities, and it is the process of Americanization and assimilation into a "disposable society" that encourages mass consumption and individualistic behavior and values (Yeampierre 2013b).

The CFL has incubated four worker cooperatives and one worker collective in Sunset Park.[3] The oldest one, formed in June 2006, is Si Se Puede! We Can Do It! and currently has fifty-one members, of whom fifteen are founding members. Beyond Care is a child care cooperative established in June 2008 and has forty-one members. Golden Steps, established in June 2011, provides elder care and has seventeen members. Kickin' It, a soccer-coaching cooperative established in September 2012, is the newest and smallest cooperative, with two founding members. In addition to the worker cooperatives, in 2009 the CFL helped found the Émigré Cooking Collective, whose members cater events and offer classes on the cuisines of their home countries.

Except for Kickin' It, whose members are young men ages eighteen to twenty-four, worker cooperative members are women (mostly Latinas from Mexico, the Dominican Republic, and Ecuador), and nearly all (90 percent) are Sunset Park residents. Worker training varies from eight to twelve weeks and covers the fundamental principles of the cooperative movement, communication skills, and strategies for group work, decision making, and business development. After a cooperative is launched, regular member meetings take place on a biweekly or monthly basis. Cooperative members pay a $40 monthly fee to cover administrative expenses, which includes child care and snacks at member meetings. In addition to membership fees and meeting attendance, cooperative members must spend three hours a month promoting the cooperative to potential clients. The CFL's Worker Cooperative Project continues to incubate these worker-owned businesses by providing office space, technical and financial assistance, and mentoring. In fact, the telephone number for the Si Se Puede! housecleaning cooperative is the same as the CFL Adult Employment Program.

As an alternative to exploitative immigrant niches, cooperatives provide workers with the opportunity to be their own boss and exercise power in shaping their economic conditions and outcomes. For example, the average hourly wage for Si Si Puede! members is $22, which is comparable to a living wage in New York City.[4] Cooperatives provide women with flexibility because they can determine their work schedules and make time to take care of other responsibilities. Members of cooperatives also report feeling less isolated. The challenges in forming and sustaining successful worker cooperatives, however, are significant, as evidenced by the failure of two worker-owned businesses.[5]

The CFL employs a top-down approach to establishing worker cooperatives in that Bransbrug selects founding members, develops the training curriculum, and, "given limited worker skills," determines in which industries to establish cooperatives. Based on feasibility research, the CFL selects industries that will "appeal to community members" and will also reflect what "people [i.e., clients and customers] are into." Another challenge is cultivating cooperative membership—how to get along with each other as well as be entrepreneurial and work collectively for the viability of the cooperative. Cooperative members must also attend meetings, recruit clients, and help market the cooperative. Bransburg emphasized that forming and sustaining worker cooperatives "is hard and complex work." In addition to an involved and labor-intensive process, multitasking ranges from locating feasible consumer markets to "empowering immigrant workers to think as entrepreneurs and not employees" (Bransburg 2013).

The CFL's long and reputable history of working with Sunset Park's immigrant families uniquely positioned the organization to pursue and lead an innovative strategy to change immigrant worker conditions and outcomes (Bransburg 2013). The new phase for the CFL's worker cooperative development initiative is to train other community organizations in the New York City metro area to incubate worker cooperatives. The CFL received New York City Council funding to "train the trainers," including Make the Road NY (which is based in Bushwick in Brooklyn) and the Westchester Square Partnership (which works with Bangladeshi immigrant women) in the Bronx.[6] Currently, the CFL is training six additional community-based organizations to form worker-owned businesses. For five years the CFL has done this work with only two staff members, but Bransburg has hired two cooperative developers and anticipates that the CFL will significantly expand its capacity to incubate worker cooperatives as well as train community-based organizations in immigrant neighborhoods throughout the region.

Occupy Sunset Park: Creating Space for Latino-Asian Immigrant Activism

Sunset Park documents the possibilities and challenges of mobilizing Asians and Latinos as a "community of interest" based on their shared class positions and daily lived experiences as working-poor immigrants. Neighborhood grassroots organizational alliances are often the key venues that provide the necessary space to form a "new politics of traditionally disadvantaged actors" (Sassen 1996, 630). In his study of neighborhood dynamics in a Los Angeles suburb, Saito (1998) argued that Latino and Asian American identities and experiences are similarly grounded and that these shared experiences extend beyond an "immigrant hypothesis," which claims that all immigrants share an ideological view whereby America is upheld as a land of opportunity and mobility is premised on individual initiative (Cheng and Espiritu 1989, 528). This shared sensibility purportedly explains the relative absence of conflict between Asian and Latino immigrants compared to, for example, Korean business owners and their black customers. Saito (1998) offers an alternative rationale for a potential Latino-Asian community of interest: "The two groups share the same neighborhoods because they have been affected by, and have fought against, *the same political and economic forces of exclusion and discrimination*" (188, my emphasis).

In pluricultural New York City, working-class immigrant Asians and Latinos share multiple neighborhood spaces throughout the city, including Manhattan's Chinatown and Lower East Side; Queens' Elmhurst, Jackson Heights, Corona, and Flushing; and, most notably, Brooklyn's Sunset Park. Numerous grassroots organizations have formed in these neighborhoods to advocate for worker and immigrant rights. In contrast to established ethnic-based nonprofit organizations vested in a social service orientation (e.g., the Brooklyn Chinese-American Association and Opportunities for a Better Tomorrow), worker centers and community advocacy organizations see Sunset Park's racial diversity as a neighborhood asset and view the cultivation of shared political and economic interests among immigrant Asians and Latinos as central to their mission. Former Sunset Park resident and activist May Lin observed that ethnic-based social service organizations often "deepen the divide" in neighborhoods such as Sunset Park. While ethnic spaces are important because they provide a safe and familiar space for new immigrants, Lin argues that "they should not be at the expense of building other types of spaces" where Asians and Latinos can come together and find common cause (Lin 2013). Yeampierre (2006) has long noted the need for "a different space" and describes UPROSE as a place for Sunset Park's Latino, Asian, and Arab youths to "build community and shared identities."[7]

The formation of alternative spaces separate from established and institutionalized venues such as community boards and neighborhood-based social service agencies is necessary to cultivate immigrant leadership (see Chapter

5). La Unión's experience with the Lutheran Medical Center's (LMC) Promise Neighborhood initiative underscores the necessity of these types of spaces for meaningful community capacity building.[8] In 2010 the LMC received $498,614 as one of the first nationwide Promise Neighborhood planning grant recipients. A key component of President Barack Obama's urban antipoverty program, Promise Neighborhoods, administered by the U.S. Department of Education, are based on the Harlem Children's Zone model, which provides a holistic and comprehensive cradle-to-college approach for improving youth development and educational outcomes. The objective of the LMC's federal grant was to support a strategic neighborhood planning ` process based on intensive and inclusive community engagement.

The LMC established the Sunset Park Promise Neighborhood Council as the governing body for the federal grant in partnership with key community-based organizations, such as the CFL, Opportunities for a Better Tomorrow, Neighbors Helping Neighbors, Community Board 7, and La Unión.[9] In addition to a stated commitment that "at least one-third of the members of the advisory board will be Sunset Park residents, Brooklyn residents who are identified as low-income, and elected officials representing Sunset Park,"[10] the LMC sponsored two public meetings in February 2011 for "residents to take an active role in helping to plan the new Sunset Park Promise Neighborhood project" (Lutheran HealthCare 2011). Translation services in Arabic, Spanish, and Chinese as well as free snacks and child care were provided to encourage community participation.

Leticia Alanis and members of La Unión participated in the Sunset Park Promise Neighborhood Council meetings, training sessions, and community assessments (Alanis 2013). Alanis shared that La Unión members often felt marginalized by the council. Despite the LMC's stated commitment for community participation, the council did not consistently provide simultaneous translation to facilitate the full inclusion of Sunset Park residents and La Unión members.[11] Moreover, Alanis, the executive director of La Unión, was not always consulted in setting the agenda for council meetings. She felt that the council heavily favored community-based organizational leaders who are overwhelmingly white, and subsequently she commented that the council was "elitist," as evidenced by a planning process that was "not inclusive of community members in decision making." Ultimately, Alanis and La Unión members withdrew their participation because Promise Neighborhoods was inconsistent with La Unión's strategy for community empowerment and building immigrant leadership. St. Jacobi's Reverend Juan Carlos Ruiz has expressed similar concern with "self-serving" social service and educational institutions, which "are not here for the common good." He described Sunset Park's extensive network of social service providers as part of a "nonprofit industrial complex" (J. Ruiz 2013).

In small but significant ways, Sunset Park facilitates alternative and innovative spaces and leadership models for Latino-Asian community building. One of these initiatives is Rice and Dreams, a people's kitchen founded by Sunset Park residents including May Lin, Lida Shao, Esther Sosa, and Amina Ali. Founders donated money to buy healthy food in bulk and cooked together as a way to connect and build a "tightly knit infrastructure" for community activism (Lin 2013). Rice and Dreams prepared meals for Occupy Sunset Park meetings, prepared and distributed food at Sunset Park, and holds a monthly community meal at St. Jacobi Church. La Unión's Leticia Alanis occasionally joins Rice and Dreams for the monthly meals.

Lin jokingly said that the name was a play on rice and beans, but in seriousness she recalled that the founding members' choice of dreams was deliberate and meant to reference a "proactive vision of the neighborhood" (Lin 2013). The 2009 rezoning campaign and struggle were reactive, and local residents wanted to create a different type of space to encourage Asian and Latino exchange and relationship building. Through the preparation and sharing of food, Rice and Dreams creates opportunities for social and political engagement among Sunset Park's multiple publics. Lin concedes that having a trilingual space is "unwielding" but that it is an "inherently political act to create that space" in order for "people to engage in self-determination" (Lin 2013). While free food is the central draw, Rice and Dreams members facilitate discussions on topics that can be opportunities for political education and debate. For example, previous mealtime discussions have focused on people's favorite part of Sunset Park as well as on the history, evolution, and use of corn.

Several Sunset Park churches are critical sites for Latino-Asian community building and often provide the physical space to accommodate grassroots social justice initiatives. Since Reverend Juan Carlos Ruiz joined St. Jacobi Church in 2011, Rice and Dreams, the Raza Youth Collective, La Unión, and Occupy Sunset Park use the church's community space for meetings and events.[12] For several months, Occupy Sandy was also based at St. Jacobi Church, which served as a central coordination and distribution point for assistance and information.[13] For weeks, thousands of volunteers were dispatched from the church with hot meals and supplies to aid devastated neighborhood residents in Brooklyn and Queens. Without consulting the church council, Reverend Ruiz made an immediate decision to open the doors to house Occupy Sandy. He credited social media and the Occupy movement's extensive grassroots infrastructure for its effective mobilization, which was "unlike a canned, traditional relief response" (J. Ruiz 2013). In fact, there was no official government relief presence in Sunset Park and many neighboring communities for days in the storm's aftermath. The solidarity of Occupy Sandy volunteers was motivated by the sense that "we are all in the same boat which is sinking" (J. Ruiz 2013).

Trinity Lutheran Church also has a social justice mission, and the church is deeply engaged in neighborhood organizing and community building. Recent events at the church's community space, La Casita, included a showing of photographs taken by the tenants of the 46th Street buildings, a conversation titled "Common Ground, Common Hope: Black and Latino Dialogue" with Dr. Cornel West and Reverend Samuel Cruz, and a showing of the film *The Central Park Five,* which included a discussion with two of the young men falsely convicted and imprisoned. Plans for a showing of Konrad Aderer's *Enemy Alien* (see Chapter 1) are currently in the works. On the occasion of a Good Friday service, Reverend Cruz sermonized about the city's controversial stop-and-frisk policy and the unconstitutional targeting of black, Latino, and poor youths of color. His political position was clear in his repeated warning that "it may be Friday, but Sunday is coming."[14] His provocative reference to Sunset Park as a modern-day Nazareth certainly presented a particular narrative about the historic and contemporary positionality of the neighborhood. Social spaces such as churches and public spaces, including the subway system and Sunset Park, represent potential spaces (as deployed by the People's Transportation Project, Rice and Dreams, and Occupy Sunset Park) to nurture alternative identities, meanings, and relationships (Hou 2010).

In addition to supporting the 46th Street rent strikers, Occupy Sunset Park's early work included protesting reductions in educational funding for neighborhood Head Start and after-school programs. Occupy Sunset Park also seeks to reclaim neighborhood public spaces. Of particular significance is a former court house building centrally located on 4th Avenue and 42nd Street that currently houses Community Board 7 and one of two NYPD applicant processing centers. The required "character interview" for the NYPD Probationary Police Officer Program is conducted at the Sunset Park center.[15] Applicants are required to dress in "business attire," which is clearly specified as "a suit or slacks and sport coat with tie" for men and "pants suit or dress or combination skirt and blouse" for women.[16] Despite the fact that Sunset Park's NYPD applicant processing center primarily handles interviews and administrative paperwork, David Galarza notes that "everyone is armed, as armed as at the precincts" (Galarza 2013). In a neighborhood that continues to struggle with police brutality and the post-9/11 detainment of Arab and South Asian immigrants at the Metropolitan Detention Center (see Chapter 1), the expanded police presence in a public building is troublesome. In April 2012, Occupy Sunset Park marched to the landmarked building and rallied to "reclaim the court house" for public use (Campbell 2012).

Occupy Sunset Park organizes annual intercommunity, multilingual events on Unity Day to commemorate Dr. Martin Luther King's birthday and on May Day in honor of International Workers Day. Occupy Sunset Park collaborates with immigrant worker centers and advocacy organizations—including the Chinese and Staff Workers Association, CAAAV: Organizing Asian Communities, and La Unión—in these mobilizations (Chin 2012b). Most recently, Occupy Sunset Park participated in the formation of a Sunset Park Unity Coalition, which La Unión's Leticia Alanis described as an exciting and promising opportunity for community building and organizing. In addition to Occupy Sunset Park activists, members of the Tenants' Association of 46th Street, Occupy Sandy, and La Unión and St. Jacobi congregants participated in the inaugural June 2013 meeting held at St. Jacobi Church. Meeting minutes noted that forty individuals attended to discuss two broad themes:

> Dialogue: 1. Identifying our strengths, and 2. Around what issues do we want to use these strengths in our community?
> Second dialogue: For what purpose should we use our strength, our power? On what themes/issues?[17]

Members of Occupy Sunset Park and La Unión were encouraged by a productive and participatory discussion and anticipate that the Sunset Park Unity Coalition's next meeting will prioritize potential action issues identified, such as affordable housing, health, education, culture, food justice, climate change, and engaging more people in the coalition (Alanis 2013; Horst 2013).

Sunset Park's initiatives to build alliances among working-poor Asians and Latinos are episodic, but without a migrant civil society consisting of community churches, worker centers, and advocacy organizations such as UPROSE, the Chinese Staff and Workers' Association, La Unión, the Sunset Park Alliance of Neighbors (SPAN), and Occupy activists, the necessary relationships and resources to bridge racial divides and mobilize collective action would not be present. As Theodore and Martin (2007) argue, these organizations "offer an alternate vision of urban development and community life" and are vital to the political incorporation of immigrants without citizenship rights. In neighborhoods such as Sunset Park, even poor immigrants with legal status are so marginalized that alternative venues for mobilizing political voice, including claims for the right to stay in their neighborhood, are necessary.

Just Sustainability in Immigrant Global Neighborhoods

Sunset Park's rezoning in 2009 was part of a piecemeal strategy to transform the city landscape and built environment to accommodate racial change while advancing a real estate–driven economic development agenda. Although Dan Doctoroff and Amanda Burden, chief architects of the city's rebuilding initiatives who have been compared to Robert Moses in remaking New York City, the legacy of Mayor Michael Bloomberg's administration includes fundamentally redesigning the city's approach to urban planning and land use. Regulatory tools to promote the public interest, such as zoning and landmarking, have been aggressively employed to privilege particular groups while excluding or marginalizing others. In the case of Sunset Park, a contextual zone will protect white homeowners while directing growth (perceived as the activity of unscrupulous immigrant developers) to transitioning neighborhood sections that sustain Sunset Park's majority working-class Asian and Latino populations. Ethnic banks are central institutional actors in the intraethnic gentrification of Sunset Park, as they underwrite immigrant developers and their market-rate condominium projects.

The waterfront is a highly contested terrain in the remaking of New York City as a global city. The decline of an industrial waterfront made room for the placement of power plants and waste transfer stations and relocated adult establishments. Sunset Park was treated as a "dumping ground," and degraded environmental conditions shaped daily life in the neighborhood and embodied the systematic pattern of disinvestment in poor urban neighborhoods (Sze 2007). New York City's remaining industrial infrastructure is increasingly centered on Sunset Park's waterfront. For some economic development practitioners, the current financial crisis underscores the importance of a diversified New York City economy. However, efforts to preserve manufacturing are not about job creation but instead are about promoting niche manufacturers that provide a vital service to New York City's creative economy. The growing presence of artists' lofts and hotels along Sunset Park's waterfront is consistent with a neoliberal urban vision centered on bolstering New York City's creative and tourism economies.

Waterfront redevelopment and reuse poses fundamental dilemmas about regional planning and social equity. Environmental justice activists and organizations protested noxious uses that presented daily hazards and diminished the welfare and health of low-income communities of color. New York City's environmental justice movement developed strong political networks to resist the devaluing of these communities, but their successes, facilitated in part by a changing real estate market, now present the most critical challenge of protecting neighborhood spaces for low-income residents who have endured decades of environmental racism. Greenways, waterfront parks, and access are the material victories of environment justice struggles and will greatly improve the living environment of poor communities of color. However, the overarching goals of self-determination, engaged citizenry in public policy and city planning decisions, and creating sustainable communities are tested again in the revalorization of waterfront industrial neighborhoods as potential sites for creative entrepreneurs and workers, recreation, and tourism. The right to stay in a neighborhood is central to community empowerment and control. Exerting that right as a strategy to counter "environmental gentrification" will require new resources and alliances (Pastor, Morello-Frosch, and Sadd 2006).

Planning for just sustainable neighborhoods requires actions and strategies that recognize "the *interdependence* of social justice, economic well-being, and environmental stewardship" (Agyeman 2005, 89, my emphasis). The issue of food justice highlights the centrality of racial equity in just sustainability planning for immigrant neighborhoods such as Sunset Park. Several CFL social workers helped establish Sunset Park's community-supported agriculture (CSA) project in 2010.[18] Now in its third season, the Sunset Park CSA is a membership-based organization in which members pay up front to farmers before the start of a growing season, and then at St. Michael's Church for approximately twenty-two weeks beginning in the second week of June, members pick up weekly shares of vegetables, fruits, and eggs produced and harvested by local farmers and orchards.

When I asked CSA member and CFL food justice coordinator Gustav Gauntlett how the Sunset Park CSA addresses food justice, Gauntlett responded that "at the end of the day, it's about freshness" (Gauntlett 2013). He explained that the CSA provides quality organic vegetables and eggs from farmers located within ninety miles of New York City. He also noted that the CSA's three-tiered membership system enables low-income families to purchase less expensive B and C shares. Finally, the CSA accepts food stamps and Supplemental Nutrition Assistance Program (SNAP) debit cards as forms of payment. Currently, the CSA has 107 family members. Gauntlett conceded a need to improve outreach to Sunset Park's low-income families. The handful of Latino members learned about the CSA through their client relationship with CFL social workers. The Sunset Park CSA is an example of redistributive populism in that the emphasis is on consumer choice and availability of fresh, locally grown produce.

For La Unión, food justice entails addressing health disparities and the prevalence of inexpensive fast food restaurants as well as creating a space for immigrants to preserve cultural traditions and participate in placemaking projects, such as designing and painting a mural. In 2010, La Unión established Granja Los Colibries by repurposing a small underutilized city-owned lot into an urban farm with chickens and a vegetable garden. Managed by twenty La Unión member families, Granja Los Colibries is a site for food production and community education. At a May 2013 gathering, a La Unión member explained the importance of the farm's chipile and jicama plants, which were grown from seeds brought from Mexico. As Mares and Peña (2010, 258) argue, "These *jardincitos* are spiritual and political symbols of a process involving nothing less than the re-territorialization of place as a home by transnational communities." The spatialization of Sunset Park's food justice landscape includes the prevalence of front yards that have been transformed into small vegetable plots by many Chinese immigrant families. Typically constructed with discarded wood and rags, as shown in Figure C.1, these hybrid public spaces grow a winter melon that is common in Asian cuisines. Resisting the Sunset Park Landmark Committee's definition of historically appropriate uses for residential front yards, these tiny gardens define Sunset Park as a working-class immigrant place.

Globalization is "deeply embedded in places," and localities such as Sunset Park represent a new neighborhood typology that exemplifies the myriad and concrete forms of this contemporary period of economic globalization (Sassen 2000b, 79; see also Clarke and Gaile 1997). Immigrant neighborhoods are the strategic spaces where "the work of globalization gets done" (Sassen 1996, 630). As microcosms for the uneven economic and political incorporation of Asian and Latino migrants, immigrant neighborhoods are integral to an urban landscape of heightening class stratification and persistent but increasingly complex patterns of race and ethnic segmentation. The potential for new class mobilizations and democratic practices is based on the transformative populism practiced by worker centers, grassroots alliances, and churches that connect and organize everyday people to challenge and resist the power relations embedded in neoliberal urbanism.

Figure C.1 Typical front-yard vegetable garden constructed with rags and wood scraps, July 2013. (*Photo taken by Tarry Hum.*)

Fault lines, however, remain deeply rooted in the differential racialization and positionality of Sunset Park's multiple publics. At a recent Occupy Sunset Park meeting, a Spanish-speaking participant raised the "problem of the Chinese taking over the neighborhood" (Horst 2013). This reaction to Sunset Park's growing Chinese population was also observed by David Galarza in his conversations with residents who expressed concerns that Chinese landlords and investors have evicted Latino tenants (Galarza 2005). The challenges for building community are deep, but the promise of Sunset Park is Latino and Chinese leaders who understand that an underlying dynamic for these racial tensions is shared exclusion from full citizenship rights, resulting in a competition for crumbs.[19] As Pulido (2006, 58) noted in her book on activism in communities of color, "Despite the possibility of close relations, those connections had to be carefully articulated and cultivated by political activists and leaders—by no means were they inevitable." Sunset Park's promise is evident in a nascent migrant civil society that forges collaborations between Asians and Latinos, which threatens the status quo. Whether it is a group of youth activists who recognize each other at a community meeting, multilingual neighborhood actions to protest gentrification or commemorate international workers, or a group of residents singing karaoke or sharing a meal in a church basement, Sunset Park residents create distinct urban spaces and activities "in defiance of the official rules and regulations" that contribute to the potentiality for transformative neighborhood change (Hou 2010, 15).

Notes

INTRODUCTION

1. Information about the New York City Economic Development Corporation's Sunset Park Vision Plan and related projects is available online at http://www.nycedc.com/project/sunset-park-vision-plan, and a video of the July 20, 2009, press event is available at http://www.nyc.gov/portal/site/nycgov/menuitem.c0935b9a57bb4ef3daf2f1c701c789a0/index.jsp?pageID=mayor_press_release&catID=1194&doc_name=http%3A%2F%2Fwww.nyc.gov%2Fhtml%2Fom%2Fhtml%2F2009b%2Fpr335-09.html&cc=unused1978&rc=1194&ndi=1. See also City of New York (2009).

2. Superstorm Sandy, one of the deadliest and most destructive hurricanes in U.S. history, hit New York City on October 29, 2012. The devastation in the Northeast was extensive, with more than one hundred fatalities and complete neighborhoods destroyed.

3. For workshops with Chinese and Mexican community members in 2009, see Spark (2011).

4. See Table 2.2.

5. The website for the Japanese American National Museum exhibition *Boyle Heights: The Power of Place* is http://www.janm.org/exhibits/bh/exhibition/exhibition.htm.

6. Founded and headed by Sara Gonzalez before her 2002 special election to the New York City Council, the Hispanic Young People's Alternatives ceased operations around 2004.

1 IMMIGRANT PLACES

1. New York City Department of City Planning (2007).

2. The five families include the Ramóns from Colombia, the Chens from China, the Snreenivasans from India, the Biases from South Carolina, and the Farruggios from Sicily (Anon. 2008c).

3. See U.S. Immigration and Customs Enforcement (n.d.).

4. The Special Registration Program—part of a larger National Security Entry-Exit Registration System to keep track of foreign visitors to the United States—required men from the following twenty-five countries to register with an immigration office: Afghanistan, Algeria, Bahrain, Bangladesh, Egypt, Eritrea, Indonesia, Iran, Iraq, Jordan, Kuwait, Lebanon, Libya, Morocco, North Korea, Oman, Pakistan, Qatar, Saudi Arabia, Somalia, Sudan, Syria, Tunisia, the United Arab Emirates, and Yemen.

5. For links to the series of articles on the New York City Police Department's surveillance of the Muslim community in the New York region, see Associated Press (n.d.).

6. The other was the Passaic County Jail in Paterson, New Jersey, which was also the subject of a two-part investigative report by Daniel Zwerdling that aired on November 17 and 18 on National Public Radio (see National Public Radio 2004).

7. See Department of Justice Office of the Inspector General (2003a, 2003b).

8. Department of Justice Office of the Inspector General (2003a, chap. 2).

9. See Center for Constitutional Rights (n.d.).

10. Konrad Aderer's documentary website is available at http://www.lifeorliberty.org/enemy-alien.

11. *New York Times* reporter Nina Bernstein (2004b) investigated the arrest and detention of a Nepalese man for videotaping a "sensitive" site and the efforts of an FBI agent who advocated for the man's release from the Sunset Park MDC, where he was held for three months in solitary confinement. See Immigration and Naturalization Service (n.d.).

12. National Conference of State Legislatures (2005).

13. Immigration and Customs Enforcement (n.d.-b).

14. Immigration and Customs Enforcement (n.d.-a).

15. Doctoroff (2006) also refers to Mayor Bloomberg and the New York City Economic Development Corporation's (n.d.-b) brochure *Major Economic Development Initiatives,* which lists projects to achieve the mayor's three priorities to make New York City more livable and business friendly and to diversify its economy.

16. For example, the Empire State Development Corporation and subsidiaries, including the Lower Manhattan Development Corporation (charged with coordinating the rebuilding of Ground Zero); the Atlantic Yards Development Corporation; and the Hudson Yards Development Corporation.

17. Attorney General of the State of New York (2012).

18. The City Comptroller's Checkbook NYC website is available at http://www.comptroller.nyc.gov/mymoneynyc/checkbooknyc/.

19. See Mayor Bloomberg's PlaNYC 2030 website, available at http://www.nyc.gov/html/planyc2030/html/home/home.shtml.

20. As of December 2013, the Flushing Commons project has not broken ground, despite trips to China to raise international finance capital. See Pasquarelli and Bragg (2013), Anuta (2013) and Sheets (2011).

21. The NYCEDC's Willets Point Development website is available at http://www.nycedc.com/project/willets-point-development.

22. The F&T Group's website at available at http://www.fandtgroup.com/.

2   MAKING SUNSET PARK

1. Brooklyn (Kings), Queens, Manhattan (New York City), Bronx, and Staten Island (Richmond) Counties make up New York City.

2. The Sandhog Project documents New York City sandhogs, and its website, available at http://www.sandhogproject.com, includes the profiles and photo gallery of multigenerations of Irish and black West Indian sandhogs who are now working on the city's largest construction project, the sixty-mile City Tunnel #3 eight hundred feet below street level.

3. A New York Transit Museum exhibit titled *Steel, Stone and Backbone* commemorates the contributions of thirty thousand workers from immigrant and African American communities who built the New York City subway system.

4. For a history of the Ansonia Clock Company including an illustration of its Brooklyn factory, see Anon. (n.d.-d).

5. For basic facts about the *Norway Times,* see Library of Congress (n.d.). The website for the *Norwegian American Weekly* is available at http://blog.norway.com/.

6. According to the Scandinavian East Coast Museum website, available at http://www.scandinavian-museum.org, Victoria Hofmo helped establish the Norwegian-American Collection, which later became the museum. The website includes photographs of 8th Avenue and the business cards of numerous former Norwegian businesses in Sunset Park. During the 1990s, Hofmo was a staff member of Community Board 7 in Sunset Park. For a profile of Hofmo, see (Bleyer 2008).

7. On July 27, 2013, the Chinese Promise Baptist Church held a thirtieth anniversary celebration and dedication service for its new church building, located at 842 41st Street.

8. The Trinity Lutheran Church website is available at http://trinitybrooklyn.org/.

9. On April 24, 2013, Reverend Cruz, UPROSE, and the Mayor's Special Initiative on Rebuilding and Resiliency (SIRR) hosted the post–Superstorm Sandy Sunset Park Community Resilience Workshop at Trinity Lutheran Church.

10. The Fort Greene meat market was relocated as part of an eighty-five–acre Atlantic Terminal Urban Renewal Program, which is now part of the contested Forest City Ratner's Atlantic Yards project (Anon. 1969c).

11. A centerpiece of President Lyndon B. Johnson's War on Poverty program, the 1964 Economic Opportunity Act established the Community Action Program, which funded neighborhood health centers (Sardell 1988).

12. Institutional neglect of the Puerto Rican community was also noted in Winnick (1990, 104): the LMC "was not universally held in high affection; many Puerto Ricans believed LMC slighted their health needs with second-rate service."

13. Irving T. Bush was independently wealthy because his father, Rufus T. Bush, who died when Irving was a young man, had sold his Brooklyn oil refinery to Standard Oil, and Irving inherited the proceeds.

14. In 1915, the Honorary Chinese Commercial Commission from the Republic of China toured New York Harbor on a steamer and docked at Bush Terminal's American-Hawaiian Steamship Company pier for a visit at the Tidewater Paper Mills Company, where the commission was particularly impressed by the paper-production process (Anon. 1915).

15. The U.S. victory against Spain in the 1898 Spanish-American War concluded with Spain ceding the islands of Puerto Rico and Guam and selling the Philippines to the United States.

16. See New York City Council Committee on Waterfronts (2005).

17. The widening of the Gowanus Expressway in the late 1950s also demolished buildings on the east side of 3rd Avenue for more than twenty blocks south of 39th Street (Ment and Donovan 1980, 73).

18. The traffic volume estimate is from New York State Department of Transportation (2006).

19. Muniz (1998) cites a 1980 study by the Housing Task Force of the Puerto Rican Center for Research and Information, Inc., that documented the share of Puerto Ricans in New York City who lived in Manhattan neighborhoods such as the Lower East Side dropped from 70 percent to less than 25 percent between 1940 and 1970.

20. New York City purchased the Brooklyn Army Terminal from the federal government in 1981.

21. This quotation is from an undated speech given by Kathryn Wylde when she was an LMC staff member in the 1970s. The speech is from Wylde's personal files.

22. In New York City, Mayor Robert F. Wagner set up the Council Against Poverty to coordinate local antipoverty programs and administer federal funding. Twenty-six New York City neighborhoods were designated as poverty areas in order for the city to receive millions of dollars of federal funding from the Office of Economic Opportunity. In addition to Sunset Park, the following Brooklyn neighborhoods were designated poverty areas: Brownsville, Williamsburg, South Brooklyn, Crown Heights, Bushwick, and Bedford-Stuyvesant. These neighborhoods were predominantly black and Puerto Rican.

23. The Housing and Urban Development Act of 1968 established Section 235 of the National Housing Act to assist low-income home buyers with a reduced interest rate as low as 1 percent. See Gotham (2000) for a study on how this program reinforced racially segregated housing patterns in Kansas City, Missouri, from 1969 to the early 1970s.

24. The Partnership for New York City was formed in 2002 with the merger of the New York Chamber of Commerce and Industry and the New York City Partnership and represents the interests of the corporate and investment leadership of New York City. For a profile of Kathryn Wylde, see Pristin (2001).

25. As New York City's first antipoverty czar, Mitchell Sviridoff advocated for the creation of a Human Resource Administration to coordinate and oversee NYC's myriad antipoverty initiatives and replace local service providers with community development corporations (Kifner 1966). During his thirteen years as vice president of the Ford Foundation, Sviridoff showed an interest in Sunset Park and the work of SPRC. He appeared in a 1980 *New York Times* photo in front of a Sunset Park building undergoing renovation (Teltsch 1980).

26. See the Sunset Park Redevelopment Committee website, available at www.sprcinc.org.

27. The LMC developed and/or manages several senior housing projects, including Harbor Hill, an 87-unit complex; Shore Hill in Bay Ridge, a 558-unit rent-subsidized senior apartment complex; Marien Heim Sunset Park, a senior housing complex that is the old site of the LMC; and Marian Heim Tower, located on Ocean Parkway. Sunset Gardens, a new 80-unit independent senior living complex, opened in 2008.

28. According to the National Register of Historic Places, Sunset Park's Historic District encompasses more than thirty-two hundred buildings on twenty-eight hundred acres. See http://www.nationalregisterofhistoricplaces.com/ny/Kings/districts.

29. As the real estate values of neighboring Park Slope and Bay Ridge have skyrocketed, Chapter 5 notes how this federal and state historic district designation creates a precedent for the contextual rezoning changes that are now being sought to protect Sunset Park from overdevelopment rather than to attract new "Yuppies," as intended in the 1980s.

30. For specific examples of the Puerto Rican community's perceptions and criticisms of the Sunset Park Restoration Committee, see Muniz (1998, 77–83).

31. The Sunset Park Landmarks Committee website is available at http://www.preservesunsetpark.org/.

32. The New York City Landmark Preservation Commission's website is available at http://www.nyc.gov/html/lpc/html/home/home.shtml.

33. The quotation in the subhead is from a young rapper's spoken word performed in the final minutes of "¡Basta Ya! Sunset Rise Up," a video on Sunset Park gentrification and the 2009 rezoning struggle. The video is available at http://vimeo.com/15192664.

34. The Hart-Cellar Act established a ceiling quota of 20,000 per country and allocated 170,000 visas to countries in the Eastern Hemisphere and 120,000 to countries in the Western Hemisphere. Family reunification categories including immediate relatives such as spouses, minor children, and parents of U.S. citizens over the age of twenty-one were exempt from these numerical quotas.

35. I conducted a survey of Sunset Park immigrant business owners in 2001 and found that the majority of Latino respondents were Dominican. The results were presented in a 2002 unpublished report titled "Sunset Park, Brooklyn's Neighborhood Economy: Firm Survey Findings and Policy Implications; Report to Congresswoman Nydia Velazquez, City Councilor Angel Rodriguez, Chang Xie, Director of the Chinese American Planning Council, Renee Giordano, Executive Director of Sunset Park Business Improvement District, and Teresa Williams, Executive Director of Southwest Brooklyn Industrial Development Corporation."

36. Dominican-born entrepreneur Fernando Mateo is president of the New York State Federation of Taxi Drivers (Hoffman 2000).

37. The website for the film includes interviews and updates on the Ortiz family and is available at http://www.pbs.org/pov/pov2001/myamericangirls/thefilm.html.

38. This estimate was given by Joe Salvo, director of the Population Division, New York City Department of Planning, at a November 2005 American Planning Association panel at New York University, but Baruch College's Robert Smith estimates an even higher range of 400,000 to 450,000.

39. Juan Carlos Ruiz (2013) noted nine churches within a three-block area of St. Jacobi and commented, "It's very competitive."

40. La Unión's website is available at http://la-union.org/.

41. Carlos Menchaca's campaign website is available at http://www.carlos2013.com/.

42. A short video of the August 20, 2013, candidates forum at the Trinity Lutheran Church that provides statements by Reverend Samuel Cruz, residents, and youth leaders about the significance of Gonzalez's absence is available at http://www.youtube.com/watch?v=O9pBmuELCaw.

43. Sara Gonzalez's Facebook page, available at https://www.facebook.com/councilgonzalez?fref=ts, includes photographs from two campaign events with Sunset Park's Chinese community on August 12 and September 5, 2013. The August 12 event was organized by Paul Mak, who appears in nearly all of the photographs posted.

44. For a summary of the bill's provisions, see Library of Congress (2005).

45. Sunset Park's 8th Avenue is the first station after the N subway line emerges from underground, leading to its Chinese reference as the "Blue Sky" station.

46. Three contiguous census tracts (104, 106, 108) encompass a twenty-four-block area from 7th to 9th Avenue and from 60th to 48th Streets, constituting a large area of the Chinese residential and commercial neighborhood. Since 1980, a full third of Sunset Park's Chinese population has resided in these three tracts.

47. U.S. Congressional District 12 elected the first Puerto Rican woman, Nydia Velasquez, to the House of Representatives. Congresswoman Velasquez continues to represent Sunset Park.

48. Numerous incidences include one in July 1993 involving 658 Chinese immigrants on a freighter and two fishing boats held off the Baja California coast for nearly a month before the Mexican and U.S. governments decided to deport the migrants. Most recently, a April 2006 incident involved 22 stowaways in a metal cargo container transported by MV Rotterdam and unloaded in a Seattle port (Turnbull et al. 2006). In 2006, Sister Ping—a prominent Manhattan Chinatown business owner—was sentenced to thirty-five years in prison for orchestrating the *Golden Venture* fiasco and her extensive dealings with in human smuggling. See Keefe (2006).

49. The website for the Arab American Association of New York is available at http://www.arabamericanny.org/.

50. For a profile of Linda Sansour on the NY1 program One on 1, see Anon. (2011).

51. Maya (2005) claimed that Community Board 7 "sold out" the community on the MDC development. In their support of the prison, the community board emphasized contracting opportunities for minority-owned businesses. See Lambert (1993).

52. See Department of Justice Office of the Inspector General (2003a, 2003b).

53. Community activists Dennis Flores and David Galarza have filmed and posted on YouTube incidences of police brutality in Sunset Park, such as "Copwatch Sunset Park Puerto Rican Parade June 12th 2005," available at http://www.youtube.com/watch?v=dIYuop5DcpM. See also Yee (2012).

54. El Grito de Sunset Park's Facebook page is available at https://www.facebook.com/ElGritoDeSunsetPark?fref=ts.

55. The New York City Police Department email notice dated June 7, 2013, was forwarded by Community Board 7 to its email list with the subject heading "CORRECTION: SUNDAY, JUNE 9TH, 2013—PUERTO RICAN DAY PARADE RESTRICTIONS (SUNSET PARK)."

56. El Grito de Sunset Park, Facebook status on June 9, 2013, available at https://www.facebook.com/ElGritoDeSunsetPark?fref=ts.

3   THE WORKING POVERTY OF NEIGHBORHOOD REVITALIZATION

1. See Fiscal Policy Institute (2012) and Anon. (2012a).

2. A location quotient, expressed as a ratio, is a measure that compares a local economy to a reference economy in order to identify specializations. Location quotients were calculated for all industries to determine which location quotients are less than zero, suggesting that local employment is less than was expected for a given industry. A location quotient equal to zero suggests that the local employment is exactly sufficient to meet local demand. A location quotient that is greater than 1.0 indicates that a given industry serves a demand for service and goods that extends beyond the local economy.

3. The Center for Family Life is the subject of a 2003 book, *Nurturing the One, Supporting the Many,* by Columbia University School of Social Work faculty Peg McCartt Hess, Brenda G. McGowan, and Michael Botsko, and a related documentary film, *A Brooklyn Family Tale.*

4. The Vision 2020 comprehensive waterfront plan, released in March 2011, includes a description of the city's six Significant Maritime and Industrial Areas (SMIAs) and notes that Sunset Park has the highest job density among the city's SMIAs. See New York City Department of City Planning (2011, Appendix B).

5. On the Triangle Shirtwaist Factory fire, see Cornell University Industrial and Labor Relations (2011).

6. Johnson (2013) and Fragrance Chen (2013).

7. See Landman (2000). Marc Landman is the owner of Jomat of New York, a manufacturer of women's sportswear and Girl Scouts uniforms.

8. The Fiscal Policy Institute (2003) study on New York City's garment industry lists world-renowned designer labels that are produced in the city, such as Calvin Klein, Jones New York, Vera Wang, and Ralph Lauren.

9. Data source is the New York State ES 202 data for the first quarter of 2010. ES 202 data is collected by the Bureau of Labor Statistics and enumerates firms that pay unemployment compensation, so the firm numbers may be an underrepresentation of the actual firm numbers.

10. For an overview of history and current development trends affecting the Midtown Garment Center, see Bleyer (2007). Real Deal Staff (2008) and Tarquinio (2008) illustrate current development pressures; as Tarquinio also indicates, much of the new hotel development in the Garment Center is the work of two Chinese American developers—Sam Chang (McSam Hotel Group) and John Lam (Lam Group). Overseeing the area's rebranding is the Fashion District BID now known as the Garment District Alliance, whose mission is to "support the Garment District's transformation into a modern, 24/7, Midtown office, dining and hotel destination," as noted on the website (http://www.garmentdistrict nyc.com/the-fashion-center/).

11. Chen (2000), Dworak (2000), and Liu (2000). May Chen is the former international vice president of UNITE HERE and manager of Local 23-25. Linda Dworak is the former executive director of the Garment Industry Development Corporation. Annie Liu is the former education and training director of the Garment Industry Development Corporation.

12. See U.S. House of Representatives, Committee on Education and the Workforce, Subcommittee on Oversight and Investigations (1998) and Center for Economic and Social Rights (1999).

13. Personal files of May Chen.

14. The number of garment manufacturers and contractors cited is obtained by zip code from the New York State Apparel Industry Task Force, which is required by New York State Labor Law Article 12A to maintain a list of registered garment manufacturers and contractors. Since registration is contingent upon meeting basic labor standards, including maintaining workers' compensation/disability insurance and providing unemployment insurance coverage, the New York State Apparel Industry Task Force list may in fact underestimate the actual numbers of firms, particularly in immigrant neighborhoods such as Sunset Park. See New York State Department of Labor (n.d.). The Fashion Center zip code is 10018, Sunset Park zip codes are 11220 and 11232, and Chinatown zip codes are 10002, 10012, and 10013.

15. Thomas (2005). Phaedra Thomas is the former executive director of the Southwest Brooklyn Industrial Development Corporation.

16. A recent Department of Labor investigation of a Long Island City contractor with a Chinese workforce found that employers handed out a "cheat sheet" with prepared answers for employees in the event they were interviewed by investigators. See Greenhouse (2008).

17. The testimonials were compiled into two monographs. See Silver, Ortiz, and Nolan (1997) and Silver, Ortiz, and Nolan (1999).

18. The Kings County Apparel Association formed in 1996 to represent Sunset Park's Chinese garment contractors in discussions held by Brooklyn Borough president Howard Golden to improve the neighborhood's garment industry (Hum 2003).

19. Phone conversation with Assemblyman Ortiz's Sunset Park office, September 6, 2012.

20. See Chinese Staff and Workers' Association (n.d.).

21. The National Mobilization Against Sweatshops "Ain't I a Woman?!" campaign continues to organize against sweatshops in the tristate region. The campaign's website is available at http://aintiawoman.org/.

22. See Good Jobs New York (2004).

23. See Lower Manhattan Development Corporation (n.d.).

24. In addition to heightened enforcement of nuisance laws, which has driven the designer knock-off trade into basements and apartments (see Wilson 2011), City Council member Margaret Chin introduced Bill 0544 in April 2011. The bill would make the purchase of a counterfeit item a misdemeanor, with a $1,000 penalty or a one-year jail sentence.

25. The Save the Garment Center website is available at www.savethegarmentcenter.org.

26. The map is available at http://dev.madeinmidtown.org/#modules/slideshow/midtown-manhattan-is-the-center-of-nycs-fashion-industry.

27. See New York City Economic Development Corporation (n.d.-d), Save the Garment Center website (http://savethegarmentcenter.org/), and Williams (2013), which features New York City designer Nanette Lepore, who describes the city's "explosion" in fashion creativity and design. Lepore produces her high-end clothing line in the Midtown Garment Center, which she argues is essential to high-quality clothing production.

28. The July 2012 New York State Department of Labor Apparel Task Force database lists the business names and addresses of the 198 garment manufacturers/contractors in Sunset Park. Based on the business address, I matched the garment shop with the property owner using the 2011 New York City Primary Land Use Tax Lot Output (PLUTO™) data.

29. See the website for Steiner Studios, available at http://www.steinerstudios.com/about/.

30. See New York City Economic Development Corporation (n.d.-b).

31. One of my most vivid memories of Sunset Park's street vendors took place in my father's backyard on a warm day in May 2010 as I watched his neighbor frying chicken wings, which he then transported by bicycle to a food cart on 8th Avenue.

32. See, for example, White (2011) and Anon. (2012c).

33. In 1979, New York City set the number of general merchandise licenses at 853 and food vending permits at 3,000. First Amendment vendors and disabled veterans are exempt from any caps. The current waiting list for a vending license is more than twenty-five years, and no names have been added to the waiting list since 1993.

34. New York City's Department of Small Business Services administers and oversees Business Improvement Districts. For more information, refer to the Small Business Services website, available at http://www.nyc.gov/html/sbs/html/neighborhood/bid.shtml.

35. The debate on a Manhattan Chinatown BID was highly contentious, and despite an unprecedented number of property owners who opposed the BID, the New York City Council approved its formation on September 21, 2011, with fifty votes in favor and zero votes in opposition. See, for example, Jan Lee's Civic Center Residents Coalition blog, available at http://www.ccrcnyc.com/search/label/Chinatown%20BID; the Chinatown Partnership Local Development Corporation website, available at http://www.chinatownpartnership.org/; and Berger (2011).

36. Giordano (2012). Renee Giordano is the executive director of the Sunset Park Fifth Avenue BID.

37. Tony Giordano is married to Renee Giordano.

38. Giordano (2012) described a survey of street vendors conducted by the BID that found that most vendors are immigrant Latino residents of Sunset Park.

39. During my interview with Renee Giordano (2012), she noted several times that 5th Avenue is restricted and that lack of enforcement accounts for the continued presence of street vendors on the commercial avenue.

40. Giordano (2012).

41. For Street Vendors Project member James Williams's testimony, see New York City Council (2008, 133) and Jessica Lee (2009).

42. City Council member Julissa Ferreras who represents Pan-Latino Corona in Queens, is quoted by Mora-Mass (2011) as describing Roosevelt Avenue as a "no-man's land" and a "poor sector of the Third World" because of the street vendors.

43. Email exchange with Miguel Hernandez, legislative aide to City Council member Sara Gonzalez, June 6, 2013.

4 IMMIGRANT GROWTH COALITIONS AND NEIGHBORHOOD CHANGE

1. According to the Financial Institutions Reform, Recovery, and Enforcement Act of 1989, minority banks are defined as banking institutions in which minorities have at least 51 percent ownership and also in which a majority of board directors or account holders as well as the community served is also predominately minority. Minorities are defined as African Americans, Native Americans, Native Alaskans, Native Hawaiians, Hispanic Americans, Asian Americans, or women (Federal Deposit Insurance Corporation 2002).

2. In the 1980s, Flushing, Queens, was the subject of much media coverage on the role of Taiwanese capital and the distinct class composition of Chinese immigrant investors in local real estate and small businesses. Increasingly, transnational capital and immigrant growth coalitions are also present in Manhattan's Chinatown and Sunset Park.

3. Transnational remittances are not a new phenomenon; however, the scale of and importance to the gross domestic product of several developing countries is new. For example, remittances are second only to oil exports in Mexico's gross domestic product. While much research and policy attention is on Mexico and Central and South America, the Philippines, India, and China also receive large volumes of remittances from immigrants in the United States.

4. For recent studies, see Singer and Paulson (2004); Bowdler (2005); and Bocian, Ernst, and Li (2006).

5. Anon. (2007c) includes two tables that ranked neighborhoods according to the number of bank branches in 2006, and Sunset Park ranked fourth among the top five neighborhoods with the most bank branches.

6. According to the Federal Deposit Insurance Corporation (www.fdic.gov), commercial real estate lending is defined as loans for construction and development, multifamily housing, and nonresidential real estate purchase and/or development.

7. A sample of the numerous articles and studies on the gentrification of Manhattan's Chinatown includes CAAAV (2008), Powell (2011), and Toy (2006).

8. Based on the Federal Reserve Board (2013) data, I enumerated the number of Asian foreign banks with U.S. offices in New York City by country: Japan(23), China (9), South Korea (8), Taiwan (7), India (5), and Pakistan (3). Hong Kong, Indonesia, Philippines, and Singapore each have 2 foreign bank offices in New York City, while Thailand and

Malaysia have 1 each. Several foreign banks have acquired U.S. banks to extend their investment presence and activity in dynamic growth markets. For example, in early January 2006, Hong Kong's Bank of East Asia (BEA) acquired the National American Bancorp in San Francisco, which according to Chief Executive David KP Li is "a significant milestone for BEA's strategic expansion in the U.S." (Bank of East Asia 2006).

9. UCB collapsed because of overleveraged loans, primarily in commercial real estate, and was acquired by East West Bank in November 2009 (Reckard 2009).

10. Twenty-nine of Cathay Bank's thirty-seven domestic branch offices are located in California, with the next largest cluster of four branches in New York City's Flushing, Queens (opened in 1986); Sunset Park, Brooklyn (opened in 2002); and Manhattan Chinatown (opened in 1997 and 2005). Similarly, UCB's fifty-five domestic branch offices are concentrated in California but include four branch offices in New York City (two in Manhattan Chinatown and one each in Flushing and Brooklyn).

11. In the past year, UCB acquired two small banks—Asian American Bank in Boston, with three bank branches in historic Boston Chinatown and the rapidly growing Asian communities of Allston/Brighton and Quincy, and Pacifica Bancorp, Inc., in the Washington state, with bank branches in Bellevue and Seattle. The acquisition of Pacifica Bancorp, Inc., marks UCB's entry into the Pacific Northwest and a further consolidation of its dominance in financing trade relations with the Pacific Rim (Anon. 2005).

12. A small news announcement released in September 2005 publicized the purchase of Great Eastern Bank and its five local branches for a sum of $28.4 million by Cathay General Bancorp (the holding company that owns Cathay Bank). A month later, newspaper accounts in Los Angeles and New York City noted that UCBH Holdings Inc. (the holding company that owns UCB) intended to expand its presence in New York City with the acquisition of Great Eastern Bank for $103.4 million. In response, Cathay Bank CEO and president Dunson K. Cheng raised Cathay Bank's bid to match UCBH and threatened to exercise Cathay Bank's 41 percent stock ownership of Great Eastern Bank to oppose a sale to UCBH (Reckard 2006). According to its shareholder rules, two-thirds of Great Eastern Bank's shareholders need to approve a sale. Despite Great Eastern Bank's preference for a merger with UCB, Cathay Bank aggressively pursued the acquisition, and its efforts ultimately succeeded with the Federal Reserve Board and New York State Department of Banking rulings that approved Cathay Bank's purchase of 100 percent of Great Eastern Bank's outstanding stock.

13. Joseph Liu is the father of the first Asian American elected official in New York City, John Liu, who frequently confronted questions regarding his father's indictment during his 2001 campaign for the New York City Council (Shifrel 2001).

14. A second incident occurred later that year in which five former members of Great Eastern Bank's board of directors were ordered by the Federal Reserve Board to make restitution for "alleged breaches of fiduciary duties, violations of law and regulations, and unsafe and unsound banking practices" (Federal Reserve Board 2002).

15. See United States Attorney, Southern District of New York (2003); Retsinas (2003a, 2003b); and Barron (2003).

16. As stated in *The People of the State of New York v. Abacus Federal Savings Bank et al.,* Indictment No. 2480-2012 in the New York Supreme Court for New York County.

17. According to the CDFI Fund online awardees/allocatees database (available at http://www.cdfifund.gov/awardees/db/basicSearchResults.asp), FAIB was awarded a Bank Enterprise Award in 2001 ($363,000), 2002 ($843,275), 2004 ($1.5 million), 2005 ($500,000), 2006 ($500,000), and 2007 ($500,000).

18. For the text of the FDIC's order to cease and desist, see Federal Deposit Insurance Corporation (2007b).

19. Banco Credito was a key lender of construction loans in Puerto Rico, and a recession that started in 1974 led to the collapse of this industry. Banco Credito was sold to two banks—Santander in Spain and Banco Popular in Puerto Rico.

20. See Scheck (2006, 76–77).

21. A 2005 study on Sunset Park remittances by a group of Hunter College students counted at least fifteen wire transfer agencies.

22. See Scott (2004).

23. The FDIC website is a repository of financial information for all FDIC insured institutions. The website includes a link to industry and bank statistics at http://www.fdic.gov/bank/statistical/. The June 30, 2012, deposit data was retrieved from this FDIC website. Manhattan Chinatown is defined by three zip codes: 10038, 10013, and 10002. Downtown Flushing is defined by two zip codes: 11355 and 11354. See also Chan (2002).

24. The most recent year for HMDA data available at this writing is 2011.

25. My analysis using 2000–2008 HMDA to look at ethnic bank lending in New York City overall found similar findings as in Sunset Park, with minimal ethnic bank involvement in home mortgage lending (Hum 2011).

26. Yu (2005). Emily Yu was a loan officer with Washington Mutual.

27. Using HMDA data, I compared bank decisions on loan applications for the purchase of a one- to four-family home by racial groups for two years—2006 (before the 2008 financial crisis) and 2011. I found that while the number of Asian applicants was roughly comparable, their denial rate increased from 17 percent to 20 percent. As Table 4.3 indicates, ethnic banks originated only 11 percent of home mortgage loans to Asian applicants in 2006 and 69 percent to Asian applicants in 2011.

28. Commercial real estate loans are defined as loans for income-producing residential properties such as condominium developments, apartment buildings, hotels, and motels as well as commercial properties, including office, retail, and industrial properties.

29. For photos of development projects in Sunset Park, see Wired New York (2005).

30. See Gabby (2009).

31. I used public records from the New York State Division of Corporations' State Records & UCC database and New York City's ACRIS, PLUTO, and DoB databases to track ownership and financing of these developments.

32. While Sunset Park is largely within the boundaries of Community Board 7, east of 8th Avenue to Ft. Hamilton Parkway—which is also considered part of Sunset Park—is in Community Board 12.

33. Based on compiling a database of the New York City DoB permit applications for Sunset Park defined by two zip codes, 11220 and 11232, for a six-month period in 2008, I reviewed the names of all property owners or LLC contacts to identify those with Asian surnames.

34. New York City DoB BIN #310139169.

35. New York City DoB BIN #310135975.

36. A June 24, 2008, search in the Yellow Pages for realtors in Sunset Park's two zip codes—11220 and 11232—resulted in 104 real estate agencies.

37. Xie (2006). Chang Xie was the director of the Brooklyn Chinese American Planning Council.

38. Kleinfield (1986) profiles several key Chinatown elites, including Mr. Lam.

39. The website for the Lam Group is available at http://www.lamgroupnyc
.com/. A 2012 interview in which John Lam details his trajectory from garment factory
owner to a real estate development is available at http://www.youtube.com/watch?v=G
-VbE2wuyrQ.
40. Manhattan Savings Institution was chartered in New York state in 1850, changed
its name to Manhattan Savings Bank in 1942, merged with Federal Republic National
Bank of New York in 1996, and in 1999 merged with HSBC Bank USA.
41. Accessed on http://www.abacus.com's link to "Who Banks with Abacus" on February 2, 2006.
42. Based on the five-year estimates from the 2007–2011 American Community
Survey.
43. For a recent analysis of rental housing costs in New York City, see Liu (2012b).
44. U.S. Department of Housing and Urban Development (n.d.).
45. For an online exhibit of photos taken by rent strikers of life in Sunset Park, see
Romano (2012). See also Neuhauser (2012).
46. Based on the 2007–2011 American Community Survey.
47. A copy of the Community Board 7 flyer is available on the Concerned Citizens of
Greenwood Heights website at http://www.ccgreenwoodhts.com/get-your-cb7-sro-illegal
-conversion-community-forum-flyer/.
48. Because the focus of this discussion on CRA pertains to small, intermediate, and
large banks, I omit the CRA requirements for wholesale and limited-purpose banks.
49. Lee (2005). Vee How Lee is the CRA director of Amerasia Bank.
50. For Cathay Bank's 2007 CRA Performance Evaluation report, see Federal Deposit
Insurance Corporation (2007a).
51. For the press release on this merger, see Lilly and Kuo (2006). Mr. Koehler now
serves as the executive vice president of the Lending Department at Carver Federal Savings
Bank.
52. See New York State Department of Financial Services (n.d.).
53. Amalgamated Bank's website is available at http://www.amalgamatedbank.com/
home/aboutus.
54. Amalgamated Bank's application for a Sunset Park (North), Brooklyn Banking
Development District, November 19, 2007. Amalgamated Bank's community development approach states, "Together with our union, not-for-profit and government partners,
the Bank offers innovative and affordable solutions" (Amalgamated Bank n.d.).
55. Much research has been conducted on the reliance of Sunset Park's undocumented
Latino population on money transfer agencies and the exorbitant fees they charge to process remittances. See, for example, Neighborhood Economic Development Advocacy Project (2006) and Thompson (2007).

5 GENTRIFYING SUNSET PARK

1. A prime example is the blog site Queens Crap: A Website Focused on the Overdevelopment and "Tweeding" of the Borough of Queens in the City of New York, available
at http://queenscrap.blogspot.com/.
2. In February 2009, Aldofo Carrión was appointed by President Barack Obama as
the director of the new White House Office on Urban Policy.
3. Spielman (2009). Lynda Spielman is the former chair of Queens Community
Board 7.

4. Scott Stringer's 2005 study is titled "Elevating Citizen Government: A Blueprint to Reform and Empower Manhattan's Community Boards," and a summary of the key proposals is available at http://mbpo.org/free_details.asp?id=65.

5. For information about this program, see Stringer (2008).

6. The Campaign for Community-Based Planning website is available at http://communitybasedplanning.wordpress.com.

7. Citywide advocacy groups for immigrant rights, labor issues, and voting rights—including the New York Immigration Coalition, the Restaurant Opportunities Center (ROC-NY), the Chinese Staff and Workers' Association, and the New York Voting Rights Consortium—have been successful in mobilizing immigrants to participate in political actions and protests.

8. Orr (2007, 3) defines the ecology of civic engagement as "the terms by which major community and institutional sectors of a city relate to one another and their role in the structure and function of local political regimes."

9. A short video by Aaron Braesher (2007), founder of Concerned Citizens of Greenwood Heights, emphasizes the views of the harbor from Sunset Park and how the proposed development would obstruct these views.

10. Comments expressed by attendees of a March 1, 2007, emergency meeting at the Brooklyn Community Board 7 regarding the 420 42nd Street development.

11. Brown (2007) profiles Aaron Brashear, Concerned Citizens of Greenwood Heights, and his videotapes of alleged illegal construction activity.

12. Rodriguez's arrest and conviction were particularly embarrassing, as he was positioned to become the next City Council Speaker. See Marzulli (2003) and Saulny (2003).

13. Anon. (n.d.-b).

14. See Kuntzman (2004).

15. September 6, 2007, meeting at the New Chinese Promise Baptist Church with Reverend Samuel Wong, members of his parish, SPAN members, and EAIA members.

16. For Mayor Bloomberg's PlaNYC 2030 website, see City of New York (2013a).

17. The EAIA frequently brings Buddhist monks to community board meetings to express a need for space.

18. September 6, 2007, meeting at the New Chinese Promise Baptist Church with Reverend Wong, members of his parish, SPAN members, and EAIA members.

19. As indicated in March 2008 by a realtor representing a condominium building on 55th Street and 7th Avenue financed by the FAIB.

20. The Savoy Bakery owner's response to Reverend Wong's concern about the need for affordable housing was that new development would also increase his congregation.

21. The DCP policy that downzoning must be accompanied by upzoning elsewhere to accommodate the need for new development is noted by Queens DCP director John Young.

22. Quoted in Steinhauer (2005, my emphasis).

23. The DCP Proposed Sunset Park Rezoning Map is available at http://www.nyc.gov/html/dcp/pdf/sunset_park/proposed_zoning.pdf.

24. Brashear and Holwin (2005).

25. ¡Basta Ya! Sunset Rise Up on Sunset Park gentrification and the rezoning debate includes clips from the numerous community protests held in the neighborhood as well as at Community Board 7 meetings.

26. See *Chinese Staff and Workers Association et al., Appellants, v. City of New York et al., Respondents,* Court of Appeals of New York, 68 N.Y.2d 359, 502 N.E.2d 176, 509 N.Y.S.2d 499 (1986), N.Y. Lexis 20850.

27. For a discussion of Sunset Park Latino-Asian collaborations, including Sunset United, UPROSE organizing on environmental justice, and Asian American Legal Defense and Education Fund and Puerto Rican Legal Defense and Education Fund collaboration in political redistricting in Sunset Park, see Hum (2002b).

28. The standard definition of housing affordability used by the U.S. Department of Housing and Urban Development is no more than 30 percent of income spent on housing costs. Spending more has been referred to as "shelter poverty" by University of Massachusetts professor Michael Stone (2004).

29. SPAN held a neighborhood summit on September 23, 2007, with the stated goal "To find unity in the diverse voices of Sunset Park and create a plan for the future development of Sunset Park that will support families and residents" (Anon. 2007a).

30. See Tucker (2008). For coverage of the community, see NY1 (2008).

31. See Bloomberg (n.d.). For an interview with DCP director Amanda Burden, see Berg (2006). At the Asian Americans for Equality's Community Development Conference on October 26, 2007, Manhattan Borough president Scott Stringer commented that the "new paradigm" of affordable housing is based on zoning and land use.

32. This point was made by Hunter College Urban Planning professor Tom Angotti in his presentation at the October 12, 2007, Queens Historical Society conference at Queens College.

33. See Wisloski (2005), which includes a photo.

34. This exchange was observed by Dan Wiley, community liaison to Congresswoman Nydia Velázquez, and relayed to me in a personal conversation on March 13, 2008.

35. Community Board 7 chair Randy Peers had the same response to concerns about 8th Avenue serving as the boundary between Community Boards 7 and 12 at a June 2007 meeting prior to the DCP rezoning study.

36. In an email dated April 16, 2008, Julia Fitzgerald summarized an Affordable Housing Working Group (AHWG) meeting held to discuss the DCP's rezoning proposal and noted that "Various members of the AHWG expressed relief that City Planning had not proposed an even greater upzoning of any of the Avenues. Several members had feared a proposal of R8A for one or more of the Avenues, which would have permitted buildings of up to 12-stories. The group discussed the removal of the west side of 8th Avenue from the rezoning proposal, and did not come to a conclusion about it."

37. Information was retrieved from the New York City Department of Finance's Automatic City Register Information System (ACRIS), an online database (available at http://a836-acris.nyc.gov/CP/) that notes real estate transactions for tax purposes.

38. New York City's 311 is a primary resource for nonemergency services and information and can be reached by telephone or online at http://www1.nyc.gov/311/index.page.

39. DoB Bin #3010882, Complaint #3444036.

40. Brownstoner (2009).

41. UPROSE used to host the Sin Freno Films Youth Film Festival to feature videos produced by youths about Sunset Park's environmental conditions.

42. Publius (2008).

43. Ibid.

44. Ibid., my emphasis.

45. The Accountable Development Principles are affordable housing, livable wage jobs, sustainable environmental practices, and an accountable process. For video footage of City Council member David Yassky and state assemblymen Jim Brennan and Hakeem Jeffries signing the document, see Anon. (2008a).

46. See Pratt Center for Community Development (n.d.).

47. The website for Towards a 21st Century City for All is available at http://www.21cforall.org/.

48. John Burns, founder of the South Park Slope Community Group: Protecting Brooklyn's Future (http://www.southsouthslope.com), served as the chair of Community Board 7's Land Use Committee, and Aaron Brashear, founder of Concerned Citizens of Greenwood Heights, founded and chairs Community Board 7's Buildings and Construction Committee.

49. Section 197-a of the New York City Charter authorizes community boards to prepare a plan to guide future neighborhood development. While the City Planning Commission and the City Council need to approve a 197-a plan, there is no provision in the City Charter that these plans be enforced. For case studies of 197-a plans, see Angotti (2008b).

50. Brashear (2008). Aaron Brashear is a founding member of Concerned Citizens of Greenwood Heights.

51. The Mayor's Community Affairs Unit oversees New York City's fifty-nine community boards, and the website—available at http://www.nyc.gov/html/cau/html/cb/about.shtml—provides information, resources, and links to the community boards.

52. See Angotti (2008a, 5).

53. The *New York Daily News* and other local media venues provided regular coverage of the Sunset Park tenant actions during the summer of 2012. See Musumeci (2012) and Morales (2012a, 2012b).

6   POWER PLANTS, SEX SHOPS, INDUSTRIAL ZONES, AND OPEN SPACE

1. The film *A Village Called Versailles* documents the Vietnamese community's protest of the landfill near their Versailles neighborhood in New Orleans. The website for the film is available at http://avillagecalledversailles.com/.

2. For the 2007 report, see La Unión de la Comunidad Latina (n.d.). See also Pastor (2007).

3. For example, Flushing, Queens, is designated a New York State Brownfield Opportunity Area and is estimated to have thirty-two brownfields.

4. See New York City Department of City Planning (2011). For press coverage, see Santora (2010).

5. Gowanus Canal was designated a federal Superfund site in March 2010 even though the Bloomberg administration proposed its own cleanup in hopes of protecting the development potential of the site. Federal cleanup will take ten to twelve years (longer than the city's projection) and will cost $300 million to $500 million (Navarro 2010).

6. For planning purposes, the DCP divided the waterfront into twenty-two reaches based on common land-use patterns, natural features, physical boundaries, and community district lines. The nautical term "reach" refers to a continuous expanse of water. Sunset Park is included in the Brooklyn East River/Upper Bay reach, which extends for twelve miles and covers most of Brooklyn's working industrial waterfront.

7. See National Trust for Historic Preservation (2007) and Pogrebin (2007).

8. See Alex Garvin & Associates (2006).

9. The ArtMostFierce blog is available at http://artmostfierce.blogspot.com/2009/01/new-factory-in-brooklyn-industrial.html. See also Stein (2009).

10. City of New York (2013b). For a video of the June 11, 2013, briefing, see Anon. (2013b).

11. The relocation of the meatpacking distribution plant was part of Fort Greene's urban renewal plan to assemble land for the MetroTech development that launched the economic restructuring of downtown Brooklyn.

12. Sunset Park Community Resilience Workshop, April 24, 2013, Trinity Lutheran Church.

13. A *New York Times* editorial (Anon. 2001) criticized the state for lack of disclosure on siting decisions that burden low-income communities of color and for exploitation of legal loopholes to avoid comprehensive environmental impact studies.

14. Improved community outreach efforts are evident at the project's website (http://www.uspowergen.com/projects/south-pier/), which is available in four languages—English, Spanish, Chinese, and Arabic—along with an explanation of the project and photographs.

15. See Egeln (2008c). In 2011, UPROSE negotiated a Memorandum of Understanding on behalf of several community groups, including Community Board 7 and the Southwest Brooklyn Industrial Development Corporation, to formalize agreements with USPowerGen regarding a cap on emissions (Yeampierre 2013a; Laufer 2013b).

16. See New York Power Authority (2006), which has a link for a photo of the ground breaking.

17. See deGalarza (2006).

18. Efforts by New York City's Department of Environmental Protection to contain the odors resulting from the treatment of raw sewage at the facility are discussed by Muessig (2008).

19. New York State Office of General Counsel (n.d.).

20. *New York Times* coverage of Mayor Giuliani's actions to close sex shops in Times Square includes Allen (1998a, 1998b).

21. Numerous news articles document the growth of adult establishments in Sunset Park after the zoning amendments. See, for example, see Kwan (1997), McPhee (2000), and Egbert (2001).

22. As of July 2013, the establishment is still located on the corner of 4th Avenue and 39th Street but is now called Peyton's Playpen Gentleman's Club.

23. Gretchen Dykstra, quoted in Toy (1996).

24. Based on a sample of three ads in the June 6, 2013, issue of *Sing Tao Daily*.

25. The UPROSE website is available at www.uprose.org. See also Boehm (2003) and Yeampierre (2007).

26. For 2012 IBZ Boundary review maps and discussion, see http://www.nycedc.com/industry/industrial/nyc-industrial-business-zones.

27. According to a 2008 Pratt Center study, New York City's manufacturing zoned land is 12,542 acres, of which 4,100 acres (33 percent) is within an IBZ (Pratt Center for Community Development 2008).

28. DCP director Amanda Burden, quoted in New York City Economic Development Corporation (2005a).

29. See New York City Department of City Planning (n.d.).

30. For a map of the Southwest Brooklyn IBZ, see http://www.sbidc.org/documents/ southwest_brooklyn_map.pdf.

31. See the New York State Empire Zone at http://esd.ny.gov/businessprograms/ empirezones.html.

32. See Hotel BPM's website at http://www.hotelbpmbrooklyn.com/ for numerous links to related media articles, including the Hotel BPM "Fact Sheet" (Hotel BPM 2012).

33. See New York City Economic Development Corporation (n.d.-c).

34. For two recent news articles describing these firms, see Berger (2012) and Kusisto (2012).

35. For an extensive profile of Brooklyn artisanal manufacturers, see Wallace (2012).

36. The city is encouraging artists to locate in city-owned buildings in Sunset Park. For photographs of potential artist spaces, see Croghan (2012).

37. Since Times Equities withdrew from project, related online materials describing the project have been taken down. Times Equities spent more than $1 million in engineering and design studies. For a blog posting that depicts one of the illustrations for the proposed Sunset Marketplace, see Steve (2008).

38. See CBRE (2013), which includes photos of the interior spaces.

39. The subhead is a quotation from shipping executive Frangiskos G. Stafilopatis, president of Home Lines Cruises Inc. in a *New York Times* article (Lueck 1986).

40. TEU is a standard industry measure to compare freight volumes. A typical containerized cargo capacity is forty feet in length, eight feet in depth, and eight feet 6 inches in height and represents two TEUs. Growth projections are cited from Port Authority of New York and New Jersey (n.d.-a).

41. See also Port Authority of New York and New Jersey (2008), Anon. (2008e) and Anon. (n.d.-a).

42. Eddie Bautista, OWN activist and former director of community planning at NY Lawyers for the Public Interest, was recognized for his work mobilizing environmental justice coalitions to support the SWMP with a mayoral appointment as director of the Office of City Legislative Affairs in 2006 (City of New York Office of the Mayor 2006).

43. City Planning Commission (2005). The Hamilton MTS facility will receive residential waste from the central portion of Brooklyn, encompassing Community Districts 2, 6, 7, 8, 9, 10, 14, 16, 17, and 18.

44. See City of New York Department of Sanitation (2007) for the meeting transcript.

45. The website for Residents for Sane Trash Solutions is available at http://sanetrash .org/.

46. The Hugo Neu Corporation, a longtime U.S.-based New York City contractor, was purchased by the Australian company Sims Metal Management in 2005. The website for Sims Metal Management is available at http://www.simsmm.com.

47. See South Brooklyn Marine Terminal (n.d.).

48. See New York City Council Committee on Waterfronts (2005) and Bagli (2006).

49. Congressman Jerrold Nadler, memorandum on Red Hook and Sunset Park/South Brooklyn Marine Terminal and Axis Group, June 9, 2006.

50. See Brodsky (2004) and Port Authority of New York and New Jersey (n.d.-b).

51. The New York State Department of Transportation has agreed to rebuild the more than sixty-year-old Gowanus Expressway. The scenarios for its reconstruction include a tunnel that is most costly but would restore 3rd Avenue and improve air quality in the neighborhood. See New York State Department of Transportation (2006).

52. Congressman Jerrold Nadler, memorandum on Red Hook and Sunset Park/South Brooklyn Marine Terminal and Axis Group, June 9, 2006. See Bagli (2004).

53. Elizabeth Yeampierre, UPROSE executive director, frequently notes that the open space ratio for Sunset Park includes Greenwood Cemetery. See New Yorkers for Parks (2009) for an open-space map of City Council District 38, which encompasses Greenwood Cemetery.

54. See New York State Department of Environmental Conservation (2004).

55. This sentiment was echoed in Sunset Park's 197-a plan regarding the tunneling options for the Gowanus Expressway: "Removal of the viaduct may also lead to increased development pressures along Third Avenue that may threaten industrial preservation and development efforts on the waterfront" (Community Board 7 2011, 9).

56. New York State Department of State (2011, my emphasis).

57. Elizabeth Yeampierre, paraphrased in Slade (2013).

58. Notes from the Sunset Park Community Resiliency Workshop with the mayor's SIRR, April 24, 2013.

59. For a video of Eddie Bautista's March 2013 talk, see Garrison Institute (2013).

60. Ibid.

61. See, for example, New York City Council Committee on Waterfronts (2005).

62. Views expressed in interviews with the executive directors of Brooklyn Economic Development Corporation (Bartolomeo 2004) and South Brooklyn Industrial Development Corporation (Thomas 2005); Commissioner Robert Walsh (2003), New York City Department of Small Business Services; former commissioner Sayu Bhojwani (2003), Mayor's Office of Immigrant Affairs; and former director Carl Hum (2012), Mayor's Office of Manufacturing and Industrial Businesses.

63. See also Voien (2012b) and Warshawer (2008).

CONCLUSION

1. Wylde was responding to a question about the conditions of Sunset Park revitalization that includes immigrant working poverty and informalization.

2. Bransburg (2013). Vanessa Bransburg is the coordinator of the Worker Cooperative Development and leads the CFL's initiative to form worker cooperatives and provide citywide training.

3. Three workers cooperatives have websites: Si Si Puede! We Can Do It! (http://www.wecandoit.coop/), Beyond Care (http://www.beyondcare.coop/about.html), and Golden Steps (http://www.goldensteps.coop/index.php).

4. Bransburg (2013).

5. Bransburg (2013) noted that two worker cooperatives related to the construction and home improvement and maintenance industries—We Can Fix It and Color Me (interior painting)—failed because of the decline in the housing industry coupled with the do-it-yourself trend.

6. New York City Council (2013b). For local coverage, see Clarke (2013).

7. UPROSE hosted its third annual two-day citywide Climate Justice Youth Summit for teens and young adults ages fourteen to twenty-four in July 2013. For news coverage, see Anon. (2013a).

8. The Sunset Park Promise Neighborhood blog, which includes photos, is available at http://sunsetparkpromise.wordpress.com/.

9. See Sunset Park Promise Neighborhood (n.d.).

10. Lutheran Medical Center (n.d., 4).

11. The blog for the Sunset Park Promise Neighborhood Council (http://sunsetpark promise.wordpress.com/news/) includes a photo of community members wearing headphones for simultaneous translation.

12. Chin (2012a) quotes Reverend Samuel Cruz and David Galarza, founders of Occupy Sunset Park.

13. For news coverage, see Feuer (2012) and Conde (2012).

14. Good Friday Service, March 29, 2013, Trinity Lutheran Church, 411 46th Street, Brooklyn 11220.

15. See New York City Police Department (n.d.-a).

16. New York City Police Department (n.d.-b, 4).

17. From Sunset Park Unity Coalition Meeting Minutes, June 14, 2013. I was given a copy of the minutes by Occupy Sunset Park.

18. The website for the Sunset Park CSA is available at http://www.sunsetparkcsa .org/.

19. My interview with Reverend Juan Carlos Ruiz (2013) started with a discussion of the July 15, 2013, anti-immigration reform rally in Washington, D.C. organized by the Black American Leadership Alliance. Reverend Ruiz described the division among people of color as "fighting over crumbs" when we should be "demanding inclusion at the table."

References

Abbott, Edith. 1924. "Federal Immigration Policies, 1864–1924." *University Journal of Business* 2 (2): 133–156.

Abel, David, and Kristen Green. 2006. "34 Hurt in Troubled Bus Line's Latest Episode." *Boston Globe,* September 6.

Abu-Lughod, Janet. 1999. *New York, Chicago, Los Angeles: America's Global Cities.* Minneapolis: University of Minnesota Press.

Adcock, Thomas. 2007. "Local Lawyers Fight Atlantic Yards Project as 'Own Law Firm.'" New York Law Journal, June 8. Available at http://www.newyorklawjournal.com/PubArticleNY.jsp?id=900005483130.

Aderer, Konrad. 2013. Interview by the author, Trinity Lutheran Church, July 12.

Adinyayev, Avi, Daniel Raucher, Tina Krekoukis, and Derek Rada. 2002. "Fresh Kills Landfill (1947–2001)." CUNY Solid Waste Disposal project, Fall. Available at http://acc6.its.brooklyn.cuny.edu/~scintech/solid/silandfill.html.

Afridi, Humera. 2005. "The Coney Island of Their Mind." *New York Times,* June 19.

Aguilar–San Juan, Karin. 2009. *Little Saigons: Staying Vietnamese in America.* Minneapolis: University of Minnesota Press.

Agyeman, Julian. 2005. *Sustainable Communities and the Challenge of Environmental Justice.* New York: New York University Press.

Akram, Susan M., and Kevin R. Johnson. 2002. "Race, Civil Rights, and Immigration Law after September 11, 2001: The Targeting of Arabs and Muslims." *New York University Annual Survey of American Law* 58 (3): 295–355.

Alanis, Leticia. 2013. Interview by the author, Sunset Park, Brooklyn, July 8.

Aldrich, Howard, and Roger Waldinger. 1990. "Ethnicity and Entrepreneurship." *Annual Review of Sociology* 16:111–135.

Alex Garvin & Associates. 2006. "Visions for New York City: Housing and the Public Realm." Report prepared for the New York City Economic Development Corporation, May. Available at http://www.streetsblog.org/wp-content/uploads/2006/08/Garvin_Report_Full.pdf.

Ali, Amina. 2013a. Telephone interview by the author, June 26.

———. 2013b. Telephone interview by the author, July 18.

Allam, Abeer. 2005. "Amid Claims of Rising Prostitution, Complaints, Followed by Arrests." *New York Times,* May 8.

Allen, Michael O. 2001. "Four Face Prison for Fraud." *New York Daily News,* December 24.

Allen, Mike. 1998a. "Giuliani Vows More Closings of Sex Shops." *New York Times,* August 30.

———. 1998b. "New York Begins to Raid and Close Adult Businesses." *New York Times,* August 2.

Amalgamated Bank. n.d. "Community Development." Available at http://www.amalgam atedbank.com/home/aboutus/communitydev.

Amateau, Albert. 2011. "City Council, Chin Pulls the Plug on Bowery Old-Timer." *The Villager,* September 22–28.

American Planning Association. 2013. "Getting Back to Business: Addressing the Needs of Rockaway Businesses Impacted by Superstorm Sandy." A report by the American Planning Association–New York Metro Chapter for the Rockaway Development & Revitalization Corporation, May. Available at http://www.nyplanning.org/docs/APA -NYM%20Business%20Recovery%20Report%20to%20RDRC.pdf.

Anderson, Kay J. 1987. "The Idea of Chinatown: The Power of Place and Institutional Practice in the Making of a Racial Category." *Annals of the Association of American Geographers* 77 (4): 580–598.

Anderson, Martin. 1964. *The Federal Bulldozer: A Critical Analysis of Urban Renewal, 1949–1962.* Cambridge, MA: MIT Press.

Angotti, Tom. 2008a. "Is New York's Sustainability Plan Sustainable?" July. Available at http://www.hunter.cuny.edu/ccpd/repository/files/is-nycs-sustainability-plan-sustain able.pdf.

———. 2008b. *New York for Sale: Community Planning Confronts Global Real Estate.* Cambridge, MA: MIT Press.

———. 2009. "Zoning without Planning." *Gotham Gazette,* May 26. Available at http:// www.gothamgazette.com/index.php/opinions/223-zoning-without-planning.

———. 2010. "Land Use and the New York City Charter." Submitted to the New York City Charter Commission. August. Available at http://www.hunter.cuny.edu/ccpd/ repository/files/charterreport-angotti-2.pdf.

Angotti, Tom, and Steven Romalewski. 2006. "Willets Point Land Use Study." Hunter College Center for Community Planning & Development, April. Available at http:// www.hunter.cuny.edu/ccpd/repository/files/willetspoint.pdf.

Anon. n.d.-a. "China Is No. 1 for Exports, Too." Available at http://mycrains.crainsnew york.com/stats-and-the-city/2011/transportation/china-is-no-1-for-exports-too.

———. n.d.-b. "The City Council's Term Limits." Gotham Gazette. Available at http:// www.gothamgazette.com/searchlight/2003.03.termlimits.shtml.

———. n.d.-c. "Inner City Press Bank Beat Archive 2005–2006: December 12, 2005." Available at http://www.innercitypress.org/bankb106.html.

———. n.d.-d. "The Rise and Fall of the Ansonia Clock Company." Available at http:// www.antiqueansoniaclocks.com/ansonia-clock-history.php.

———. 1908. "Problem of Freight Congestion." *New York Times,* November 29.

———. 1909. "To Enlarge Bush Stores: Boston Delegation Here to Study the Method of Handling Goods." *New York Times,* September 21.

———. 1910. "Bush Terminal Lofts." *New York Times,* July 17.

————. 1915. "Chinese Merchants See Port Facilities." *New York Times*, June 5.

————. 1918. "Bush Terminal Plant Largest of Its Kind." *New York Times*, January 1.

————. 1919. "Italian Strikers Fire on Workmen Going to Piers." *New York Times*, October 28.

————. 1924. "Cooperatives Open Housing Exhibition." *New York Times*, February 27.

————. 1945. "Our Men Move into and out of the Fighting Fronts." *New York Times*, January 10.

————. 1957. "Norton Lilly Moving to Newark after 52 Years at Bush Terminal in Brooklyn." *New York Times*, September 24.

————. 1960. "Puerto Rican Lawyer Sets Up a Savings Concern in the Bronx." *New York Times*, May 3.

————. 1961. "Transport News: Inquiry Is Ended." *New York Times*, November 4.

————. 1965. "Text of President's Speech on Immigration," *New York Times*, October 3.

————. 1969a. "Bush Terminal to Close Piers." *New York Times*, February 1.

————. 1969b. "City Aide Deplores Closing of Piers at Bush Terminal." *New York Times*, February 5.

————. 1969c. "City Picks Site in Sunset Park for Fort Greene Meat Market." *New York Times*, August 19.

————. 1979. "Brooklyn Brownstones: Two Tours Scheduled." *New York Times*, October 18.

————. 1981a. "House Tours for an Autumn Weekend." *New York Times*, October 15.

————. 1981b. "Incinerator Closing in South Brooklyn." *New York Times*, January 3.

————. 2001. "The Turbine Mess." *New York Times*, March 20.

————. 2005. "Pacifica Bancorp Buyout Complete." Puget Sound Business Journal, November 1. Available at http://www.bizjournals.com/seattle/stories/2005/10/31/daily12.html.

————. 2007a. "All Out to the Sunset Park Summit Sept. 23rd." Sunset Park Autonomous Zone, August 27. Available at http://sunsetparkzone.blogspot.com/search?updated-min=2007-01-01T00%3A00%3A00-05%3A00&updated-max=2008-01-01T00%3A00%3A00-05%3A00&max-results=17.

————. 2007b. "Memories of New York's Only Chinese-Norwegian Fusion Restaurant." February 25. Available at http://lostnewyorkcity.blogspot.com/2007/02/memories-of-new-yorks-only-chinese.html.

————. 2007c. "Poor Can't Bank on Branches." *New York Daily News*, September 17.

————. 2008a. "Hakeem Jeffries vs. Development Gone Wild." Video uploaded on May 31. Available at http://www.youtube.com/watch?v=m7rtszDTjL4.

————. 2008b. "How Immigrants Saved Social Security." *New York Times*, April 2.

————. 2008c. "Mayor Bloomberg's 2008 State of the City Address." *New York Times*, January 17.

————. 2008d. "Shipments through Port Authority Spike 425%." Going Coastal, July 1. Available at http://goingcoastal.wordpress.com/2008/07/01/shipments-through-port-authority-spike-425/.

————. 2011. "*One On 1*: Arab American Association Director Finds Time For It All." NY1, July 25. Available at http://www.ny1.com/content/shows/one_on_1_archives_qz/143662/one-on-1—arab-american-association-director-finds-time-for-it-all.

————. 2012a. "Immigrants and Small Business." *New York Times*, June 30.

————. 2012b. "Reader Says Sunset Park Vending Bill Is a Boon for the Neighborhood." Sunset Park Chronicles, April 21. Available at http://www.sunsetparkchron.com/2010/04/21/reader-says-sunset-park-vending-bill-is-a-boon-for-the-neighborhood/.

————. 2012c. "Sunset Park." Eat in Translation, January 1. Available at http://www .eatingintranslation.com/sunset_park/.

————. 2013a. "Hundreds of Young Adults Attend UPROSE NYC Climate Justice Youth Summit." News 12 Brooklyn, July 27. Available at http://brooklyn.news12 .com/news/hundreds-of-young-adults-attend-uprose-nyc-climate-justice-youth -summit-1.5781140.

————. 2013b. "Mayor Bloomberg Presents 'A Stronger, More Resilient New York.'" Video uploaded June 11, length 54:55. Available at http://www.youtube.com/ watch?v=w7TtVB2fJCc.

————. 2013c. "US DOT Orders Fung Wah Bus to Immediately Cease Passenger Service." CBS New York, February 6. Available at http://newyork.cbslocal.com/2013/02/26/ us-dot-orders-fung-wah-bus-to-immediately-cease-passenger-service/.

Anuta, Joe. 2012. "EDC and Shulman's Development Group Admit to Illegal Lobbying." *TimesLedger*, July 3.

————. 2013. "Huge Flushing Commons Project Delayed, Again." Crain's New York Business, October 30. Available at http://www.crainsnewyork.com/article/20131030/ REAL_ESTATE/131039989.

Aponte-Parés, Luis. 1998. "Lessons from *El Barrio*—The East Harlem Real Great Society/Urban Planning Studio: A Puerto Rican Chapter in the Fight for Urban Self-Determination." *New Political Science* 20 (4): 399–420.

Appelbaum, Alec. 2007. "Housing Advocate Brad Lander to Run for DeBlasio's Council Spot." New York Magazine, November 16. Available at http://nymag.com/daily/ intel/2007/11/housing_advocate_brad_lander_t.html.

Argento, Mike. 2013. "Golden Venture 20 Years Later Today: Many Lives Remain in Limbo." York Daily Record, June 6. Available at http://www.ydr.com/history/ ci_23362804/golden-venture-20-years-later-many-lives-remain.

Armstrong, Regina, and Tina Lund. 2005. "Up from the Ruins: Why Rezoning New York City's Manufacturing Areas for Housing Makes Sense." Manhattan Institute, Rethinking Development Report No. 2, June. Available at http://www.manhattan -institute.org/html/rdr_02.htm.

Asian American Legal Defense and Education Fund. 2004. "Special Registration: Discrimination and Xenophobia as Government Policy." Available at http://www.aaldef .org/docs/AALDEF-Special-Registration-2004.pdf.

————. 2012. "AALDEF Preliminary Response to LATFOR Redistricting Maps' Impact on Asian Americans." Press release, January 26. Available at http://aaldef.org/ press-releases/press-release/aaldef-preliminary-response-to-latfor-redistricting-maps -impact-on-asian-americans.html.

Associated Press. n.d. "AP's Probe Into NYPD Intelligence Operations." Available at http://www.ap.org/Index/AP-In-The-News/NYPD.

————. 2012. "Superstorm Sandy Deaths, Damage and Magnitude: What We Know One Month Later." Huffington Post, November 29. Available at http://www.huffington post.com/2012/11/29/superstorm-hurricane-sandy-deaths-2012_n_2209217.html.

Attorney General of the State of New York. 2012. "In the Matter of the Investigation by Eric T. Schneiderman, Attorney General of the State of New York, of New York City Economic Development Corporation, Flushing–Willets Point–Corona Local Development Corporation, and Coney Island Development Corporation." Assurance No. 12-068, July 2. Available at http://www.ag.ny.gov/sites/default/files/press -releases/2012/AOD-No-12-068.pdf.

Babin, Janet. 2012. "A Wider Panama Canal Could Lead to a NY Boom, but City May Not Be Ready." Transportation Nation, March 9. Available at http://transportation nation.org/2012/03/09/a-wider-panama-canal-could-lead-to-a-ny-boom-but-city-may-not-be-ready/.

Bagli, Charles V. 1998. "Holding On in the Garment Center; Shops Struggle with Soaring Rents in a Shrinking District." *New York Times,* March 2.

———. 2004. "Is a Blue-Collar Future a Luxury on the Waterfront?" *New York Times,* February 4.

———. 2006. "Shipping Is Up in Brooklyn but Future Is Shaky." *New York Times,* June 29.

———. 2008a. "Lease Ends Uncertainty for Red Hook Cargo Docks." *New York Times,* April 25.

———. 2008b. "Trade Center to Get Tenant from China." *New York Times,* June 3. Available at http://www.nytimes.com/2008/06/03/nyregion/03tower.html?_r=0.

Baker, Al, and Joseph Goldstein. 2011. "After an Earlier Misstep, a Minutely Planned Raid." *New York Times,* November 15.

Bank of East Asia. 2006. "BEA Group to Acquire National American Bancorp to Enter the San Francisco Market." Press release, January 3. Available at http://www.hkbea.com/FileManager/EN/Content_2396/20060103e1.pdf.

Bao, Xiaolan. 2002. "Sweatshops in Sunset Park: A Variation of the Late 20th Century Chinese Garment Shops in New York City." *International Labor and Working-Class History* 61:69–90.

Barbanel, Josh. 2004. "Remaking or Preserving the City's Face." *New York Times,* January 18.

Barron, James. 2003. "Chinatown Bank Endures Run as Fear Trumps Reassurances." *New York Times,* April 23.

Barry, Dan. 1995. "The Fading Neon of Times Square's Sex Shops; Elusive, Undisputed King of Midtown Pornography May Be Forced Out of Business." *New York Times,* October 28.

Bartlett, Josey. 2013. "Day after Willets Point Rally Helen Marshall Approves Proposed Mall." *Queens Chronicle,* July 1.

Bartolomeo, Joan G. 2004. Interview by the author, Brooklyn Economic Development Corporation, November 17.

Bayoumi, Moustafa. 2006. "Arab America's September 11th." *Nation,* September 25.

Bell, Daniel. 1973. *The Coming of Post-Industrial Society.* New York: Basic Books.

Bennett, Drake. 2013. "Mortgage Fraud Prosecutors Pounce on a Small Bank." *Business-Week,* January 31.

Bennett, Robert A. 1985a. "Bank's Closing Incenses Depositors in Chinatown." *New York Times,* June 25.

———. 1985b. "Deposits of Chinatown Bank Sold." *New York Times,* June 27.

———. 1985c. "F.D.I.C. Seeks Merger for Chinatown Bank." *New York Times,* June 26.

Benoit, David. 2013. "The Top 50 U.S. Banks by Assets." *Wall Street Journal,* September 26.

Berg, Nate. 2006. "Interview: New York City Planning Director Amanda Burden." Planetizen, October 9. Available at http://www.planetizen.com/node/21476.

Berger, Joseph. 2003. "Over 100 Years, the Williamsburg Bridge Has Diversified a Borough." *New York Times,* June 22.

———. 2011. "Chinatown to Join Roster of Business Improvement Districts." *New York Times,* September 21.

———. 2012. "Instead of Industrial Giants, Brooklyn Has Niche Factories." *New York Times,* August 7.

———. 2013a. "In Brooklyn Neighborhood, Multiplying Massage Parlors Cause Residents to Fret." *New York Times,* June 25.

———. 2013b. "Prostitution Investigation at Day Spas Results in 19 Arrests." *New York Times,* July 11.

Bernhardt, Annette, Siobhan McGarth, and James DeFilippis. 2007. *Unregulated Work in the Global City: Employment and Labor Law Violations in New York City.* New York: Brennan Center for Justice, New York University Law School.

Bernstein, Fred A. 2011. "A New Start for an Ambitious Queens Condo Complex." *New York Times,* September 1.

Bernstein, Nina. 2004a. "Detainees' Lawyers Sue over Secret Jail Recordings." *New York Times,* May 5.

———. 2004b. "In F.B.I., Innocent Detainee Found Unlikely Ally." *New York Times,* June 30.

———. 2004c. "2 Men Charge Abuse in Arrests after 9/11 Terror Attack." *New York Times,* May 3.

———. 2005. "Record Immigration Changing New York's Neighborhoods." *New York Times,* January 24.

———. 2006a. "Judge Rules That U.S. Has Broad Powers to Detain Noncitizens Indefinitely." *New York Times,* June 15.

———. 2006b. "Making It Ashore, but Still Chasing U.S. Dream." *New York Times,* April 9.

Bhojwani, Sayu. 2003. Interview by the author, New York City Immigrant Affairs office, March 13.

Binder, Frederick M., and David M. Reimers. 1995. *All the Nations under Heaven: An Ethnic and Racial History of New York City.* New York: Columbia University Press.

Bleyer, Jennifer. 2007. "Pins and Needles." *New York Times,* December 2.

———. 2008. "When Brooklyn Was Norway." *New York Times,* July 25.

Bloomberg, Michael. n.d. "The New Housing Marketplace: Creating Housing for the Next Generation." Available at http://www.nyc.gov/html/hpd/downloads/pdf/10yearHMplan.pdf.

———. 2005. "Protecting and Growing New York City's Industrial Job Base." New York City Industrial Policy report, January. Available at http://www.nycedc.com/industry/industrial.

Bluestone, Barry, and Bennett Harrison. 1982. *The Deindustrialization of America: Plant Closings, Community Abandonment, and the Dismantling of Basic Industry.* New York: Basic Books.

Bluestone, Daniel M. 1991. "'The Pushcart Evil': Peddlers, Merchants and New York City's Streets, 1980–1940." *Journal of Urban History* 18 (1): 68–92.

Blumenthal, Ralph. 1972. "Sunset Park Learns Why It Went Downhill." *New York Times,* April 5.

Bocian, Debbie Gruenstein, Keith S. Ernst, and Wei Li. 2006. "Unfair Lending: The Effect of Race and Ethnicity on the Price of Subprime Mortgages." Center for Responsible Lending, May 31. Available at http://www.responsiblelending.org/mortgage-lending/research-analysis/rr011-Unfair_Lending-0506.pdf.

Boehm, Jason. 2003. "United Puerto Ricans of Sunset Park." The Brooklyn Rail: Critical Perspectives on Arts, Politics. and Culture, April 1. Available at http://www.brooklynrail.org/2003/04/local/united-puerto-ricans-of-sunset-park.

Bonavoglia, Angela. 1977. "A Festival of Brownstone Expertise." *New York Times,* September 29.

Bowdler, Janis. 2005. "Jeopardizing Hispanic Homeownership: Predatory Practices in the Homebuying Market." National Council of La Raza, May 25. Available at http://www.nclr.org/index.php/publications/jeopardizing_hispanic_homeownership_predatory_practices_in_the_homebuying_market/.

Bradsher, Keith. 1989. "Bank Merger Plan Stirs Puerto Rico." *New York Times,* July 13.

Braesher, Aaron. 2007. "420 42nd St—10 Story Monster in Sunset Park, Bklyn, NY." Video, 2:56 minutes. Posted to YouTube, January 24. Available at http://www.youtube.com/watch?v=3AzGxCJ2Wxs.

Bransburg, Vanessa. 2013. Telephone interview by the author, July 11.

Brash, Julian. 2011. *Bloomberg's New York: Class and Governance in the Luxury City.* Athens: University of Georgia Press.

Brashear, Aaron. 2008. Interview by the author, Brooklyn Community Board 7, February 20.

Brashear, Aaron, and Mic Holwin. 2005. "Up with Downzoning: Development in 'Neighborhood Brooklyn' and Its Impact on Communities." The Brooklyn Rail: Critical Perspectives on Arts, Politics, and Culture, November 1. Available at www.brooklynrail.org/2005/11/local/up-with-downzoning.

Brenner, Neil, and Roger Keil. 2006. *The Global Cities Reader.* New York: Routledge.

Brenner, Neil, Jamie Peck, and Nik Theodore. 2005. "Neoliberal Urbanism: Cities and the Rule of Markets." Available at http://murrum.wikispaces.com/file/view/Brenner-Peck-Theodore_Neoliberal_urbanism.pdf.

Breton, Raymond. 1964. "Institutional Completeness of Ethnic Communities and the Personal Relations of Immigrants." *American Journal of Sociology* 70 (2): 193–205.

Briggs, Vernon M. 1989. "Immigration Policy and Its Impact: The Relevance for New York." Briggs Volume 3, Paper #53, Cornell University. Available at http://digitalcommons.ilr.cornell.edu/briggsIII/12/.

Brodsky, Robert. 2004. "Opposition Grows as City Holds Hearing on Cross Harbor Tunnel." *Queens Chronicle,* June 3.

Brooklyn Borough President. 2005. "Brooklyn Borough President Recommendation." Available at http://www.brooklyn-usa.org/Pages/ULURP_Hearings/public_hearing_9-22a.htm.

Brooklyn Historical Society. 1989. *Brooklyn's Hispanic Communities.* Brooklyn, NY: Brooklyn Historical Society.

Brown, Eliot. 2007. "Brooklynite Uses YouTube to Battle Development." *New York Sun,* March 1.

Browning, E. S. 1994. "A New Chinatown Grows in Brooklyn." *Wall Street Journal,* August 31.

Brownstoner. 2007. "420 42nd Street Building Gets Cut in Half." March 12. Available at http://brownstoner.com/brownstoner/archives/2007/03/420_42nd_street_2.php.

———. 2009. "CB7 Votes in Favor of Sunset Park Rezoning Plan." Brownstoner: Brooklyn Inside and Out, May 21. Available at http://www.brownstoner.com/blog/2009/05/cb7-votes-in-fa/.

Brugge, Doug. 2013. "The Biggest Public Health Threat Nobody Is Talking About." Available at http://talkingpointsmemo.com/cafe/the-biggest-public-health-threat-nobody-is-talking-about.

Brugge, Doug, Andrew Leong, and Amy Law. 2003. "Environmental Health and Safety in Boston Chinatown." In *Asian Americans: Vulnerable Populations, Model Interventions, and Clarifying Agendas,* edited by Lin Zhan, 43–67. Boston: Jones and Bartlett.

Brugge, Doug, Edna Rivera-Carrasco, Jean Zotter, and Alice Leung. 2010. "Community-Based Participatory Research in Boston's Neighborhoods: A Review of Asthma Case Examples." *Environmental & Occupational Health* 65 (1): 38–44.

Buettner, Russ. 2012. "Abacus Bank Charged with Mortgage Fraud." *New York Times,* May 31.

Buiso, Gary. 2007. "New View Feud—Fight for Historic Lookout." *Park Slope Courier,* May 5.

Burks, Edward. 1972. "Sharp Rise in Brooklyn Welfare Cases." *New York Times,* April 23.

Bush, Irving T. 1916. "The Real Estate and Industrial Future of Brooklyn." *New York Times,* December 10.

CAAAV. 2008. "Converting Chinatown: A Snapshot of a Neighborhood Becoming Unaffordable and Unlivable." Available at http://caaav.org/publications/ConvertingChina townReport.pdf.

Camayd-Freixas, Erik. 2008. "Interpreting after the Largest ICE Raid in US History: A Personal Account." Available at http://graphics8.nytimes.com/images/2008/07/14/ opinion/14ed-camayd.pdf.

Campbell, Zach. 2012. "Occupy Sunset Park: Seeking Change in Many Languages." Brooklyn Bureau, April 10. Available at http://www.bkbureau.org/2012/04/10/ occupy-sunset-park-seeking-change-in-many-languages/.

Cappi, Sal. 2008. Personal email correspondence with the author, June 10.

Cardinale, Vanessa. 2013. Interview by the author, Trinity Lutheran Church, July 8.

Cardwell, Diane. 2007. "City Hopes to Allow More Offices in Garment Center." *New York Times,* February 15.

Cardwell, Diane, and Charles V. Bagli. 2007. "Deputy Mayor Leaving to Run Bloomberg L.P." *New York Times,* December 7.

Caro, Robert A. 1974. *The Power Broker: Robert Moses and the Fall of New York.* New York: Random House.

Caskey, John P. 1994. "Bank Representation in Low-Income and Minority Urban Communities." *Urban Affairs Quarterly* 29 (4): 617–638.

Castells, Manuel. 1998. *The Information Age.* Oxford, UK: Blackwell.

Cathay Bank. 2013. "Cathay Bank History." Available at https://www.cathaybank.com/ About-Us/Cathay-Bank-History.

CBRE. 2013. "Liberty View Industrial Plaza: Make It in America, Make It in Brooklyn." Available at http://www.cbre.us/o/outerboroughs/AssetLibrary/Liberty%20View%20 Industrial%20Plaza%20updated%203.13.pdf.

Center for Constitutional Rights. n.d. "Turkmen v. Ashcroft." Available at http://ccrjus tice.org/ourcases/current-cases/turkmen-v.-ashcroft.

Center for Economic and Social Rights. 1999. "Treated Like Slaves: Donna Karan, Inc. Violates Women Workers' Human Rights." Available at http://cesr.live.radicaldesigns. org/downloads/Treated%20Like%20Slaves%20DK%20Inc.pdf.

Center for an Urban Future. 2007. "A World of Opportunity." Available at http://nyc future.org/images_pdfs/pdfs/IE-final.pdf.

Cerne, Frank. 1995. "Lutheran Medical Center." *Hospitals & Health Networks* 69 (March 6): 50–51.

Chan, Sewell. 2008. "City Raids 'Counterfeit Triangle,' Shutting 32 Storefronts." *New York Times,* February 26.

Chan, Yek Kuang. 2002. "Flushing Has Become the Second-Largest Banking Area in New York; Deposits Exceed $3 billion." *Sing Tao Daily,* September 17.

Chang, Nancy. 2002. *Silencing Political Dissent: How Post–September 11 Anti-Terrorism Measures Threaten Our Civil Liberties.* New York: Steven Stories.

Charles, Nick. 1994. "A Red-Letter Day for Chinese." *New York Daily News,* February 4.

Chen, David W., and Michael Barbaro. 2010. "Agency Owes Millions to City, an Audit Finds." *New York Times,* April 27.

Chen, Denny. 2013. Interview by the author, Sunset Park, Brooklyn, July 1.

Chen, Fragrance. 2013. Interview by the author, St. Jacobi Lutheran Evangelical Church, July 20.

Chen, May. 2000. Interview by the author, New York, October 27.

———. 2010. Interview by the author, CUNY Murphy Institute, New York, February 5.

Cheng, Lucie, and Yen Espiritu. 1989. "Korean Businesses in Black and Hispanic Neighborhoods: A Study of Intergroup Relations." *Sociological Perspectives* 32 (4): 521–534.

Cheng, Lucie, and Philip Q. Yang. 1998. "Global Integration, Global Inequality, and Migration of the Highly Trained to the United States." *International Migration Review* 32 (3): 626–653.

Cheng, Wendy. 2013. "The Changs Next Door to the Diazes: Suburban Racial Formation in Los Angeles's San Gabriel Valley." *Journal of Urban History* 39 (1): 15–35.

Chin, Heather J. 2012a. "Occupy Sunset Park Continues to Grow." Home Reporter, November 11. Available at http://www.homereporternews.com/news/general/occupy -sunset-park-continues-to-grow/article_15651dbe-0cab-11e1-a07c-001cc4c002e0 .html.

———. 2012b. "Occupy Sunset Park Marks King's Birthday." Home Reporter, January 19. Available at http://www.homereporternews.com/news/general/occupy-sunset -park-marks-king-s-birthday/article_443b8d9a-42ba-11e1-84f0-001871e3ce6c.html

Chin, Margaret M. 2005. *Sewing Women: Immigrants and the New York City Garment Industry.* New York: Columbia University Press.

Chinese Staff and Workers' Association. n.d. "A Brief History of Chinese Staff." Available at http://www.cswa.org/www/our_history.asp.

City of New York. 2004. "New York City Charter: As Amended through July 2004." Available at http://home.nyc.gov/html/charter/downloads/pdf/citycharter2004.pdf.

———. 2009. "Mayor Bloomberg Announces Programs to Expand the Reactivation of Brooklyn's Working Waterfront." Official Website of the City of New York, July 20. Available at http://www1.nyc.gov/office-of-the-mayor/news/335-09/ mayor-bloomberg-programs-expand-reactivation-brooklyn-s-working-waterfront.

———. 2013a. "PlaNYC 2030." Available at http://www.nyc.gov/html/planyc2030/ html/home/home.shtml.

———. 2013b. *A Stronger, More Resilient New York.* PlaNYC report, released June 11. Available at http://www.nycedc.com/resource/stronger-more-resilient-new-york.

City of New York Department of Sanitation. 2007. "Environmental Justice Informational Meeting: Proposed Hamilton Avenue Converted Marine Transfer Station." Transcript, April 12. Available at http://www.nyc.gov/html/dsny/downloads/pdf/swmp _implement/mts/NYSDECNS/transcriptMTS/HAMILTON.pdf.

———. 2011. "City Environmental Quality Review: Environmental Assessment Statement Short Form." Contracts for Export of Municipal Solid Waste from the Borough of Brooklyn, Traffic, Air and Noise Analyses, Supplemental Report to the Environmental Assessment Statement Form, CEQR Number: 11-Dos-009k, September.

Available at http://www.nyc.gov/html/dsny/downloads/pdf/ShortTermContracts/Final_Bk.pdf.

City of New York Office of the Mayor. 2006. "Mayor Bloomberg Announces Appointments to Offices of State and City Legislative Affairs." Press release, July 23. http://www.nyc.gov/portal/site/nycgov/menuitem.c0935b9a57bb4ef3daf2f1c701c789a0/index.jsp?pageID=mayor_press_release&catID=1194&doc_name=http%3A%2F%2Fwww.nyc.gov%2Fhtml%2Fom%2Fhtml%2F2006b%2Fpr258-06.html&cc=unused1978&rc=1194&ndi=1.

City Planning Commission. 2005. "In the Matter of an Application Submitted by the Department of Sanitation Pursuant to Section 197-c of the New York City Charter, for Site Selection of Property Located at 488 Hamilton Avenue (Block 625, Part of Lot 2 and Part of Lot 250), Community District 7, Borough of Brooklyn, for Use as a Marine Transfer Station." C 050176 PSK, April 13. Available at http://www.nyc.gov/html/dcp/pdf/cpc/050176.pdf.

Claffey, Mike. 2002. "Bank Bosses Sentenced, 2 Get Light Jail Time, 2 Get Probation in $1M Fraud Case." *New York Daily News*, January 9.

Clark, Alfred E. 1968. "Brooklyn Plant to Shut Down after Strike Lasting 5 Months." *New York Times*, June 23.

Clarke, Erin. 2013. "Bronx Co-Op Gives Female Immigrants Business Savvy Edge." NY1, January 11. Available at http://bronx.ny1.com/content/top_stories/175313/bronx-co-op-gives-female-immigrants-business-savvy-edge.

Clarke, Katherine. 2013. "Times Square Marriott Marquis Sold in Controversial $20M Deal." The Real Deal, December 12. Available at http://therealdeal.com/blog/2013/12/12/marriott-marquis-sold-in-controversial-20m-deal/.

Clarke, Susan, and Gary Gaile. 1997. "Local Politics in a Global Era: Thinking Locally, Acting Globally." *AAPSS Annals* 551:28–43.

Cohen, Mark Francis. 1996a. "Cold Days for Finnish Society." *New York Times*, January 14.
———. 1996b. "New Tactic in Sex Zone War." *New York Times*, May 12.

Cohler-Esses, Larry. 2005. "Brooklyn's Abu Ghraib." *New York Daily News*, February 20.

Colangelo, Lisa L. 2003. "Banking on 100M Boost." *New York Daily News*, November 21.

Cole, Robert J. 1970a. "Banco de Ponce Expanding Here." *New York Times*, January 31.
———. 1970b. "Puerto Rican Bank Here Stresses Public Service." *New York Times*, July 25.

Collins, Glenn. 2005a. "Condo Project Threatens a Storied Line of Sight." *New York Times*, April 8.
———. 2005b. "In Chinatown, Good Luck Comes with a Good Lock." *New York Times*, July 8.

Community Board 7. 2011. "New Connections/New Opportunities: Sunset Park 197-a Plan." Available at http://www.nyc.gov/html/dcp/pdf/community_planning/bk7_sunset_park_197a.pdf.

Community Development Financial Institutions Fund. 2013. "CDFI Certification." Available at http://www.cdfifund.gov/what_we_do/programs_id.asp?programID=9.

Compton, Matt. 2012. "President Obama Delivers Remarks on Immigration." The White House Blog, June 15. Available at http://www.whitehouse.gov/blog/2012/06/15/president-obama-delivers-remarks-immigration.

Conde, Arturo. 2012. "Occupy Sandy's Spirit of Solidarity Resonates with Latino Values." ABC News, November 8. Available at http://abcnews.go.com/ABC_Univision/News/occupy-sandy-latino-soul-activism/storynew?id=17667896

Confessore, Nicholas. 2006a. "Perspectives on the Atlantic Yards Development through the Prism of Race." *New York Times,* November 12.
———. 2006b. "A Spoonful of Foreign Culture Helps Western Medicine Go Down." *New York Times,* June 4.
Connell, Rich, and Frederick M. Muir. 1993. "Woo Stand, Bank's Practices Differ." *Los Angeles Times,* March 5.
Cordero-Guzman, Hector R. 2005. "Community Based Organizations and Migration in New York City." *Journal of Ethnic and Migration Studies* 31 (5): 889–909.
Cordero-Guzman, Hector R., Robert C. Smith, and Ramon Grosfoguel, eds. 2001. *Migration, Transnationalization, and Race in a Changing New York.* Philadelphia: Temple University Press.
Cornell University Industrial and Labor Relations. 2011. "The 1911 Triangle Factory Fire." Available at http://www.ilr.cornell.edu/trianglefire/index.html.
Cowan, Lisa, and Brad Lander. 2013. "A Flood of Compassion . . . But Not Much Justice." October 29. Available at http://bradlander.com/blog/2013/10/29/a -flood-of-compassion-but-not-much-justice.
Cristillo, Lou. 2004. Interview by the author, New School for Social Research, December 3.
Croghan, Lore. 2012. "Brooklyn Army Terminal Mixes Affordable Artists' Studios with Manufacturers." *New York Daily News,* September 5. Available at http://www.nydaily news.com/new-york/brooklyn/brooklyn-army-terminal-mixes-affordable-artists -studios-manufacturers-article-1.1152930.
Crosman, Penny. 2012. "Why Banco Popular Is Changing Its Name and Digital Strategy." American Banker, March 27. Available at http://www.americanbanker.com/ issues/177_60/Banco-Popular-rebranding-upgrading-digital-channels-1047878-1 .html.
Curan, Catherine. 2002. "Chinatown Apparel Firm Defies the Area's Odds." *Crain's New York Business,* September.
Curran, Winifred, and Susan Hanson. 2005. "Getting Globalized: City Policy and Industrial Displacement in Williamsburg, Brooklyn." *Urban Geography* 26:461–482.
Dailey, Jessica. 2012. "Garment District to Be Wiped Off the Map, Rebranded." Curbed NY, July 25. Available at http://ny.curbed.com/archives/2012/07/25/garment_district _to_be_wiped_off_the_map_rebranded.php.
Daniel, Mac. 2006. "Fung Wah Bus Line Faces State, Federal Scrutiny." *Boston Globe,* September 7.
Davila, Arlene. 2004. *Barrio Dreams: Puerto Ricans, Latinos, and the Neoliberal City.* Berkeley: University of California Press.
Davis, Mike. 2000. *Magical Urbanism: Latinos Reinvent the US City.* London: Verso.
Deane, Daniela. 2003. "Mortgage Rates' Fall Continues; 30-Year Loans Now Average Just 5.61%." *Washington Post,* March 14.
Dear, Michael. 2002. "Los Angeles and the Chicago School: Invitation to a Debate." *City and Community* 1 (1): 5–32.
deGalarza, Grito. 2006. "Too Many Fear Those We Pay to Protect." Blog, December 3. Available at http://gritodegalarza.blogspot.com/.
Delehanty, Daniel. 2005. Interview by the author, New York State Banking Department, August 2.
Department of Justice Office of the Inspector General. 2003a. "The September 11 Detainees: A Review of the Treatment of Aliens Held on Immigration Charges in

Connection with the Investigation of the September 11 Attacks." Available at http://www.usdoj.gov/oig/special/0306/.

———. 2003b. "Supplemental Report on September 11 Detainees' Allegations of Abuse at the Metropolitan Detention Center in Brooklyn, New York." Available at http://www.usdoj.gov/oig/special/0312/final.pdf.

Diaz, David R. 2005. *Barrio Urbanism: Chicanos, Planning, and American Cities.* New York: Routledge.

Doctoroff, Daniel L. 2006. "No Small Plans: The Rebirth of Economic Development in New York City." *IEDC Economic Development Journal* 5 (2): 17–23. Available at http://web.cued.org/EDJournal/Spring_06/No_Small_Plans.pdf.

Dodds, Jerrilynn D. 2013. "The Dome and the Grid." Saudi Aramco World, November–December 1996. Available at http://www.saudiaramcoworld.com/issue/199606/the.dome.and.the.grid.htm.

Dreier, Peter, John Mollenkopf, and Todd Swanstrom. 2001. *Place Matters: Metropolitics for the Twenty-First Century.* Lawrence: University Press of Kansas.

Duggan, Lisa. 2003. *The Twilight of Equality: Neoliberalism, Cultural Politics, and the Attack on Democracy.* Boston: Beacon.

Dunaief, Daniel. 2004. "Big Boost for Small Banks Funds from City, State." *New York Daily News,* May 24.

Dunn, Julia. 2009. "Pay it Forward: Group Responds to Subway Fare Hike with Free Swipes." The Indypendent, June 25. Available at http://www.indypendent.org/2009/06/25/pay-it-forward-group-responds-subway-fare-hike-free-swipes.

Durand, Jorge, Douglas S. Massey, and Rene M. Zenteno. 2001. "Mexican Immigrants to the United States: Continuities and Changes." *Latin America Research Review* 36 (1): 107–127.

Durkin, Erin. 2012. "Re-drawn Map Would Form Asian-Majority District in Brooklyn." *New York Daily News,* January 30.

Dworak, Linda. 2000. Interview by the author, Garment Industry Development Corporation, September 7.

Dymski, Gary, Wei Li, Carolyn Aldana, and H. H. Ahn. 2010. "Ethnobanking in the United States: From Antidiscrimination Vehicles to Transnational Entities." *International Journal of Business & Globalisation* 4 (2): 163–191.

Dymski, Gary, and L. Mohanty. 1999. "Credit and Banking Structure: Insights from Asian and African-American Experience in Los Angeles." *American Economic Review Papers and Proceedings* 89 (2): 362–366.

Eaton, Leslie. 2006. "New Orleans Mayor Closes a Disputed Landfill Used for Debris from Hurricane." *New York Times,* August 16.

Edroso, Roy. 2009. "Groups Sues [*sic*] Planners to Stop Sunset Park Rezoning." *Village Voice,* August 21.

Egbert, Bill. 2001. "City Fighting Surge of Sunset Park Porn." *New York Daily News,* May 11.

Egeln, Harold. 2008a. "Biz Leaders Eye Long-Vacant Sunset Park Federal Building." *Brooklyn Eagle,* July 10.

———. 2008b. "Southwest Brooklyn Blackouts Largest in City This Year." *Brooklyn Eagle,* July 22.

———. 2008c. "Sunset Park Power Plant: Is Proposal 'Green' Enough?" *Brooklyn Eagle,* April 4.

———. 2009. "Sunset Park Re-Zoning Hearings Bring Information and Protests." *Brooklyn Daily Eagle,* May 15.

El-Faizy, Monique, and Maki Becker. 1999. "Indicted Bank's Getting a New Owner." *New York Daily News,* December 11.

Engquist, Erik, and Matthew Sollars. 2008. "Sunset Park Plan Draws Ire of Business Group." *Crain's New York Business,* July 8. Available at http://www.crainsnewyork .com/apps/pbcs.dll/article?AID=/20080708/FREE/444740779/-1/breaking.

Ennis, Thomas W. 1955. "Demolitions Pose Housing Problem." *New York Times,* June 26.

Espiritu, Yen L., and Paul M. Ong. 1994. "Class Constraints On Racial Solidarity among Asian Americans." In *The New Asian Immigration in Los Angeles and Global Restructuring,* edited by Paul Ong, Edna Bonacich, and Lucie Cheng, 295–321. Philadelphia: Temple University Press.

Fainstein, Susan. 2001. *The City Builders: Property Development in New York and London, 1980–2000.* Lawrence: University of Kansas Press.

———. 2005. "The Return of Urban Renewal: Dan Doctoroff's Grand Plan for New York City." *Harvard Design Magazine* (22). Available at http://www.gsd.harvard.edu/ images/content/5/4/540416/fac-pub-fainstein-Return-of-Urban-Renewal-final.pdf.

Fainstein, Susan S., and Norman I. Fainstein. 1982. "Neighborhood Enfranchisement and Urban Redevelopment." *Journal of Planning Education and Research* 2 (11): 11–18.

Fasenfest, David, Jason Booza, and Kurt Metzger. 2004. "Living Together: A New Look at Racial and Ethnic Integration in Metropolitan Neighborhoods, 1990–2000." Center on Urban and Metropolitan Policy, The Living Cities Census Series, Brookings Institution. Available at http://www.brookings.edu/~/media/research/files/reports/2004/4/ demographics%20fasenfest/20040428_fasenfest.

Federal Deposit Insurance Corporation. 2002. "FDIC Law, Regulations, Related Acts." Available at http://www.fdic.gov/regulations/laws/rules/5000-2600.html.

———. 2007a. "Community Reinvestment Act Performance Evaluation: Cathay Bank." Available at http://www2.fdic.gov/crapes/2007/18503_070402.pdf.

———. 2007b. "In the Matter of First American International Bank: Order to Cease and Desist, FDIC-07-095b." August 3. Available at http://www.fdic.gov/bank/individual/ enforcement/2007-08-05.pdf.

———. 2009. "United Commercial Bank Fact Sheet: Discussion of Additional Issues." Press Release, November 9. Available at http://www.fdic.gov/news/news/press/2009/ pr09201c.html.

Federal Reserve Board. 2002. "Press Release." July 8. Available at http://www.federal reserve.gov/boarddocs/press/enforcement/2002/20020708/default.htm.

———. 2013. "Structure Data for the U.S. Offices of Foreign Banking Organizations." Available at http://www.federalreserve.gov/releases/iba/201306/bycntry.htm.

Fernandez, Manny. 2006. "A Study Links Trucks' Exhaust to Bronx Schoolchildren's Asthma." *New York Times,* October 29.

———. 2007. "Housing Takes Bigger Bite of New Yorkers' Incomes, Census Data Shows." *New York Times,* September 13.

Feuer, Alan. 2012. "Occupy Sandy: A Movement Moves to Relief." *New York Times,* November 9.

Fine, Janice. 2006. *Worker Centers: Organizing Communities at the Edge of the Dream.* Ithaca, NY: Cornell University Press.

Fink, Carolee. 2011. Vice President, New York City Economic Development Corporation. Telephone interview by author, July 15.

Fiscal Policy Institute. 2001. "Economic Impact of the September 11 World Trade Center Attack." Available at http://www.fiscalpolicy.org/sep28WTCreport.pdf.

————. 2003. "NYC's Garment Industry: A New Look?" Available at http://fiscalpolicy
.org/NYC%20sGarmentIndustry.pdf.

————. 2007. *Working for a Better Life: A Profile of Immigrants in New York State Economy.*
Available at http://www.fiscalpolicy.org/publications2007/FPI_ImmReport_Work
ingforaBetterLife.pdf.

————. 2012. "Immigrant Small Business Owners: A Significant and Growing Part of the
Economy." Immigration Research Initiative, June. Available at http://fiscalpolicy.org/
wp-content/uploads/2012/06/immigrant-small-business-owners-FPI-20120614.pdf.

Fischer, Muriel. 1973. "Factory Will Be a Hospital; City and State Aid." *New York Times,*
March 25.

Fitch, Robert. 1993. *The Assassination of New York.* Brooklyn, NY: Verso.

Fitzgerald, Julia. 2007. Interview by the author, Neighbors Helping Neighbors, Sunset
Park, Brooklyn, December 5.

————. 2008. Interview by the author, Community Board 7, Sunset Park, Brooklyn,
March 13.

Foderaro, Lisa W. 2012. "Huge Rooftop Farm Is Set for Brooklyn." *New York Times,* April 5.

Foggin, Mark. 2006. "Testimony at the New York City Council Subcommittee on Zon-
ing and Franchises." September 19. Available at http://legistar.council.nyc.gov/
LegislationDetail.aspx?ID=450250&GUID=FA7013CB-BDA1-4C55-BB04
-DF513350DAE5&Options=&Search=.

Foner, Nancy. 2001. "Transnationalism Then and Now: New York Immigrants Today and
at the Turn of the Twentieth Century." In *Migration, Transnationalization, and Race
in a Changing New York,* edited by Hector R. Cordero-Guzman, Robert C. Smith,
and Ramon Grosfoguel, 35–57. Philadelphia: Temple University Press.

Foner, Nancy, and Roger Waldinger. 2013. "New York and Los Angeles as Immigrant
Destinations: Contrasts and Convergences." In *New York and Los Angeles: The Uncer-
tain Future,* edited by David Halle and Andrew A. Beveridge, 343–357. New York:
Oxford University Press.

Fragomen, Austin T. 1997. "The Illegal Immigration Reform and Immigrant Responsibility Act of 1996: An Overview." *International Migration Review* 31 (2): 438–460.

Fredrickson, Tom. 2003. "Chinatown Bank Calculates Damage." *Crain's New York Business,* May 5.

————. 2004. "Asian Banks Reorient—Flood into NY Market; Could Lead to Saturation?" *Crain's New York Business,* September 13.

————. 2006. "NY's Immigrants Stranded by Banks." *Crain's New York Business,*
August 7.

Freeman, Joshua B. 2000. *Working Class New York: Life and Labor since World War II.* New
York: New Press.

Friedman, Adam. 2009. "Transforming the City's Manufacturing Landscape." In *From
Disaster to Diversity: What's Next for New York City's Economy,* the edited by Jonathan
P. Hicks and Dan Morris, 21–37. New York: Drum Major Institute.

Fung, Ernest. 2008. Interview by the author, United Commercial Bank, Manhattan Chinatown, April 22.

Furman Center for Real Estate and Urban Policy. 2013. "Sandy's Effect on NYC Housing." Available at http://furmancenter.org/files/publications/SandysEffectsOnHous
ingInNYC.pdf.

Gabby. 2009. "The Sunset Park Condo That Helped Fuel the Rezone Fire." Brownstoner,
March 27. http://www.brownstoner.com/blog/2009/05/the-sunset-park/.

Gaber, John. 1994. "Manhattan's 14th Street Vendors' Market: Informal Street Peddlers' Complimentary Relationship with New York City's Economy." *Urban Anthropology* 23 (4): 373–408.

Galarza, David. n.d. "In the First Person." Available at http://earthjustice.org/50states/2013/david-galarza.

———, David. 2005. Interview by the author, Sunset Park, Brooklyn, April 24.

———. 2013. Interview by the author, Trinity Lutheran Church, July 8.

Gallagher, Frank. 1908. "South Brooklyn Is Port of Future." *New York Times,* May 3.

Garrison Institute. 2013. "Eddie Bautista: The Waterfront Justice Project." Video, uploaded April 24. Available at http://www.youtube.com/watch?v=Ith5JBMAGek&feature=share.

Gauntlett, Gustav. 2013. Telephone interview by the author, July 9.

Geiger, Daniel. 2013a. "Bid for Big Complex Boosts South Brooklyn." *Crain's New York Business,* August 25.

———. 2013b. "Huge B'klyn Complex to Get Its Navy Yard Moment." *Crain's New York Business,* September 5.

———. 2013c. "Key Bloomberg Player Pinsky Takes Private Gig." *Crain's New York Business,* July 16.

———. 2013d. "Navy Yard Head Sails to Big Developer." *Crain's New York Business,* June 13.

Gendar, Alison. 2004. "Queens Sgt. Faces D-Day Wife, Pals Defend 1st Soldier Tried in Iraq POW Abuse as Verdict Nears." *New York Daily News,* September 3.

Genn, Andrew. 2005. Interview by author, New York City Economic Development Corporation, date.

Giordano, Renee. 2012. Interview by the author, Sunset Park 5th Avenue Business Improvement District office, June 26.

Giridharadas, Anand. 2007. "India's Edge Goes beyond Outsourcing." *New York Times,* April 4.

Goldstein, Joseph. 2012. "Kelly Defends Surveillance of Muslims." *New York Times,* February 27.

González, Juan. 2013. "New York City Poised to Elect Its Most Progressive Government in 50 Years." Video clip and transcript, Democracy Now! September 12. Available at http://truth-out.org/video/item/18797-juan-gonzález-new-york-city-poised-to-elect-its-most-progressive-government-in-50-years.

Good Jobs New York. 2004. "The LMDC: They're In the Money; We're in the Dark." Reconstruction Watch, August. Available at http://www.goodjobsfirst.org/sites/default/files/docs/pdf/lmdc_report.pdf.

Goodman, Amy, and Juan González. 2012. "Occupy Sunset Park: 99% Solidarity Takes Root in Brooklyn Community Where Tenants Stage Rent Strike." *Democracy Now!* transcript, September 17. Available at http://www.democracynow.org/seo/2012/9/17/occupy_sunset_park_99_solidarity_takes.

Goodstein, Laurie, and Tamar Lewin. 2001. "Victims of Mistaken Identity, Sikhs Pay a Price for Turbans." *New York Times,* September 19.

Gotham, Kevin Fox. 2000. "Separate and Unequal: The Housing Act of 1968 and the Section 235 Program." *Sociological Forum* 15 (1): 13–37.

———. 2002. "Beyond Invasion and Succession: School Segregation, Real Estate Blockbusting, and the Political Economy of Neighborhood Racial Transition." *City & Community* 1 (1): 83–111.

Gottdiener, Mark, and Ray Hutchison. 2000. *The New Urban Sociology*. Boulder, CO: Westview.

Gray, Billy. 2012. "The Sun Also Rises: Sunset Park's Booming Artisanal Economy." Commercial Observer, February. Available at http://commercialobserver.com/2013/02/the-sun-also-rises-sunset-parks-booming-artisanal-economy/.

Greenhouse, Steven. 2001. "Pay Case Does Not Help All of City's Deliverymen." *New York Times,* January 18.

———. 2003. "Day to Day, but Making a Living; Immigrant Laborers' Wages Top Minimum, Study Finds." *New York Times,* April 11.

———. 2004a. "Janitors Say Supermarkets Are Still Locking Them In." *New York Times,* December 25.

———. 2004b. "Workers Say Late Shifts Often Mean Locked Exits." *New York Times,* June 18.

———. 2008. "Queens Factory Is Found to Owe Workers $5.3 Million." *New York Times,* July 23.

Greenwood, Davydd J., William F. Whyte, and Ira Harkavy. 1993. "Participatory Action Research as a Process and as a Goal." *Human Relations* 46 (2): 175–192.

Grosfugel, Ramon. 1999. "Puerto Rican Labor Migration to the United States: Modes of Incorporation, Coloniality, and Identities." *Review: Fernand Braudel Center* 22 (4): 503–521.

Gross, Jill. 2005. "Business Improvement Districts in New York City's Low-Income and High-Income Neighborhoods." *Economic Development Quarterly* 19:174–189.

Hackworth, Jason. 2002. "Postrecession Gentrification in New York City." *Urban Affairs Review* 37 (6): 815–843.

———. 2007. *The Neoliberal City: Governance, Ideology, and Development in American Urbanism*. Ithaca, NY: Cornell University Press.

Halcrow, Fleming, MDS Transmodal, Duncan Maritime, Moffatt & Nichol Engineers, Zetlin Strategic Communications, and Hirani Engineering. 2005. "CPIP Consortium, Port of New York & New Jersey: Comprehensive Port Improvement Plan; Volume 1: The Plan." Available at http://www.panynj.gov/about/pdf/cpip/v1_plan.pdf.

Halpern, Robert. 1995. *Rebuilding the Inner City: A History of Neighborhood Initiatives to Address Poverty in the United States*. New York: Columbia University Press.

Harris, Alisa. 2010. "High BIDs." Worldmag, April 24. Available at http://www.bryant park.org/about-us/press/20100424-wmg.html.

Harrison, Bennett, and Barry Bluestone. 1988. *The Great U-Turn: Corporate Restructuring and the Polarizing of America*. New York: Basic Books.

Hartocollis, Anemona. 2004. "A Little Congee May Make the Medicine Go Down." *New York Times,* November 14.

Harvey, David. 2003. "The Right to the City." *International Journal of Urban and Regional Research* 27 (4): 939–941.

Harwood, Stacy Anne. 2005. "Struggling to Embrace Difference in Land-Use Decision Making in Multicultural Communities." *Planning Research and Practice* 20 (4): 355–371.

Harwood, Stacy Anne, and Dowell Myers. 2002. "The Dynamics of Immigration and Local Governance in Santa Ana: Neighborhood Activism, Overcrowding and Land-Use Policy." *Policy Studies Journal* 30 (1): 70–91.

Haslip-Viera, Gabriel. 1996. "The Evolution of the Latino Community in New York City: Early Nineteenth Century to the Present." In *Latinos in New York: Communities in*

Transition, edited by Gabriel Haslip-Viera and Sherrie Baver, 3–29. Notre Dame, IN: University of Notre Dame.

Hauser, Christine. 2008. "City Agents Shut Down 32 Vendors of Fake Items." *New York Times,* February 27.

Havens, Chris. 2010. Interview by the author, Brooklyn Heights, June 23.

Hawkins, Andrew J. 2012. "Surge in Shipping Has New York Hot on L.A.'s Heels." Crain's New York Business, August 5. Available at http://www.crainsnewyork.com/article/20120805/TRANSPORTATION/308059971.

Hess, Adam. 2006. "Sunset Park Is Fast Becoming New York's Hot Neighborhood." *Real Estate Weekly,* March 8.

Hess, Peg McCartt, Brenda G. McGowan, and Michael Botsko. 2003. *Nurturing the One, Supporting the Many.* New York: Columbia University Press.

Hicks, Jonathan P. 1997. "Albany Lawmakers Agree on Redrawn 12th District." *New York Times,* July 31.

———. 2001. "Jailed Vieques Protesters Remain Unbowed." *New York Times,* May 31.

Higgins, Michelle. 2013. "Brooklyn's New Gentrification Frontiers." *New York Times,* March 8.

Hing, Bill Ong. 1993. *Making and Remaking Asian America through Immigration Policy, 1850–1990.* Stanford, CA: Stanford University Press.

Historic Districts Council. 2013. "Six to Celebrate 2013." Available at http://hdc.org/program-events/six-to-celebrate/six-to-celebrate-2013-neighborhoods.

Hochberg, Mina. 2013. "6 Bargains in Sunset Park." HGTV FrontDoor, April 1. Available at http://www.frontdoor.com/places/6-bargains-in-sunset-park.

Hoffman, Claire. 2003. "Globalization's Underside: Sex Trafficking in Brooklyn." *Brooklyn Rail,* August 1. Available at http://brooklynrail.org/2003/08/local/globalizations-underside-sex-trafficking-in-brooklyn.

Hoffman, Jan. 2000. "Dynamism, Put to Work for Livery Drivers." *New York Times,* April 28.

Horst, Ian. 2013. Telephone interview by the author, July 18.

Hotel BPM. 2012. "Hotel BPM Fact Sheet." Available at http://www.hotelbpmbrooklyn.com/bpm-press-kit.pdf.

Hou, Jeffrey, ed. 2010. *Insurgent Public Space: Guerrilla Urbanism and the Remaking of Contemporary Cities.* London: Routledge.

Howe, Marvine. 1986. "Bodegas Find Prosperity amid Change." *New York Times,* November 19.

———. 1987. "City's Third Chinatown Is Emerging in Brooklyn." *New York Times,* September 13.

Huege, Janet. 2006. "Brooklyn Hits New Hights [*sic*]." *New York Post,* April 1. Available at http://www.masseyknakal.com/news/pdf/Sarn_On_Greenwood_Heights_nypost.pdf.

Hum, Carl. 2012. Interview by the author, Sunset Park, Brooklyn, September 15.

Hum, Tarry. 2002a. "Asian and Latino Immigration and the Revitalization of Sunset Park, Brooklyn." In *Intersections and Divergences: Contemporary Asian Pacific American Communities,* edited by Linda Vo and Rick Bonus, 27–44. Philadelphia: Temple University Press.

———. 2002b. "Redistricting and the New Demographics: Defining 'Communities of Interest' in New York City." Available at http://www.apa.nyu.edu/coi/pdf/redistricting.pdf.

————. 2003. "Mapping Global Production in New York City's Garment Industry: The Role of Sunset Park, Brooklyn's Immigrant Economy." *Economic Development Quarterly* 17 (3): 294–309.

————. 2005. "Immigration Grows to Half of New York's Labor Force." *Regional Labor Review* (Spring/Summer): 22–29.

————. 2006. "New York City's Asian Immigrant Economies: Community Development Needs and Challenges." In *Jobs and Economic Development in Minority Communities: Realities, Challenges and Innovation,* edited by Paul Ong and Anastasia Loukaitou-Sideris, 176–202. Philadelphia: Temple University Press.

————. 2011. "Minority-Owned Banks in New York City: Is the Community Reinvestment Act Relevant?" *Journal of Civil Rights and Economic Development,* Symposium Issue, *The Fall of the Economy: How New York Can Rise to the Challenge* 25 (3): 501–524.

Immergluck, Dan. 2004. *Credit to the Community: Community Reinvestment and Fair Lending Policy in the United States.* Armonk, NY: M. E. Sharpe.

Immigration and Customs Enforcement. n.d.-a. "Removal Statistics." Available at http://www.ice.gov/removal-statistics/.

————. n.d.-b. "Secure Communities." Available at http://www.ice.gov/secure_communities/.

Immigration and Naturalization Service. n.d. "List of Deaths in ICE Custody, October 2003–December 6, 2012." Available at http://www.ice.gov/doclib/foia/reports/detaineedeaths2003-present.pdf.

Ingrassia, Robert. 2001. "Rev. Al Is Released, and Hits the Streets; Leads Vieques Rally, March to Site of Fatal Crash." *New York Daily News,* August 18.

Irazábal, Clara. 2012. "Beyond 'Latino New Urbanism': Advocating Ethnurbanisms." *Journal of Urbanism* 5 (2/3): 241–268.

Iritani, Evelyn. 2007. "California Bank Goes after China." *Los Angeles Times,* March 28. Available at http://articles.latimes.com/2007/mar/28/business/fi-bank28.

Jackson, Kenneth T. 1987. *Crabgrass Frontier: The Suburbanization of the United States.* Oxford: Oxford University Press.

Jacobs, Jane. 1961. *The Death and Life of Great American Cities.* New York: Vintage Books.

Johnson, James H., Jr., and Melvin L. Oliver. 1989. "Interethnic Minority Conflict in Urban America: The Effects of Economic and Social Dislocations." *Urban Geography* 10:449–463.

Johnson, Kirk. 1998. "Report Shows a Strong and Diverse Job Growth for New York City." *New York Times,* March 5.

Johnson, Leila. 2013. Interview by the author, St. Jacobi Lutheran Evangelical Church, July 20.

Jones, Richard Lezin, and Kevin Flynn. 2001. "Officer in Accident Spent up to 12 Hours Drinking, Police Say." *New York Times,* August 8.

Jones-Correa, Michael. 1998. *Between Two Nations: The Political Predicament of Latinos in New York City.* Ithaca, NY: Cornell University Press.

Kamber, Michael. 2001. "On the Corner: New York's Undocumented Day Laborers Fight for Their Piece of the Big Apple." Village Voice, July 24. Available at http://www.villagevoice.com/issues/0130/kamber.php.

Kappstatter, Bob. 2006. "Carrión Defends Board Firings." *New York Daily News,* June 21.

Kavanaugh, Shane Dixon. 2012. "A New Dawn for Sunset Park: Collection of Old Factory Spaces Lures Artists, Other Users." Crain's New York Business, May 20. Available at http://www.crainsnewyork.com/article/20120520/REAL_ESTATE/305209992.

Kaysen, Ronda. 2012. "Brooklyn's Industrial Space Retools for a New Era." *New York Times,* September 25.

Keefe, Patrick Radden. 2006. "The Snakehead: The Criminal Odyssey of Chinatown's Sister Ping." *New Yorker,* April 24.

———. 2013. "A Path Out of Purgatory." *New Yorker,* June 6. Available at http://www.newyorker.com/online/blogs/comment/2013/06/golden-venture-immigration-reform.html.

Kennedy, Marie. 1996. "Transformative Community Planning: Empowerment through Community Development." Working Paper prepared for the 1996 Planners Network Conference, Renewing Hope, Restoring Vision: Progressive Planning in Our Communities.

Kennedy, Marie, Chris Tilly, and Mauricio Gaston. 1990. "Transformative Populism and the Development of Community of Color." In *Dilemmas of Activism: Class, Community, and the Politics of Local Mobilization,* edited by Joseph M. Kling and Prudence S. Posner, 302–324. Philadelphia: Temple University Press.

Kerr, Peter. 1985. "Bank in Chinatown Closed by Federal Officials." *New York Times,* June 23.

Kifner, John. 1966. "Plan to Aid Poor Widely Praised." *New York Times,* June 28.

Kihss, Peter. 1953a. "Flow of Puerto Ricans Here Fills Jobs, Poses Problems." *New York Times,* February 23.

———. 1953b. "Puerto Rico Combats Exodus by a Drive to Raise Incomes." *New York Times,* February 24.

Kim, Claire J., and Taeku Lee. 2001. "Interracial Politics: Asian Americans and Other Communities of Color." *PS: Political Science and Politics* 34 (3): 631–637.

Kleinfield, N. R. 1986. "Mining Chinatown's 'Mountain of Gold.'" *New York Times,* June 1.

Koehler, Charles. 2005. Interview by the author, Community Capital Bank, Sunset Park, Brooklyn, June 29.

Kramer, Louise. 2002. "Lust for Hispanic Market Turns into Love Fest." *Crain's New York Business,* July 22.

Kranz, Matt. 2004. "Banks Market to Asian Communities: Branches Profit as They Meet Growing Need." *USA Today,* September 22.

Krugman, Paul. 2009. "How Did Economists Get It So Wrong?" *New York Times,* September 2.

Kugel, Seth. 2006. "Leaving New York, with Bodega in Tow." *New York Times,* October 29.

Kuntzman, Gersh. 2004. "She's City 'Cancel' Woman." *New York Post,* May 3.

Kurashige, Scott. 2004. "The Many Facets of Brown: Integration in a Multiracial Society." *Journal of American History* 91 (1): 56–68.

———. 2008a. "Crenshaw and the Rise of Multiethnic Los Angeles." *Afro-Hispanic Review* 27 (1): 41–58.

———. 2008b. *The Shifting Grounds of Race: Black and Japanese Americans in the Making of Multiethnic Los Angeles.* Princeton, NJ: Princeton University Press.

Kusisto, Laura. 2012. "Mini-Manufacturers Try Factory Life." *Wall Street Journal,* August 16.

Kwan, Susan. 1997. "Nabe Sees Red over Porn Biz." *New York Daily News,* July 25.

Kwong, Peter. 1987. *The New Chinatown.* New York: Farrar, Straus & Giroux/Hill and Wang.

———. 1994. "Chinese Staff and Workers' Association: A Model for Organizing in the Changing Economy?" *Social Policy,* 25 (2): 30–38.

———. 1997. *Forbidden Workers: Illegal Chinese Immigrants and American Labor.* New York: New Press.

———. 2009. "Answers about the Gentrification of Chinatown." *New York Times,* September 16. Available at http://cityroom.blogs.nytimes.com/2009/09/16/answers-about -the-gentrification-of-chinatown/?_r=0.

Kwong, Peter, and JoAnn Lum. 1988. "How the Other Half Lives Now." *The Nation,* June 18.

Kwong, Peter, and Dusanka Miscevic. 2005. *Chinese America: The Untold Story of America's Oldest New Community.* New York: New Press.

Labaton, Stephen. 1999. "Agreement Reached on Overhaul of U.S. Financial System." *New York Times,* October 23.

Lai, Clement. 2012. "The Racial Triangulation of Space: The Case of Urban Renewal in San Francisco's Fillmore District." *Annals of the Association of American Geographers* 102 (1): 151–170.

Lai, Zenobia, Andrew Leong, and Chi Chi Wu. 2000. "The Lessons of the Parcel C Struggle: Reflections on Community Lawyering." *UCLA Asian Pacific American Law Journal* 6 (1): 1–43.

Lambert, Bruce. 1993. "U.S. to Open Jail, Despite Snags." *New York Daily News,* December 19.

Lamphere, Louise, ed. 1992. *Structuring Diversity: Ethnographic Perspectives on the New Immigration.* Philadelphia: Temple University Press.

Lander, Brad. 2006. "Testimony to the New York City Council Land Use Committee in Support of Resolution 141, to Create 'Industrial Employment Districts.'" September 19. Available at http://prattcenter.net/news-events/news/support-resolution-141.

Lander, Brad, and Laura Wolf-Powers. 2004. "Remaking New York City: Can Prosperity Be Shared and Sustainable?" Departmental Papers, City and Regional Planning, Pratt Institute. Available at http://repository.upenn.edu/cplan_papers/43/.

Landman, Marc. 2000. Interview by the author, Sunset Park, Brooklyn, September 26.

Laufer, Jeremy. 2013a. Email correspondence with the author, December 11.

———. 2013b. Interview by the author, Community Board 7, Sunset Park, Brooklyn, June 6.

Lauinger, John. 2008. "City Council Members Warn Mayor Bloomberg on Willets Point Plan." *New York Daily News,* August 13.

La Unión de la Comunidad Latina. n.d. "Health and Housing Report." Available at http:// www.citylimits.org/images_pdfs/pdfs/healthandhousingreport.pdf.

Laurentz, Robert. 1980. "Racial/Ethnic Conflict in the New York City Garment Industry, 1933–1980." Unpublished Ph.D. dissertation, SUNY, Binghamton.

Lee, Denny. 2000. "Immigrants Work in Parlors Offering More Than Massages." *New York Times,* November 12.

Lee, Jennifer 8. 2009. "Sunset Park Rezoning Plan Prompts Concerns." *New York Times,* May 14.

Lee, Jessica. 2009. "Sunset Park Sidewalk Clash." The Independent, May 14. Available at http://www.indypendent.org/2009/05/14/sidewalk-clash/.

Lee, Vee How. 2005. Interview by the author, Flushing, Queens, October 5.

Legal Aid Society. 2013. "Legal Aid Society and Weil Win Major Victory for Hundreds of Sandy Evacuees." Press release, May 16. Available at http://www.legal-aid.org/

en/mediaandpublicinformation/inthenews/legalaidandweilmajorvictoryhundredsof
sandyevacuees.aspx.

Leong, Andrew. 1997. "The Struggle over Parcel C: How Boston's Chinatown Won a Victory in the Fight against Institutional Expansionism and Environmental Racism."
Institute for Asian American Studies Publications, Paper 22. Available at http://scholar
works.umb.edu/iaas_pubs/22.

Levitan, Mark. 1998. *Opportunity at Work: The New York City Garment Industry.* New
York: Community Service Society of New York.

Levitt, Peggy. 2001. "Transnational Migration: Taking Stock and Future Directions."
Global Networks 1 (3): 195–216.

Levy, Clifford J. 1997. "Court Outlaws New York District Drawn Up to Aid Hispanic
Voters." *New York Times,* February 27.

Lewin, Tamar, and Gustav Niebuhr. 2001. "Attacks and Harassment on Middle Eastern
People and Mosques." *New York Times,* September 18.

Lewis, Bertha. 2006. "Supporting Atlantic Yards: 'Simply Not Enough Housing in Brooklyn.'" *City Limits,* July 31. Available at http://www.citylimits.org/content/articles/
viewarticle.cfm?article_id=1953.

Ley, David. 2010. *Millionaire Migrants: Trans-Pacific Life Lines.* West Sussex, UK:
Blackwell.

Li, Peter S. 1994. "Unneighbourly Houses or Unwelcome Chinese: The Social Construction of Race in the Battle over 'Monster Homes' in Vancouver, Canada." *International
Journal of Comparative Race and Ethnic Studies* 1:14–33.

Li, Wei. 2005. "Beyond Chinatown, Beyond Enclave: Reconceptualizing Contemporary
Chinese Settlements in the United States." *GeoJournal* 64 (1): 31–40.

———. 2009. *Ethnoburb: The New Ethnic Community in Urban America.* Honolulu: University of Hawaii Press.

Li, Wei, Gary Dymski, Yu Zhou, Maria Chee, and Carolyn Aldana. 2002. "Chinese-
American Banking and Community Development in Los Angeles County." *Annals of
the Association of American Geographers* 92 (4): 777–796.

Li, Wei, Yu Zhou, Gary Dymski, and Maria Chee. 2001. "Banking on Social Capital
in the Era of Globalization: Chinese Ethnobanks in Los Angeles." *Environment and
Planning A* 33:1923–1948.

Liang, Zai. 2001. "Demography of Illicit Emigration from China: A Sending Country's
Perspective." *Sociological Forum* 16 (4): 677–701.

Library of Congress. n.d. "About Norway Times = Nordisk tidende: Brooklyn, N.Y.
(1984–2008)" Available at http://chroniclingamerica.loc.gov/lccn/sn84037021/.

———. 2005. "H.R. 4437 (109th): Border Protection, Antiterrorism, and Illegal Immigration Control Act of 2005." Available at https://www.govtrack.us/congress/
bills/109/hr4437#summary/libraryofcongress.

Lieberman, Beth. 2004. "Density, Zoning, and Class in New York City." *MONU Magazine on Urbanism* 2 (January): 11–14. Available at http://www.monu.org/monu2/
Density,%20Zoning%20and%20Class%20in%20NYC.pdf.

Light, Ivan. 1974. "From Vice District to Tourist Attraction: The Moral Career of American Chinatowns, 1880–1940." *Pacific Historical Review* 43 (3): 367–394.

———. 2002. "Immigrant Place Entrepreneurs in Los Angeles, 1970–1999." *International Journal of Urban and Regional Research* 26 (2): 215–228.

Light, Ivan, and Edna Bonacich. 1988. *Immigrant Entrepreneurs: Koreans in Los Angeles,
1965–1982.* Berkeley: University of California Press.

Lii, Jane H. 1995. "65 Cents an Hour—A Special Report: Week in Sweatshop Reveals Grim Conspiracy of the Poor." *New York Times,* March 12.

Lilly, David, and Joseph Kuo. 2006. "Carver Bancorp Receives Regulatory Approvals for Community Capital Bank Acquisition." Press release, September 25. Available at http://www.snl.com/irweblinkx/file.aspx?IID=112079&FID=2817794.

Lim, James. 2013. Telephone interview by the author, July 25.

Lin, Jan. 1998. *Reconstructing Chinatown: Ethnic Enclave, Global Change.* Minneapolis: University of Minnesota Press.

———. 2011. *The Power of Urban Ethnic Places: Cultural Heritage and Community Life.* New York: Routledge.

Lin, May. 2013. Interview by the author, Lower East Side, July 2.

Lipsitz, George. 2007. "The Racialization of Space and the Spatialization of Race: Theorizing the Hidden Architecture of Landscape." *Landscape Journal* 26:10–23.

Lipton, Eric. 2004. "New York Port Hums Again, with Asian Trade." *New York Times,* November 22.

Lissner, Will. 1969. "U.S. Study Finds City's Poorest Are Puerto Ricans in the Slums." *New York Times,* November 17.

Liu, Annie. 2000. Interview by the author, Garment Industry Development Corporation, New York, October 12.

Liu, John C. 2012a. "Liu Calls on Bloomberg to Change EDC's 'Law-Breaking' Culture." Press release, July 9. Available at http://comptroller.nyc.gov/newsroom/liu-calls-on-bloomberg-to-change-edcs-law-breaking-culture/.

———. 2012b. "Rents through the Roof! A Statistical Analysis of Unaffordable Rents in New York City." Available at http://comptroller.nyc.gov/wp-content/uploads/documents/Rents-through-the-Roof.pdf.

———. 2013. "EDC'S Times Square Giveaway Cost Taxpayers $344.9 Million." Press conference, February 12. Available at http://www.youtube.com/watch?v=eUbkBlG3uQE.

Lobo, Arun Peter, Ronald J. O. Flores, and Joseph J. Salvo. 2002. "The Impact of Hispanic Growth on the Racial/Ethnic Composition of New York City Neighborhoods." *Urban Affairs Review* 37 (5): 703–727.

Lobo, Arun Peter, and Joseph J. Salvo. 1998. "Changing US Immigration Law and the Occupational Selectivity of Asian Immigrants." *International Migration Review* 32 (3): 737–760.

———. 2013. "A Portrait of New York's Immigrant Melange." In *One Out of Three: Immigrant New York in the Twenty-First Century,* edited by Nancy Foner, 35–63. New York: Columbia University Press.

Logan, John R., Richard D. Alba, and Wenquan Zhang. 2002. "Immigrant Enclaves and Ethnic Communities in New York and Los Angeles." *American Sociological Review* 67:299–322.

Logan, John R., and Harvey L. Molotch. 1987. *Urban Fortunes: The Political Economy of Place.* Berkeley: University of California Press.

Logan, John R., and Charles Zhang. 2010. "Global Neighborhoods: New Pathways to Diversity and Separation." *American Journal of Sociology* 115 (4): 1069–1109.

Long, Colleen. 2007. "Credit Giuliani for New Times Square?" *USA Today,* December 28. Available at http://usatoday30.usatoday.com/news/politics/2007-12-28-1612178948_x.htm.

Lopez, Mark Hugo, and Ana Gonzalez-Barrera. 2013. "High Rate of Deportations Continue under Obama Despite Latino Disapproval." Pew Research Center,

September 19. Available at http://www.pewresearch.org/fact-tank/2013/09/19/high-rate-of-deportations-continue-under-obama-despite-latino-disapproval/.

Lowe, Lydia, and Douglas Brugge. 2007. "Grassroots Organizing in Boston Chinatown: A Comparison with CDC-Style Organizing." In *Acting Civically: From Urban Neighborhoods to Higher Education,* edited by Susan Ostrander and Kent Portney, 44–71. Lebanon, NH: University Press of New England.

Lower Manhattan Development Corporation. n.d. "Partial Action Plan 010: Lower Manhattan Revitalization Projects and Lower Manhattan Tourism." Available at http://www.renewnyc.com/FundingInitiatives/PartialActionPlans.aspx.

Lueck, Thomas J. 1986. "New York Port Changes with Shifting Economy." *New York Times,* June 1.

Lui, Mary Ting Yi. 2003. "Examining New Trends in Chinese American Urban Community Studies." *Journal of Urban History* 29 (2): 173–185.

Luk, Chiu. 2005. "Contextualizing the Emergence of New Chinatowns: An Introduction." *GeoJournal* 64 (1): 1–6.

Luo, Michael. 2004. "Weary Owners Struggle to Stay Afloat in Cutthroat Competition." *New York Times,* February 21.

Lutheran HealthCare. 2011. "LFHC Calling on Neighbors to Help Build a 'Cradle-to-Career' Pathway for Our Children." Press release, January 27. Available at http://www.lutheranmedicalcenter.com/News/PressReleases/Detail/?id=208.

Lutheran Medical Center. n.d. "Sunset Park Promise Neighborhood—Planning: Memorandum of Understanding." Available at http://www2.ed.gov/programs/promiseneighborhoods/2010/mou/u215p100311.pdf.

Lutz, Jaime. 2013. "Arch Angels: China Has a Gift for Sunset Park." *Brooklyn Paper,* April 18.

Maantay, Juliana. 2002. "Industrial Zoning Changes in New York City: A Case Study of 'Explusive' Zoning." *Projections 3: The MIT Journal of Planning: Planning for Environmental Justice.* Available at http://www.lehman.cuny.edu/deannss/geography/publications/MaantayArticle_Projections.pdf.

Macchiarola, Frank J., and Joseph G. Diaz. 1993. "Minority Political Empowerment in New York City: Beyond the Voting Rights Act." *Political Science Quarterly* 108 (1): 37–57.

Maitland, Leslie. 1978. "Despair in Sunset Park and Hope, Too." *New York Times,* December 8.

Maly, Michael. 2005. *Beyond Segregation: Multiracial and Multiethnic Neighborhoods in the United States.* Philadelphia: Temple University Press.

Marcuse, Peter. 1990. "New York City's Community Boards: Neighborhood Policy and its Results." In *Neighbourhood Policy and Programme,* edited by Naomi Carmon, 145–163. New York: St. Martin's.

———. 1997. "The Enclave, the Citadel, and the Ghetto: What Has Changed in the Post-Fordist US City." *Urban Affairs Review* 33 (2): 228–264.

Mares, Teresa M., and Devon G. Peña. 2010. "Urban Agriculture in the Making of Insurgent Spaces in Los Angeles and Seattle." In *Insurgent Public Space: Guerrilla Urbanism and the Remaking of Contemporary Cities,* edited by Jeffrey Hou, 241–254. London: Routledge.

Mark-Viverito, Melissa. 2012. "Taking on Our Fair Share of the City's Waste Burden." Huffington Post, July 19. Available at http://www.huffingtonpost.com/melissa-markviverito/nyc-trash_b_1686656.html.

Marsico, Richard. 2005. "Democratizing Capital: The History, Law, and Reform of the Community Reinvestment Act." *New York Law Review* 49:717–726.

Marwell, Nicole. 2004. "Privatizing the Welfare State: Nonprofit Community-Based Organizations as Political Actors." *American Sociological Review* 69:265–291.

Marzulli, John. 2003. "Ex-Pol Begs for Mercy before Sentence." *New York Daily News,* February 27.

Massey, Douglas, and Nancy Denton. 1993. *American Apartheid: Segregation and the Making of the Underclass.* Cambridge, MA: Harvard University Press.

Massey Knakel Realty Services. n.d. "Bowery Development Opportunity for Sale." Advertisement. Available at http://www.masseyknakal.com/listingimages/setup/pdf/135 _Bowery_Street-Setup.pdf.

Matasar, Ann B., and Joseph N. Heiney. 2002. *The Impact of Geographic Deregulation on the American Banking Industry.* Westport, CT: Quorum Books.

Matasar, Ann B., and Deborah D. Pavelka. 2004. "Minority Banks and Minority Communities: Are Minority Banks Good Neighbors?" *International Advances in Economic Research* 10 (1): 43–57.

Mauk, David C. 1997. *The Colony That Rose from Sea: Norwegian Maritime Migration and Community in Brooklyn, 1850–1930.* Champaign: University of Illinois Press.

Maya, Violetta. 2005. Interview by the author, Lutheran Medical Center, December 18.

McCarthy, T. C. 2002. "Fuzhou Province Immigration Increasing, Rivaling Cantonese. Immigrants Moving to Eighth Avenue, Brooklyn." Translated by Wendy Szeto. *World Journal,* June 16. Available at http://www.voicesofny.org/2002/06/ nycma-voices-25-news-news_1/.

McCormick, Lynn, Efrain Borrero, Sam Imperatrice, and Rupesh Manglavil. 2012. "A Role for Manufacturing in the Real Estate Capital of the World? Furniture and Apparel in New York City." *Progressive Planning Magazine* 190:27–30.

McGeehan, Patrick. 2005. "Port of New York Imports Rise Faster Than Places to Put Them." *New York Times,* March 17.

McGeehan, Patrick, and Griff Palmer. 2013. "Displaced by Hurricane Sandy, and Living in Limbo." *New York Times,* December 6.

McGeehan, Patrick, and Ray Rivera. 2008. "Ex-Official Cleared to Continue Work on Big City Projects." *New York Times,* March 26.

McGowan, Kathleen. 1999. "The Waterfront." City Limits, January 1. Available at http:// www.citylimits.org/content/articles/viewarticle.cfm?article_id=2349.

McNees, Molly, Nina Siule, Olivia Flores, and Robert Smith. 2005. "Mexican Immigrant Health in New York: Findings from the Community Health Survey." Unpublished report, Mexican Health Project, Lutheran Medical Center, Brooklyn, New York.

McPhee, Michele. 2000. "Brooklyn's Red Light District, Porn Sports Move from Times Square." *New York Daily News,* June 11.

McShane, Larry. 2013. "Controller Liu: Luxury Times Square Marriott Marquis Hotel Could Cost City Taxpayers $344 Million Due to 'Worst' Deal in City's History." *New York Daily News,* February 12.

Mello, William. 2002. "The Legacy of Pete Panto and the Brooklyn Rank-and-File Committee." *Italian American Review* 9 (1): 1–14.

Menchaca, Carlos. 2013. Interview by the author, City Council Campaign Office, Sunset Park, Brooklyn, July 8.

Ment, David, and Mary S. Donovan. 1980. *The People of Brooklyn: A History of Two Neighborhoods.* Brooklyn, NY: Brooklyn Rediscovery, Brooklyn Educational and Cultural Alliance.

Migration Policy Institute. 2007. "Proposed Points System and Its Likely Impact on Prospective Immigrants." May, No. 4. Available at http://www.migrationpolicy.org/pubs/pointssystem_051807.pdf.

Miraftab, Faranak. 2004. "Invited and Invented Spaces of Participation: Neoliberal Citizenship and Feminists' Expanded Notion of Politics." *Feminists Confront Empire,* Special issue of *Wagadu* 1. Available at http://appweb.cortland.edu/ojs/index.php/wagadu/article/viewfile/378/719.

Mitchell, Katharyne. 1993. "Multiculturalism, or the United Colors of Capitalism?" *Antipode* 25 (4): 263–294.

———. 2004. *Crossing the Neoliberal Line: Pacific Rim Migration and the Metropolis.* Philadelphia: Temple University Press.

Miyares, Ines M. 2004. "Changing Latinization of New York City." In *Hispanic Spaces, Latino Places: Community and Cultural Diversity in Contemporary America,* edited by Daniel D. Arreola, 145–166. Austin: University of Texas Press.

Moody, Kim. 2007. *From Welfare State to Real Estate: Regime Change in New York City, 1974 to the Present.* New York: New Press.

Monserrate, Hiram, Tony Avella, John Liu, Leroy C. Comrie, Helen Sears, Eric N. Gioa, James Sanders Jr., David Weprin, Letitia James, Mathieu Eugene, Charles Barron, Lewis A. Fidler, Annabel Palma, David Yassky, Albert Vann, James Vacca, Bill de Blasio, Joel Rivera, Rosie Mendez, Diana Reyna, Miguel Martinez, Sara M. Gonzalez, Joseph Addabbo Jr., Thomas White, Darlene Mealy, Vincent J. Gentile, James Gennaro, Inez Dickens, and G. Oliver Koppell. 2008. "Letter to New York City Deputy Mayor of Economic Development Robert Lieber." April 21. Available at http://www.thefreelibrary.com/Nearly+30+City+Council+Members+Call+Willets+Point+Plan+'Unacceptable'-a01611497350.

Morales, Mark. 2012a. "Sunset Park Tenant Who Was Fighting Slumlord to Make Repairs Is Now Fighting to Get Better after Attack." *New York Daily News,* July 23.

———. 2012b. "Sunset Park Tenants Use Their Own Photos of Shoddy Conditions of Their Apartment Buildings as Subjects for Art Show." *New York Daily News,* August 2.

———. 2013. "Sunset Park and Greenpoint on Prestigious 'Six to Celebrate' Neighborhood List." *New York Daily News,* January 3.

Mora-Mass, Elizabeth. 2011. "Roosevelt Avenue 'Out of Control.'" *El Correo De Queens,* December 19. Translation available at http://voicesofny.org/2011/12/roosevelt-avenue-out-of-control/.

Morawetz, Nancy. 2000. "Understanding the Impact of the 1996 Deportation Laws and the Limited Scope of Proposed Reforms." *Harvard Law Review* 113 (8): 1936–1962.

Moses, Paul. 2004. "Hard Knocks: Justice Is Not Served at Brooklyn's 'Abu Ghraib.'" *Newsday,* September 21.

Moss, Mitchell. 2006. "New York City in the 21st Century." *IEDC Economic Development Journal* 5 (2): 7–16.

Muessig, Ben. 2008. "Less Think at Owls Head." The Brooklyn Paper, July 10. Available at http://www.brooklynpaper.com/stories/31/27/31_27_less_stink_at_owls_head.html.

Muller, Thomas. 1993. *Immigrants and the American City.* New York: New York University Press.

Muniz, Vicky. 1998. *Resisting Gentrification and Displacement: Voices of Puerto Rican Women of the Barrio.* New York: Garland.

Murphy, Jarrett. 2006a. "Dumping on Everyone Else: Trash Plan Relieves Our Neighborhoods, but West of the Hudson, It's Just More of the Same Old Garbage from

New York City." *Village Voice,* July 25. Available at http://www.villagevoice
.com/2006-07-25/news/dumping-on-everyone-else/.

———. 2006b. "Save the 'Burbs! Flushing Homeowners Lead the Growing Queens Quest
for Landmark Status." *Village Voice,* April 11.

Murphy, Patrick. 2010. Interview by the author, New York City Economic Development
Corporation, January 14.

Musumeci, Natalie. 2012. "Sunset Park Tenants Fear They Live in a Firetrap." *New York
Daily News,* July 11.

———. 2013. "Men-shocka! Challenger Carlos Menchaca Unseats Sara Gonzalez in Sunset Park Council Primary." *Brooklyn Paper,* September 11. Available at http://www
.brooklynpaper.com/stories/36/37/dtg_menchacaupset_2013_09_13_bk.html.

National Conference of State Legislatures. 2005. "The Real ID Act of 2005 (Contained
in P.L. 109-13)." Available at http://www.ncsl.org/research/transportation/real-id-act
-of-2005.aspx.

National Public Radio. 2004. "Jailed Immigrants Allege Abuse." November 17–18. Available at http://www.npr.org/series/4184282/jailed-immigrants-allege-abuse.

National Trust for Historic Preservation. 2007. "11 Most Endangered Historic Places:
Brooklyn's Industrial Waterfront." Available at http://www.preservationnation.org/
issues/11-most-endangered/locations/brooklyns-industrial-waterfront.html#.Uq-8Rv
RDtbQ.

Navarro, Mireya. 2010. "Gowanus Canal Gets Superfund Status." *New York Times,*
March 2.

———. 2013a. "Hundreds of Storm Evacuees in Hotels Face Evictions." *New York Times,*
September 24.

———. 2013b. "Judge Orders Extension of Hotel Program for Hurricane Sandy Evacuees." *New York Times,* May 15.

———. 2013c. "Relying on Hotel Rooms for Thousands Uprooted by Hurricane Sandy."
New York Times, March 29.

Negrete, Citlalli. 2013. Interview by the author, Sunset Park, July 10.

Neighborhood Economic Development Advocacy Project. 2006. "Promoting Financial
Justice for Immigrant New Yorkers." Conference report, August. Available at http://
www.nedap.org/news/documents/FORUMREPORTfinal.pdf.

Nelson, Bruce. 2001. *Divided We Stand: American Workers and the Struggle for Black
Equality.* Princeton, NJ: Princeton University Press.

Ness, Immanuel. 2005. *Immigrants, Unions, and the New U.S. Labor Market.* Philadelphia:
Temple University Press.

Neuhauser, Alan. 2012. "Rent-Strikers Hope to Form Co-Op to Solve Housing
Woes." DNAinfo New York, September 13. Available at http://www.dnainfo.com/
new-york/20120913/sunset-park/rent-strikers-hope-form-co-op-solve-housing-woes.

Nevard, Jacques. 1959. "Continued Bias in Pier Hirings Is Charged by 2 Negro Leaders."
New York Times, September 15.

Newman, Andy. 2007. "Shake-up of Board Is Defended." *New York Times,* May 26.

Newman, Kathe, and Philip Ashton. 2004. "Neoliberal Urban Policy and New Paths of
Neighborhood Change in the American Inner City." *Environment and Planning A*
36:1151–1172.

New Partners for Community Revitalization. 2007. "Brownfields Breakthrough: A Report
on New York's Community Revitalization Tool for the Future." January. Available at
http://npcr.net/pages/legislation_and_policy/docs/BrownfieldJournalFinal.pdf.

New York City Council. 2005. "Report of the Human Services Division, Committee on Civil Service and Labor, Int. No. 629." June 7.

———. 2006. "Transcript of the Minutes of the Subcommittee on Zoning and Franchises." September 19. Available at http://legistar.council.nyc.gov/Legislation Detail.aspx?ID=450250&GUID=FA7013CB-BDA1-4C55-BB04-DF513350DAE5& Options=&Search=.

———. 2008. "Transcript of the Minutes of the Joint Committees on Consumer Affairs and Immigration." November 14. Available at http://legistar.council.nyc .gov/MeetingDetail.aspx?ID=76246&GUID=EF6B9F0B-0B32-4586-ABF7-7908B 943FC0E&Options=&Search=.

———. 2010. "Intro #0036-2010: A Local Law to Amend the Administrative Code of the City of New York, in Relation to Vending in Sunset Park, Brooklyn." Available at http://legistar.council.nyc.gov/LegislationDetail.aspx?ID =649933&GUID=42875FFF-0A9A-4086-8187-1FA7A83B1A89&Options=ID% 7cText%7c&Search=0036.

———. 2013a. "Legislation Details (with Text): File # Int 0434-2010, Version A." Available at http://www.nyc.gov/html/dca/downloads/pdf/general_vendor_law_rules .pdf.

———. 2013b. "Speaker Quinn Announces Selection of Participants for Worker Cooperative Development Training Program." Press release, January 3. Available at http:// council.nyc.gov/html/pr/010312workers.shtml.

New York City Council Committee on Waterfronts. 2005. "Oversight: The Status of Job Development in the Port of New York." Briefing paper, January 12. Available at http:// legistar.council.nyc.gov/LegislationDetail.aspx?ID=443493&GUID=A195F58F -BF97-421B-8EA1-C61C865EE2DA&Options=&Search=.

New York City Department of Buildings. n.d. "Building on My Block." Available at http:// a810-bisweb.nyc.gov/bisweb/my_community.jsp.

New York City Department of City Planning. n.d. "Hudson Yards—Approved! Original Proposal as Adopted." Available at http://home2.nyc.gov/html/dcp/html/hyards/pro posal.shtml.

———. 1996. *The Newest New Yorkers: 1990–1994.* New York: New York City Department of City Planning.

———. 2007. *The Jamaica Plan: Final Environmental Impact Statement.* Available at http://www.nyc.gov/html/dcp/html/env_review/jamaica.shtml.

———. 2011. "Vision 2020: New York City Comprehensive Waterfront Plan." Official Website of the City of New York, March. Available at http://www.nyc.gov/html/dcp/ pdf/cwp/vision2020_nyc_cwp.pdf.

———. 2013. "Community District Needs: Fiscal Year 2013 for the Borough of Brooklyn. Community Board 7 Statement of Needs." Available at http://www.nyc.gov/ html/dcp/pdf/pub/bkneeds_2013.pdf.

New York City Economic Development Corporation. n.d.-a. "Industrial Space Modernization RFP." Available at http://www.nycedc.com/opportunity/industrial- space-modernization-rfp.

———. n.d.-b. *Major Economic Development Initiatives.* Brochure. Available at http:// www.nycedc.com/sites/default/files/filemanager/Resources/Brochures/Initiatives _Brochure.pdf.

———. n.d.-c. "NYC? Industrial Industries." Available at http://www.nycedc.com/ industry/industrial.

————. n.d.-d. "Why NYC? Fashion Industries." Available at http://www.nycedc.com/industry/fashion#8.

————. 2005a. "Mayor Michael R. Bloomberg Introduces New Initiatives to Support New York City's Industrial Sector." Press release, January 19. Available at http://www.nycedc.com/press-release/mayor-michael-r-bloomberg-introduces-new-initiatives-support-new-york-citys-industrial.

————. 2005b. "NYCEDC Leases 25th Street Pier to LaFarge." Press release, April 11. Available at http://www.nycedc.com/press-release/nycedc-leases-25th-street-pier-lafarge.

————. 2006. "Mayor Bloomberg and Governor Pataki Announce $36 Million for Environmental Cleanup and Redevelopment of Bush Piers." Press release, April 20. Available at http://www.nycedc.com/press-release/mayor-bloomberg-and-governor-pataki-announce-36-million-environmental-cleanup-and.

————. 2007a. "NYC Economic Development Corporation Signs Lease with Axis Group for 74-Acre Brooklyn Site." Press release, February 26. Available at http://www.nycedc.com/press-release/nycedc-signs-lease-axis—group-74-acre-brooklyn-site.

————. 2007b. "NYCEDC Selects Time Equities and Brooklyn Economic Development Corporation to Redevelop Federal Building #2 in Sunset Park." Press release, May 23. Available at http://www.nycedc.com/press-release/nycedc-selects-time-equities-and-brooklyn-economic-development-corporation-redevelop.

————. 2009. "Sunset Park Waterfront Vision Plan." Available at http://portnyc-sbmt.com/Portals/127644/pdfs/sunset_park_vision_plan.pdf.

————. 2010. "Mayor Bloomberg Breaks Ground on New Municipal Recycling Facility in Sunset Park." Press release, October 25. Available at http://www.nycedc.com/press-release/mayor-bloomberg-breaks-ground-new-municipal-recyling-facility-sunset-park.

New York City Independent Budget Office. 2010. "Sidewalk Standoff: Street Vendor Regulations Are Costly, Confusing, and Leave Many Disgruntled." Fiscal Brief, November. Available at http://www.ibo.nyc.ny.us/iboreports/peddlingnovember2010.pdf.

New York City Police Department. n.d.-a. "Application Process." Available at http://www.nyc.gov/html/nypd/html/careers/application_overview.shtml.

————. n.d.-b. "Candidate Resource Booklet." Available at http://www.nyc.gov/html/nypd/downloads/pdf/applicant_processing/Candidate_Resource_Booklet_2009.pdf.

New York City Small Business Services. 2011. "Mayor Bloomberg and Speaker Quinn Announce 22 New Initiatives to Help Small Industrial Businesses Stay and Grow in New York City," Press release, June 7. Available at http://www.nyc.gov/portal/site/nycgov/menuitem.c0935b9a57bb4ef3daf2f1c701c789a0/index.jsp?pageID=mayor_press_release&catID=1194&doc_name=http%3A%2F%2Fwww.nyc.gov%2Fhtml%2Fom%2Fhtml%2F2011a%2Fpr195-11.html&cc=unused1978&rc=1194&ndi=1.

New York City Special Initiative on Rebuilding and Resiliency. 2013. "A Stronger, More Resilient New York." Available at http://www.nyc.gov/html/sirr/html/report/report.shtml.

New Yorkers for Parks. 2009. "City Council District Profiles." Available at http://www.ny4p.org/research/d-profiles/38.pdf.

New York Power Authority. 2006. "Power Authority Starts Construction of Wall around Sunset Park Facility; Breaks Ground at 23rd and 3rd Street." Press release, July 13. Available at http://www.nypa.gov/press/2006/060713a.htm.

New York State Banking Department. 2010. "10 Years In: A Review of the Banking Development District Program." May. Available at http://www.dfs.ny.gov/banking/bddreview.pdf.

New York State Department of Environmental Conservation. 2004. "Environmental Restoration Record of Decision: Bush Terminal Landfill Piers 1–4 Site; Brooklyn, Kings County, New York Site Number B00031-2." March. Available at http://www.dec.ny.gov/docs/remediation_hudson_pdf/rodb000312.pdf.

New York State Department of Financial Services. n.d. "Approved Banking Development Districts." Available at http://www.dfs.ny.gov/banking/bddapp.htm.

New York State Department of Labor. n.d. "Apparel Industry Task Force." Available at http://www.labor.state.ny.us/workerProtection/LaborStandards/workprot/garment.asp.

New York State Department of State. 2011. "Department of State Announces $6.5 Million in Brownfield Opportunity Areas Program Grants." Press release, April 20. Available at http://www.dos.ny.gov/press/2011/BOA_Grants.html.

New York State Department of Transportation. 2006. "Gowanus Project." Available at Available at https://www.dot.ny.gov/regional-offices/region11/projects/project-repository/gowanus/index.html.

New York State Office of General Counsel. n.d. "Legal Memorandum LU03: Municipal Regulation of Adult Uses." Available at http://www.dos.state.ny.us/cnsl/lu03.htm.

New York University. 2006. "South Bronx Environmental Health and Policy Study." Available at http://www.icisnyu.org/south_bronx/admin/files/HandoutWagnerOct162006.pdf.

Ngai, Mae. 2007. "Nationalism, Immigration Control, and the Ethnoracial Remapping of America in the 1920s." *OAH Magazine of History,* July, pp. 11–15.

Nicolle-Grist, Lisa. 2005. Interview by the author, Neighbors Helping Neighbors, Sunset Park, March 31.

NPR Staff. 2012. "Finding an Anchor for a Life Set Adrift by a Shipwreck." National Public Radio, June 7. Available at http://www.npr.org/2013/06/07/189222117/finding-an-anchor-for-a-life-set-adrift-by-a-shipwreck.

NY1. 2008. "Community Board 3 Rezoning Meeting." Video clip uploaded on May 13. Available at http://www.youtube.com/watch?v=WqXmI4QYncI.

O'Brien, Rory. 1998. "An Overview of the Methodological Approach of Action Research." Available at www.web.ca/~robrien/papers/arfinal.html.

Occupy Wall Street. 2012. "Today: Sunset Park Rent Strikers to Hold Sleep-in and People's Inspection." July 18. Available at http://occupywallst.org/article/today-sunset-park-rent-strikers-hold-sleep-and-peo/.

Ohrstrom, Lysandra. 2008. "The Local: Rezoning Anxiety Rends Garment District." *New York Observer,* February 29. Available at http://www.observer.com/2008/local-garment-district.

Oliver, Melvin, and Thomas Shapiro. 1995. *Black Wealth/White Wealth: A New Perspective on Racial Inequality.* New York: Routledge.

Ong, Paul M. 1984. "Chinatown Unemployment and the Ethnic Labor Market." *Amerasia Journal* 11 (1): 35–54.

Ong, Paul M., and Tania Azores. 1994. "The Migration and Incorporation of Filipino Nurses." In *The New Asian Immigration in Los Angeles and Global Restructuring,* edited by Paul M. Ong, Edna Bonacich, and Lucie Cheng, 164–195. Philadelphia: Temple University Press.

Ong, Paul M., and R. Varisa Pataporn. 2006. "Asian Americans and Wealth." In *Wealth Accumulation and Communities of Color in the United States: Current Issues,* edited by Jessica Gordon Nembhard and Ngina Chiteji, 173–190. Ann Arbor: University of Michigan Press.

Onishi, Norimitsu. 1994. "Where Cocoa Is King." *New York Times,* March 13.

Orr, Marion, ed. 2007. *Transforming the City: Community Organizing and the Challenge of Political Change.* Lawrence: University Press of Kansas.

Oser, Alan S. 1996. "Immigrants again Renew Sunset Park." *New York Times,* December 1.

Osofsky, Gilbert. 1963. *Harlem: The Making of a Ghetto.* New York: Harper Torchbooks.

Park, Edward J., and John S. W. Park. 2005. *Probationary Americans: Contemporary Immigration Policies and the Shaping Of Asian American Communities.* New York: Routledge.

Park, Kyeyoung, and Russell Leong. 2008. "How Do Asian Americans Create Places? From Background to Foreground." *How Do Asian Americans Create Places: Los Angeles & Beyond,* special issue of *Amerasia Journal* 34 (3): vii–xiv.

Pasquarelli, Adrianne. 2012. "Fashion BID Seeks New Label for Itself: A Changing District Wants Distance from Its Garment Past." *Crain's New York Business,* June 10.

Pasquarelli, Adrianne, and Chris Bragg. 2013. "Big Project Is Missing in Flushing." *Crain's New York Business,* February 2.

Passel, Jeffrey S., Randy Capps, and Michael Fix. 2004. "Undocumented Immigrants: Facts and Figures." Urban Institute Immigration Studies Program, January 12. Available at http://www.urban.org/UploadedPDF/1000587_undoc_immigrants_facts.pdf.

Pastor, Kate. 2007. "Tenants with Asthma Fight to Breathe Easy." *City Limits,* June 18.

Pastor, Manuel, Rachel Morello-Frosch, and Jim Sadd. 2006. "Breathless: Pollution, Schools, and Environmental Justice in California." *Policy Studies Journal* 34 (3): 337–362.

Pear, Robert. 2012. "Limits Placed on Immigrants in Health Care Law." *New York Times,* September 17.

Pecorella, Robert F. 1989. "Community Governance: A Decade of Experience." *Proceedings of the Academy of Political Science* 37 (3): 97–109.

Perez-Pena, Richard. 2003. "Study Finds Asthma in 25% of Children in Central Harlem." *New York Times,* April 19.

Pew Hispanic Center. 2006. "Modes of Entry for the Unauthorized Migrant Population." Available at http://pewhispanic.org/files/factsheets/19.pdf.

Phillips-Fein, Kim. 2013. "The Legacy of the 1970s Fiscal Crisis." *The Nation,* May 6. Available at http://www.thenation.com/article/17383/legacy-1970s-fiscal-crisis#.

Pincus, Adam. 2009. "Time Equities Abandons Two Brooklyn waterfront Projects." *Real Deal,* February 25. Available at http://therealdeal.com/blog/2009/02/25/time-equities-abandons-two-brooklyn-waterfront-projects/.

Pogrebin, Robin. 2007. "Brooklyn Waterfront Called Endangered Site." *New York Times,* June 14.

Pollard, Jane S. 1996. "Banking at the Margins: A Geography of Financial Exclusion in Los Angeles." *Environment and Planning A* 28:1209–1232.

Polsky, Sara. 2012. "Sunset Park Tries for 'Neo-Soho' Vibe with New Artist Lofts." Curbed, March 1. Available at http://ny.curbed.com/archives/2012/03/01/sunset_park_tries_for_neosoho_vibe_with_new_artist_lofts.php.

Port, Bob. 2001. "Sweatshop Suit Today: Garment Workers to File." *New York Daily News,* February 12.

Port Authority of New York and New Jersey. n.d.-a. "Comprehensive Port Improvement Plan: Section 2, Purpose and Need for the Project." Available at http://www.panynj.gov/about/pdf/cpip/cpip_assess/2.pdf.

———. n.d.-b. "Cross Harbor Freight Program." Available at http://www.crossharbor study.com/.

————. 2008. "Port of New York and New Jersey Sets Cargo Record in 2007; Plans for Expansion Announced." Press Release, March 20. Available at http://www.panynj.gov/press-room/press-item.cfm?headLine_id=969.

Porter, Eduardo. 2005. "Illegal Immigrants Are Bolstering Social Security with Billions." *New York Times,* April 5.

Portes, Alejandro. 1981. "Modes of Structural Incorporation and Present Theories of Labor Immigration." In *Global Trends in Migration: Theory and Research on International Population Movements,* edited by M. Kritz, C. B. Keely, and S. M. Tomasi, 279–297. New York: Center for Migration Studies.

Portes, Alejandro, and Robert L. Bach. 1985. *Latin Journey: Cuban and Mexican Immigrants in the United States.* Berkeley: University of California Press.

Portes, Alejandro, Manuel Castells, and Lauren Benton, eds. 1989. *The Informal Economy: Studies in Advanced and Less Developed Countries.* Baltimore: Johns Hopkins University Press.

Portes, Alejandro, Luis E. Guarnizo, and William Haller. 2002. "Transnational Entrepreneurs: An Alternative Form of Immigrant Economic Adaptation." *American Sociological Review* 67:278–298.

Portes, Alejandro, and Rubén G. Rumbaut. 1990. *Immigrant America: A Portrait.* Berkeley: University of California Press.

Portes, Alejandro, and Min Zhou. 1992. "Gaining the Upper Hand: Economic Mobility among Immigrant and Domestic Minorities." *Ethnic and Racial Studies* 15:491–522.

Powell, Michael. 2011. "Her Chinatown Home Is 'Underperforming.'" *New York Times,* August 15.

————. 2012. "Police Monitoring and a Climate of Fear." *New York Times,* February 27.

Pratt Center for Community Development. n.d. "One City/One Future." Available at http://prattcenter.net/projects/sustainable-community-development/one-city/one-future.

————. 2007. "Sunset Park Voices in the Rezoning Process." Sustainable Community Development report, December 17. Available at http://www.prattcenter.net/pubs/PrattCenter-Sunset_Park_Rezoning.pdf.

————. 2008. "Protecting New York's Threatened Manufacturing Space." Available at http://prattcenter.net/issue-brief/protecting-new-yorks-threatened-manufacturing-space.

Pratt Institute. n.d. "Pratt Center." Available at http://www.pratt.edu/support_pratt/pratt_gives_back/pratt_center/.

Pressar, Patricia. 1995. *A Visa for a Dream: Dominicans in the United States.* Needham Heights, MA: Allyn and Bacon.

Preston, Julia. 2012. "Record Number of Foreigners Were Deported in 2011, Officials Say." *New York Times,* September 7.

Pristin, Terry. 2001. "On the Run to the Halls of the Boardroom Power." *New York Times,* January 3.

Prokesch, Steven. 1993. "New York City Planners Seek New Uses for Industrial Areas." *New York Times,* January 15.

Publius [David Au]. 2008. "The Manifesto." Save Sunset Park blog, March 8. Available at http://savesunsetpark.blogspot.com/2008_03_01_archive.html.

Pulido, Laura. 2006. *Black, Brown, Yellow, and Left: Radical Activism in Los Angeles.* Berkeley: University of California Press.

Rath, Jan, and Robert Kloosterman. 2000. "Outsiders' Business: A Critical Review of Research on Immigrant Entrepreneurship." *International Migration Review* 34 (3): 656–680.

Raymond, Janice G., and Donna M. Hughes. 2001. "Sex Trafficking of Women in the United States: International and Domestic Trends." Unpublished report. Available at http://www.uri.edu/artsci/wms/hughes/sex_traff_us.pdf.

Real Deal Staff. 2007. "Sunset Park Also Rises." *Real Deal,* October 24. Available at http://therealdeal.com/issues_articles/sunset-park-also-rises/.

———. 2008. "Architects Drafting a Better Office Space in Garment District." *Real Deal,* July. Available at http://ny.therealdeal.com/articles/architects-drafting-a-better-office-space-in-garment-district.

Reckard, E. Scott. 2003. "Do Minority Banks Lend Enough to Other Minorities?" *Los Angeles Times,* July 2.

———. 2006. "Banks Wrestle for Larger Share of Chinese American Market." *Los Angeles Times,* February 10.

———. 2009. "United Commercial Bank Is Shut Down, Sold to East West Bancorp." *Los Angeles Times,* November 7.

Reichl, Alexander. 1999. *Reconstructing Time Square.* Lawrence: University of Kansas Press.

Retsinas, Greg 2003a. "Bank Officer, Still on Run, Is Charged with Fraud." *New York Times,* April 23.

———. 2003b. "In a Bank Run, Money Outtalks a Bullhorn." *New York Times,* April 24.

Reynolds, Francis. 2012. "Weathering Super Storm Sandy in Chinatown." The Nation, November 1. Available at http://www.thenation.com/video/170970/weathering-super-storm-sandy-chinatown.

Rivera, Ray. 2012. "Groups Admit to Lobbying Illegally to Aid Mayor's Plans." *New York Times,* July 3.

Robbins, Liz, and Mike McIntire. 2004. "A True Champion of Grand Plans and Tiny Details; With the Zeal of an Athlete, Doctoroff Pursues Olympics." *New York Times,* May 16.

Robert. 2007. "Sunset Park to Enter Downzoning Olympics." March 28. Available at http://ny.curbed.com/archives/2007/03/28/sunset_park_to_enter_downzoning_olympics.php.

Roberts, Sam. 2005. "In Manhattan, Poor Make 2¢ for Each Dollar to the Rich." *New York Times,* September 4.

———. 2011. "Filing Challenge to Census, City Says 50,000 Weren't Counted in 2 Boroughs." *New York Times,* August 10.

Rodriguez, Cindy Y. 2011. "Ydanis Rodriguez Arrested: New York City Council Member Hit and Arrested during Police Raid at Zuccotti Park." Huffington Post, November 15. Available at http://www.huffingtonpost.com/2011/11/15/ydanis-rodriguez-arrested-hit-occupy-wall-street-raid_n_1094645.html.

Rodriguez, Juan Carlos. 2012. "NY's Abacus Bank Charged with Mortgage Fraud." May 31. Available at http://www.law360.com/articles/345776/ny-s-abacus-bank-charged-with-mortgage-fraud.

Rogers, David. 1990. "Community Control and Decentralization." In *Urban Politics: New York Style,* edited by Jewel Bellush and Dick Netzer, 143–186. Armonk, NY: M. E. Sharpe.

Rohter, Larry. 1985. "New York's Thriving Hispanic Banks." *New York Times,* August 11.

Romano, Denise. 2012. "Rent Strikers Showcase Their Struggles." Home Reporter and Sunset News, August 8. Available at http://www.homereporternews.com/news/general/rent-strikers-showcase-their-struggles/article_3df37e5c-e0d5-11e1-8a3b-0019bb2963f4.html?mode=story.

————. 2013. "Residents Fight 'Adult Toy' Store—and Win." *Home Reporter,* May 29.

Rose, Joel. 2013. "Time for Superstorm Sandy Evacuees to Check Out of Hotels." National Public Radio, October 3. Available at http://www.npr.org/2013/10/03/228910696/ superstorm-sandy-evacuees-hotel-rooms.

Rosen, Rae, Susan Wieler, and Joseph Pereira. 2005. "New York City Immigrants: The 1990s Wave." Federal Reserve Bank of New York Report, Current Issues in Economics and Finance, Vol. 11, No. 6 (June). Available at http://www.ny.frb.org/research/ current_issues/ci11-6.pdf.

Rosenthal, Elisabeth. 2000. "Chinese Town's Main Export: Its Young Men." *New York Times,* June 26.

Ross, Barbara. 1999. "Garment Exec Facing Bank Fraud Charges Said Hiding Out in China." *New York Daily News,* December 6.

Ruben. 2009. "The New Factory: In Brooklyn, an Industrial Artists' Colony." Art Most Fierce blog, January 15. Available at http://artmostfierce.blogspot.com/2009/01/new -factory-in-brooklyn-industrial.html.

Ruiz, Albor. 2002. "New Outcry over Jailed Immigrants." *New York Daily News,* March 25.

Ruiz, Cynthia. 2013. Interview by the author, St. Jacobi Evangelical Lutheran Church, July 20.

Ruiz, Juan Carlos. 2013. Interview by the author, St. Jacobi Evangelical Lutheran Church, July 20.

Sadovi, Maura Webber. 2013. "Industry City Investors Hope 'Made in Brooklyn' Lures Tenants." *Wall Street Journal,* September 17.

Saenz, Rogelio, Maria Cristina Morales, and Maria Isabel Ayala. 2004. "The United States: Immigration to the Melting Pot of the Americas." In *Migration and Immigration: A Global View,* edited by Maura Isabel Toro-Morn and Marixsa Alicea, 211–230. Westport, CT: Greenwood.

Saito, Leland. 1998. *Race and Politics: Asian Americans, Latinos, and Whites in a Los Angeles Suburb.* Champaign: University of Illinois Press.

Salazar, Christian. 2013. "What Future for the City's Waterfront?" Gotham Gazette, April 10. Available at http://www.gothamgazette.com/index.php/environment/ 4221-what-future-for-the-citys-waterfront.

Samers, Michael. 2002. "Immigration and the Global City Hypothesis: Towards an Alternative Research Agenda." *International Journal of Urban and Regional Research* 26 (2): 389–402.

Sanchez, George. 2001. "Excerpt from the Presidential Address to the American Studies Association, November 9, 2001." Available at http://www.janm.org/exhibits/bh/ resources/sanchez_article.htm.

————. 2004. "'What's Good for Boyle Heights Is Good for the Jews': Creating Multi-racialism on the Eastside during the 1950s." *American Quarterly* 56 (3): 633–661.

Sanchez Korrol, Virginia. 1983. *From Colonia to Community: The History of Puerto Ricans in New York City.* Berkeley: University of California Press.

————. 2005. "Building the New York Puerto Rican Community, 1945–1965: A Historical Interpretation." In *Boricuas in Gotham: Puerto Ricans in the Making of Modern New York City,* edited by Gabriel Haslip-Viera, Angelo Falcon, and Felix Matos Rodriquez, 1–20. Princeton, NJ: Markus Wiener.

Sandberg, Lisa. 1997. "Center Toils for Sweatshop Workers." *New York Daily News,* January 3.

Sandercock, Leonie. 2003. "Integrating Immigrants: The Challenge for Cities, City Governments, and the City-Building Professions." Working Paper Series, Research on Immigration and Integration in the Metropolis, Vancouver Centre of Excellence.

Sandomir, Richard. 2005. "Latino Bank Teams Up with Mets." *New York Times,* March 23.

Sanjek, Roger. 1998. *The Future of Us All: Race and Neighborhood Politics in New York City.* Ithaca, NY: Cornell University Press.

————. 2000. "Color-Full before Color Blind: The Emergence of Multiracial Neighborhood Politics in Queens, New York City." *American Anthropologist* 102 (4): 762–772.

Santora, Marc. 2010. "New York's Next Frontier: The Waterfront." *New York Times,* November 5.

Santos, Fernanda. 2008a. "A Confrontation over the Future of Willets Point." *New York Times,* August 13.

————. 2008b. "4 Brooklyn Neighborhoods Lose Power." *New York Times,* July 21.

Santucci, Christina. 2007. "City Council Downzones Sections of Flushing." *Queens Courier,* October 11.

Sardell, Alice. 1988. *The U.S. Experiment in Social Medicine: The Community Health Center Program, 1965–1986.* Pittsburgh, PA: University of Pittsburgh Press.

Sassen, Saskia. 1988. *The Mobility of Labor and Capital: A Study in International Investment and Labor Flow.* London: Cambridge University Press.

————. 1990. "Economic Restructuring and the American City." *Annual Reviews in Sociology* 16:465–490.

————. 1991. *The Global City: New York, London, Tokyo.* Princeton, NJ: Princeton University Press.

————. 1994. *Cities in a World Economy.* Thousand Oaks, CA: Pine Forge.

————. 1996. "Cities and Communities in the Global Economy: Rethinking Our Concepts." *American Behavioral Scientist* 39:629–639.

————. 2000a. "Forward." In *Latino Metropolis,* edited by Victor M. Valle and Rodolfo D. Torres, ix–xiii. Minneapolis: University of Minnesota Press.

————. 2000b. "The Global City: Strategic Site/New Frontier." *American Studies* 41 (2/3): 79–95.

Saulny, Susan. 2003. "Ex-Councilman Sentenced to 4 Years in Bribery Case." *New York Times,* June 18.

Scheck, Anne. 2006. "Credit Lending, the American Way." *Independent Banker,* September. Available at http://www.icba.org/files/ICBASites/PDFs/msf0906.pdf.

Schwartz, Joel. 1993. *The New York Approach: Robert Moses, Urban Liberals, and Redevelopment of the Inner City.* Columbus: Ohio State University Press.

Schwartz, John. 2012. "US Ports Expand, with an Eye on Panama." *New York Times,* August 21.

Scott, Allen J. 2006. "Creative Cities: Conceptual Issues and Policy Questions." *Journal of Urban Affairs* 28 (1): 1–17.

Scott, Allen J., and Edward W. Soja, eds. 1996. *The City: Los Angeles and Urban Theory at the End of the Twentieth Century.* Berkeley: University of California Press.

Scott, Janny. 2004. "Bank Branches, Sprouting Like Weeds." *New York Times,* February 7.

Segal, Valerie. 2003. Interview by the author, Center for Family Life, October 21.

Seidman, Karl F. 2005. *Economic Development Finance.* Thousand Oaks, CA: Sage.

Selver, Paul. 1974. "Community Boards Meet Vital Need." *New York Times,* December 1.

Semple, Kirk. 2013. "Take the A Train to Little Guyana." *New York Times,* June 8.

Semple, Kirk, and Jeffrey E. Singer. 2012. "Chinatown Gambling Raid May Reveal Cultural Divide." *New York Times,* July 5.

Sengupta, Somini. 1996. "Illegal Van Express Overtakes Slow Transit to Chinatown." *New York Times,* July 7.

Shaman, Diana. 1979. "Local Boards Now Crucial to the Process of Change." *New York Times,* July 1.

Shanmuganathan, Premala, Merlin Stone, and Bryan Foss. 2004. "Ethnic Banking in the USA." *Journal of Financial Services Marketing* 8 (4): 388–400.

Shao, Lida, Rebecca Giordano, May Lin, and Sunset Park Residents. 2010. *¡Basta Ya! Sunset Rise.* Video, 33 minutes. Available at http://vimeo.com/15192664.

Sheets, Connor Adams. 2011. "Commons Eyes China Cash." *TimesLedger,* July 13.

Shephard, George F. 1919. "Uncle Sam, Wholesale Warehouseman." *New York Times,* December 7.

Shifrel, Scott. 2001. "Kin's Guilt Clouds Fate of Hopeful Liu Says Dad Not Guilty." *New York Daily News,* March 11.

Sietsema, Robert. 2009. "Market Watch: Albino Bitter Melon and More at Fei Long Market in Brooklyn." *Village Voice,* August 26. Available at http://blogs.villagevoice.com/forkintheroad/2009/08/market_watch_wh.php.

Sikh Coalition. 2008. "Making Our Voices Heard: A Civil Rights Agenda for New York City's Sikhs." April. Available at http://www.sikhcoalition.org/documents/pdf/RaisingOurVoicesReport.pdf.

Silver, Sheldon, Felix W. Ortiz, and Catherine Nolan. 1997. "Behind Closed Doors: A Look into the Underground Sweatshop Industry." Unpublished report by the New York State Assembly Sub-Committee on Sweatshops, November.

———. 1999. "Behind Closed Doors II: Another Look into the Underground Sweatshop Industry; The Second Report by the New York State Assembly Sub-Committee on Sweatshops." Unpublished report, September.

Silverman, Robert M., Henry L. Taylor, and Christopher Crawford. 2008. "The Role of Citizen Participation and Action Research Principles in Main Street Revitalization." *Action Research* 6 (1): 69–93.

Simon, Rachel. 1995. "New York City's Restrictive Zoning of Adult Businesses: A Constitutional Analysis." *Fordham Urban Law Journal* 23 (1): 187–219.

Singer, Audrey, and Anna Paulson. 2004. "Financial Access for Immigrants: Learning from Diverse Perspectives." The Brookings Institution Policy Brief, Conference Report #19.

Slade, Holly. 2013. "Rebuilding from the Ground." *New York World,* April 2. Available at http://www.thenewyorkworld.com/2013/04/02/rebuilding-from-the-ground-up/.

Small, Mario Luis. 2006. "Neighborhood Institutions as Resource Brokers: Childcare Centers, Interorganizational Ties, and Resource Access among the Poor." *Social Forces* 53 (2): 274–292.

Smith, Christopher J. 1995. "Asian New York: The Geography and Politics of Diversity." *International Migration Review* 29 (1): 59–84.

Smith, Neil. 2002. "New Globalism, New Urbanism: Gentrification as Global Urban Strategy." *Antipode* 32 (2): 427–450.

Smith, Neil, and James DeFilippis. 1999. "The Reassertion of Economics: 1990s Gentrification in the Lower East Side." *International Journal of Urban and Regional Research* 23:638–653.

Smith, Robert C. 1996. "Mexicans in New York: Membership and Incorporation in a New Immigrant Community." In *Latinos in New York: Communities in Transition,* edited by Gabriel Haslip-Viera and Sherrie L. Baver, 57–103. Notre Dame, IN: University of Notre Dame Press.

Soadwa, Akua. 2008. Interview by the author, New York State Banking Department, March 27.

South Brooklyn Marine Terminal. n.d. "Introducing America's Automotive Gateway." Brochure. Available at http://portnyc-sbmt.com/Portals/127644/pdfs/axis_sbmt_brochure_2011.pdf.

Spark. 2011. "New Immigrant Leaders in Sunset Park." Blog for the Center for Family Life's New Immigrant Leadership Project, July 18, 2011. Available at http://cflspark.wordpress.com/2009/06/10/new-immigrant-leaders-in-sunset-park/.

Spielman, Lynda. 2009. Interview by the author, Flushing, Queens, June 25.

Spinola, Steven. 2008. "New York City Still Building and Selling, Despite a Tightening Financial Market." The ResidentialNYNYC.com Condominium Report, Spring. Available at http://www.rebny.com/pdf_files/Luxury%20Living%20Spring%202008.pdf.

Squires, Gregory D., and Charis E. Kubrin. 2005. "Privileged Places: Race, Uneven Development, and the Geography of Opportunity in Urban America." *Urban Studies* 42 (1): 47–68.

Stein, Joshua David 2009. "The New Factory: In Brooklyn, an Industrial Artists' Colony." *New York Magazine,* January 11. Available at http://nymag.com/news/features/all-new/53346/.

Steinhauer, Jennifer. 2005. "Housing Boom Echoes in All Corners of the City." *New York Times,* August 4. Available at http://www.nytimes.com/2005/08/04/nyregion/04housing.html?pagewanted=all&_r=0.

Stern, Walter H. 1961. "City's Pulse Felt at Bush Terminal." *New York Times,* May 28.

Stern, William J. 1999. "The Unexpected Lessons of Times Square's Comeback." *City Journal,* Autumn. Available at http://www.city-journal.org/html/9_4_the_unexpected.html.

Steve. 2008. "Can This Be This?" Brooklyn Row House blog, August 26. Available at http://www.brooklynrowhouse.com/sunset_marketplace.

Stiroh, Kevin, and Philip E. Strahan. 2003. "Competitive Dynamics of Deregulation: Evidence from U.S. Banking." *Journal of Money, Credit, and Banking* 35:801–828.

Stone, Michael E. 2004. "Shelter Poverty: The Chronic Crisis of Housing Affordability." *New England Journal of Public Policy* 20, 1. Available at http://scholarworks.umb.edu/nejpp/vol20/iss1/16.

Strahan, Philip E. 2003. *The Real Effects of U.S. Banking Deregulation.* The Federal Reserve Bank of St. Louis, July/August. Available at http://research.stlouisfed.org/publications/review/03/07/Strahan.pdf.

Street Vendors Project. 2006. "Peddling Uphill: A Report on the Conditions of Street Vendors in New York City." Available at http://www.scribd.com/doc/18948529/Peddling-Uphill.

Stringer, Scott M. 2008. "Community Planning Fellowship Program: Annual Report, Fall 2007–Spring 2008." Available at http://mbpo.org/uploads/Fellowship%20Annual%20Report%202007-2008.pdf.

———. 2010. "Recommendations to the New York City Charter Revision Commission." May. Available at http://www.mbpo.org/uploads/policy_reports/CharterRevisionReport2.pdf.

Stumpf, Melisa. 2013. "Women Rule—Gonzalez Honors Women of Distinction." *Home Reporter,* March 27.

Sullivan, Mercer L. 1993. "Puerto Ricans in Sunset Park, Brooklyn: Poverty amidst Ethnic and Economic Diversity." In *In the Barrios: Latinos and the Underclass Debate,* edited by Joan Moore, 1–25. New York: Russell Sage Foundation.

Sung, Thomas. 2005. Interview by the author, Abacus Federal Savings Bank, Manhattan Chinatown, May 12.

Sunset Park 5th Avenue BID. 2007. "'Plaza del Mercado Unido': The Uniting of Two Business Districts." Unpublished monograph.

Sunset Park Promise Neighborhood. n.d. "Who Are We?" Available at http://sunsetpark promise.wordpress.com/who-is-the-sppn/.

Sunset Park Restoration Committee. 1979. "Sunset Park: A Time Remembered." Unpublished monograph.

Sussman, Nadia. 2011. "Struggling to Stitch." *New York Times,* March 21. Video. Available at http://www.nytimes.com/video/2011/03/21/nyregion/100000000735431/ garmentlabor.html.

Sviridoff, Mitchell. 1994. "The Seeds of Urban Revival." *Public Interest* 114 (Winter). Available at http://www.questia.com/library/1G1-15139620/the-seeds-of-urban-revival.

Swarns, Rachel L. 2004. "Program's Value in Dispute as a Tool to Fight Terrorism." *New York Times,* December 21.

Sze, Julie. 2007. *Noxious New York: The Racial Politics of Urban Health and Environmental Justice.* Cambridge, MA: MIT Press.

Tarquinio, Alex J. 2008. "Budget Hotels for the Garment District." *New York Times,* June 18.

Taylor, Kate. 2012. "East River Trash Project Receives Federal Permit." *New York Times,* July 22.

———. 2013. "Mayoral Candidates Wrestle over Waste Removal." *New York Times,* June 2.

Tchen, Jack Kuo Wei. 1999. *New York before Chinatown: Orientalism and the Shaping of American Culture, 1776–1882.* Baltimore: Johns Hopkins University Press.

Teltsch, Kathleen. 1980. "In Borough Park, Jewish-Italian-Hispanic Self-Help Leads to a Grant." *New York Times,* December 19.

Thabit, Walter. 2003. *How East New York Became a Ghetto.* New York: New York University Press.

Theodore, Nik, and Nina Martin. 2007. "Migrant Civil Society: New Voices in the Struggle over Community Development." *Journal of Urban Affairs* 29 (3): 269–287.

Thomas, Jo. 1994. "Sludge Still Causes a Stink in Sunset Park." *New York Times,* October 3.

Thomas, June Manning. 1994. "Planning History and the Black Urban Experience: Linkages and Contemporary Implications." *Journal of Planning Education and Research* 14 (1): 1–11.

Thomas, Phaedra. 2005. Interview by the author, Southwest Brooklyn Industrial Development Corporation, Sunset Park, May 10.

Thompson, Gabriel. 2007. "Immigrants Push Western Union to Share the Wealth." *The Nation,* May 11. Available at http://www.thenation.com/article/immigrants-push -western-union-share-wealth.

Tierney, John. n.d. "Giuliani's Legacy: A Change in the Way New Yorkers Think about Crime, Welfare, Quality of Life, Squeegee Men." Available at http://www.gotham gazette.com/commentary/91.tierney.shtml.

Timmons, Heather. 2008. "Cost-Cutting in New York, but a Boom in India." *New York Times,* August 11.

Toy, Vivian S. 1996. "New York Zoning against Sex Shops Is Upheld as Fair." *New York Times,* October 24.

———. 2006. "Luxury Condos Arrive in Chinatown." *New York Times,* September 17.

Trapasso, Clare. 2014. "Nordstrom Rack to Move to Skyview Center in Flushing, Queens." *New York Daily News,* January 7.

Tucker, Karen. 2006. "Is the Intermediate Small Bank Exam Right for Your Bank?" Community Developments: 2005 CRA Changes and the Intermediate Small Bank in Review. Available at http://www.occ.gov/static/community-affairs/community -developments-investments/summer06/istheintermediate.html.

Tucker, Maria Luisa. 2008. "Runnin' Scared: Lower East Side Rezone Sparks Border War in Chinatown." *Village Voice,* May 20.

Turcotte, Jason. 2009. "6M S/F Brooklyn 'Regeneration' Is a Work of Art." *Real Estate Weekly,* April 22.

Turnbull, Lornet, Kristi Heim, Sara Jean Green, and Sanjay Bhatt. 2006. "15 days in a Metal Box, to Be Locked Up." *Seattle Times,* April 6. Available at http://seattletimes .com/html/localnews/2002914004_smuggling.html

Turnovsky, Carolyn. 2003. "*Soy Mexicano, Soy Colombiano,* I'm American: An Intersection of Cultures among Day Laborers in New York City." Paper presented at the annual meeting of the American Sociological Association, Atlanta, Georgia, August 16. Available at http://citation.allacademic.com/meta/p_mla_apa_research_citation/ 1/0/6/8/5/pages106854/p106854-1.php.

Uchitelle, Louis. 2007. "The Richest of the Rich, Proud of a New Gilded Age." *New York Times,* July 15.

United States Attorney, Southern District of New York. 2003. "U.S. Arrests Five in $10 Million Bank Fraud Scheme at Abacus Bank in New York's Chinatown." Press release, December 18. Available at http://www.justice.gov/usao/nys/pressreleases/December 03/abacuscomplaintpr.pdf.

Urban Justice Center. 2005. "Behind Closed Doors: An Analysis of Indoor Sex Work in New York City." Sex Workers Project, Executive Summary. Available at http://sex workersproject.org/downloads/BehindClosedDoorsES.pdf.

U.S. Census Bureau. 2012. "Statistical Abstract of the United States: Section on Transportation." Available at http://www.census.gov/prod/2011pubs/12statab/trans.pdf.

U.S. Department of Housing and Urban Development. n.d. "Affordable Housing." Available at http://portal.hud.gov/hudportal/HUD?src=/program_offices/comm _planning/affordablehousing/.

U.S. House of Representatives, Committee on Education and the Workforce, Subcommittee on Oversight and Investigations. 1998. "The American Worker at Crossroads Project: Hearing on Worker Exploitation in New York City Garment Industry." March 31. Available at http://archives.republicans.edlabor.house.gov/archive/hearings/105th/oi/ awp33198/wl33198.htm.

U.S. Immigration and Customs Enforcement. n.d. "Overview." Available at http://www .ice.gov/about/index.htm.

US Power Generating Company. 2008. "Astoria Generating Company Announces South Pier Improvement Project to Provide Cleaner Air and More Reliable Power in Sunset Park Community and NYC." SPIP Public Participation Materials and Meeting Summaries, April. Available at http://www.dec.ny.gov/docs/permits_ej_operations_pdf/ gpublic1.pdf.

Valenzuela, Abel, Jr. 2001. "Day Laborers as Entrepreneurs?" *Journal of Ethnic and Migration Studies* 27 (2): 335–352.

————. 2003. "Day Labor Work." *Annual Review of Sociology* 29:307–333.

Valenzuela, Abel, Jr., and Edwin Melendez. 2003. "Day Labor in New York: Findings from the NYDL Survey." UCLA Center for the Study of Urban Poverty. Available at http://www.sscnet.ucla.edu/issr/csup/pubs/papers/pdf/csup3_NYDLS.pdf.

Velázquez, Nydia. 2013. "Despite Reforms, SBA's Sandy Response Lags." Report prepared by Democrats of the House Committee on Small Business, May. Available at http://www.house.gov/velazquez/images/SBASandyReport052013.pdf.

Vitullo-Martin, Julia. 2008. "Mayor Bloomberg: Right on Neighborhoods, Right on Immigration." Available at http://www.manhattan-institute.org/email/crd_newsletter 01-08.html.

Vo, Linda Trinh. 2004. *Mobilizing an Asian American Community*. Philadelphia: Temple University Press.

————. 2008. "Building a Vietnamese American Community: Economic and Political Transformation in Little Saigon, Orange County." *How Do Asian Americans Create Places: Los Angeles & Beyond,* special issue of *Amerasia Journal* 34 (3): 84–109.

Voien, Guelda. 2012a. "Artisanal Boom Creates Demand for NYC Factory, Warehouse Space." *Real Deal,* August 16. Available at http://therealdeal.com/blog/2012/08/16/artisanal-boom-creates-demand-for-local-factory-space/.

————. 2012b. "60 Creative Office Rentals Hit Sunset Park Market." *Real Deal,* March 9. Available at http://therealdeal.com/blog/2012/03/09/60-creative-office-rentals-hit-sunset-park-market/.

Wacquant, Loic. 2004. "Decivilizing and Demonizing: Remaking the Black American Ghetto." In *The Sociology of Norbert Elias,* edited by Steven Loyal and Stephen Quiley, 95–121. Cambridge: Cambridge University Press.

Waldinger, Roger. 1996. *Still the Promised City? African-Americans and New Immigrants in Postindustrial New York, 1940–1990.* Cambridge, MA: Harvard University Press.

Wallace, Benjamin. 2012. "The Twee Party: Is Artisanal Brooklyn a Step Forward for Food or a Sign of the Apocalypse? And Does It Matter When the Stuff Tastes So Good?" *New York Magazine,* April 15. Available at http://nymag.com/news/features/artisanal-brooklyn-2012-4/.

Walsh, Robert. 2003. Interview by the author, New York City Small Business Services, October 5.

Ward, David. 1971. *Cities and Immigrants: A Geography of Change in Nineteenth Century America.* New York: Oxford University Press.

Warren, Barbara. 2000. "Taking Out the Trash: A New Direction for New York City's Waste." Organization of Waterfront Neighborhoods and Consumer Policy Institute/Consumers Union, May 31. Available at http://www.consumersunion.org/pdf/trash%20report.pdf.

Warshawer, Gabby. 2008. "Brokers Target Creative Types for Sunset Park Workspaces." *Real Deal,* September 16. Available at http://therealdeal.com/blog/2008/09/16/brokers-targeting-creative-types-for-st1place-wst-on-st1placename-wst-on-sunset-st1placename-st1placetype-wst-on-park-workspaces-st1placetype-st1place/.

Weiner, Anthony D. 2007. "Many More Banks in New York City (But Only for Some)." U.S. House of Representatives report, August 9. Available at http://www.nytimes.com/packages/pdf/nyregion/city_room/20070910_weinerbankreport.pdf.

Wessel, David. 2005. "As Rich-Poor Gap Widens in U.S., Class Mobility Stalls." *Wall Street Journal,* May 13.

Whalen, Carmen. 2002. "Sweatshops Here and There: The Garment Industry, Latinas, and Labor Migration." *International Labor and Working-Class History* 61:45–68.

White, Stuart. 2011. "Exploring Sunset Park's Less-Traveled Chinatown." City Spoonful New York City Food and Culture, May 2. Available at http://www.cityspoonful.com/sunset-park-chinatown-crawl/.

Wilder, Craig Steven. 2000. *A Covenant with Color: Race and Social Power in Brooklyn.* New York: Columbia University Press.

Wiley, Dan. 2008a. Interview by the author, Brooklyn Heights, May 15.

———. 2008b. Interview by the author, Brooklyn Heights, August 14.

Williams, Margaret Cheatham. 2013. "American Made: Nanette Lepore." Video, available at http://www.nytimes.com/2013/12/01/business/that-made-in-usa-premium.html.

Wilson, Michael. 2011. "Catching Counterfeiters, a Real Cat-and-Mouse Game." *New York Times,* July 15.

Winnick, Louis. 1990. *New People in Old Neighborhoods.* New York: Russell Sage Foundation.

———. 1991. "Letter from Sunset Park." *City Journal,* Winter.

Wired New York. 2005. "Sunset Park Development." Post #1, August 21. Available at http://www.wirednewyork.com/forum/showthread.php?t=7075.

Wisloski, Jess. 2005. "Sealed with a Kiss: Ratner, Mayor, ACORN Agree on Housing Plan." *Brooklyn Paper,* May 28.

Wisniewski, Mary. 2005. "Banks Look to Hispanics; Increase Outreach Efforts in Hopes of Attracting Customers." *Chicago Sun-Times,* May 2.

Wong, Janelle S. 2006. *Democracy's Promise: Immigrants and American Civic Institutions.* Ann Arbor: University of Michigan Press.

Wong, Samuel. 2004. Interview by the author, Chinese Promise Baptist Church, January 8.

Wylde, Kathryn. 2005. Interview by the author, Bay Ridge, Brooklyn, May 7.

Xie, Chang. 2006. Interview by the author, Chinese American Planning Council, January 13.

———. 2013. Telephone interview by the author, July 19.

Yago, Glenn, Hyman Korman, Sen-Yuan Wu, and Michael Schwartz. 1984. "Investment and Disinvestment in New York, 1960–80." *ANNALS of the American Academy of Political and Social Science* 475:28–38.

Yarrow, Andrew L. 1991. "Development Not Even a Contender on Brooklyn's Waterfront." *New York Times,* August 21.

Yau, Patrick. 2005. Interview by the author, First American International Bank, Sunset Park, Brooklyn, June 7.

———. 2013. Telephone interview by the author, June 26.

Yeampierre, Elizabeth. 2006. Interview by the author, UPROSE, Sunset Park, Brooklyn, July 26.

———. 2007. "Comments." *Progressive Planning Magazine,* April 22. Available at http://www.plannersnetwork.org/2007/04/comments-2/.

———. 2013a. Email correspondence with the author, December 13.

———. 2013b. Interview by the author, UPROSE, Sunset Park, Brooklyn, March 28.

Yee, Vivian. 2012. "In Subway, Activist Records Stop-and-Frisk He Says Proves Its Dark Side." *New York Times,* July 26, 2012. Available at http://cityroom.blogs.nytimes.com/2012/07/26/in-subway-activist-records-stop-and-frisk-he-says-proves-its-dark-side/.

Yiftachel, Oren. 1998. "Planning and Social Control: Exploring the 'Dark Side.'" *Journal of Planning Literature,* 12 (2): 395–406.

Yoneda, Yuka. 2013. "Could This Massive 'Seaport City' Save NYC from Future Storms?" Inhabitat New York City, June 16. Available at http://inhabitat.com/nyc/could-this-massive-seaport-city-save-nyc-from-future-storms/.

Yost, Mark. 2012. "New Clothes for a Historic Neighborhood." *Wall Street Journal,* July 25.

Yu, Emily. 2005. Telephone interview by the author, June 15.

Zhou, Min. 1992. *Chinatown: The Socioeconomic Potential of an Urban Enclave.* Philadelphia: Temple University Press.

————. 2001. "Chinese: Divergent Destinies in Immigrant New York." In *New Immigrants in New York,* edited by Nancy Foner, 141–172. New York: Columbia University Press.

Zhou, Min, Jo-Ann Adefuin, Angie Chung, and Elizabeth Roach. 2000. "How Community Matters for the After-School Life of Immigrant Children: Structural Constraints and Resources in Inner-City Neighborhoods." Unpublished working paper, Carnegie Endowment for International Peace.

Zhou, Min, Margaret M. Chin, and Rebecca Y. Kim. 2013. "The Transformation of Chinese American Communities: New York vs. Los Angeles." In *New York and Los Angeles: The Uncertain Future,* edited by David Halle and Andrew A. Beveridge, 358–382. New York: Oxford University Press.

Zhou, Min, and John R. Logan. 1991. "In and Out of Chinatown: Residential Mobility and Segregation of New York City's Chinese." *Social Forces* 70:387–407.

Zhou, Yu. 1998. "How Do Places Matter: A Comparative Study of Chinese Communities in Los Angeles and New York City." *Urban Geography* 19 (6): 531–553.

Zhuang, Zhong, Lan Ding, and Haizheng Li. 2008. "China's Pulp and Paper Industry: A Review." Unpublished paper, School of Economics, Georgia Institute of Technology. Available at http://www.cpbis.gatech.edu/files/papers/CPBIS-FR-08-03%20Zhuang_Ding_Li%20FinalReport-China_Pulp_and_Paper_Industry.pdf.

Zonta, Michela. 2004. "The Role of Ethnic Banks in the Residential Patterns of Asian Americans: The Case of Los Angeles." Unpublished Ph.D. dissertation, UCLA.

Zraick, Karen. 2007. "Towering Trouble on 42nd Street—Construction of New Residential Building Is Just More Overdevelopment, Critics Say." *Park Slope Courier,* February 29.

Zukin, Sharon. 1987. "Gentrification: Culture and Capital in the Urban Core." *Annual Reviews in Sociology* 13:129–147.

————. 1991. *Landscapes of Power: From Detroit to Disney World.* Berkeley: University of California Press.

————. 2010. *Naked City: The Death and Life of Authentic Urban Places.* New York: Oxford University Press.

Index

Tarry Hum is Professor of Urban Studies at Queens College and Graduate Center, City University of New York.

E. San Juan Jr., *The Philippine Temptation: Dialectics of Philippines–U.S. Literary Relations*

Carlos Bulosan and E. San Juan Jr., eds., *The Cry and the Dedication*

Carlos Bulosan and E. San Juan Jr., eds., *On Becoming Filipino: Selected Writings of Carlos Bulosan*

Vicente L. Rafael, ed., *Discrepant Histories: Translocal Essays on Filipino Cultures*

Yen Le Espiritu, *Filipino American Lives*

Paul Ong, Edna Bonacich, and Lucie Cheng, eds., *The New Asian Immigration in Los Angeles and Global Restructuring*

Chris Friday, *Organizing Asian American Labor: The Pacific Coast Canned-Salmon Industry, 1870–1942*

Sucheng Chan, ed., *Hmong Means Free: Life in Laos and America*

Timothy P. Fong, *The First Suburban Chinatown: The Remaking of Monterey Park, California*

William Wei, *The Asian American Movement*

Yen Le Espiritu, *Asian American Panethnicity*

Velina Hasu Houston, ed., *The Politics of Life*

Renqiu Yu, *To Save China, To Save Ourselves: The Chinese Hand Laundry Alliance of New York*

Shirley Geok-lin Lim and Amy Ling, eds., *Reading the Literatures of Asian America*

Karen Isaksen Leonard, *Making Ethnic Choices: California's Punjabi Mexican Americans*

Gary Y. Okihiro, *Cane Fires: The Anti-Japanese Movement in Hawaii, 1865–1945*

Sucheng Chan, *Entry Denied: Exclusion and the Chinese Community in America, 1882–1943*